Royal Insurance

LONDON
COMMUTER
GUIDE

Royal Insurance

LONDON
COMMUTER
GUIDE

Caroline McGhie

Good Books

PUBLISHED IN ASSOCIATION WITH ROYAL INSURANCE
BY GOOD BOOKS (GB PUBLICATIONS LIMITED),
LAGARD FARM, WHITLEY, WILTS SN12 8RL

A CIP CATALOGUE RECORD FOR THIS BOOK IS AVAILABLE
FROM THE BRITISH LIBRARY.
ISBN 0 946555 23 0

ASSOCIATE EDITOR: ELVIRA ROMANS
COVER AND INSIDE DESIGN: DESIGN/SECTION, FROME
COVER ILLUSTRATION: RICHARD BEARDS
ILLUSTRATIONS AND MAPS: VINCENT DESIGN
RAIL TRAVEL INFORMATION: BARRY DOE

TYPESETTING BY DP PHOTOSETTING, AYLESBURY, BUCKS
MADE AND PRINTED IN GREAT BRITAIN BY
BUTLER & TANNER LTD, FROME

CONTENTS

FOREWORD

"When a man is tired of London, he is tired of life", wrote Dr Johnson, "for there is in London all that life can afford."

True though the great doctor's words remain, there are some 450,000 of us who prefer to balance a working life in the metropolis with a home elsewhere. It is to help both existing and intending commuters that Royal Insurance have sponsored this new guide.

The Royal has for long been associated with home ownership, whether as an insurer of premises and contents or through the provision of endowment policies for mortgage repayment. In recent times this association has been extended through the acquisition of several estate agency chains.

Royal Insurance therefore recognise the value of accurate information on which to base a house move, and Caroline McGhie has brought together in these 350 or so pages an abundance of useful data. But this is not merely a reference work; Caroline's commentaries, laced with anecdotes, historical asides and lively observations, make the book an excellent read in its own right, even for those not contemplating an immediate change of address.

David Parry
Managing Director
Royal Life Holdings

INTRODUCTION

If the Nineties deliver what they promise, then the seduction of city dwellers by the countryside will continue to be a powerful dynamo driving the property engine. Slump or no slump, the yearning to swap traffic jams for hedgerows, dirty pavements for honest mud, ghetto-blasters for birdsong, is not to be quenched.

No London dinner party finishes without its stock-in-trade conversation about moving to the country. Couples who have reached pivotal points in their lives are especially prone to restlessness. Those with new prams in the hallway find themselves applying a Mary Poppins test to their children's environment – and usually it fails miserably. Older couples whose children have left home also feel the urge to restructure their lives along new principles. Alone together at last. But as these two critical stages are likely to span 16 years or more, the result is that some people may spend a third of their lives wondering whether or not to make the leap.

Pressure of work, leisure-packed weekends, and simply not knowing at which point of the compass to start looking, often deter a serious exploration of the possibilities. And those who do make the jump, too often do so in the dark. The longed-for move out of the city then can end up as quick and ill-considered as an unwanted pregnancy. A single day out in the country, a walk round one pretty village, and they're ready for a lifetime of commuting. The reality is that a manageable commute coupled with an enhanced lifestyle is possible only after careful consideration of a wide range of occasionally complex factors.

Londoners in particular are notorious for their scatter-gun househunting technique. One minute a couple are looking for a cottage near Tunbridge Wells; next minute you hear they have bought a little place outside Ipswich. The mobility of modern life means that househunters seldom have roots to return to. Buying a home is the ultimate consumer choice – a whole lifestyle off the peg.

In the last two decades Londoners have left the city at the rate of 58,000 a year. Some were making a straightforward quality-of-life choice. Others were refugees from the Eighties property boom, when soaring prices effectively squeezed people further and further away from the centre. For these people, the move to the country was a matter of calculation – mortgage plus season ticket. Improved quality of life was a bonus. According to the Office of Population Censuses and Surveys, most of them headed into East Anglia or to the South-west.

Before joining the trend, therefore, it is worth understanding why some areas attract more people than others, and why some are more fashionable than others (the two are not necessarily the same). East Anglia and the South-west became the places to move to in the last decade largely because the traditionally popular counties such as Hertfordshire, Buckinghamshire, Berkshire, Surrey, Hampshire and parts of East and West Sussex, had simply become saturated with commuters and overpriced. In these counties the cost of a country cottage, the centrepiece of the rural dream, grew out of all proportion to the humble architecture of what is essentially an agricultural labourer's dwelling.

Kent has always lagged behind on the property catwalk. This is partly because so much of the northern part of the county is seriously industrial, and because the rest of it sometimes feels squashed between London and the sea. Essex had the misfortune of being branded the land of the spiv, the natural homing ground for East Enders made good. The ambivalence about Essex is not new, however. For the Victorians it was just much too close to the fever-ridden marshes of the east coast – to the extent that the marshfolk in some parts are still considered oddballs. Even Hertfordshire has had to struggle to keep its end up. It lacks enduring stone as a local building material, with the result that it suffers from a shortage of the large period houses that often set the tone of a neighbourhood. Northamptonshire has the stone but lacks a strong cultural centre. There is no city or town of sufficient style to attract the middle classes, who never want to be too far away from theatres, specialist food shops and bespoke upholsterers.

It was for these reasons, aided by the shorter journey times achieved by the railway electrification programme, that prospective commuters began to look beyond these counties to the west and further east. Two predictable things then happened. Fuelled by the new demand, property prices in these areas rose phenomenally during the boom; then fell back much harder than elsewhere during the slump. The prediction now is that these are the key areas which will recover fastest when the market starts to move again.

Nineteen ninety-two and 1993 are unlikely to produce dramatic changes in house prices in any region. But as we come out of the recession the number of sales going through will pick up. As the wheels of the market are oiled in this way, so the depressing overhang of properties for sale will be diminished. Once the balance between supply and demand is restored then the building societies predict marginal increases in prices starting to occur.

Fluctuating market conditions are not the only thing to be wary of. The dream of wellington boots in the back porch, fresh eggs from the farm and an old-fashioned village school for the children often does not marry with reality. Gourmets, for instance, need to consider their sources of supply: they may not realise how important the local Tesco or corner delicatessen is until they lose it. The fruitfulness of neighbouring fields is no guarantee of local availability either. The pick of the fruit and vegetable crops will often go straight to a supermarket chain, leaving only second-best for the local shops. Unless you enjoy repeated journeys into town, country life often means living out of the freezer.

The biggest mistake is to make the move without identifying what it is you really want. A friend put it like this: "I moved to the centre of the village, but what I hadn't realised was that we wanted walks from the back door, literally. We wanted views. And we wanted friends. Now we routinely drive an hour to go to dinner parties. In fact, if we had known then what we know now, we would have chosen the other side of Oxford." Ensuring you find the right social niche is important. And it is worth remembering that the weather tends to speak with a louder voice in the country. Cold and ice command real respect, and the wellington boots are a necessity, not a fashion accessory.

Though it may be the husband who provides the decisive impetus to move, it is often the wife who is more profoundly affected. He vanishes back into his old life in the city each day while she has to make a completely new set of friends and establish a new role. This is not always easy. There are villages where you need 15 years of residence under your belt before you really belong; others require you to show some commitment to local activities. Some villages accept commuters more readily than others.

But village life has so much to offer – indeed Londoners spend half their time trying to create an urban equivalent. The slower pace of life, the give-and-take, the sense of community, are things we all long for. Having a magnificent landscape parked permanently outside your back door is impossible to quantify in terms of how much it boosts your spiritual well-being and quality of life. The siege-mentality that city life induces can be safely swopped for something altogether more friendly.

Rural England evolved with a strong sense of social hierarchy which in many villages is still in place. These are the villages – where the big house is still a residence, old trades have been handed down through the generations, and old cottages stand haphazardly around the green – which are the jewels in the country property market. You can be absolutely certain that wherever you find villages with cohesive centres, period architecture and a sense of the past, you also find the highest property prices. You can be equally sure that wherever the modern developer has been too heavy-handed the prices are bound to drop. This is a simple, observable rule of the property market which too many builders still haven't grasped. An appetite for golden eggs brings the inevitable tragedy of expiring geese.

For an intending commuter, the first consideration in

any move must be the length and convenience of the rail journey. Decide which London terminus you want to arrive at. If you work in the City, for instance, London Bridge and Liverpool Street win hands down over Paddington and Victoria. The conventional wisdom is that the journeys on either side of the main commute (from home to the station and from the London terminus to the place of work) are best kept down to 15 minutes each side. The maximum sensible number of changes en route is two: with each extra change you increase the chance of a missed connection or other unforeseen delay. Psychologists say that the stress involved in commuting is largely due to the suppression of our "fight or flight" response in just these kinds of situation.

As to the main commute, most people find that a 90-minute journey is the maximum tolerable limit – a time-band which has an inevitable influence on property prices. But it is no good looking at a map to estimate your probable journey time – the British Rail timetables make nonsense of geography. As you'll see throughout this book, places on the outskirts of London are often further away in terms of journey time than more distant county towns. Speed of journey is not the only factor to consider, however. Frequency of service is just as important. If you miss your train, how long will you have to wait for the next one? It's especially important if you need to be flexible and don't want to turn into an office clock-watcher.

The purpose of this book is to do as much as possible of the initial homework for you. As any diligent househunter would, we have followed the railway lines out of London in all directions and identified villages within reach of every station. We have tried to encapsulate the character of each town and village and to give an idea of what kinds of property are to be found there, and how much they cost. The detail is by no means comprehensive, but it should be sufficient to give you an idea of whether or not a place is worth going to see. It is not intended as a guide to schools, but if a local school has a reputation good enough to make itself felt in the local property market, then I have tried to include a mention of it. The table at the head of each station entry, prepared by transport and travel consultant Barry Doe in association with British Rail, will give you an idea of what you need to know about journey times, frequency of service and annual season ticket prices.

Many people – estate agents, parish clerks, local councils and tourist centres – have been generous with their time and knowledge, for which I am most grateful. I would particularly like to thank all the researchers who worked on the project – Nicky Hughes and Beryl Downing, fellow property writers on **The Independent on Sunday**, together with Jenny Knight, Dawn Smith, Leni Gillman and the indefatigable Marilyn Bodoh. I would also like to say that I could not have completed this book without the two wise men at my side – my publisher Graham Tarrant and my husband Richard Girling. Thanks, too, must go to Royal Insurance, sponsors of the book, and in particular to Roy Sully.

Useful sources of further information include the **Shire County Guides** (Shire Publications Ltd), which catalogue all the things to see and do in each county, and **The Villages of Britain** series (Countryside Books), which are marvellous repositories of oral history prepared by the Women's Institute. Anyone wanting a comprehensive guide to independent schools should contact the Independent Schools Information Service, 56 Buckingham Gate, London SW1.

Some explanation of the rail travel information given for each station is necessary. (For more detailed information, readers should consult the **British Rail Passenger Timetable** or British Rail itself.)

Journey time

This is the time taken by the **fastest** train in a normal off-peak hour to the relevant London terminus. On Network SouthEast services peak-hour trains usually take a little longer owing to additional stops, but InterCity services are often a little faster with fewer stops. Any significant differences between peak and off-peak services are indicated. Where there is no off-peak service, the peak-hour journey time is quoted.

Peak trains

This represents the number of **through** trains per hour arriving at the relevant terminus between 0730 and 0930. (A reasonable band either side of these times has been allowed for to take into account trains arriving at times like 0725 or 0935.) Where frequency is particularly low, or on branchlines where a change is necessary, this is indicated.

Off-peak trains

This is the total number of (non-overtaken) **through** trains to the relevant terminus in a normal off-peak hour. Any special cases, such as where services are only available by changing trains, are indicated.

Season ticket

The price quoted is that for the **Standard Class Annual**. The cost of a weekly season is obtained by dividing the annual rate by 40. A monthly season is the weekly rate × 3.84. These are the only rates on offer so that, for example, a season for six months is charged at six times the monthly rate with no further discount. However, it is possible to buy any season ticket for any length of time above a month, in odd days, at pro rata the monthly rate. **First Class** season tickets, where available, are 1.5 times the standard rate.

Out-of-town annual season ticket holders can pay a supplement of around £250pa (£375pa first class) which will incorporate a **Travelcard** with their season ticket. **Travelcards** offer unlimited travel on BR trains, tubes and buses in the Greater London area and normally cost £952.

Season tickets are valid to any appropriate London terminus. For example, tickets from Brighton to London cover not only the services shown to Victoria or London Bridge, but also to Cannon Street, Blackfriars, Waterloo and Charing Cross by changing at London Bridge. Similarly, tickets from stations on the Bristol/Paddington line are also valid to Waterloo via Staines.

Charing Cross/Waterloo (East) ....

All trains to Charing Cross stop at Waterloo (East), and many also serve London Bridge. In the peak hours on these lines there are also additional trains into Cannon Street.

LIVERPOOL STREET
— TO —
NORWICH

SHENFIELD

Journey time: *25 min*　　　| **Peak trains:** *11 per hour*
Season ticket: *£1396*　　　| **Off-peak trains:** *4 per hour*

Shenfield is a mutated village but nonetheless the greengrocer and butcher know you by name. There are three parts to it: the village itself, with bread-and-butter Victorian and Thirties streets; Hutton Mount, where avenues of five-bedroom, double-garaged detached houses (£200,000–£500,000) peep out from between the trees; and Hutton Village, which is strictly Sixties, congested but more affordable. It is on London's doorstep, just outside the M25, with the result that the station car park is so crowded that parking creeps up the side roads.

INGATESTONE

Journey time: *33 mins*　　　| **Peak trains:** *4 per hour*
Season ticket: *£1508*　　　| **Off-peak trains:** *2 per hour*

This is a village with small town pretensions and about 3,000 inhabitants, many of them East Enders who have moved up and out. Its best features are a collection of 19th-century almshouses and the high street, which is on a reassuringly human scale. One of its greatest attractions is the European School, to which parents send their children from all over Essex. Many of the passengers drive south to avoid the parking problems at Chelmsford, though they lose with one hand what they gain with the other because it is more difficult to get a seat at Ingatestone.

CHELMSFORD

Journey time: *35 min*　　　| **Peak trains:** *7 per hour*
Season ticket: *£1680*　　　| **Off-peak trains:** *4 per hour*

Chelmsford has just billowed with new developments. Broomfield and Links Drive are the right side of the railway tracks, Boarded Barns the wrong side. The space-age Sainsbury superstore is at Springfield. Property prices start at £40,000 for a studio flat, rising to £250,000 for five bedrooms and a large garden. The surrounding countryside, despite its savaging from developers, still contains some wonderful surprises. The station lays claim to being the busiest in the country, funnelling 12,000

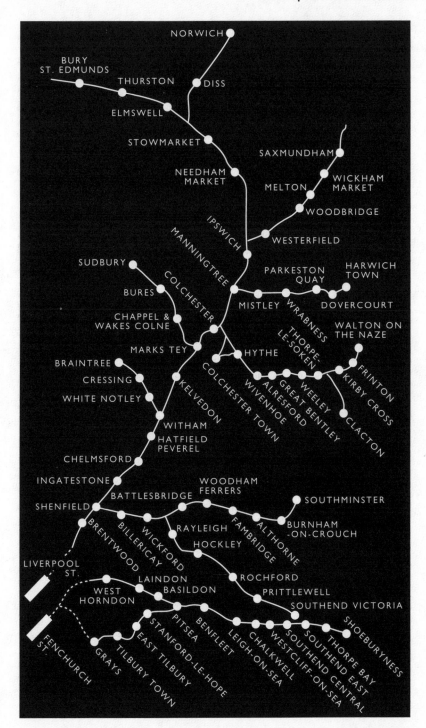

people each morning into London. Extra trains start here, rather than further up the line, in an attempt to provide more seats.

Close in on the east flank of the town is **Sandon**, a village distinguished by its remarkable Turkey Oak, one of the best outside Kew, which throws a tent of leaves over the entire village green. Two-bedroom cottages just off the green cost around £80,000, while a five-bedroom Georgian house would fetch £300,000. Modern four-bedroom houses are £150,000. The village is very much a dormitory, protected by the A12 bypass – though the roar of the traffic is still audible in some of the houses. The excellent comprehensive school has a large sixth form and draws children from further afield, including places like Maldon and South Woodham Ferrers.

A little further out is **Danbury**, larger than most people's concept of the archetypal village and on a main road (the A414). It has its own shops and pubs, some of them 16th-century, and the common, woods and lakes are big attractions. A period house with four bedrooms would cost £180,000 at least. "It's a commuter village but not posh. It's not a don't-touch-me place. Everyone and his grandmother goes there on Sundays for a walk," was how one local pundit described it. The heather and bracken of Danbury and Lingwood Commons (National Trust) provide one of the few known breeding grounds for the Rosy Marbled Moth. Blake's Wood also offers 100 acres of hornbeam and chestnut coppice carpeted with bluebells in the spring. **Little Baddow**, scarcely separated from Danbury, is much more snooty. It has a village green, little boutiques, a cricket pitch and huge six-bedroom houses on The Ridge that sell for £200,000 to £800,000.

Another classic commuter village is **Stock**, with its cluttered narrow streets, pond and village green, though it suffers from the traffic on the B1007. It has its own wine store, post office, general store, newsagent, butcher, greengrocer, fish shop and antique shops, and a wealth of societies from flower-arranging to drama and the British Legion. There are some staunch churchgoers. Opinions of village life vary. One who moved away after five years describes it thus: "I never got to know anyone. They were all at work. It is well-to-do, overpriced, snobby. People tend to talk about things that don't mean anything, like the weather or Lady So-and-So's hat." A Tudor house with a quarter of an acre on the main road would cost £220,000; a three-bedroom modern semi in the region of £100,000.

To the west of Chelmsford is a whole clutch of picturesque villages. **Writtle** is close in enough to be a suburb, with a number of 16th-and 17th-century houses costing up to £250,000. Its green and duck pond are the envy of the county. Highlands Park, a picture of beautiful decay, stands fenced off with its grounds open to the public. It provides the setting for the annual Chelmsford Spectacular, when people take their own deckchairs to hear classical music and watch synchronised firework displays.

Nearby is a collection of hamlets, linked to Chelmsford by a Tuesday and Saturday bus, where four- to five-bedroom houses cost anything from £200,000 to £400,000. **Mashbury** is without a pub or shop or jumble sales, but remarkable for its togetherness. **Good Easter** has one of the oldest barns in the county and a village green with a pump on it. **High Easter** is the prettiest, with a general store, a post office and a restaurant. And there are **Chignall Smealy** and **Chignall St James**, which have plenty of timbered houses but seem to lack a social or geographical focus. **Pleshey**, on the other hand, is particularly sought after because of its thatched cottages, post office, church, and motte-and-bailey castle. Houses here rarely come on the market.

HATFIELD PEVEREL

Journey time: *49 min*
Season ticket: *£1796*

Peak trains: *2 per hour*
Off-peak trains: *2 per hour*

Commuterland in the lee of the A12. A two-bedroom period cottage in **Hatfield Peverel** would start at £70,000; a four-bedroom period house with an acre of land would fetch upwards of £220,000.

WITHAM

Journey time: *47 min*
Season ticket: *£1880*

Peak trains: *6 per hour*
Off-peak trains: *3 per hour*

The smart set don't live in **Witham** itself, which has become a town that people shop in (no large department store) or pass through on their way to the station. Dorothy L. Sayers was not so proud, however. She lived and wrote in Newland Street and a little plaque is there to prove it. The town still serves as the social hub for the surrounding villages which feed commuters on to the fast mainline train services to Liverpool Street. Car parking spaces are plentiful, both in the station itself and at the nearby Labour Party offices.

The conservationist lobby is strong, with old stalwarts belonging to the Witham and Countryside Society; culture vultures join the Witham Operatic and Dramatic Society. The whole of the 18th- and 19th-century high street has been designated a conservation area. Apart from the Bramston Sports Centre there is little for the young. The nearest cinema is miles away in Colchester or Chelmsford. In the Seventies the town was identified as a London overspill, which is why it now contains five modern estates. Old two-bedroom terrace houses cost £45,000. New first-time-buyer properties are priced at £65,000.

The surrounding villages are significantly more expensive, with three-bedroom period houses in the £150,000–£200,000 range. Scarcely separated from Witham itself is **Chipping Hill**, with the Woolpack Inn, a triangular green and a manor house. The view from here was described by Horace Walpole in 1749 as "sweet meadows falling down a hill and rising again on the other side of the prettiest winding stream you ever saw". **Wickham Bishops**, set on a hill a couple of miles out, looks down its nose at the others. **Great Braxted** is slightly cheaper, as is **Great Totham** which is further from the station. The yachting fraternity flock to **Tollesbury** 12 miles away, where there is a large modern marina on a creek of the Blackwater.

Branchline to Braintree via White Notley and Cressing

Through trains: 2 per hour (peak)/ I per hour (off-peak)
Journey time: 60 min (from Braintree)
Season ticket from Braintree: £1936

Only since May 1990 has there been a through train service to Liverpool Street on this line, introduced as a result of vigorous lobbying by the Witham and Braintree Rail Users Association. People still tend to take the shuttle into Witham and wait five minutes for a fast connection. The snag is that the last through train to Braintree leaves Liverpool Street at 2200, which makes London theatre trips arduous. A campaign to get a later train is under way.

There are only about 30 London commuters who use **White Notley**, and most of them live within walking distance. The station is kept open because there is a level crossing here, and it remains

Traditional Essex
weatherboard house

cheaper for British Rail to keep it manned than it would be to modernise it. **Cressing** is another walk-to-the-station village. The station building itself is coming apart at the seams and British Rail is trying to sell and build a new one nearby. The village has 1,400 inhabitants, three pubs, a general store, a newsagent, a butcher, a post office and a hairdresser. It also has its own primary school, though the nearest secondary schools are in Braintree. A three-bedroom bungalow could be bought for £70,000 to £90,000. Old Cressing, part of which is a conservation area, is scissored from new Cressing by the main road. As one parish councillor put it, "Nobody would ever describe it as quaint, or even picturesque, but it is a good working village". **Braintree** is the birthplace of the Crittall window and about as pretty – definitely not a first choice for those seeking views from the sitting room window. Yet there are whole estates built on the outskirts which are full of former Londoners, happy to swop the East End for a slower pace of life, better schools and no traffic jams. Property prices are comparatively low.

KELVEDON

Journey time: *59 min*	Peak trains: *4 per hour*
Season ticket: *£1888*	Off-peak trains: *2 per hour*

Kelvedon is sought after for its strong village heartbeat. St Peter's church and the Kelvedon Players organise endless activities. It has a regular Thursday market which sells everything from buttons and WI jam to fruit and veg. Once people have settled here, they rarely move out. Two-up-two-downs start at £50,000, while a converted barn or something with four or five bedrooms is likely to be in the £200,000–£500,000 bracket. **Feering**, less than two miles away, is almost umbilically linked. It has a new community centre and village school, an art club, a village orchestra and choir, a WI flower-arranging club, bowls, badminton, Scouts, Guides. The villages share a cricket club. On May Day the pubs stay open all day while the village green throbs with dancers. Newcomers quickly become assimilated. The commuter influx has put property prices up – nothing for under £70,000 here – and out of reach of some locals, but there is an affordable housing scheme built on land provided at low cost by a local farmer.

MARKS TEY

Journey time: *65 min*	Peak trains: *4 per hour*
Season ticket: *£1944*	Off-peak trains: *2 per hour*

All the Teys, **Marks Tey**, **Little Tey** and **Great Tey**, are within a 10-minute drive of this or Colchester station. Parking at both is difficult. Marks Tey has large Seventies estates where you can buy a two-bedroom house for £50,000 or a four-bedroom detached for £90,000. Little Tey, next door, is also a grazing ground for first- and second-time buyers. Great Tey is a little more remote, with its own village shop, post office and village hall. **Coggeshall**, a couple of miles from this and Kelvedon station, is much more seductive, wonderfully medieval, with Paycocke's House (National Trust) one of the most famous Tudor houses in the country.

Branchline to Sudbury via Chappel & Wakes Colne and Bures

No through trains. Trains to Marks Tey: 1 per hour
Journey time: 97 min (from Sudbury)
Season ticket from Sudbury: £2156

Villagers living down this branchline would be just as likely to drive in and catch one of the more frequent trains from Colchester. **Chappel** and **Wakes Colne** are two villages sewn together by a vast and spectacular Victorian viaduct. The River Stour, crossed by a

Thatched cricket
pavilion, Bures

small bridge, marks the line which slices **Bures** up between Essex and Suffolk. It therefore has two of everything, from parish clerks downwards. The cricket club and green are picturesque – matches are watched by the sheep kept by the vicar in the field next door. There is conspicuous wealth here, and some weekend cottages. The odd pop musician sweeps through in his Rolls Royce. A little two-bedroom Victorian cottage costs £60,000; a modern detached three-bedroom house will cost £80,000 or more, while a four-bedroom house in half an acre might reach £180,000. Sadly, the number of children at the primary school has dwindled from 120 to 60.

Sudbury's irresistible charms compensate for the inconvenience of the journey for the brave few who commute from here. The jumble of historic cottages, churches and grander gabled houses, Gainsborough's birthplace among them, sit in the arm of the River Stour, cushioned by water meadows. The market square is filled with stalls on Thursdays and Saturdays. The Sudbury Dramatic Society raised money to establish the Quay Theatre which is also the home of the Sudbury Light Operatic Society, the cinema and the jazz club. Down towards the water meadows there are the tennis club, the rowing club and the cricket club. The new Kingfisher Leisure Pool provides a dash of Disneyland with flume rides, a wave machine and giant bouncing rubber balls.

A few commuters choose to live in the town and walk to the station, or even drive to Marks Tey or Colchester. First-time-buyer studios start at £30,000, and for £40,000 you might get a dilapidated terraced Victorian house to restore. There is the occasional one-bedroom cottage, too, which would cost £60,000, but anything with four bedrooms would start at £90,000 to £130,000. Steer clear of the Great Cornard, originally a London overspill zone and still stigmatised as such.

Most people opt for the villages. **Long Melford**, three and a half miles out, is one of the most admired in the county with an achingly lovely long main street (hence the name of the village) which eventually erupts on to the green and a cathedral-sized church. The Hall is National Trust. The Green is one of *the* addresses. A four-bedroom house with beams, peg-tile roof and an inglenook fireplace would cost £230,000, though you can get tiny one-bedroom cottages for as little as £60,000. The village has its own school, post office, grocery stores, butcher and baker. It crawls with antique dealers and American tourists in the summer.

Lavenham, four miles from Sudbury, is another film-set medieval village, with restaurants, dried flower and teddy bear shops, 300 listed buildings and the home of the Suffolk Preservation Society. It is beyond the 10-mile belt round Colchester and therefore a bit too hard to reach at the end of a long day to be considered seriously by regular commuters. **Cavendish** on the River Stour is another with a village green, antique shops and restaurants, but think hard about the journey before you look at it.

COLCHESTER

Journey time: *49 min*	**Peak trains:** *8 per hour*
Season ticket: *£2052*	**Off-peak trains:** *4 per hour*

People have time for **Colchester**, which is the oldest town in Britain, built on the foundations of a Roman temple. The little medieval alleyways in the old quarter harbour specialist shops such as an Italian shoe shop and a teddy bear shop, while the two pedestrianised shopping centres serve up all the usual chain stores. There are any number of societies including the archaeological, jazz and folk and choral. It has two theatres – The Mercury which is a repertory company, and St Mary's Arts Centre in a converted church which puts on a mix of concerts and shows – and there is also a cinema with four screens. Colchester Leisure World is an impressive new multi-sports stadium. Annual events include the two-day Summer Show held in June and the rather bizarre Oyster Feast in October, to which assorted media figures are invited to gorge themselves.

The Colchester bag is brimming with goodies. The Colnes (see page 22) are handsome but not glamorous. **Earls Colne**, two miles away, is the biggest and is distinguished for having a gas supply – no dreaded oil tank lurking at the bottom of the garden. It is self-contained, with a supermarket, restaurants, banks, and individual shops in the period high street. There are a few modern one-off executive houses which fetch between £140,000 and £200,000. **White Colne** is merely a ribbon settlement along the main A604 to Earls Colne and it has no shop. But properties along the main road come considerably cheaper – priced at possibly 20 per cent less than on quieter roads. **Colne Engaine** is the most desirable of this group. It has a classic village green, framed with period houses, a village shop, a pub, a church and a primary school. You need £100,000 to £150,000 to start looking for a house here.

Eight Ash Green is also highly prized. The A604 cuts through the centre, skirting the green and the little houses that circle it. It has a village store, a primary school, a church and a garage *and* gas supply. It has a mix of houses, from ex-local authority selling at £50,000 to £60,000, to small peg-tiled timbered cottages at £100,000; or you might get a Thirties semi in half an acre for £150,000. **Fordham**, on the River Colne, is rather more dislocated. It does a kind of vanishing act half way through the main street, then gives you a second helping as you turn the bend. Children travel up to 20 miles to Colchester Royal Grammar School (boys) or The County High (girls) if they can get a place.

The Horkesleys are not greatly loved, though you could pick up a cottage in **Little Horkesley** for £130,000. **Stoke-by-Nayland**, however, eight miles from Colchester, is where the poetry begins and drunken timber-frame houses splashed with Suffolk pink wash begin to colour the landscape. It is set high on a ridge over the Stour with a church that commands a giddy view of Constable country in all directions. **Boxford**, a couple of miles further out, is as pretty and quieter.

Line to Clacton or Walton on the Naze via Colchester Town, Hythe, Wivenhoe, Alresford, Great Bentley, Weeley, Thorpe-le-Soken, Kirby Cross and Frinton

Through trains: 1 off-peak*
Journey time to Liverpool St: 86 min (from Clacton)
Trains to Colchester: 1 per hour
Season ticket from Clacton: £2308

* Clacton, Thorpe-le-Soken, Wivenhoe only. Other stations: change at Colchester

Wivenhoe is subject to commuter clotting. It is a little quayside town which grows lumps of commuter cars each day, left there by those who want to avoid the stressful drive into Colchester (which can take 45 minutes). Parking space is so precious that the public car park, which is meant for shoppers only, is locked between 5.30pm and 8.45am. Local councillors have even considered buying houses to knock them down, simply to create more parking spaces.

The village is gradually metamorphosing from a working port where the oyster catch was all important, to a boating village with craft shops that attract local artists and writers. The pubs bulge with students at certain times of year and parties of foreign students at others, brought in by Essex University, based in the tower blocks in Wivenhoe Park. It is distinct from Colchester five miles away, cushioned by green fields which are fiercely defended from development. There is pressure for new housing estates on the old shipyards as they close. The ferry to Rowhedge (rowed by an old woman who smoked a pipe) has long gone. Detached period houses on the quayside cost over £100,000. Smaller three-bedroom Victorian terrace houses start at under £60,000. It has an infant and a primary school, and local societies including the Gilbert and Sullivan Society, the Wivenhoe Players and the Pantomime Group. There is also an annual regatta.

Great Bentley is chiefly notable for the extraordinary size of its village green. At 45 acres it swallows the cricket green, two football pitches and the annual gymkhana – and the houses on it are the ones to aim for. A bungalow with four bedrooms and a swimming pool sold last year (1991) for £150,000, but something with three bedrooms off the green might cost £80,000. There is a baker, a general store that sells everything from secondhand fire engines to candles, a primary school and allotments for residents only.

Clacton-on-Sea may one day find itself a conservation area. It epitomises the pre-war seaside resort, where those with fond memories of holidays in bed-and-breakfasts and days on the pier might choose to buy their final bungalow and take up a round of golf on Sundays. The average three-bedroom semi costs £60,000, while the two-up-two-down comes in cheaper at £40,000. Described by some as being full of "East Enders-made-good driving their Range Rovers".

My dear, if you live in **Frinton-on-Sea**, you have arrived. That is to say that you have certainly distanced yourself from that "frightful candyfloss and razzmatazz" in Clacton. The old railway level-crossing gates are the heavenly portals to Frinton. Outside is where the modern estates are put, and it isn't Frinton proper. For Frinton is very proper. There are no pubs, and the beach is free of ice-cream sellers. It is genteel, with a strong churchgoing community. It also has its commuters who use the direct trains to Liverpool Street. Solicitors, doctors, dentists and accountants are attracted to the cavernous houses, servants' quarters and tennis courts included, worth over £200,000, that sit in swathes of garden in The Avenues. There is no problem buying olive oil here. Connaught Avenue, with its designer clothes shops, jewellers and delicatessens, is known as the Bond Street of Essex. The local clubs and societies cover three foolscap pages, but it is bridge evenings that make the world go round, coupled with the Frinton Arts and Music Society, the annual tennis tournament and the 18-hole links.

You get sand as fine but house prices considerably cheaper in **Walton on the Naze**. There are regulation seaside resort chip shops and a pier, but the main attractions are the sheltered inlets behind The Naze where the yacht club is. The saltings and mudflats, designated as a Site of Special Scientific Interest, are a staging post for flocks of migrating birds and there are monthly guided walks.

Kirby le Soken, two miles away, is sought after because of its proximity to Frinton. It was originally threaded on to a single long main street, in the Essex tradition, but has since sprung bungaloid growths around it. One village shop has closed, leaving one remaining, plus a secondhand dress shop. Everybody knows everybody in this village. Cottage windows are papered with posters flagging local events, and gardens are regularly thrown open to the public for good causes. "You cannot be lonely. If your are, you need only weed your front garden and you would spend all day chattering," says the chair of the Frinton and Walton Heritage Trust.

MANNINGTREE

Journey time: *72 min*   **Peak trains:** *3 per hour*
Season ticket: *£2288*   **Off-peak trains:** *1 per hour*

This station is often preferred to Colchester because it is marginally easier to park the car (though nothing is free) and easier to get a seat. **Manningtree** town itself has a charming frontage on to the Stour, known as the Walls, where homeowners think their houses are worth £150,000, though they tend to stick at that price. Legoland executive houses have leached onto it. The social life is mixed – old skippers and commuters drink together in the pubs – and the Manningtree Society and Stour Music Society add a cultural note.

East Bergholt is one of the set-piece villages in this area, sprawly but prime commuter territory, where houses go for up to 10 per cent more than similar ones nearby. Constable wrote of it in 1776: "I even love every stile and stump and every lane in the village". He painted it enough times, and the cottage he used as a studio is still there – as is Willy Lott's cottage, which he made famous by painting. It doesn't seethe with tourists quite as much as other local sightseeing spots. A late Georgian house with three bedrooms might sell for over £100,000. A modern four- or five-bedroom detached house that would sell for £90,000 in Ipswich would fetch at least £10,000 more here. Houses at **Flatford Mill**, the hamlet nearby, are similarly fought over. The mill was owned by Constable's father and painted by the man himself.

Dedham is positively stockbroker now, and, in spite of the paralysing tourist influx in the summer, it is a place that people still dream of moving to. Sir Alfred Munnings's home lies just to the south. Those who live in the high street are martyrs to the tourists who make parking and shopping impossible. Vendors tend to think their houses are worth substantially more than comparable houses in other villages. One resident of 17 years remembers how quiet it used to be. "It looks beautiful at eight o'clock at night when nobody is here." Her commuting husband used to park in a field to catch the train at Manningtree. Now he will stubbornly wait three hours to get on a train that allows him a seat.

Branchline to Harwich Town, via Mistley, Wrabness, Harwich Parkeston Quay and Dovercourt

Peak trains: 2 per hour (3 from Harwich P.Q.)
Off-peak trains: I per hour (change at Manningtree)
Journey time: 103 min (from Harwich Town)
Season ticket from Harwich Town: £2312

While Manningtree benefits from the stops made by fast trains coming through from Harwich and Norwich, the small stops out along the tidal estuary towards Harwich do not. Properties are scattered and isolated along this out-of-the-way bit of coastline, and the journey, which usually involves a change at Manningtree, is a deterrent.

IPSWICH

Journey time: *65 min*	**Peak trains:** *3 per hour*
Season ticket: *£2768*	**Off-peak trains:** *2 per hour*

Ipswich itself is described as a town of convenience, good for shopping. There is a theatre and a live rock venue. Two-bedroom terrace houses to the east, near the well-respected Northgate comprehensive, can be bought for around £38,000; three-bedroom semis for £55,000 and detached houses for £65,000 to £80,000. The prices rise when you get close to a park, especially Christchurch Park where the private schools are. Here a three-bedroom Victorian semi will cost £90,000; a substantial family house £200,000.

The Shotley Peninsula, in the tongue of land just below Ipswich, is where the naturalists and yachting types gather. It has the River Orwell to one side, the Stour to the other and oozing mudflats between that attract wildfowl and waders. **Stutton** is the popular village here, on the Alton Reservoir which is the sailing centre. **Shotley Gate** at the tip provides a vantage point from which to watch the ships ploughing in and out of Harwich.

Eight miles to the west of Ipswich is **Hadleigh**, a classic period market town, untouched by the deadening hand of huge supermarket chains. It is a model collection of medieval and Georgian houses, and provides everything that a small town should, from wine bars and interior designers to banks and solicitors. But the young consider it dreary. A small two-bedroom Tudor cottage here would cost £55,000, while a large Georgian town house would fetch £150,000. Just two miles beyond it is **Kersey**, where the price of the houses depends on how desperate people are to buy their fantasy. The hillside, running steeply down to a watersplash and up again, is stacked with remarkable lichen-cloaked half-timbered houses, built 500 years ago on the profits of the cloth industry. One homeowner there recently wanted £140,000 for a house that the estate agent had valued at £125,000, though it would have been worth £100,000 anywhere else.

Continuing west you have to beware the flight path of the low-flying Phantoms that come screaming out of RAF Wattisham. Cottages close to it will sell for possibly £25,000 less than the equivalent £150,000 cottage elsewhere.

To the east is **Woodbridge**, one of the most sought-after towns in this part of Suffolk. It has its own station (see branchline to Lowestoft below) but people would be just as likely to drive into Ipswich to catch the train. High ranking, high salaried types buy up the 16th-century houses round this old port on the Deben estuary. It is serious boating country. You can buy a three-bedroom terrace close to the ancient weatherboarded tide-mill and old quayside buildings in the town itself for £70,000 to £80,000 with on-road parking. Or you could spend £270,000 on a period house with six bedrooms and exposed beams. It also has its own highly respected co-educational school (Woodbridge School) and a prep.

● Branchline to Saxmundham via Westerfield, Woodbridge, Melton, and Wickham Market

No through trains. Trains to Ipswich: 1 every 2 hours
Journey time: 120 min (from Saxmundham)
Season ticket from Saxmundham: £3272

Much of this remarkable coast is just too far for daily commuters.

People are more likely to move here if they have to reach London only once or twice a week. With no through train service at all, you have to change at Ipswich. None of these little stations are staffed either, so if the train is late you are kept stewing in ignorance on the platform. According to the East Suffolk Travellers Association, the last train out of Ipswich (at 2150) is financed by the County Council rather than British Rail.

Those who can't afford Woodbridge (see Ipswich above) might consider **Little** and **Great Bealings** or **Grundisburgh** (pronounced Grundsbra), which is popular with families because it has a good primary school, or **Ufford** which is very pretty and unspoilt. **Wickham Market** is also an unpretentious little town with a market square fringed with white-fronted Georgian houses.

Or you could journey to **Saxmundham** and head for **Aldeburgh** – respectable, but, as E.M.Forster fondly put it, "a bleak little place, not beautiful". People retire and take second homes there, only intending to commute during the summer months. Prices vary from £60,000 for a two-bedroom cottage in the town centre to £500,000 for nine bedrooms, five bathrooms and 25 acres. The internationally renowned music festival is held down the road at **Snape**. Or there are the huge seaside holiday villas at Tudoresque **Thorpeness** that go for £90,000 to £200,000.

Beyond the Sizewell power station, which is not everyone's idea of a scenic embellishment, you come to the villages of **Westleton** and **Middleton**. These are hugely popular with escapees from the City who want to don Barbours, wellies and tweed hats and visit those wonderful vanishing cliffs at Dunwich (National Trust) or the Royal Society for the Protection of Birds reserve at Minsmere. Westleton has a village green and duck pond to go with its Suffolk thatch, colour wash and wattle-and-daub cottages. A cottage in either village might cost £85,000 to £150,000, but you could get a three-bedroom end-of-terrace for £55,000. **Yoxford** is worth thinking about because it is soon to be bypassed and it has mains gas. **Peasenhall** is also pretty, and **Framlingham** provides the nearest classic country town, with a market square and old castle at its heart, though it is rather too far for commuters.

NEEDHAM MARKET

Journey time: *94 min*	Peak trains: *1 per hour**
Season ticket: *£3104*	Off-peak trains: *1 every 4 hours**

* Change at Ipswich

Needham Market has plenty of old houses, some with Georgian facades, and a wondrous 15th-century chapel with a roof that sent Pevsner into orbit. He described it as "a whole church with nave, aisles and clerestory seemingly in the air". Buyers are drawn to the villages to the south-west that bask in the reflected glow of nearby Lavenham. **Hitcham** has the crucial ingredients of shop and garage, and a densely packed parish calendar, but the property prices are a fraction lower than those around Stowmarket. **Bildeston** has all the black and cream wickerwork architecture of a town built on the profits of the medieval clothing industry, and one of the most perfect rows of cottages running off the Square. It also has restaurants and a doctor's surgery. To the east of Needham Market the houses have much humbler origins. Prices tend to be lower simply because the properties here are smaller.

STOWMARKET

Journey time: *77 min*	Peak trains: *2 per hour*
Season ticket: *£3132*	Off-peak trains: *1 per hour*

Stowmarket has a strategic position just on the lip of the Suffolk prairie. Beyond the A45 all the last dimples in the countryside have been ironed flat, and the trees and hedges unpicked from a landscape which blazes yellow with rape in the summer. It is a good, old-fashioned market town where local businesses have established themselves over generations. A two-bedroom Victorian terrace house will cost around £38,000; a four-bedroom modern estate house £50,000. **Haughley**, however, is pretty enough to have been colonised by commuters to Bury or Ipswich, combining new developments on the outskirts with an intimate old village street and a green with a 60-ton parish coalhouse upon it, built in 1861. It also has shops, restaurants, a doctor's surgery, and a vet. **Wetherden** has not been developed quite so much, and its preoccupations are firmly agricultural and horsy. Newmarket is not that far away, and point-to-points are regular and well attended. A three-bedroom thatched cottage in either village could be expected to cost £90,000 to £100,000.

Branchline to Bury St Edmunds via Elmswell and Thurston

No through trains. Trains to Ipswich: 1 every 2 hours
Journey time: 100 min (from Bury St Edmunds)
Season ticket from Bury St Edmunds: £3256

This area is not nearly as popular with London commuters as that served by the fast electric trains to Diss. Both **Elmswell** and **Thurston** are earmarked for expansion by the local authority. British Rail's skip-stop policy means that most trains roar straight through to Bury, with only the occasional one deigning to stop in the mornings and evenings.

Bury St Edmunds could be forgiven for regarding itself as the capital of East Anglia. As atmospheric as Norwich, Cambridge or King's Lynn, it sits right at the heart of the region on the conjunction of the A45, A143 and A134. On the rail network it stands on the watershed, suspended 28 miles from Cambridge and Ipswich. People travel west via Cambridge, east via Ipswich. Georgian and medieval houses crowd the centre, and in summer the tourists flock in to see the abbey ruins. The livestock market is on Wednesdays, and the covered market on Wednesdays and Saturdays. British Sugar has made it the base for one of its major production plants. West Suffolk Hospital is also there, and so is the Greene King brewery. Victorian terrace houses stand in appropriately named streets – Queens Road, Kings Road, Albert Crescent and so on. The two-bedroom version starts at around £55,000. Between-the-wars detached houses further out can be bought at £80,000 for three bedrooms, while something more lavish at an address like Home Farm Lane will cost at least £130,000.

Three miles to the north is **Culford**, best known for its mixed day and boarding public school. To the north-west you rapidly enter the Fens, and most people tend to prefer the more undulating landscape to the south. But **Fornham St Martin** on the northern edge is worth mentioning because it is soon to be relieved by a bypass, with property prices expected to pick up as a result. Four-bedroom houses skirting the Fornham Park golf course sell at £98,000. **Fornham All**

Suffolk half-timber and
thatch cottage

Saints is an older village altogether, centred around the church and village green. Four-bedroom houses here might fetch £95,000.

To the south is **Horringer** (once known as Horningsheath) with a set-piece church and green beside the entrance to Ickworth House (National Trust). The green is framed by neat cottages in plastered timber, flintwork and white brick that sell in an instant. Or there is **Cockfield**, an extraordinary cluster of hamlets, each with its own green, where a five-bedroom period house with three reception rooms might sell for £175,000. A mile away is **Great Green**, where you have village cricket on summer Sunday afternoons and four-bedroom detached houses selling at £120,000.

DISS

Journey time: *89 min*	Peak trains: *2 per hour*
Season ticket: *£3516*	Off-peak trains: *1 per hour*

Diss is extremely popular with commuters because the trains whistle through to London. During the property boom of the late Eighties the town expanded, a few computer companies moved in and prices went up. It currently has a population of around 7,500, and still has a weekly Friday market, though it no longer includes livestock. It has an indoor swimming pool, squash and tennis courts, and an 18-hole golf course but no cinema. In the town itself (which has mains gas) the streets to look at are around Denmark Street and Friends Road, where older Georgian houses mix with Fifties houses. A Fifties semi with three bedrooms might sell for £65,000, while a four-bedroom detached with large garden might fetch £125,000.

People say it is better to live south of the town rather than to the north where Norfolk starts, and where the villages tend to have fewer shops and amenities. But **Dickleburgh**, three miles to the north, has its own village stores, post office and doctor's surgery, and has just been bypassed. Or you could look west to **Redgrave**, which has a village green, post office and primary school. Much closer to Diss is **Palgrave**, which has a preponderance of artists, including a cartoonist, who live in the plastered and thatched cottages and regularly show their work. It has a post office-cum-shop, a green and a primary school. Locals complain that the school is cramped Victorian, but it cannot expand because it is built on common land. The only pub closed several years ago and the bar in the village hall is only open occasionally.

South-west is **Mellis**, a tiny scattered village with the most extraordinarily large 1,400-acre green. It has no pub, post office or shop, and the most talked-about feature is the common. The Suffolk Wildlife Trust likes to delay the hay-cutting in order to allow the wild flowers to reseed, but some villagers worry that so much dried grass represents a fire hazard. The green is bisected by the main railway line which can be noisy, depending which way the wind is blowing. Children attend the primary school here, then go to secondary school in Eye, but at sixth form level they have to move on to Framlingham.

For a very lively village life it would be better to look east to **Hoxne** (rhymes with oxen) which is set around the village green with an outstanding half-timbered priory with herring-bone brickwork. It has its modern estates, close to the primary school. The clubs and societies vary from the Ramblers to Hoxne Players, and there is a weekly youth club for teenagers that throws the occasional disco. The village has two pubs, three shops and a petrol pump. Country dancing around the maypole is a must, as is the Harvest Breakfast on the green in the autumn. A weighty breakfast is followed by a rousing church service. A small terrace house

Georgian farmhouse,
south Norfolk

here could be had for around £50,000, but something bigger with three bedrooms would start at £80,000.

Eye, four miles south, is a typical sleepy Suffolk market town on the River Dove, with a pharmacy, butcher, greengrocer, fabric shop, bank and post office, and an old castle. Though it is no longer a borough, it still has its mayor and deputy mayor. It attracts lots of London commuters and buzzes with societies. These include the Eye Business Association, the Gardening Club, the Eye Theatre, the Eye Bach Choir, old-time dancing and a ladies' cricket team called The Eye Catchers. It has a primary school and a small hospital that caters mainly for the elderly. Gardening is competitive – residents throw their gardens open to the public. And church fund-raising activities are frequent and impressive. A four-bedroom thatched cottage with a separate annexe at **Yaxley**, two miles away, would hit the market with a price tag of around £139,500.

NORWICH

Journey time: *105 min*	**Peak trains:** *3 per hour*
Season ticket: *£3788*	**Off-peak trains:** *1 per hour*

Very few people commute this far, though the attractions of **Norwich** are strong especially since the Broads and the Norfolk beaches are a car drive away. The hospitals and the University of East Anglia swell the ranks of the middle-class professionals in the city. It retains a strong sense of history as well as managing to be a vibrant shopping centre. To be within easy reach of the station you need to look at the south-east of the city where Victorian houses range from £43,000 for a two-bedroom walk-into-the-sitting-room terrace; to £80,000 for a three-bedroom semi; and £200,000 for a double-fronted detached villa. On a modern estate you could buy a three-bedroom semi for between £49,000 and £53,000, or a larger detached four-bedroom house for £85,000 to £90,000.

LIVERPOOL STREET
— TO —
SOUTHEND

BRENTWOOD

Journey time: *31 min*	**Peak trains:** *9 per hour*
Season ticket: *£1280*	**Off-peak trains:** *3 per hour*

People are fond of **Brentwood** because of its traditional high street with independent shops and its convenient position. It is right on Junction 28 of the M25, yet within walking distance of fields and woods. It exudes a sense of wealth, even among the young. Ford, the car manufacturer, has a strong presence as property owner as well as employer. Modern estates have been grafted on to gracious Victorian terraces and Thirties cul-de-sacs. The Homesteads, for instance, is one where mansion-sized houses are packed as tight as country cottages to create a feeling of village intimacy. A four-bedroom property here would cost £160,000. Brentwood's adult population empties into London every weekday, but many of them opt to catch the train at Shenfield (a recent survey showed that 15–20 per cent of commuters there were not local) for the faster service.

SHENFIELD

Journey time: *25 min*	**Peak trains:** *11 per hour*
Season ticket: *£1396*	**Off-peak trains:** *4 per hour*

See **Liverpool Street to Norwich** (page 16).

BILLERICAY

Journey time: *30 min*	**Peak trains:** *10 per hour*
Season ticket: *£1532*	**Off-peak trains:** *4 per hour*

Billericay is quiet, respectable and genteel. House prices are not as high as at Shenfield or Brentwood, but they are more expensive than Chelmsford. The town is close enough to the open countryside to attract a steady drift of people from London's East End. A private golf course is being built on the Chelmsford side. To park your car in the station car park you have to strike up a close relationship with the car park attendant, or join a waiting list which is several years long. And remember, there are between 3,000 and 4,000 season ticket holders to compete with.

WICKFORD

Journey time: *36 min*	**Peak trains:** *10 per hour*
Season ticket: *£1712*	**Off-peak trains:** *4 per hour*

People who live in **Wickford** consider themselves superior to those who live in Basildon but inferior to those from Rayleigh. Commuters pour in from the Dengie peninsula to catch the fast trains here, rather than take the stopping service on the Southminster branchline. Some of the trains stop at Stratford East, where people can switch painlessly to the London Underground. The town is a tumour of Sixties estates built on to the village of Shotgate, with green belt on three sides. You could spend £73,000 on a three-bedroom semi, or well over £100,000 on a house with four bedrooms. Where estates are more cramped, houses are cheaper. Starter homes are just under £50,000.

Branchline to Southminster via Battlesbridge, Woodham Ferrers, Fambridge, Althorne and Burnham-on-Crouch

Through trains: 2 per hour (peak)/1 per hour (off-peak)
Journey time: 80 min (from Southminster)
Season ticket from Southminster: £1908

British Rail class this as a branchline. But it differs from other branchlines in that during peak hours (and occasionally at other times during the day) the trains run straight through to Liverpool Street, so you are spared having to change trains.

South Woodham Ferrers is almost other-worldly, epitomising all that the Essex Design Guide had to say about the use of traditional materials and regional styles. Building began in 1976, which makes it one of the more recent attempts to create a planned new town instead of a rash of new developments. Banks are made to look like barns. Everything has steep pitch roofs and eaves, and the William de Ferrers school doubles as a public library, a police station and the hall for the amateur dramatic society. Planning regulations are fierce. You need permission for double glazing, and satellite dishes are out. The Round Table and other similar organisations are strong in a place where people are all newcomers together, forging links for the first time. "It is a real *thirtysomething* place. There are no old

Riverside apartments,
Burnham-on-Crouch

people and no poor people. It is said that the children may grow up with a warped view of life," said one local resident. One-bedroom houses start at £46,000, four-bedroom detached houses at £110,000. The Marsh Farm Country Park offers 320 acres of reclaimed marshland in which to walk the dog.

At **Fambridge** you enter yachting country. It has a post office and a general stores and is encircled by new estates. A bungalow on one of these would cost £100,000, and detached houses start at £120,000. **Althorne** is a tiny hamlet, half a mile from its station on the river. It is mostly modern, with a post office and a pub. A semi there costs £55,000 upwards, a bungalow £80,000, and a detached house £90,000 to £120,000. It is **Burnham-on-Crouch**, however, which is the real yachting capital of the Dengie peninsula, known as the pearl or the Cowes of the East Coast. Burnham Week attracts hundreds of yachts and visitors every year. The town has a mix of Victorian, Georgian and classic Essex weatherboarded cottages, and a huge modern complex of flats built on the quay, popular with weekenders. Those overlooking the river with mooring rights start at £160,000, while the smallest flats go for £50,000–£70,000. An older two-bedroom cottage could be had for £65,000.

Southminster suddenly seems remote at the end of the line, and house prices drop accordingly. It is a close farming community on the very edge of the marshes that stretch timelessly off into the North Sea. A three-bedroom semi here would cost £55,000. A grander house on the outskirts with a paddock would be upwards of £150,000. Southminster has its own primary school, cricket and football teams and choral society. **Tillingham**, to the north, is the archetypal Essex village with weatherboarded cottages, a green, a church and a pub. A two-bedroom cottage in a terrace starts at £50,000; a four-bedroom detached house in an acre would cost £150,000. Then there is **Bradwell-on-Sea**, still within reach of Southminster station. It has a village green fringed with cottages, and Bradwell Lodge, a Georgian house overlooking the Blackwater, with internal decorations by Robert Adam. Its church, St Peter's-on-the-Wall, is one of the earliest in England, built in 654, though only the nave remains. Close by is a marina and bird reserve, but the area is stigmatised by the presence of the nuclear power station.

RAYLEIGH

Journey time: *41 min*	Peak trains: *9 per hour*
Season ticket: *£1772*	Off-peak trains: *3 per hour*

This is where the large local Sainsbury is, where people from many of the surrounding towns come to do their shopping. **Rayleigh** mushroomed in the Thirties, and considers itself up-market of Basildon and Wickford. A two-bedroom bungalow here now costs £70,000, with three-bedroom houses at £80,000 and four bedrooms at £120,000 upwards. The nearby village of **Hullbridge** has the dubious honour of being dubbed by *The Sun* as the sexiest place in England. The reasons given were no more exciting than its high per capita birthrate and a local councillor's claim that the place is so boring that people have nothing better to do than stay at home and make babies. The village should be valued more for the fact that it sits on the Crouch Estuary, and if you join any part of the sea wall there you can walk along it as far as Battlesbridge, there to enjoy one of the few slivers of Essex landscape which have remained unsullied by modern pressures.

HOCKLEY

Journey time: *45 min*
Season ticket: *£1780*

Peak trains: *9 per hour*
Off-peak trains: *3 per hour*

The Southend area was developed in the 1890s, and the further you come inland from the tip, the more modern it becomes. **Hockley** and **Hawkwell**, roughly six miles inland, have mostly Sixties and Seventies houses, costing around £100,000 for three to four bedrooms. Hockley Woods is the place for Sunday walks, with drinks at The Bull afterwards.

ROCHFORD

Journey time: *49 min*
Season ticket: *£1780*

Peak trains: *9 per hour*
Off-peak trains: *3 per hour*

Rochford is a plain town with a square surrounded by banks and specialist shops including a delicatessen, a tea and coffee shop, and a watch repairer. The market is held here once a week. Hall Road is the smart address. The houses here have huge gardens that run down to the golf course, and you'll need up to £500,000 to buy. The town tends to feel overshadowed by Southend. It has a lake popular with the local anglers on Sundays. The choice of shops has improved with the opening of a new lakeside shopping centre off the M25 at Thurrock 10 miles away. **Ashingdon**, three miles away, offers lower property prices. A one-bedroom starter home on a new development here can be had for as little as £40,000, with two-bedroom Fifties bungalows at £60,000. It has a pub, a few shops and a baker, and it sits in a patch of Essex that is genuinely rural.

PRITTLEWELL

Journey time: *53 min*
Season ticket: *£1780*

Peak trains: *9 per hour*
Off-peak trains: *3 per hour*

Prittlewell is a restrained northern suburb of Southend. People who travel this line have seen the service improve dramatically in the last decade. "I'll tell you how bad it used to be," says one commuter. "About 10 years ago I sent a bottle of wine to the station manager just because my train was on time. Then 77 consecutive journeys were 10 minutes late."

SOUTHEND VICTORIA

Journey time: *55 min*
Season ticket: *£1796**

Peak trains: *9 per hour*
Off-peak trains: *3 per hour*

* **Also valid from Southend Central/East**

See Southend on the **Fenchurch Street to Shoeburyness** line (page 41). Most people prefer to use that line because the journey is quicker.

FENCHURCH STREET
—— TO ——
SHOEBURYNESS

WEST HORNDON

Journey time: *28 min*   **Peak trains:** *4 per hour*
Season ticket: *£1236*   **Off-peak trains:** *3 per hour*

Classic between-the-wars and post-war suburbia has sprouted at **West Horndon** because of the sheer convenience of the rail service, though it somehow remains rural and most of the 1930s bungalows have 150ft gardens, many of them backing onto fields. The station attracts commuters along the A128 from Brentwood who find it easier to drive south and catch the train here than tangle with the traffic in Brentwood or Basildon. A semi-detached bungalow sells for between £83,000 and £100,000, and a detached one for around £140,000 to £150,000.

LAINDON

Journey time: *33 min*   **Peak trains:** *9 per hour*
Season ticket: *£1424*   **Off-peak trains:** *3 per hour*

Laindon station has the advantage of an extra platform. A number of services start from here, and its commuters are guaranteed a seat. The down-market area is known locally as Alcatraz, where three-bedroom terrace houses cost around £40,000. The better area is Langdon Hills which is within a few minutes' walk of the station, where modern detached houses sell for about £150,000 to £160,000.

BASILDON

Journey time: *28 min*   **Peak trains:** *7 per hour*
Season ticket: *£1452*   **Off-peak trains:** *4 per hour*

Basildon has virtually swallowed up Laindon and Pitsea. As one of the eight new towns planned after World War Two to absorb people and industry from London, it exists as a kind of joke to people who once thought we could be weaned away from commuting. The planners decided people could live and work in the same place – industrial development was zoned to the north of the town – and for this reason it was built without a station. They finally had to bow to pressure and build one in the Seventies. The town's phenomenal rate of growth has not been without its problems. Older residents feel increasingly uneasy about walking alone at night, and the centre has to be heavily policed. You could buy a two-bedroom house for just under £50,000 and a three-bedroom one for around £60,000. The Kingswood area, close to the centre of town, is probably slightly more up-market than the rest, where a three-bedroom semi costs £95,000.

PITSEA

Journey time: *40 min*	Peak trains: *7 per hour*
Season ticket: *£1540*	Off-peak trains: *4 per hour*

Pitsea is rather more friendly than Basildon proper, with a defined centre and an open-air market in the sea of ex-council housing. Pitsea Mount offers some of the best private housing very close to the station, with two-bedroom semi-bungalows costing £80,000 and four-bedroom detached houses with garages costing just over £92,000.

BENFLEET

Journey time: *36 min*	Peak trains: *8 per hour*
Season ticket: *£1620*	Off-peak trains: *4 per hour*

The Southend Travellers Association says this is the busiest station on the entire line, serving a huge catchment area swollen with Sixties development. **Benfleet** itself is little more than ribbon development along the A130, and it is hard to find anything you could define as a centre. Three-bedroom semis cost about £65,000 and detached executive houses with four or five bedrooms cost £200,000.

The station also attracts commuters from **Canvey Island**, which is really the scrag end of Essex. So much of it lies below sea level that houses tend to offer views of the sea wall or oil refineries, and property is cheap. You can get a little one bedroom house for £35,000 to £40,000 or a three-bedroom semi for around £60,000. Traffic in and out of the island strangles the only two roads linking it to the mainland. Peter de Savary is behind plans to build 4,300 houses which might be accompanied by a new station just south of Benfleet.

LEIGH-ON-SEA

Journey time: *39 min*	Peak trains: *8 per hour*
Season ticket: *£1672*	Off-peak trains: *4 per hour*

Leigh blends a certain eccentricity (of the take-the-tricycle-rather-than-the-bus kind) with airs and graces, and is more sought after than its neighbours. The old town in particular is worth just going to see, since it retains its historical integrity as a working fishing village. You can watch the boats landing their catches, and the cockle sheds are well stocked. The two- or three-bedroom terrace cottages rarely come on the market and are quickly snapped up, for £70,000 or more, when they do.

Birdwatchers are treated to endless sightings of migratory birds that stop off at Two Tree Island, a stretch of saltmarsh that was once a refuse dump. And Hadleigh Country Park offers 100 acres of grazed downland with birds, butterflies and urbanised wildlife. Many of the larger Victorian houses have been filleted into flats. Something with one bedroom might sell at £35,000, two bedrooms at £40,000 to £45,000. Unconverted Twenties and Thirties houses up on the cliffs go for £100,000–£125,000.

CHALKWELL

Journey time: *41 min*
Season ticket: *£1676*
Peak trains: *7 per hour*
Off-peak trains: *4 per hour*

The Chalkwell Hall estate is extremely popular, being south of the London Road, close to the Fenchurch Street line and the bracing breezes from the sea-front. Large detached Victorian houses with four bedrooms cost £150,000 to £200,000.

WESTCLIFF-ON-SEA

Journey time: *43 min*
Season ticket: *£1688*
Peak trains: *8 per hour*
Off-peak trains: *4 per hour*

Westcliff is a dignified old Victorian lady of a town which has managed to fend off the encroaching seaside tat. Sadly, however, her densely layered streets of 19th-century houses, many of them now converted into flats, tend to be jammed with cars that can't find anywhere to park. Average prices of flats range from around £35,000 for one bedroom to £45,000 for two. The Cliff Gardens run all the way along the cliffs to Southend.

SOUTHEND CENTRAL

Journey time: *45 min*
Season ticket: *£1700**
Peak trains: *8 per hour*
Off-peak trains: *4 per hour*

* £1796 if also valid from Southend Victoria

Southend has spent the last few decades adjusting to the death of the Great British Holiday, while simultaneously adapting itself as a London dormitory. It remains popular with day trippers and bank holiday weekenders, and hasn't lost the brash, kiss-me-quick, ice cream and candyfloss feel of the Fifties. Strolling along the Prom is still a popular Sunday morning pastime. Education is a draw to jaded Londoners. Four of the eight grammar schools in Essex are to be found in Southend. The other four are divided between Colchester and Chelmsford. The one-and-a-quarter-mile pier, which miraculously survived a fire in 1976 and being cut by a boat 10 years later, is now being restored.

The Access credit-card company and the administrators of VAT are both large local employers. The shopping centre is now pedestrianised, though it is outdone in choice of shops by Basildon and the huge Lakeside development at Thurrock. Southend has its own airport with flights to France, Holland, Belgium, Denmark, Germany and Sweden, and charter flights to Malta, Portugal, Palma and Malaga. The sailing fraternity is strong. There are seven yacht clubs either side of Southend, in the stretch between Thorpe Bay and Leigh Old Town.

Average house prices run from £50,000 for a two-bedroom house, £60,000 or over for a three-bedroom semi, and £130,000–£150,000 for five to six bedrooms.

Sea-front property, Southend

SOUTHEND EAST

Journey time: *48 min*
Season ticket: *£1716**

Peak trains: *7 per hour*
Off-peak trains: *4 per hour*

* *£1796 if also valid from Southend Victoria*

This is the area known as **Southchurch**. A great web of residential streets extends from Southend Central to Thorpe Bay, stitched together by a long main road of shops and offices. A three-bedroom semi on one of the nicest roads – Southchurch Boulevard or Arlington Road, for example – will cost around £86,000. In less popular streets the price drops to around £70,000. Two- or three-bedroom terrace houses sell for around £53,000.

THORPE BAY

Journey time: *51 min*
Season ticket: *£1736*

Peak trains: *7 per hour*
Off-peak trains: *3 per hour*

Thorpe Bay is the most expensive part of Southend, and even those who live on the fringe-of-the-fringe say they live there. Detached houses with four to five bedrooms, built early this century, sell for around £200,000. Those on the sea-front might go for anything up to £400,000. The private golf club and the Conservative Club feature large on the social circuit, which is fuelled with new money and is anxious to dissociate itself from anything too down-market. There is only one pub. The place excites envy in its neighbours, as described by one local cricketer with typical Essex bluntness. "When you played against Thorpe Bay, you bowled at the batsman, not the wicket."

SHOEBURYNESS

Journey time: *54 min*	**Peak trains:** *5 per hour*
Season ticket: *£1764*	**Off-peak trains:** *3 per hour*

With its sprawling council estates and industrial zones, **Shoeburyness** has little to offer other than cheapness. A three-bedroom house can be had for around £58,000. It also has a beach which is good for windsurfing, sailing and jet skiing. There are a few small houses right on the beach that sell for around £70,000, but the marginally more salubrious part lies to the north. Here a new estate is being developed which includes everything from starter homes for £45,000 to five-bedroom houses for £250,000.

   Barling nearby offers profound contrast with little 300-year-old cottages selling for between £60,000 and £90,000, depending on condition. A period house with a paddock in this area would cost at least £250,000. Alternatively there is **Great Wakering**, with its church, pubs and shops. A two-bedroom cottage here would cost between £60,000 and £70,000, with a modern four-bedroom chalet in a quarter of an acre at around £170,000.

FENCHURCH STREET
— TO —
PITSEA

(via Tilbury)

GRAYS

Journey time: *32 min*	**Peak trains:** *6 per hour*
Season ticket: *£1288*	**Off-peak trains:** *2 per hour*

Grays was built in two surges – one in the late 19th century and one in the Thirties – and is now enjoying something of a renaissance as one of the busiest commercial centres in this part of Essex. The most sedate area to live is **North Grays** where the roads are filled with large 1930s houses. The four-bedroom detached variety would cost between £125,000 and £140,000. **North Stifford** is another popular part, with the remnants of the old village intact, though the 15th-century cottages that could sell for around £140,000 are now surrounded by modernity. The vast much-trumpeted Lakeside shopping centre at Thurrock, two to three miles away, with undercover parking for 9,000 cars, is challenging shoppers' loyalty to Basildon and Southend. Though Grays itself is a good secondary shopping centre and has small outlets of the big chains. Nearby is the site of the new Chafford Hundred development where between 4,000 and 5,000 new houses are being built on the old chalk pits beside the M25 and the Dartford Tunnel. It has everything from one-bedroom flats for £20,000 to £55,000 up to four-bedroom houses selling for around £125,000, with maisonettes, semis and terrace housing between.

TILBURY TOWN

Journey time: *36 min*	**Peak trains:** *6 per hour*
Season ticket: *£1392*	**Off-peak trains:** *2 per hour*

Tilbury itself bears all the warts and eyesores that the 20th century could have thrown at it. When the ships coming up the Thames got so big that they couldn't squeeze up to London any more, Tilbury became the main dock and developed a dock complex so huge it can be seen for miles around. Housing is very council-orientated and cheap. Tenants have been buying their properties and, regardless of age, you pay £45,000 to £50,000 for a three-bedroom house. The Tilbury loop has abandoned the use of first class carriages since British Rail has found there is little call for them. **Tilbury Riverside** burgeoned on the back of the new boat-trains to Europe in the 1850s. Now the only ferry that ploughs in and out is that which goes to Gravesend. The station has had a closure notice served on it by British Rail, but at the time of going to press the outcome is still to be decided. There is an hourly shuttle to Tilbury Town and the occasional peak service through to Fenchurch Street.

EAST TILBURY

Journey time: *42 min*	**Peak trains:** *4 per hour*
Season ticket: *£1516*	**Off-peak trains:** *2 per hour*

There are strangely rural, forgotten-about pockets in this town that has no bus service. Around quiet corners you come suddenly upon dirt tracks that open up long walks beside the Thames. The Bata shoe company was started here by Czechoslovakians who built their own flat-roofed houses, schools and cinema. The factory is still open but many of the houses have been sold on the open market. The old Bata office block has now been converted into flats which sell in the low £40,000 range. The older turn-of-the-century terraces cost about £65,000, but you can also buy the ubiquitous four-bedroom detached house for about £70,000 to £75,000. The station itself is antiquated, with an old timber platform, and the level-crossing gates are operated manually.

"It's called the Misery Line. I can honestly say I haven't come into work for a whole week ever without a problem," says one commuter. British Rail says it has plans to spend £200m on new Networker trains, and £100m on track and signalling improvements in the years 1993–97. The overcrowding on the line – it carries 500,000 passengers a week – is caused by the inexorable growth of new housing over the last 20 years that has not been accompanied by any commensurate expansion of the rail service.

STANFORD-LE-HOPE

Journey time: *46 min*
Season ticket: *£1540*

Peak trains: *4 per hour*
Off-peak trains: *2 per hour*

There are a few late 19th-century streets near the station, but otherwise most of **Stanford-Le-Hope** is an eruption of low-cost Sixties housing that engulfed **Corringham** and **Coryton** as far as the big oil refineries on the edge of the Thames. Three-bedroom semis are priced at about £65,000 to £70,000, standard four-bedroom detached houses at £90,000 and the most expensive in the range would probably sell for about £120,000 at the most. From here people might prefer to travel by rail up to Pitsea and change to the main line into Fenchurch Street, rather than take the slow and indirect route through Tilbury.

PITSEA

Journey time: *40 min*
Season ticket: *£1540*

Peak trains: *7 per hour*
Off-peak trains: *4 per hour*

See **Fenchurch Street to Shoeburyness** (page 40).

LIVERPOOL STREET
— TO —
KING'S LYNN

BROXBOURNE

Journey time: *28 min*
Season ticket: *£1260*

Peak trains: *5 per hour*
Off-peak trains: *4 per hour*

The railway came to **Broxbourne** in 1840. Victorian houses immediately started going up around the station, and it has been commuter country ever since. To the south of it is a soothing pocket of countryside where the New River lazes across the meadows. Other relics of the rural past, including Broxbourne Woods, have been retained by conversion into parkland. The Lea Valley Regional Park runs for 23 miles from Bromley-by-Bow through Broxbourne to Ware, making Broxbourne a handy resort for boating and holiday chalets – strategically placed near the all-singing, all-dancing leisure pool with its wave-machine, sauna and solarium. There has been a huge amount of new development. Detached houses on the more residential western side of the town can sell for up to £250,000; smaller three-bedroom houses to the east fetch between £80,000 and £110,000. There is a prestigious out-of-town Marks & Spencer and Tesco development at Cheshunt to the south, the first of its kind, which has parking spaces for 1,800 cars. Cheshunt also has a golf course, a wet-and-dry sports centre and a "fitness factory".

Broxbourne doesn't stop before **Hoddesdon** begins, though the atmosphere becomes rather more industrial. Hoddesdon is tightly bound by the green belt and it has a proper town centre with 17th-century buildings set around the old clock tower – an area busy with stalls on market day. Houses on the west and south sides are more desirable, being removed from the more industrial east. In the mix of Victorian, Thirties and Sixties houses you could buy a three-bedroom semi for £80,000 to £110,000. Larger houses, such as those in the privacy of College Road, sell for around £200,000.

LINE TO HERTFORD EAST (see map)

RYE HOUSE

Journey time: *50 min*
Season ticket: *£1308*

Peak trains: *3 per hour*
Off-peak trains: *2 per hour*

Rye House sits on the northern edge of Hoddesdon, on the finger of

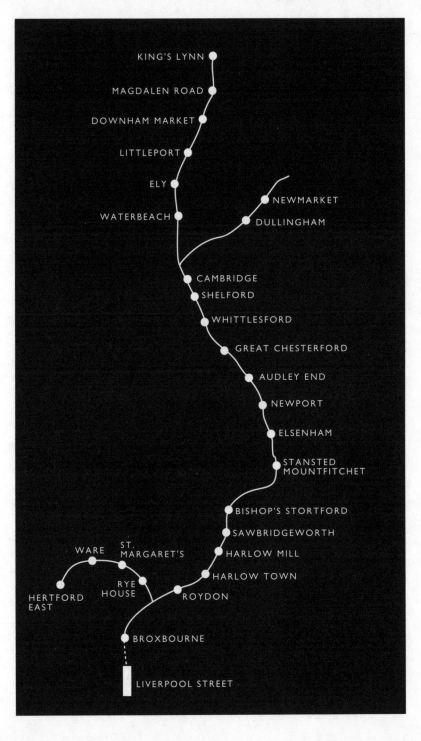

the Lea Valley Regional Park where the remains of the old Rye House gatehouse still stand. There was once a thriving nursery garden industry here. In the Thirties, says the local council, the Lea Valley had "the world's largest accumulation of glasshouses". Between 1968 and 1971 much of the old nursery land was surrendered to housing, thus creating what is now known as the Hundred Acre Estate, attached to the north side of Hoddesdon. Here you can buy a basic terrace house for £70,000; a three-bedroom semi for £95,000. Elsewhere in Rye House, property tends to be fairly cheap. Two-bedroom Victorian terraces can be bought for £50,000 unrestored; £65,000 restored. The relative modesty of the houses here is ironic when you remember that there was once a plan to make Rye House into a kind of genteel pleasure garden. The plans were buried when Sir Giles Gilbert Scott's huge power station arrived. There is certainly nothing genteel about the entertainments at Rye House Stadium: go-kart, speedway and greyhound racing.

ST MARGARET'S

Journey time: *52 min*	**Peak trains:** *3 per hour*
Season ticket: *£1388*	**Off-peak trains:** *2 per hour*

The village here is **Stanstead St Margaret's**, divided from **Stanstead Abbots** by the River Lea. A new bypass has reduced the amount of through traffic from 19,000 vehicles a day to 9,000. It is a fast-growing village with new houses going up all the time. There are no shops or post office but it does have two pubs and a special school for the disabled. The Crown pub used to be called the House Up A Tree because it had a tree-house to which people used to take their pints in the summer. The old malt industry lingers like a ghost. Disused cowls and chutes litter the skyline, and the smell of it still hangs over the terraced cottages and modern estates in Stanstead Abbots. There are some small shops and a post office on this side of the river, with playing fields and sports club just outside at St Margaretsbury. Stanstead Abbots has a voluntary-aided primary school attached to the church. Most of the older children attend secondary schools in Hertford or North Hoddesdon. The Stansteads have a marina with narrow boats, cruisers and rowing boats for hire. Property prices in both villages are similar to those in Hoddesdon.

WARE

Journey time: *56 min*	**Peak trains:** *3 per hour*
Season ticket: *£1476*	**Off-peak trains:** *2 per hour*

People say that this is where the chimney pots stop and the

countryside begins. **Ware** is a good old market town which hasn't been spoilt, and beyond it lies what the estate agents like to call the golden box – a group of handsome villages in a landscape which, despite its proximity to London, preserves a feeling of real remoteness. The town has a strong sense of history. The main local employer is Glaxo, whose factory has all the grandeur of a country house set in parkland by the river. In developing new sites it has dug up Roman remains. There were also bodies from the Black Death, shipped out along the River Lea for burial outside London. What Hertfordshire sent in return was water – channelled to the East End by way of the New River, a canal built in the early 17th century. Much of the town's wealth was created by the malting industry, and many of the old maltings have been converted into flats, mini-Docklands style, with prices that once were just as crazy. In these more sober times you could buy a one-bedroom flat on the water for just over £50,000; a two-storey flat with a sitting room the size of a football pitch for £110,000. It is a very charming place to live. The narrow boats still come past, there is a chandlery on the quayside, and there are some very pretty walks along the riverbank. These enable you to view the extraordinarily delicate old gazebos behind the houses in the high street, where the gardens run down to the river.

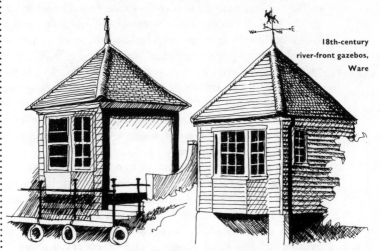

18th-century
river-front gazebos,
Ware

The town centre also contains quite a few mews houses, developed from the old stables and courtyards behind the high street. One of these would cost between £58,000 and £72,000 for one or two bedrooms. Ordinary two-bedroom Victorian cottages cost around £65,000; larger five-bedroom town houses around £175,000. There are some smart modern houses closer to the golf course on the south side of the town, where something with four bedrooms and a double garage would fetch up to £200,000. The town has lots of clubs and societies, which show themselves off once a year during Ware Week. There are indoor and outdoor heated swimming pools, cricket on the Old Hertfordians Ground, Hertford Rugby Club at Hoe Lane, and Ware Football Club. For major shopping, however, most people prefer Hertford.

The villages are in a quite different price zone. Footballers, pop stars and television personalities lurk down these country lanes, and you could easily pay up to £500,000 for an ex-farmhouse with acreage. **Great Amwell** is both the most expensive and the prettiest, with the New River draped in willows. Here it widens to a pool with two islands in it. These hold monuments to the New River's creator, the engineer Sir Hugh Myddleton, and floodlit concerts are sometimes given from them in the summer. Two miles away are the imposing buildings of Haileybury College. A period house with five bedrooms and two acres in Great Amwell could easily cost £400,000, though at the other end of the scale you might find a little two-up-two-down in need of modernisation for £45,000. The village has an annual flower show and every so often it opens its gardens to the public.

To the east is **Hunsdon**. Its timbered and weatherboarded cottages, village school and friendly atmosphere all contribute to its great appeal. Saturday coffee mornings are a regular event in the village hall, and there are societies for toddlers, tennis players and the elderly. Small Victorian cottages cost around £73,000, with the weatherboarded versions more in the region of £80,000. There are a great many larger houses too. Three-bedroom cottages can be expected to cost at least £150,000 and farmhouse-sized properties between £250,000 and £350,000. New houses are also being built in small handfuls, for those at managing director level, priced at £260,000 for five bedrooms.

In the precious northern belt are villages like **Standon** and **Puckeridge** in the Rib Valley. Standon is favourite, with its wide curving high street, timber-frame houses and village school. St Edmund's Roman Catholic College is a few miles to the west. Property prices are similar to those in Hunsdon. Puckeridge has a twisting high street and more the feel of a small town about it, with Sixties and Seventies developments tacked on. More new development may follow as a result of the expansion of Stansted airport. An older two-bedroom terrace here would cost £67,000; a new four-bedroom house £140,000. The Puckeridge and Thurlow hunt rides out from Brent Pelham nearby.

Braughing is a film-set village built at the confluence of the River Quin with the Rib. The approach to it is by way of a ford that occasionally floods. The colour-washed cottages have often been used as backdrops to television feature films, and some have superb pargeting. The smallest cottage here would cost around £72,000, with prices rising to about £400,000 for the larger period houses.

HERTFORD EAST

Journey time: *59 min*	**Peak trains:** *3 per hour*
Season ticket: *£1508**	**Off-peak trains:** *2 per hour*

* Also valid at Hertford North

See Hertford on **Moorgate/Kings Cross to Stevenage** line (page 89), for faster journey time into London.

CONTINUATION OF MAIN LINE TO CAMBRIDGE

ROYDON

Journey time: *40 min*	**Peak trains:** *3 per hour*
Season ticket: *£1408*	**Off-peak trains:** *1 per hour*

Roydon is quite a commuter haven, being handsome enough to have a conservation booklet written about it, but not chocolate-boxy. Some of the houses are genuinely Georgian; others have false Georgian fronts. The village revolves around the church, the green and the high street, which has many listed buildings. The school still thrives, though the village has lost a couple of shops including its butcher. It still has a bakery, chemist, part-time doctor's surgery, hairdresser, wine bar and a gunshop in the old forge. Other historical relics – unused – include village stocks and lock-up. Roydon has a flower festival every other year; the tennis court is well used, and the Roydon Players can be relied upon for local drama. A chalet-style bungalow with four bedrooms and two and a half acres here will cost around £200,000.

HARLOW TOWN

Journey time: *34 min*	**Peak trains:** *7 per hour*
Season ticket: *£1492*	**Off-peak trains:** *2 per hour*

It has to be said that many people hate **Harlow** in spite of its parks and Henry Moore sculptures (most of which are now so valuable that they have had to be put away in museums). The New Town was created in 1947 as a series of four large residential zones in a rural setting, each with its own infrastructure. The population jumped from 4,000 to over 80,000, mostly as a result of London overspill. Harlow has a good shopping centre at Broad Walk, its own nightclub, bingo hall and the Towngate Theatre. There is a sports centre, and Harlow Pool has aquatubes, a trimnasium, solarium and dance studio. The two large industrial estates on the edge of the town accommodate such companies as BP, Rank Hovis McDougall and Beecham.

Most of the houses were built with three bedrooms and small gardens, originally for rent. One of these is likely to cost between £60,000 and £65,000, depending on whether it has central heating and replacement windows. Those areas that still retain some association with the past tend to be more expensive. A house at The Stow, for example, may carry a premium of around £2,000. There are also some purpose-built private estates where a link-detached house (joined to its neighbour by the garage) will cost £90,000; a genuine detached house up to £110,000.

HARLOW MILL

Journey time: *48 min*   **Peak trains:** *3 per hour*
Season ticket: *£1540*   **Off-peak trains:** *1 per hour*

This is the station for some of Harlow's smarter parts – Mark Hall North, for instance, where a three-bedroom house still costs £62,000. **Harlow Old Town** is very popular because of the older period properties it contains. A house here is likely to cost £10,000 more than its nearest equivalent in the New Town. There are many pretty villages to the east. At **Fyfield** or **Moreton**, for example, you could buy a reasonably spacious bungalow for £165,000 or a discreet country house with six bedrooms and 11 acres for £600,000. People who live in this area are not famous for their liking of Harlow and are more likely to nip south and use the Central Line tube from Chipping Ongar.

SAWBRIDGEWORTH

Journey time: *51 min*   **Peak trains:** *3 per hour*
Season ticket: *£1624*   **Off-peak trains:** *1 per hour*

Sawbridgeworth is a low-rise town set in the fields and woods between Harlow and Bishop's Stortford, and – though at this point you are in Hertfordshire – this is where you begin to see the distinct local building styles of Essex: steep tiled gables and dormers, overhanging upper storeys, timber and weatherboarding. The town has two primary schools and enough shops for day-to-day needs, including bakers and butchers. There are all the usual societies, plus a lacemakers' group, the Sawbridgeworth Musical Youth Theatre, and the Old Malt House Music Society. In a strange reversal of trends, the old cinema has been turned into a Catholic church. Horse-riding is popular with local children. Flats in the converted Old Maltings by the station are particularly popular with commuters. A one-bedroom flat here will cost £45,000; a two-bedroom flat £64,000; and a three-bedroom house between £85,000 and £100,000.

BISHOP'S STORTFORD

Journey time: *34 min*	Peak trains: *7 per hour*
Season ticket: *£1728*	Off-peak trains: *3 per hour*

Bishop's Stortford is a wealthy little market town surrounded by very pretty villages. Aircraft coming in and out of Stansted airport fly around it to avoid causing any distress to those who live here. It has a good shopping centre, with a Sainsbury, a Tesco and the usual chainstores. A market is still held on most Thursdays in the market square. The town buzzes with local activities, including both operatic and amateur dramatic societies. The Juicy Duck Disco caters for ravers, and there are a couple of wine bars.

The older, more attractive buildings are in North Street, Windhill and the Old High Street. It is possible to buy a two-bedroom house in Bishop's Stortford for as little as £50,000; but a three-bedroom semi would take you over the £80,000 mark, and you should expect to pay £120,000 for a four-bedroom detached. The better side of town is the north-west corner. The private boys' school Stortford College is here, and the houses are large and secluded. Prices range beween £200,000 and £250,000. There is an equestrian centre at Hallingbury Hall, Little Hallingbury, and stables at Thorley.

To the west are the Hadhams. **Much Hadham** is probably the smartest village in the area. Its fashionable status derives from the fact that the Bishop of London once took up residence here, and subsequent bishops kept the palace going for centuries. It has a charming mix of Elizabethan cottages, 18th-century town houses and Victorian alms-houses. As in any village, the sizes and prices of the houses span a very wide range. You might buy a two-up-two-down for £65,000. At the other extreme, one of the larger houses with land is reputed to have sold for as much as £1.7m.

Further north are the Pelhams. **Stocking Pelham** is a particularly pretty village where a good country house with three acres could easily reach £300,000. A house complete with its own airstrip recently went for £230,000.

To the south-east is **Hatfield Broad Oak**, built on the edge of Hatfield Forest – more than 1,000 acres of National Trust woodland donated by the Puckeridge and Essex hunts. It is a handsome old village full of Georgian buildings, where property prices are probably five per cent higher than in Bishop's Stortford. There is some post-war development south and east of the high street. Hatfield Broad Oak has a post office-cum-general store, a butcher and wet fish shop, and an antique shop. Time does not stand still, however: the former craft shop now sells computers. The influx of commuters and working wives who are out of the village during the day, and so shop elsewhere, is making life difficult for the shopkeepers. Barrington Hall, a grand country house set in parkland, is now the office of a perfume company. You do get the occasional stray aircraft overhead, but for the most part they disturb other villages such as Great Hallingbury.

STANSTED MOUNTFITCHET

Journey time: *62 min*	Peak trains: *3 per hour*
Season ticket: *£1772*	Off-peak trains: *1 per hour*

The expansion of **Stansted** airport cannot but have a huge effect on the area surrounding it. The new passenger terminal opened in spring 1991 and the airport is growing steadily towards its predicted passenger total of eight million a year. Major road improvements are providing better links with the M11. **Manuden** is one of the nicest villages within striking distance of the railway station – a tiny one-and-a-half-street village on the River Stort with some very pretty jettied timber-frame houses. A three-bedroom detached bungalow in poor condition might cost around £95,000; a four-bedroom thatched 16th-century cottage would be likely to fetch £200,000.

ELSENHAM

Journey time: *65 min*	Peak trains: *3 per hour*
Season ticket: *£1808*	Off-peak trains: *1 per hour*

Elsenham offers a good view of the air traffic in and out of Stansted but strangely it is little affected by the noise. Its two most prominent features are a village pump in a domed octagonal well-house, and Elsenham Hall, a late Georgian red-brick mansion by the church. The village has seen a lot of new development in the last 10 years, and the range of property types and prices is large, from £40,000 to over £200,000. A three-bedroom modern house would cost around £72,000; a five-bedroom detached Edwardian house with an acre of ground might fetch £250,000. Shops include a butcher, greengrocer, post office and general store, and Bishop's Stortford is nearby for major shopping. It is a very horsy kind of a village, with plenty of activities: WI, gardening club, allotment association, cricket, football and keep fit clubs. The eponymous jam factory is not as huge as you would expect.

Ugley just to the north does not deserve its misleading name, and **Quendon**, too, is very pretty. The big house, Quendon Park, is surrounded by a wooded deer-park and has a good William and Mary south front. A tiny two-bedroom lath-and-plaster cottage could be bought for £76,000; a four-bedroom semi is likely to fetch £195,000.

To the north-east on the young River Chelmer is **Thaxted**, an impressive old village with a guildhall that broods over the open market place and an old windmill at the end of Fishmarket Street which has been restored as a museum. The church, with 181ft spire and medieval roofs, is one of the finest in Essex. Thaxted's problem is that it lies beneath the flight path to Stansted airport, but people are so attached to it that they don't seem to mind. Many of them move house within the village, and some Londoners have second homes here. A two-bedroom terrace house will cost around £53,000; a three-bedroom detached house £98,000.

NEWPORT

Journey time: *71 min*	**Peak trains:** *3 per hour*
Season ticket: *£1876*	**Off-peak trains:** *1 per hour*

Newport has always been a more expensive place to live than neighbouring Saffron Walden, to which it long ago lost its market. It has a fine main street of gracious houses, all within easy reach of the station and the M11. A five-bedroom house with a quarter of an acre and a tennis court would cost around £235,000. An added attraction is Newport Grammar School for boys – an ex-grammar but still highly respected.

Essex begins to get pricey here, with a collection of very pretty villages. South-west of the station are **Clavering**, with its cluster of cottages around the church, and **Rickling Green**. The latter has a picture-book green with a cricket pitch appropriately overlooked by a pub called The Cricketers. A two-bedroom semi here would cost around £95,000.

Nearer to the station, only a mile to the west, is **Wicken Bonhunt**, very small and exclusive, where a five-bedroom bungalow will cost around £325,000. Another mile brings you to **Arkesden**, by a little stream called Wicken Water. Thatched cottages spread themselves around a green, and there is a good 16th-century hall and 13th- to 14th-century church. A three-bedroom thatched cottage would be likely to fetch around £160,000.

On the east side is **Widdington**, also very small and expensive, a hilltop village with cottages around the green and larger houses hidden in the lanes. A four-bedroom detached house would cost around £260,000; a small lath-and-plaster cottage around £95,000. **Debden** is another thatched village on the way to nowhere. The occasional two-bedroom modern semi could be bought here for around £60,000. More interestingly for rural dreamers, a number of old barns are being converted into houses. Some are being sold as shells at around £65,000; finished homes sell for up to £210,000.

AUDLEY END

Journey time: *56 min*	**Peak trains:** *4 per hour*
Season ticket: *£1908*	**Off-peak trains:** *2 per hour*

There is little more at **Audley End** than the station itself. The town it serves is **Saffron Walden**, which is one of the few places in this extremely wealthy part of the country where the less well off and the young can afford to buy. There is still some Quaker pride here: the town has a Waitrose but no other major retailers have moved in. The shops are old-fashioned, family-run firms that go back over several generations. Goddards the butchers, for example, have been here for centuries. The huge common, once used for grazing cattle and medieval tournaments, now serves as a fairground and recreation area. Its most puzzling feature is a rare turf maze – archaeologists still don't understand its purpose. Friends co-educational private school is a draw for many of the families who come to live here. There are quite a few inexpensive modern estates. A two-bedroom flat will cost around £37,000; a three-bedroom semi around £56,000; and a three- or four-bedroom detached house between £65,000 and £70,000. Older one-bedroom cottages start at £50,000, and Thirties semis around £76,000. The town can be rather touristy in summer, which some people might consider a drawback.

The villages nearby are beyond the reach of most local young couples. At **Wendens Ambo**, right beside the station, one of the (very few) four-bedroom modern houses would be likely to fetch around £185,000. The more substantial five-bedroom, three-reception room houses built in the Sixties would sell for £245,000. The lane to the church has some particularly appealing cottages. **Littlebury** nearby is also expensive, with a good collection of lath-and-plaster cottages on the tip of the Chiltern foothills near the site of an Iron Age camp. A 150-year-old two-up-two-down will cost £60,000; a converted barn would be likely to fetch well over £300,000.

On the east side of Audley End is **Wimbish** – little more than a smattering of houses through the lanes. The presence of an Army barracks pulls the prices down to Saffron Walden levels. **Hempstead**, Dick Turpin's birthplace, is very popular though the road to it is winding and slow. A five-bedroom farmhouse would cost around £235,000; a modern four-bedroom house around £160,000. To the north-east, on the map closer to Great Chesterford (the next station) though there is no road between them, is **Hadstock**, a pretty village with thatched cottages around a green. Two-bedroom flats in the converted manor house have been selling for just under £100,000.

GREAT CHESTERFORD

Journey time: *79 min*	**Peak trains:** *2 per hour*
Season ticket: *£1952*	**Off-peak trains:** *1 per hour*

Little and **Great Chesterford** are both extremely prestigious, being close enough to attract people working in Cambridge. The River Cam tiptoes through both and in Great Chesterford it is overlooked by a large watermill converted into flats. A one-bedroom unit here would cost around £55,000. The village has a family grocer and a few other shops, and some very stylish early houses, one of which has some spectacular pargeting. An ordinary three-bedroom house without period details will cost at least £160,000.

WHITTLESFORD

Journey time: *83 min* | **Peak trains: *3 per hour***
Season ticket: *£2000* | **Off-peak trains: *1 per hour***

Whittlesford is ideally situated close to Cambridge and the M11 but it is a very small village and prices are on a par with neighbouring **Duxford**, which is the more obvious place to look. Most people know Duxford for its airfield, which houses part of the collection of the Imperial War Museum. In addition to the permanent display of historic aircraft there are flying displays and pleasure flights in the summer. There are some nice old pubs and some thatched cottages, though these have been rather swamped by the new estates and bungalows. A two-bedroom detached bungalow will cost around £80,000; a three-bedroom detached house £95,000.

   Sawston has an image problem caused by the large council estates with which it is surrounded. What draws many people to it, however, is the presence of a Cambridge Village College (see Cambridge below). Small one-bedroom houses cost around £45,000; three-bedroom semis in the region of £60,000.

SHELFORD

Journey time: *88 min* | **Peak trains: *2 per hour***
Season ticket: *£2068* | **Off-peak trains: *1 per hour***

Great Shelford and **Little Shelford**, with **Stapleford** into which they merge at the base of the Gog Magog Hills, all ooze prosperity. This is where the Cambridge wealthy – businessmen and London commuters rather than academics – choose to make their homes. The houses are large and secluded, with parks and other green open spaces to enhance the feeling of spaciousness. There are plenty of shops, including a boutique. Period houses in Great Shelford's Mingle Lane and Gog Magog Way, which leads to the Gog Magog Golf Club, are thought to have particular appeal, with price tags of over £500,000 for eight or nine bedrooms. You don't have to be rich to live here, however. A new development close to the station offers two-bedroom starter homes at £57,000. Sawston Village College, one of the much-admired Cambridge Village Colleges (see Cambridge below), is the local secondary school.

CAMBRIDGE

Journey time: *68 min* | **Peak trains:** *4 per hour*
Season ticket: *£2148* | **Off-peak trains:** *2 per hour*

See **Kings Cross to Grantham** (page 78).

The property market in **Cambridge** has a mind of its own, being heavily influenced by the constant comings and goings of university academics and the staff of the high-tech industries that have thrived in the university's shadow. During the Eighties the explosion of scientific, medical and agricultural companies based on university research was known as the Cambridge Phenomenon – and predictably it delivered an upward thrust to local house prices. Though prices have now fallen back, the turnover of properties is still fairly brisk and the number of people working in the area has increased. Because this beautiful but still quite tiny city is bursting at the seams, it is not surprising that a whole new village, with homes for up to 5,000 people, was being planned, as well as a new town for up to 10,000 more. However both of these plans have been shelved for the moment. There is also talk of filling the green space between the city and the A45 with houses.

To the north lie the Science Park and the stark flat landscape of the Fens. It is the south, therefore, that most people prefer. The station is here, and so are the better schools, including The Perse co-educational private school. The area closest to the station, around Tennyson Road, is popular with young couples. Two-bedroom Victorian terraces in this area cost £70,000. On the other side of the tracks they cost £60,000. Larger four-bedroom Victorian houses in the station area will cost around £130,000. The Kite, so called because of its diamond shape, is another favoured address, close to the new shopping centre. A two-bedroom Victorian house here would cost around £75,000. Alternatively, to the west, there is Newnham – an old-established residential area where a typical bay-fronted three-bedroom Victorian house would cost £90,000 to £95,000.

Modern timber-style house, Cambridge

The most expensive, exclusive and attractive village in the area has to be **Grantchester**, two miles to the south. As a student Rupert Brooke lived here at the Old Vicarage, now occupied by Jeffrey Archer. Brooke's best-remembered lines, "Stands the Church clock at ten to three?/And is there honey still for tea?", are a reference to his time in Grantchester. The village's many attractions include walks along the Cam, pretty but crowded pubs, and pretty cottages that sell for enormous sums. You could possibly get a small two-bedroom Victorian terrace for £80,000; but a five-bedroom house with a large garden near the millpond is likely to fetch £450,000.

To the west of Cambridge is **Comberton**. This is a good village for families since it contains one of the highly regarded Cambridge Village Colleges. A handful of these were built to embody the ideas of Henry Morris, who was chief education officer at Cambridge from 1922 to 1954. He believed that secondary schools could be run like small colleges, serving several villages while at the same time fulfilling their cultural needs and providing adult education. Property prices in the villages (excluding Grantchester) generally tend to be much lower than those in Cambridge itself. A three-bedroom semi on a Sixties estate will cost around £60,000 to £65,000.

Due west of Cambridge is **Madingley** – worth looking at because of the stunning views across to the spires and towers of Cambridge, seen against the backdrop of the Gog Magog hills. Much of the village is owned by the university, and the hall is now a hostel for graduates. Prices are probably up to 10 per cent lower than Grantchester's.

The countryside in the north looks markedly less friendly. **Histon**, having long been the base of the Chivers jam-making enterprise, is almost a small town now, with shops, sub-branches of banks, building societies and garages. Its main attraction is its proximity to **Impington**, which has a Village College designed in the early Thirties by Walter Gropius and Max Fry. It is also close to Girton, home not only of Girton College but also of Girton Golf Club. A three-bedroom semi-detached in Histon will cost £60,000 to £65,000.

In the east, on the edge of fens which can sometimes look like the edge of the world, are **Swaffham Bulbeck** and **Swaffham Prior**. They are eight miles from Cambridge, but worth considering if you want to escape the academic atmosphere which affects some of the other villages. Both are remarkably unspoiled and have some charming period cottages. At Swaffham Prior (where the poet Edwin Muir once lived) you could buy a detached cottage with two double bedrooms for £85,000.

The A45 is an important dividing line in the east. Anything to the south of it, where the countryside starts to ripple again, will command a higher price. **Fulbourn** serves as a Cambridge suburb, with new developments encroaching on the older houses and thatched cottages. There is a range of shops, a primary school and a mill which is open to the public. Nearby is Fulbourn Fen, an educational nature reserve. There is also a large Victorian mental hospital. A three-bedroom semi on a new estate will cost £65,000; a four-bedroom detached house with two bathrooms around £135,000; a four-bedroom period house over £200,000.

Branchline to Newmarket via Dullingham

No through trains. Trains to Cambridge: 1 per hour
Journey time: 120 min (from Newmarket)
Season ticket from Newmarket: £2264

Dullingham is quite remote, probably suited to two-car families, and it stands out as expensive in an otherwise low-priced area. It is very pretty, with thatch-and-clunch cottages, an old farm and stables, and a village green. A small thatched cottage would cost around £75,000; a four- or five-bedroom modern detached house between £110,000 and £175,000. The village shop has gone, but Tesco provides a coach service into **Newmarket**. This is the place to live if you are a fancier of horseflesh. The town lives and breathes racing. The chalk downland is peppered with stud farms, shelter belts and exercise areas, with the National Stud at Newmarket Heath. Strings of horses can be seen each day trailing through the town to the specially designed horsewalks leading to the gallops. There are two racecourses – the Rowley Mile and the July. A large house with stabling and acreage could cost anything from £200,000 to £500,000. But you can still get small, unmodernised two-bedroom houses for £30,000–£40,000. The co-educational Japanese boarding school Shi-Tenoji is nearby.

Beyond Cambridge there are no through trains at the moment but later this year (1992) the line is due to be electrified and Ely and King's Lynn services will operate through to Kings Cross, taking about 100 minutes. (Currently the journey time is 129 minutes, changing at Cambridge.) The option of changing at Cambridge for Liverpool Street will remain.

Stations between Cambridge and King's Lynn: Waterbeach, Ely, Littleport, Downham Market, Magdalen Road
Season ticket from King's Lynn: £2584

The trains out of **Waterbeach** in the morning are full of children on their way to school in Cambridge or Ely. The village does have its own primary school, however, attached to the community centre. Here you can also take evening classes, or join the Waterbeach Players, or the brass band. Waterbeach has an Army barracks, a post office, hardware store, grocer, cobbler, fish-and-chip shop, butchers and bakers, and several pubs. There is a Tesco three miles away at Milton. The Waterbeach Feast, a procession of floats and stalls, is held every June and traditionally at this time the local women have always made frumenty – boiled wheat in a thick sweet milk-and-sugar sauce with raisins. The best houses are the classic Cambridge brick houses around the village green, which have a preservation order on them. A three-bedroom semi in Waterbeach is likely to cost around £60,000.

Cottenham, also on the edge of the fens close to Waterbeach station, has a Village College in its favour but it has expanded rather brutally. Its population has doubled in only 20 years. A two-bedroom Victorian terrace will cost just over £55,000.

Ely had remained aloof, cut off from Cambridge by the fens for so long that the Eighties property boom arrived as something of a shock. Some of the older residents have been heard to claim that they haven't let anyone from outside the area cross their threshold for 30 years or more. Now, however, people tend to move here as a cheaper alternative to Cambridge. There are a few brave London commuters, and some Londoners with second homes. A house with a view of Ely's remarkable 11th-century cathedral is usually thought more desirable than a home in one of the villages. It is a very small, compact city with a tiny high street, though it does have both a Tesco and a Sainsbury. Georgian houses sit quite happily alongside Thirties semis, and there are no distinct up-market areas. A three-bedroom semi might cost around £55,000; an older, larger town house around £80,000 to £100,000. There are dramatic and choral societies for those inspired by the theatrical fen landscapes. King's School is situated close to the cathedral.

Some people are also attracted to the area by thoughts of the Good Life – the cottage with a productive vegetable garden, a few ducks and a goat. Villages to the south and west, such as **Witchford**, **Sutton**, **Haddenham**, and **Stretham**, are the most sought after. You should expect to pay around £50,000 for a two-bedroom semi; between £85,000 and £110,000 for a four-bedroom detached.

Littleport is a thriving little fen town with some beautiful old houses as well as plenty of new estates and more to come. The thatched bank and thatched electrical shop are attractive local curiosities. A completely restored turn-of-the-century house with four bedrooms will cost £100,000; a new house with the same number of bedrooms £83,000. Littleport is due to get a new leisure and sports centre but it already has countless sports clubs (at least three of them involving badminton). Littleport Village College provides evening classes. Secondary-age children go to school in Ely. Littleport has plenty of day-to-day shops including a wonderful bakery, a butcher and fishmonger, and a clothes shop. "The best thing about living here is that there are such beautiful sunsets, flooding across acres and acres of open sky," says one enraptured local resident. Some of the older people are keenly superstitious and fond of weather-prediction – grasshoppers in a ditch mean foul weather for Thursday week.

Downham Market is popular with people who are taking early retirement. Estate agents say that nine out of 10 people looking for properties here are about to stop work. It is a pleasant Norfolk town with plenty of shops, a floodlit football ground, a swimming pool, and a half-built industrial estate on the outskirts. It used to be an inland port but today the river is a thing to walk beside rather than a busy thoroughfare for imports and exports. It is the kind of place where you can leave your

200-year-old brick-and-flint
farmhouse, Downham Market

car unlocked all day, and where you don't have to queue in the supermarket. A two-bedroom turn-of-the-century terrace house will cost around £35,000; a three-bedroom semi £45,000; a three-bedroom detached house £55,000.

Magdalen Road station really serves **Watlington**, a village which already has a great deal of new development and is likely to get even more. It has a couple of shops, a primary school and a doctor's surgery. A three-bedroom detached house would cost around £53,000.

The old port of **King's Lynn** has a definite appeal for birdwatchers, who can be seen in their anoraks and wellington boots scanning the sky with their binoculars. The marshes and mudflats of the Wash are a great attraction for waterfowl and waders. The riverside is a favourite spot for watching the fishermen come in, though Fisher Fleet, the fishermen's quarter, can get a little smelly. Architecturally, much of the stuffing was knocked out of King's Lynn as old buildings were replaced by housing estates. The conservationists now have a firm grip on what is left – a historic legacy which includes the merchants' houses of Nelson Street, Queen Street and King Street – most of which are now used as offices. The King's Lynn Arts Centre has a gallery and theatre, and in the summer there is an annual music and arts festival, usually attended by one of the Royals (Sandringham is only eight miles away). It is the biggest shopping centre for miles around, with Body Shop being one of the latest arrivals. A three-bedroom semi on a new estate will cost roughly £45,000. Among the older properties you could pick up a small three-bedroom terrace house for £35,000. Even the most expensive old town houses will probably not exceed £100,000.

KINGS CROSS TO GRANTHAM

BROOKMANS PARK

To Moorgate only
Journey time: *35 min*
Season ticket: *£1212*

Peak trains: *3 per hour*
Off-peak trains: *2 per hour*

This is the world of personalised number plates and golf courses, the playground to Potters Bar. Large expensive houses, some of them sealed behind tall hedges, have been built between lakes and woodlands in the grounds of two long-demolished country houses called Brookmans and Gobions. The railway arrived in 1926, and gradually suburbia ate up the surrounding fields. The price of a four-bedroom house in **Brookmans Park** can vary between £200,000 and £1m.

WELHAM GREEN

To Moorgate only
Journey time: *38 min*
Season ticket: *£1268*

Peak trains: *3 per hour*
Off-peak trains: *2 per hour*

Welham Green is definitely a step down from Brookmans Park. The village offers a mix of private developments and council estates built around a centre with a green, shops and a garage. A three-bedroom detached house could be bought for £120,000 – possibly 50 per cent cheaper than an equivalent house in Brookmans Park.

HATFIELD

To Kings Cross
Journey time: *24 min*
Season ticket: *£1380*
Peak trains: *4 per hour*
Off-peak trains: *2 per hour*

To Moorgate
Journey time: *41 min*
Season ticket: *£1380*
Peak trains: *3 per hour*
Off-peak trains: *2 per hour*

Hatfield is probably the dreariest of the new towns in this area, though the council is now investing a lot of money in trying to inject a little more fun. It has a new American-style shopping centre, the Galleria, with a nine-screen cinema and a drive-in McDonald's. There is also a new leisure centre with a swimming pool, plus the older swimming pool which is celebrated for having the largest hyperbolic paraboloid roof in Europe.

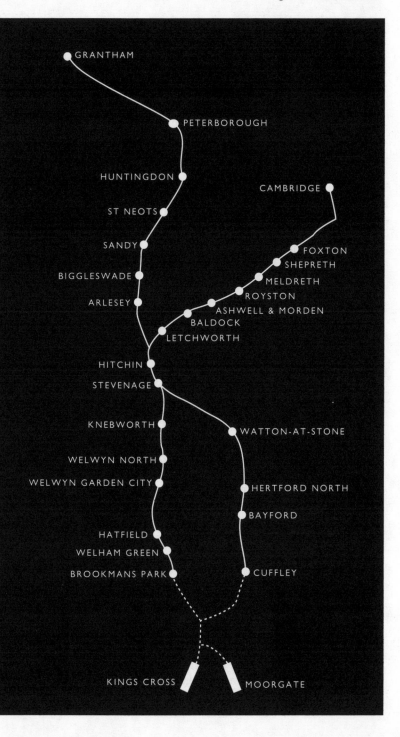

Hatfield's advantages lie in its strategic position – being close to the A1, the M25, and only a wingbeat from Kings Cross by train – and in offering lower house prices than surrounding areas. Its greatest public attraction is Hatfield House, built in the early 17th century by Robert Cecil at the top of the hill, one of the first houses to be lit by "Edison-Swan electric incandescent light bulbs", patented in 1879.

Most people prefer the red-brick houses of Old Hatfield to the Thirties-style, bypass variegated houses and shopping parades of the 1948 New Town. A cottage with two bedrooms in Old Hatfield would be likely to cost around £70,000, though a flat of similar size would be slightly cheaper at £65,000. There aren't many large properties, but a three- or four-bedroom detached house will cost from £130,000 upwards. Two of the best roads are The Ryde, which has detached houses and bungalows, and Ellenbrook, where there is a mix of Thirties semis and detached houses. The lowest price for something with three bedrooms here would be £100,000. In New Hatfield the starting price for a three-bedroom semi is around £75,000, rising to around £130,000. Ex-council terrace houses can be picked up for just under £60,000.

WELWYN GARDEN CITY

To Kings Cross	To Moorgate
Journey time: *27 min*	Journey time: *44 min*
Season ticket: *£1528*	Season ticket: *£1528*
Peak trains: *4 per hour*	Peak trains: *3 per hour*
Off-peak trains: *2 per hour*	Off-peak trains: *2 per hour*

Ebenezer Howard, with his chief architect Louis de Soissons, designed **Welwyn Garden City** around the commuter. Early residents in the Twenties had to wade through the builders' mud in their wellington boots to get to the station, and changed into their city shoes on the train. The fusion of garden and city still remains very attractive, and the original cottagey houses behind perfectly clipped hedges are very much sought after, though some newcomers are deterred by the fact that some of them are on 99-year or 999-year leases from the council, which were inherited from the Welwyn Garden Company. The utilitarian planning means that there is very little sense of one street being more up-market than any other. The wide main shopping boulevards now look strangely dated, and local shops and businesses tend to feel they have lost out to the bustle and variety of St Albans nearby. There is, however, a John Lewis department store, and the new Howard Centre close to the station has added new life to the shopping scene. Sports enthusiasts are well catered for by the Goslings Sports Stadium and there are two 18-hole golf courses for devotees of the game.

The best side of the town is the west, where a three-bedroom house with a garage in a quiet tree-lined road could cost £135,000. It is possible, however, to buy a one-bedroom house or maisonette at just over £50,000. The town is still evolving, and large new private estates are being built near the Panshanger aerodrome. Here you can buy anything from studios at just over £40,000 to large executive houses at £200,000.

Modern "executive" home, Wheathampstead

There is some very pretty, rolling wooded countryside around Welwyn Garden City, and those who prefer an older village could look at **Wheathampstead** to the west. As you approach the charming high street from the direction of St Albans you pass a small quay on the River Lea, and then a converted watermill which now contains a harberdasher, a secondhand clothes shop, a butcher and offices. The village has two primary schools, from which children move on to secondary schools in Harpenden and St Albans. There is a library, four churches of different denominations, and lots of clubs and societies, including wine-making and archery clubs, cricket and tennis. You could pay well over £100,000 for a small cottage in this area. Nearby is Brocket Hall, where Lady Caroline Lamb once emerged naked from a soup tureen. It is used to host rather more sober occasions now that Lord Brocket has converted it into a hotel and conference centre.

Old Welwyn, just to the north of Welwyn Garden City, is so much more refined and mature than its upstart neighbour. It has a mix of houses from two-up-two-downs with tiny courtyard gardens, priced at around £80,000, to larger four-bedroom cottages fronting the road at £150,000 to £160,000. On the edge, away from the shops in the main street, is a new executive development called Danesbury Park. A four-bedroom, box-shaped house here will cost £155,000; a five-bedroom one £200,000.

WELWYN NORTH

Journey time: *31 min*	**Peak trains:** *3 per hour*
Season ticket: *£1564*	**Off-peak trains:** *2 per hour*

The village best served by this station is **Digswell**, which consists of large detached houses with secluded gardens sewn into the lanes behind high hedges – some of them dominated by the huge viaduct built to carry the Great Northern Railway over the valley. Houses tend to be sold very discreetly, and are not cheap. Those with large gardens are in the £700,000 to £800,000 bracket. Last year the house formerly occupied by Enid Blyton's illustrator, Eileen Soper, went on the market at £245,000. The garden, much of which had been left to the Royal Society for the Protection of Birds, was so overgrown that the agent couldn't even photograph the house properly.

Tewin is another wooded dormitory, but the sale of the village by the Cowper estate in 1919 led to its rapid expansion, with large new estates leeching on. The Upper Green is still used for tennis, cricket and football matches. The cheapest three-bedroom modernised cottage on the green would cost just under £100,000; larger four- and five-bedroom detached houses in large gardens fetch around £300,000.

The Ayots to the west, like Digswell, are very exclusive: **Ayot St Peter**, perched on a hilltop, and **Ayot St Lawrence**, with its narrow lanes walled between hedgebanks. The latter also has a popular old pub, the Brocket Arms, a post office, and George Bernard Shaw's house, the late Victorian Shaw's Corner, where he lived until his death in 1950. The house, which has Shaw's writing hut at the bottom of the garden, is in the hands of the National Trust. The village's most prominent landmark, however, is the extraordinary neo-classical parish church, viewed like an 18th-century folly across a meadow. House prices range from £200,000 up to £800,000.

KNEBWORTH

Journey time: *35 min*	**Peak trains:** *3 per hour*
Season ticket: *£1728*	**Off-peak trains:** *2 per hour*

As is the case with most towns and villages in this area, there is an old and a new **Knebworth**. Old Knebworth grew up around the big house and parkland. The newer part was built around the railway station, which arrived at the turn of the century. Lutyens tried his hand with some cottages in Deard's End Lane and Park Lane, and he also produced a golf clubhouse and the remarkable church of St Martin. The village has all the day-to-day shops you would need, covering everything from videos to fast-food; it also has its own dentist, doctor and Indian restaurant. It is hugely popular with commuters, many of whom never escape from the sound of the trains. Because the railway line runs right through the middle, many of the older, quainter cottages back straight on to it. A two-bedroom cottage in this position would cost £70,000 to £80,000. More expensive houses are to be found in Oakfields Road and Oakfields Avenue, where you might have to pay £250,000 to £300,000 for a Twenties house with a mature garden backing on to open fields. In Deard's End Lane, a Lutyens house will cost £300,000 to £400,000. There are plenty of local activities and clubs, from cricket to amateur dramatics and old-time dancing, and there is a two-week annual summer festival. This is aside from the rock festivals at Knebworth House.

Waiting for trains at Knebworth is made slightly more pleasant by the presence of a huge grapevine, planted when the station opened, with its roots in the platform itself. The station master has been known to harvest up to 55lb of grapes from it and make five or six gallons of wine. The station refit a couple of years ago caused much consternation over disturbance to the vine, but somehow it has managed to survive.

Many people prefer the atmosphere of the smaller, more rural villages such as **Datchworth** to the east, where the community spirit remains strong and anyone who falls ill, or who can't fetch the children from school, soon finds their needs catered for. Pony paddocks abound. There are several riding stables in the area and local farms put on shows at weekends. It has general stores, a primary school and a much-loved sports pavilion where badminton and squash are played, with a rugby field behind it. There is a mix of property spread between a web of greens, from three-bedroom semis selling at around £100,000 to the kind of place that comes with an acre of ground, tennis court, and price tag of around £360,000. Barry Norman lives here.

STEVENAGE

To Kings Cross	To Moorgate
Journey time: *24 min*	Journey time: *49 min*
Season ticket: *£1824*	Season ticket: *£1824*
Peak trains: *5 per hour*	Peak trains: *2 per hour*
Off-peak trains: *4 per hour*	Off-peak trains: *nil*

Stevenage offers something like safety-net housing for people who can't afford Hertfordshire's plusher towns and villages. It isn't attractive, but the house prices are low by comparison and the train service is excellent. The station is served not only by the Royston and Peterborough commuter services but also by the InterCity 125s on the East Coast line into Kings Cross and trains going to Moorgate down the Cuffley loop (see page 91). The New Town developments have streets romantically named after famous explorers, cathedrals, inventors, cricketers and so on, but in reality they offer little more than the uniformity of the three-bedroom mid- and end-terrace. Most are designed according to what is called the Radburn principle, which means that pedestrians and traffic are kept well apart. Houses in the better areas such as Martin's Wood, Shephall and Broadwater, might fetch around £70,000. Those in the less well-liked areas such as St Nicholas and Bedwell Crescent might be had for £50,000. There is also a sea of council housing, now peppered with repossessions, some brought about by the redundancies made by large local employers such as British Aerospace and Marconi. A three-bedroom repossessed semi can be picked up for £55,000.

The beauty of the large modern shopping centre is that it is genuinely traffic-free. The various neighbourhoods, including the industrial area, are joined to each other, and to the centre, by cycleway, a cleverly designed miniature road network which at peak periods takes up to 1,100 people per hour on their way to and from school or work. The shopping centre offers excellent choice, with all the major chain stores as well as a large range of retail warehouses such as B&Q and Texas Homecare. At Poplars there is a giant Sainsbury superstore. The covered market is open three days a week, and the stalls for the outdoor market go up on Wednesdays and Saturdays.

Stevenage is very strong on computers and technology, both in the businesses it attracts to its huge industrial parks, which employ 20,000 people, and in its educational facilities. The College of Further Education prides itself in its computer and technology courses. There is also an Information Technology Centre, The Open Terminal community computer centre and The Heathcote community computer centre. Leisure facilities are lavish, too. The huge leisure centre accommodates both the Gordon Craig Theatre and an exhibition hall. Nearby is a heated indoor swimming pool, and there are three 18-hole golf courses. The place for Sunday walks is Fairlands Valley Park, where there is a sailing and fishing lake, a boating lake and a bandstand for open-air concerts.

The Old Town, "Hilton" in E.M. Forster's *Howards End*, is greatly cherished and property prices are proportionately higher. A two-bedroom cottage would cost just under £80,000; a three-bedroom detached double-fronted house with bay windows just under £140,000. On Stevenage's margins are some sedate, tree-lined roads that attract the middle-class professionals – Rectory Lane, Chancellor's Road and Granby Road, for example, where a detached house with four or five bedrooms and a large garden may cost upwards of £150,000. A new development here offers similarly large houses fetching between £180,000 and £200,000.

There is also a huge leap in house prices between the New Town and the villages that surround it. **Benington** in the east, for example, has picture-postcard village green and timbered cottages, and is very sought after – though it does also have its share of new developments and local authority housing. A one-bedroom flat would cost just under £50,000 (compared with just over £40,000 in Stevenage). An older house with five bedrooms would take you into the £230,000 range.

Walkern is much busier, with a high street that takes quite a bit of traffic, and with new estates that have sprung up around the old dovecote and pond, and by the chequer-brick Manor Farm. A modern two-bedroom house will cost just over £60,000; an older cottage of the same size may cost £5,000 more. A larger, four-bedroom house is likely to fall into the range of £180,000 to £200,000. Two-bedroom town houses in the old brewery sell for around £75,000.

Aston is also popular and much closer to Stevenage, though it is a little hemmed in by the latter and has had its own struggle to restrict development – the field in the village centre has been fiercely defended. Most of the new housing is kept to small developments in cul-de-sacs. A three-bedroom detached house built a couple of decades ago would cost around £125,000; a large four-bedroom detached would cost £135,000. A roomy 17th-century cottage would be likely to fetch over £200,000.

Distinctive late Victorian cottage, Old Stevenage

HITCHIN

Journey time: *33 min*	Peak trains: *5 per hour*
Season ticket: *£1896*	Off-peak trains: *4 per hour*

Hitchin has managed to retain its character better than some of the surrounding towns. Parts of the centre still remain in a medieval time-warp – the market place, the lanes leading off it to the cathedral-sized St Mary's church and the River Hiz. Tilehouse Street, now relieved of much of its through traffic, remains just as medieval England must have known it; and Bancroft has been admired as one of the best urban streets in England. It is a classic small market town, once famous for straw plaiting, surrounded by popular commuter villages. The shopping centre is adequate for everyday needs. In the town itself a two-bedroom terrace house in Tilehouse Street would fetch between £80,000 and £150,000, though it might only be very small. Larger three-bedroom semis on the south side of the town can be bought for around £80,000. The Avenue, Wymondley Road and Benslow Lane are quiet leafy roads only 15 minutes' walk from the station, and contain some rather grand houses. A three- to four-bedroom house built in Wymondley Road could be bought for between £170,000 and £190,000. The large Victorian and Edwardian houses in The Avenue tend to sell for between £170,000 and £200,000.

The villages of **Gosmore** and **Charlton** to the south are very close to Hitchin and therefore desirable. Gosmore has a green and some very pretty old houses. You could spend anything from £60,000 for a tiny cottage to £200,000 for a bungalow in an acre of land. **Pirton** also scores because it isn't linear like many of the other villages in the area, but has a good, compact round shape which somehow affects the social dynamics and makes it a more convivial place to live. A three-bedroom detached house might cost between £120,000 and £160,000; a smaller, three-bedroom end-of-terrace £80,000.

Great Wymondley and **Little Wymondley** also loom in the Hitchin firmament, the irony being that Little Wymondley is by far the larger of the two. Great Wymondley is little more than an untidy crossroads with a few cottages, a pub, and the humps of a medieval castle. Little Wymondley is being relieved of traffic by a bypass, but prices are still a little depressed. A three-bedroom ex-council terrace here will sell for around £53,000.

St Ippollits (sometimes just called Ippollits, and spelled in a variety of different ways) is a rather pretty hilltop village with smartly painted timbered houses and a dominating church which gives the village its name. An ex-council three-bedroom house will cost £80,000, though more stylish period properties will sell for much more. Commuters from St Ippollits and the Wymondleys also have the option of travelling from Stevenage, where car-parking is easier.

LINE TO CAMBRIDGE (see map)

LETCHWORTH

Journey time: *37 min*	Peak trains: *3 per hour*
Season ticket: *£1948*	Off-peak trains: *2 per hour*

You need to make sure your face fits in **Letchworth**. This was the first garden city, and the dream is still intact, as wholesome as a Hovis advert. To those who come from elsewhere to live – and to the groups of Japanese architects who come to gawp at it in summer – it can seem strange indeed. Ebenezer Howard's social experiment attracts a distinct type of middle-class teetotaller, full of good intentions and disposed to vegetarianism. Great joy is still taken in the fact that there is only one pub, The Black Squirrel (where it is best not to be seen). There was once the Skittles Inn, but it sold only lemonade and ginger beer and has now been turned into a community centre called The Settlement. Pleasant evenings are spent in patchwork groups, making friendly quilts, or in other craft activities whose fruits are apt to appear at craft fairs. The beauty of all this is that it is quite safe to roam the streets at night. The town is altogether too serious to have a major shopping centre, and the supermarket is on the outskirts of an industrial estate.

The sought-after properties are the original garden city houses which have a rural calm about them. The cottages in Nevells Road, Icknield Way and Wilbury Road are worth just going to look at. A four-bedroom detached house in Nevells Road will cost just under £120,000. The larger detached original houses are to be found in Sollershott West and East, and The Broadway. The cheapest houses in one of these leafy boulevards will cost around £380,000.

"Outsiders think the people in Letchworth are crazy. It is very tight-knit socially, artistic and rather like a commune," said one who is now devoted to the town and wouldn't live anywhere else. It can afford to be particularly proud of its schools. Not only does it have two well-known public schools, St Francis College for girls and St Christopher's for boys (the latter known for its relaxed approach and amazing vegetable gardens), but it also has two well-respected comprehensives, Highfield and Fernhill. The town is still growing, and properties on the new estates tend to be much cheaper than in the Garden City proper. A three-bedroom detached house on the Lordship Farm estate, for instance, will cost £85,000. A four-bedroom house on the Manor Park estate will cost £150,000.

Of the villages close by, **Norton** has a haphazard charm, a good pub and a common that offers 63 acres of woodland and deer. It also has the local leisure centre, used by the townsfolk of Letchworth.

Willian is made endearing by its duck pond and some very old houses, but property in both these villages rarely comes on the market.

BALDOCK

Journey time: *40 min*	Peak trains: *3 per hour*
Season ticket: *£1964*	Off-peak trains: *2 per hour*

Baldock is a classic small market town, with an old coaching history and a much-admired wide main street. People enjoy living here, and like to protect the place from further development. Unfortunately, however, their zeal sometimes backfires. Plans for a long-awaited bypass have finally been abandoned because the three wrangling action groups could not agree a route. The main asset for shoppers is a vast and impressive Tesco superstore in a converted neo-Classical hosiery factory which also once enjoyed a brief life as a film studio. The price paid is that the smaller, traditional high street shops have suffered. The town does still muster a butcher and a baker, plus plenty of solicitors and estate agents, antique shops and a steak house.

Almost anywhere in Baldock is nice to live. There are streets of timber-frame and colour-wash, Georgian and Victorian houses and some modest modern estates. Even the council estates are arranged in well-kept, tree-lined avenues. A reasonably new one-bedroom flat will cost around £45,000; a four-bedroom modern house with *en suite* bathroom £120,000 to £130,000. A rather extraordinary Georgian house with four bedrooms and a ballroom was sold last year for £140,000. Baldock is just within range of people who work in Cambridge (20 miles), and this is reflected in the property prices. It is also attractive for its secondary school. Knight's Templar Comprehensive has a high reputation for academic achievement and is the preferred choice of many parents who could afford to have their children educated privately.

ASHWELL & MORDEN

Journey time: *45 min*	Peak trains: *3 per hour*
Season ticket: *£2012*	Off-peak trains: *2 per hour*

Though the station is too far outside the village to walk, there is a taxi service that whisks commuters home through the lanes in the evening. **Ashwell** is a commuter dormitory which manages to retain a ferociously active village social life. There is a playgroup, a babysitting circle, a stage school and a dance school and every year the Ashwell Show grows less like a village flower show and more like a county horse show. It really is *the* chic village to live in this rather flat bit of countryside. The attraction lies in its sense of complete self-containment and in the preservation of its architecture. Timber-framed cottages, some cob, are followed by dignified Georgian town houses. It has a pretty church in clunch and flint, and a primary school that is not only highly thought of educationally but is also a social engine to the village. It has a bakery, three pubs, a pharmacy, a doctor's surgery, a dentist, a weaver and a potter. People expect their houses to sell at a premium in Ashwell, so you have to be ready for this when you go house-hunting. A two-up-two-down here might cost £60,000 – £10,000 more than it would fetch a few miles away in Royston. Some of the larger cottages will cost between £200,000 and £275,000.

Kelshall sits in the foothills of the Chilterns, and from here you have views right across the prairies of Bedfordshire and Cambridgeshire. It is an extrememly well-kept and close-knit village. A five-bedroom house with two-thirds of an acre is likely to fetch around £275,000. **Therfield** is another proud old Chilterns village whose agricultural heritage goes back a very long way, as the long barrows on Therfield Heath testify. A four-bedroom thatched cottage will cost £175,000; a three-bedroom one £150,000.

ROYSTON

Journey time: *49 min*	**Peak trains:** *3 per hour*
Season ticket: *£2100*	**Off-peak trains:** *2 per hour*

Royston is suffering a little from small-town-recession symptoms, with some shop fronts going dark from time to time. It sits on the borders of Hertfordshire and Cambridgeshire, so people have the choice of two education systems. It offers cheap housing and convenience. In addition to the railway line it also has easy access to the A10, M25, A1 and M11. Traditionally the south side of town is thought to be better than the north, where some of the housing estates have been built at a very high density – and where a new Tesco is opening. Property prices start at around £30,000 for a one-bedroom flat, rising to £60,000 for a three-bedroom semi and £115,000 for a four-bedroom detached house with two bathrooms. The modern houses tend to be cheaper than the older Victorian/Edwardian ones which offer more room. The heath, which has a golf course on it, is attractive for walking and riding.

The surrounding countryside offers a wide choice of villages. **Barley**, to the south-east, is a no-frills village with a strong local community, pretty walks and an all-purpose village shop. The Barley Players put on summer and Christmas shows, and there is a good local riding school. Its greatest assets are an early Tudor restored town house, used for village activities and harvest suppers, and a small village cage, or lock-up, which remains as a curiosity. A two-bedroom bungalow on a large plot will cost £130,000. The village's position on the chalk toes of the Chilterns accounts for the villagers' historic nickname – "the little men from the hills".

Three-bedroom period cottage, near Royston

Barkway is rather more elegant, with a wonderful array of timber-framed and Georgian brick houses. One of these with six bedrooms and parking on the main street will cost £180,000. A three-bedroom detached will cost £125,000. It still has its own village school, but the rolls are falling. **Bassingbourn**, to the north, also has an impressive main street lined with period houses. The nearby army barracks does not affect house prices. A very spacious five-bedroom detached house with four reception rooms will cost £160,000. An older thatched semi would sell for £95,000.

MELDRETH

Journey time: *55 min*	**Peak trains:** *2 per hour*
Season ticket: *£2100*	**Off-peak trains:** *1 per hour*

This is fruit-growing country, so **Meldreth** is well supplied with orchards. It still has a small green, and beneath a spreading chestnut tree are the old village stocks and a whipping post. It is an enormously welcoming village, though it is rather scattered. The primary school is well regarded, as is the Melbourn College for 11- to 16-year-olds. Leisure opportunities include tennis, cricket, croquet, and the Super-Troupers dramatic society. Village people may also use the riding stables attached to the Meldreth Manor School for children with cerebral palsy. The village contains a mix of old thatched cottages and new developments, though much of the newer housing seems very uniform. Ex-council semis sell for £60,000, with privately built semis around £10,000 more. A four-bedroom detached house will fetch around £125,000. For a sought-after address in Chiswick End Road, however, you might have to pay up to £300,000 for a secluded thatched cottage.

Melbourn is across the fields. Its attractions include two restaurants and a very strong community spirit. Property prices are similar to those in Meldreth.

SHEPRETH

Journey time: *58 min*
Season ticket: *£2100*

Peak trains: *2 per hour*
Off-peak trains: *1 per hour*

The feature of **Shepreth** village centre is a stream with two old mills on its banks. There are some pretty thatched cottages and several modern closes built in the late Sixties and Seventies. The village has a shop-cum-post office, an antique shop, a nursery school and two trout farms. The houses tend to be larger than those in Meldreth, and those backing on to open fields in Frog End are probably the best. A four-bedroom detached house with two bathrooms here will cost between £135,000 and £200,000. Annual village events include a horticultural show, harvest festival and the Shepreth festival of arts and crafts. Several artists live in the area, and one of the results is a rather curious art-bus that serves as a mobile studio. It is a horsy area – including even a few horse-and-carriages.

FOXTON

Journey time: *60 min*
Season ticket: *£2100*

Peak trains: *2 per hour*
Off-peak trains: *1 per hour*

Foxton is attractive and quiet, with a pretty but tiny green and some good timber-frame houses in the long main street. The village has two churches, a shop-cum-post office and a pub. The Foxton Forum meets to hear speakers invited to address them on specialist subjects. There are all the usual societies for women, toddlers and the elderly, plus the formidable Foxton Gardeners Association which organises a regular September show. The village is best known to outsiders for being the subject of a highly praised historical book, *The Common Stream*, by local author Rowland Parker, published in 1975. The older thatched cottages don't come up for sale very often, but might be expected to fetch anything between £120,000 and £200,000 depending on their condition.

Barrington nearby has a huge set-piece green with thatched cottages on one side and a fine church on the other. The Cambridge factor is a significant influence on prices. Houses on the green come up for sale once in a lifetime and might fetch anything between £200,000 and £325,000. There are some modern developments discreetly tucked away in cul-de-sacs, where four-bedroom detached houses sell for around £105,000. An acre or two of land, however, could put the price up to £160,000. Clunch, the chalk-stone used so extensively in local building, was quarried nearby.

CAMBRIDGE

Journey time: *59 min*	**Peak trains:** *3 per hour*
Season ticket: *£2148*	**Off-peak trains:** *2 per hour*

See **Liverpool Street to King's Lynn** (page 58).

CONTINUATION OF MAIN LINE TO GRANTHAM

ARLESEY

Journey time: *39 min*	**Peak trains:** *2 per hour*
Season ticket: *£1936*	**Off-peak trains:** *2 per hour*

You are on to the Bedfordshire plains here, where the low, sprawly, yellow-brick villages can seem monotonous and unimaginative after the variety of Hertfordshire. **Arlesey** itself lays claim to being the longest linear village in the country, with a high street of Victorian brick houses, many of which have been extended at the back to provide bathrooms and kitchens. A two-bedroom mid-terrace house could be bought for £45,000. Two social fixtures in the year are the Agricultural Show and the Wives' Pram Race. Its immediate neighbour, **Stotfold**, is another large village dominated by the local yellow brick, with a similar mix of Victorian and modern housing at similar prices. Stotfold has the additional advantage of having a secondary school, being close to the A1M, and offering the choice of whisking down the motorway for the better train service from Stevenage. Letchworth and Baldock are also nearby.

Henlow is the village where sports and showbiz personalities come to revitalise at the Henlow Grange health farm. Henlow has a few shops and pubs and good sports facilities. County cricket matches are sometimes played at The Pyghtles. The proximity of RAF Henlow influences prices and a four-bedroom detached house here might cost £95,000. Other villages worth looking at in this catchment area are **Meppershall**, **Lower Stondon** and **Clifton**.

BIGGLESWADE

Journey time: *44 min*	Peak trains: *2 per hour*
Season ticket: *£1948*	Off-peak trains: *2 per hour*

Biggleswade has a population of around 12,500 and is very much a dormitory town – to Cambridge and Bedford as well as to London. It is a town of yellow-brick houses and market gardening, set on the River Ivel which was once just navigable from the sea. Greene King have a brewery here, which may explain why there are so many pubs. Shops are adequate, though people tend to go to Cambridge for major purchases. Proximity to the A1 means that Stevenage is also easily accessible. One-bedroom flats start at £35,000; three-bedroom semis at £65,000. One of the more highly regarded streets is London Road, where large four-bedroom houses can be bought for £150,000. It is a busy road, however, and seems to have less appeal for incomers than it does for people moving locally.

Those in search of the rural idyll must go west to **Ickwell Green**, whose village green has a cricket club and a maypole on it, and is fringed with colour-wash, brick-and-tiled cottages. There is the odd modern house, too. A three-bedroom terrace would sell for around £55,000 to £60,000. **Old Warden** is even more picturesque, having been preserved in aspic by the Shuttleworth Estate. The cottages are thatched, with gingerbread trimmings and chimney pots, and very few of them ever reach the open market. But its very presence is a magnet to the area, attracting people to the neighbouring villages. The Shuttleworth Collection of historic aircraft is a major attraction to visitors, especially on flying days. **Northill**, the third village in the cluster, is not quite so rarefied. The occasional modern house has crept in beside the older cottages around the pub and the duckpond at the centre. A two-bedroom thatched semi will cost around £95,000. There are stables in the area and it is fairly horsy.

SANDY

Journey time: *48 min*	Peak trains: *2 per hour*
Season ticket: *£1960*	Off-peak trains: *2 per hour*

Sandy is plain as can be, an old Bedfordshire market town that has sponged up overspilling Londoners into its large council estates and yellow-brick streets. It is perhaps a shade cheaper than Biggleswade. The

Royal Society for the Protection of Birds has its headquarters outside the town at Sandy Lodge, and there are some pleasant woodland walks. Two of the more expensive places to live are the large Victorian houses along Bedford Road, which can be a little noisy because of proximity to the A1; and the modern houses on the river-front at Mill Lane. One of these will cost you up to £250,000, despite having to be approached through a housing estate.

Beeston, on the southern edge of Sandy, is divided by the A1, and quite a few properties are blighted by it. Nevertheless, the conservation area with the green, old thatched cottages and blacksmith's forge offers pleasant relief from some of the other, drearier villages in the area. **Tempsford**, to the north, is also spliced by the A1. Its wartime aerodrome was used by the Special Operations Executive to drop secret agents into occupied France, and it was from here that Glenn Miller took off for his final flight.

Semi-detached
thatched cottage,
Bedfordshire

Potton, to the east, is the size of a small town, with a population of 5,000. Its market square is much admired, though the only way to live in it would be to buy a flat over one of the shops. The likely price is £45,000 to £55,000 for one bedroom. Otherwise property in the town tends to be cheaper than Biggleswade or Sandy. It is the headquarters of the eponymous Potton company, makers of neo-Tudor self-build home kits.

ST NEOTS

Journey time: *57 min*	**Peak trains:** *4 per hour*
Season ticket: *£2096*	**Off-peak trains:** *2 per hour*

St Neots is considerably prettier than many of the towns in the area, and larger too, with a population of 25,000 or more. Yet it has the atmosphere of a backwater. In part this is due to the condition of the rather fine market square, where many of the buildings need renovating and some of them are boarded up. The shopping centre has lost out to Cambridge and Bedford. Teenagers are especially at a loose end in the evenings. There is no cinema, so they tend to end up door-hanging around the market square. There are plenty of daylight activities, however. Cricket and rugby are played on the huge, 160-acre common; and there is an operatic society called the St Neots Players which puts on productions at the Civic Centre. There is also an annexe of Huntingdon Technical College.

The River Ouse contributes both colour and charm. There is a rowing club and two marinas. People come to St Neots to mess about in boats and fish, or to walk the Ouse Valley trail. Unsurprisingly, some of the nicest places to live are close to the river. **Eaton Ford**, for example, was once a riverside village in its own right. It has now been absorbed by the town and offers some of the most expensive housing. The period architecture, combined with the St Neots Golf Club and the river meadows, have pushed the price of a three-bedroom semi here up to £60,000. A four-bedroom detached house with a separate dining room and single garage will sell for around £105,000 – about the same as an older three-bedroom cottage.

Also popular is Old St Neots, in the area around the market square and shops, with walks in the woods of Priory Park. A three-bedroom house on a 20-year-old estate such as Birdlands will cost about £75,000; a four-bedroom house around £95,000. Slightly cheaper is **Eaton Socon**, another former village drawn into the St Neots fold, where houses tend to be arranged in terraces. A three-bedroom semi could be bought for between £52,000 and £55,000; a four-bedroom detached for £80,000. It has the advantage of being on the A1, convenient for commuting to Stevenage or Hatfield, and it is competitively priced.

People looking for a village home tend to head for the east, where the countryside starts to undulate a little – though property prices also begin to rise as you get closer to Cambridge. **Great Gransden, Little Gransden** and **Waresley** have pretty Elizabethan thatched cottages and are particularly popular with professional couples. A three-bedroom house in one of these villages would fetch around £130,000. **Eltisley** is slightly cheaper – pretty but not quite so special, with an extraordinarily large village green and a lovely thatched cricket pavilion which is used for meetings as well as cricket matches. The village has no shop but it does have a post office and a popular primary school that also serves other villages nearby. There are two small new housing estates popular with young families, and there are some bungalows for the elderly. A three-bedroom detached house would cost around £115,000 here – more than the equivalent in St Neots but less than in the Gransdens.

To the north-west is Grafham Water, a huge man-made reservoir that draws people from miles around for walking, water skiing, windsurfing and other watersports. **Perry** was a village that had little to say for itself before Grafham Water was made, but now it has some new housing with price tags of around £85,000 for four bedrooms. One possible drawback of living near open water is that flies can be a problem in the summer.

HUNTINGDON

Journey time: *64 min*
Season ticket: *£2276*

Peak trains: *4 per hour*
Off-peak trains: *2 per hour*

Most people will probably prefer the neighbouring villages to **Huntingdon** itself, though the old county town is not unattractive. Oliver Cromwell lived here, and the old school which both he and Samuel Pepys once attended has been turned into a Cromwell Museum. The house-price boom of the Eighties brought quite a few Londoners in search of cheaper housing, so there is a well-established body of commuters. Cheap housing still exists here. There is a mass of ex-council housing to be had on the Oxmoor estate, where you could buy a three-bedroom house for around £35,000. The truth is, however, that people tend to spend their lives trying to move out of this area rather than in. The better addresses are in Hartford and Sapley, where the period properties add a touch of class to the newer developments and bungalows. An older house with four bedrooms in either area will cost around £110,000; a large bungalow with three to four bedrooms will cost £85,000 – about the same as a new four-bedroom house on a small development.

Across the remarkable 14th-century bridge in **Godmanchester**, the tone is raised by some pretty, pastel-coloured 16th-, 17th- and 18th-century houses, and by pleasant walks along the Great Ouse to Portholme Great Meadow, which is ablaze with wild flowers in spring. Much of Godmanchester is a designated conservation area, and there are some particularly fine houses in Post Street, Earning Street and The Causeway, where some of the gardens run down to the river. A large older house here is likely to fetch between £140,000 and £200,000, though a garden on the river will push it up towards the £300,000 mark. At the opposite extreme, a one-bedroom starter home on the new estate can be had for between £35,000 and £40,000. Not far to the west is **Brampton**, where Pepys lived and where the Brampton Racecourse is. It still retains its village green, though there have been a lot of new developments. The RAF station here is nothing to worry about because its function is purely administrative.

St Ives, five miles to the east, also has more charm than Huntingdon, with a pot-pourri of building styles along the quay and a smattering of pubs and restaurants. The centre is a conservation area, and the threadwork of alleyways between Market Hill and the riverside is particularly intriguing. It grew up on the site of a large Easter Fair, and is the St Ives of the nursery rhyme.

Close to it, nudging the Fens, are some of the most desirable villages in the area. **Hemingford Abbots**, formerly part of the Ramsey Abbey estate, seduces everyone with its thatched cottages and lovely walks. It is full of successful local businessmen and young couples attracted like moths to the Cambridge lamplight – all waxed jackets, Land Rovers and labradors. "You know if someone comes from Hemingford Abbots because they talk down to you," says one local resident. "There is a lot of pride in the village. If there is an art exhibition in the area, it will always be held in Hemingford Abbots." For the young, there are two-up-two-down courtyard houses selling for £70,000 to £72,000. The wealthier aim for the small urban palaces in Common Lane. Some of these have river frontages and might sell for up to £750,000. The walks are idyllic, along footpaths that cross the meadows to Houghton Mill. This is an early Ouse watermill, in a beautiful setting that gets rather touristy in the summer. Those with less money might look next door to **Hemingford Grey**, which is the poor relation living off the Hemingford name. There are many more family-sized houses here. A four-bedroom modern house would cost around £120,000.

Houghton and **Wyton**, linked by a main street, are also cheaper because they are that much further from the A1. The high street has a family butcher and a small tearoom; the housing market offers a mix of old and new. Those looking in Wyton should take the presence of the RAF base into account if a price looks unexpectedly low. A two-up-two-down will cost £65,000; a four-bedroom modern estate house around £95,000. To the north is **Woodhurst**, a perfect example of a ring village. A family house with large garden could be bought here for £150,000, though some of the five-bedroom houses on new developments will fetch no more than £115,000.

Due north of Huntingdon are **Little** and **Great Stukeley** (where John Major lives), which offer a reasonable mix of old and new houses, council estates and chalet bungalows. A modern house with six bed-rooms, three bathrooms, four reception rooms, stabling for six horses and an acre and a half of land in Great Stukeley is likely to cost around £300,000. More modest family houses can be bought for £150,000. Aircraft noise could be a problem if you stray too close to the USAF at Alconbury.

PETERBOROUGH

Journey time: *50 min*	Peak trains: *4 per hour*
Season ticket: *£3452*	Off-peak trains: *3 per hour*

The tower of the Norman cathedral, which contains the tomb of

Catherine of Aragon, is just about the only thing of beauty in **Peterborough**. It is visible from almost anywhere in the city and is illuminated at night. What the city lacks in aesthetics, however, it might be said to gain in purpose-built leisure facilities – cathedrals of contemporary life. The Queensgate shopping centre's malls and squares, in marble, glass and steel, are air-conditioned, American-style. There is an 11-screen cinema, the largest roller-skating centre in Europe, an ice rink, a rowing and canoeing centre, an indoor cricket stadium and three golf courses. The Wirrina sports stadium is used both for athletics championships and for concerts. The city is ringed with fast roads and bypasses, making life easy for drivers and pedestrians too. The Key Theatre, opened in 1973, keeps the culture vultures happy with everything from opera and ballet to Christmas panto. And the Peterborough Arts Centre, in an old farmhouse at Orton Goldhay, puts a crafty-vegetarian spin on photography, music and the theatre.

There is a plentiful supply of cheap housing for first-time buyers. It is question of working your way around the various Ortons. **Orton Goldhay** has shoals of ex-council terrace properties selling at around £35,000 for three bedrooms, £36,500 for four. At **Orton Malborne** there are more private houses in the mix, but prices remain similar. A three-bedroom terrace house might cost £30,000 to £35,000; a three-bedroom semi £45,000; a three-bedroom detached £50,000. Prices rise sharply in the sumptuous, newly built estates of **Orton Wistow**, where a family-sized house can cost anything up to £200,000. Similarly expensive properties can also be found in **Werrington** and **Gunthorpe**, both of which still retain a core of older housing too. Much of central Peterborough is to be avoided, especially the repetitive drab of the older terraces. Westown is one of the more popular inner areas, where three-bedroom semis with gardens sell at around £49,500. For real one-upmanship, there are the houses in Thorpe Park Road, Thorpe Road and Westwood Road, where Thirties houses in voluminous gardens sell at anything over £100,000 to the city's doctors, dentists and solicitors. The less wealthy middle classes find themselves in Longthorpe and Netherton, where there is a range of older houses. A three-bedroom end-of-terrace would cost around £44,000; a four-bedroom detached house £70,000 to £80,000.

To the east of Peterborough is stark fenland. Those who are interested will find it expertly interpreted at the Wildfowl and Wetlands Centre at Peakirk. Most people find it too glum, and head determinedly for the undulating landscape and stone villages to the west. But, for those who are undeterred, **Whittlesey** in the east is set right in the fens. Just to the south of it is King's Dyke, designed to introduce a sharp kink into the network of navigable waterways and so limit the size of vessels passing between the Rivers Nene and Ouse. The village has a brickworks, but is still dwarfed by the huge flatness that surrounds it. A two-bedroom

detached bungalow might cost £44,000; an older three-bedroom detached house £85,000. **Thorney**, slightly further north, was kept intact as
an estate village throughout the 19th century and so has a greater sense of
history. The rather mock-Jacobean water tower adds a flourish to the
skyline. An older three-bedroom semi here will cost £42,000.

The villages to the south of Peterborough are also somewhat
lacking in visual appeal. **Yaxley**, being so close to the A1, offers the
convenience of an easy commute to the towns both north and south.
Technically it is a village, though it has all the amenities and proliferating
housing estates of a small town. There is also a significant American
influence on the housing market here, due to the proximity of Alconbury.
The old part of Yaxley is the most sought after – particularly the thatched
cottages that skirt the village green with the old village pump in the centre.
These rarely come up for sale, but you could expect to pay well over
£100,000 if they did. Run-of-the-mill three-bedroom semis fetch around
£45,000; four-bedroom detached houses £70,000. The countryside
around is not for those who want conventional beauty. "It can seem
hideous because there are no hedgerows, no trees and no hills. But it grows
on you," said one who had been converted. Large tracts of it between
Yaxley and Fletton have been earmarked for new housing development.
The old brick pits will be replaced by what is currently being referred to
as the new Southern Township.

Villages to the west of the A1 tend to feel a little cut off by it.
Crossing is difficult because of the volume of traffic, and it is a known
accident blackspot. It is now being turned into a three-lane highway,
which means that the traffic noise will be brought that much closer to
villages such as **Folksworth**, **Haddon** and **Stilton**.

North and west of Peterborough are the best areas to look. **Market
Deeping** and its satellites **Deeping St James** and **Deeping Gate** ("Deeping"
is a reference to the deep meadows on the banks of the River Welland) are
a major attraction. Market Deeping is an attractive old town with wide
streets, some old stone houses and pubs, and with good old-fashioned
butchers and bakers mixed in between the antique shops. It has its own
leisure centre, library and health centre, and an industrial zone including
such light industries as fireplace manufacturers and double-glazing
specialists. There are two primary schools and a good comprehensive. The
eight-mile drive to Peterborough station is only a matter of minutes along
the A1. An older stone house with four bedrooms, a garage and central
heating (the Deepings are on mains gas) will cost around £130,000. A
three-bedroom semi will fetch £48,000 – considerably more than its
counterpart in Peterborough. A four-bedroom detached house on a
modern estate would cost around £62,000; a more lavish one-off modern
house in half an acre around £150,000.

The stone villages in the Deepings corridor are all desirable and have been protected from over-development. They include **Maxey**, **Barnack**, **Ufford** and **Helpston**, the last being where the poet John Clare lived in the 19th century, and where he wrote his poems about the agricultural changes he saw going on around him. A three-bedroom semi in Helpston, or any other of these villages, would be likely to cost around £45,000. A large thatched cottage with four bedrooms and a garage might cost £115,000. Due west of Peterborough you find a similar kind of charm in villages such as **Wansford**, where a Grade II listed house with four bedrooms and three reception rooms might cost £140,000. The village has a combined post office and shop serving a population of about 450. A beautiful stone packhorse bridge links the two halves across the River Nene. The Fitzwilliam hunt meets outside the Haycock Hotel. Close by is **Elton**. It has some good 17th-century houses, with Elton Hall just to the south and a lock on the Nene just to the west. A small two-bedroom cottage in Elton might cost £79,000. All these villages benefit from being close to Stamford, which is a pretty medieval town and a very good antidote to Peterborough.

GRANTHAM

Journey time: *72 min*	Peak trains: *3 per hour*
Season ticket: *£3968*	Off-peak trains: *1 per hour*

A solid band of commuters, many of whom arrived in **Grantham** on the crest of the 1988 housing boom, still solemnly take the London train each day. In those heady, boom-time days, around 80 per cent of the people looking for houses in and around the town came from outside the area. Now around 90 per cent of the buyers are local. What everyone knows about Grantham is that Mrs Thatcher was born here, in North Parade. Not quite so many people remember that Sir Isaac Newton was born here too. Mrs Thatcher was educated at Kesteven and Grantham Girls' School, which is still doing for girls what Kings does for boys. The town also has a college of further education offering courses in building, business studies, engineering and general studies. There are golf courses at Belton Park and Stoke Rochford, and good fishing on the River Witham.

Some recent new development is lying unfinished, sitting out the recession. Some builders are switching their output from executive houses to starter homes for young couples. At the lower end of the market, two-bedroom terrace houses start at around £31,000; three-bedroom terraces stretch to just under £40,000. Modern three-bedroom detached houses start at around £55,000 and go up to £70,000; four-bedroom detached houses which might have fetched £125,000 in the boom have now fallen back to around £75,000. Because those areas that shot up in price the furthest tend also to have fallen back the furthest, Grantham has found itself particularly hard hit by the slump. The best roads to live in are probably those leading out towards the villages of Manthorpe and Belton. Large detached houses set well back from the road sell for between £125,000 and £140,000.

The limestone hills around Grantham contain some pretty stone villages, particularly in the west. **Barrowby**, for instance, stands high enough to afford good views across the Vale of Belvoir. An old stone family-sized house here might cost £120,000; a smaller three-bedroom terrace house around £55,000. **Denton** is another handsome stone village which used to be part of the Welby estate. Denton Reservoir nearby is popular with anglers, and has some pretty pathways along its banks. There is some modern housing in the mix, and a small council estate. You could expect to pay £90,000 for a three-bedroom detached house with a double garage; £55,000 for a semi.

Closer to Grantham is **Harlaxton**, which is sufficiently attractive to have been designated a conservation area and hasn't been abused by unimaginative modern development. It owes much of its style to the Gregory family, who built the eye-catching manor house in the early 19th century, plus some of the Regency-style houses in the village. A pretty country cottage with three bedrooms, garaging and stables, might cost £125,000.

Perhaps two of the most exclusive villages are **Manthorpe** and **Belton** to the north, sandwiched by Belton Hall and its magnificent park, now in the hands of the National Trust. Little ever comes up for sale in Belton, but if you were lucky you could expect to pay £180,000 for something with four or five bedrooms.

Early 20th-century farmhouse, Grantham area

MOORGATE/KINGS CROSS
—— TO ——
STEVENAGE

CUFFLEY

To Moorgate

Journey time: *37 min*	Peak trains: *5 per hour*
Season ticket: *£1144*	Off-peak trains: *2 per hour*

Cuffley is prime commuter country, much of it built in stockbroker Tudor style on what was once a wooded hillside. Though the character of the houses is intensely suburban, the village is still surrounded by proper farmland. Some of the large bungalows in their ample gardens have had new houses squeezed in beside them. Two-bedroom flats can be bought for around £57,500; four-bedroom semis around £100,000. In The Ridgeway, mansions backing on to woodland start at around £300,000 and go up to well over £500,000.

A vociferous group of conservationists opposed the building of a golf course on nearby farmland; and the parish council is seeking permission to turn some agricultural land back into common. The village has enough shops to provide practically two of everything, and it has its own primary school. Older children go to Potters Bar or Goff's Oak. Leisure activities include the Cuffley Players and an operatic society, plus football club, cricket and bowls. There is also a tennis club, but it has a two-year waiting list. People ride here, too, though the shortage of bridle-paths means that they have to take to the roads. The Round Table is a force to be reckoned with. It organises the annual Cuffley and Goff's Oak Carnival (or vice versa, since the villages take it in turns to put their name first), and the village fireworks display.

BAYFORD

To Moorgate

Journey time: *41 min*	Peak trains: *3 per hour*
Season ticket: *£1324*	Off-peak trains: *2 per hour*

Bayford is significantly more rural than Cuffley. It is set quietly in the heart of the Broxbourne woods, which are full of footpaths and bridle-ways, and is not so overburdened with modern development. The older Georgian houses have a pleasing presence as a result. The village is rather spread out, and has both a pond and an open space which it treats as a green. Cricket is played on it, but dogs are not allowed. There is no post office or shop, and most people stock up from Waitrose or Tesco in Hertford. The village has its own mixed infants and junior school, but older children must go to Hertford. Every year villagers open their gardens to the public.

Together with its neighbours – **Brickendon**, **Little Berkhamsted**, **Epping Green** and **Bayfordbury** – Bayford exudes wealth and charm, and there is little point harbouring any ambition to live here unless you're looking in the £200,000 to £500,000 bracket. Brickendon is little more than a tiny hamlet set around a green, half a mile's walk from Bayford. Little Berkhamsted is delightfully wooded and has some lovely weather-boarded cottages opposite the church. Bayfordbury is perhaps not so exclusive since it has the B158 running through it.

HERTFORD NORTH

To Moorgate	To Kings Cross
Journey time: *45 min*	Journey time: *26 min*
Season ticket: *£1508**	Season ticket: *£1508**
Peak trains: *5 per hour*	Peak trains: *nil*
Off-peak trains: *2 per hour*	Off-peak trains: *1 per hour*

* Also valid at Hertford East

Hertford is a surprisingly small, old-fashioned county town, protected by a quilt of green belt at the junction of the Rivers Beane, Lea and Mimram. It is possible to take a boat south to the sea from here by negotiating a series of locks. Much of the town centre is a conservation area, charmingly provincial considering its proximity to London, where family firms still thrive alongside all the antique shops, the busy cattle market and the Saturday street market. It has a county court, county hospital and all the other public buildings you would expect of an administrative centre, the 1939 county hall on its hilltop being the most ostentatious.

The Round Table has a strong presence and organises the annual carnival. Other prominent social groups include the Company of Players, based at the Little Theatre; the Dramatic and Operatic Society, which organises the annual theatre week; and the organisers of the annual horse show. There are also choral and art societies, and a symphony orchestra. There is quite a sporting fraternity too: cricket club, canoe club, Hertford Football Club, the Old Hertfordians Rugby Club, and fishing in streams made famous by Izaak Walton in *The Compleat Angler*.

Hertford is generally more expensive than other nearby towns, partly because of its status as the county town. Commuters have a good choice of routes into London. The Moorgate/Kings Cross trains from Hertford North provide easy changes to the London Underground at Finsbury Park or Highbury & Islington. Or, if you prefer, there are trains to Liverpool Street from Hertford East (page 51), which connect with the Underground at Seven Sisters and Tottenham Hale. So many people scuttle through the short cuts converging on Hertford North station in the morning that there is a prescribed route known locally as the Commuter Trail. Not many of them live in the area immediately behind the station, which is dominated by council estates, but there are plenty of good streets within walking distance.

At the cheaper end of the market, modern town houses can be bought for around £75,000 or £80,000. For middle-range, three- and four-bedroom houses with generous gardens you should look in the Fordwich area. Here you will find semis at around £120,000; detached houses around £150,000. For more extravagant housing see High Molewood and Great Molewood, where large detached houses and chalet bungalows spread themselves along unmade private roads surrounded by woodland. Five bedrooms, two bathrooms and four reception rooms in Thirties architectural style might cost £335,000. The smartest suburb to the north is **Bengeo**. People moving to Hertford are often so completely fixated on Bengeo that they will consider living nowhere else. It has a parade of shops and two boutiques – one for chic brides and the other for chic babies. A six-bedroom house in an acre or two of garden might cost £450,000.

However great the appeal of Bengeo for commuters, it is the south side of town which locals consider to be the more desirable. The large Victorian and Edwardian houses of Queen's Road and Highfield Road, enlivened by the occasional architectural curio, sell at around £400,000 for six bedrooms. This is also where two of the more highly regarded schools – Simon Balle, which is co-educational, and Richard Hale, for boys – are to be found.

In the centre of Hertford, upwardly mobile young couples are attracted to the riverside, where terrace cottages were originally built for

Period country house, Herts

mill or malt workers. In the last decade Folly Island has been mercilessly gentrified, regardless of the shortage of parking places, and tiny two-bedroom houses with small gardens now cost around £75,000 to £80,000. The second bedroom tends only to be cot-sized, so those with growing families have to think of moving on.

Outside Hertford, **Hertingfordbury** is probably one of the most exclusive villages in the area. The thriller writer Frederick Forsyth has a house here. The village has no more than 20-odd houses with a cricket pitch and two pubs, a church and a bridge over the Mimram. Its quaintness easily projects house prices through the £500,000 barrier.

WATTON-AT-STONE

To Moorgate	To Kings Cross
Journey time: *42 min*	Journey time: *32 min*
Season ticket: *£1656*	Season ticket: *£1656*
Peak trains: *2 per hour*	Peak trains: *nil*
Off-peak trains: *nil*	Off-peak trains: *1 per hour*

Watton-at-Stone is submerging its pretty face in a tide of new development. The main street is where the older properties are – yellow- and red-brick houses, jettied timber and plaster. A two-bedroom house, without garage, on a modern estate might cost around £69,000; a four-bedroom modern detached around £170,000. One of the more recent development plans has been to convert an old salmon-smoking factory into flats. The village combines the best of both worlds by being intensely rural (and horsy), and yet close enough to London for theatre and other trips. There is cricket, football and – a most unusual asset – tennis on floodlit courts; plus a flower club and other village societies. It also has the Heath Mount private infant and junior schools.

STEVENAGE

To Moorgate	To Kings Cross
Journey time: *49 min*	Journey time: *24 min*
Season ticket: *£1824*	Season ticket: *£1824*
Peak trains: *2 per hour*	Peak trains: *5*
Off-peak trains: *nil*	Off-peak trains: *4 per hour*

See **Kings Cross to Grantham** (page 69).

ST PANCRAS
— TO —
LEICESTER

Up to Bedford the majority of trains serve Kings Cross Thameslink rather than St Pancras. They then go on to Farringdon, City Thameslink and Blackfriars, or to Moorgate (peak hours only). Season ticket prices quoted are for St Pancras/Kings Cross Thameslink only.

ST ALBANS

Journey time: *22 min*	Peak trains: *9 per hour*
Season ticket: *£1400*	Off-peak trains: *5 per hour*

Forget the villages around **St Albans**. The attractions of the town itself, with its medieval centre focused around the cathedral, are such that it has become one of the smartest places to live north of London. Georgian and Edwardian town houses snuggle against quaint old cottages and 15th-century coaching inns. In these cramped but charming streets in the town centre conservation area you could buy a two-up-two-down cottage for around £75,000.

St Albans has excellent communications. It lies roughly equidistant from the M1 and A1, only a few miles from the A25, and the train journey into London is so fast that, in terms of time, it's hardly further from the City than Clapham is. In the last decade some of the country's biggest accountancy firms have moved here, including Peat Marwick and Price Waterhouse.

The shopping centre feels reassuringly traditional: there are old-fashioned individual shops, antique shops and art galleries, and a mews where hand-crafted goods are sold. The Civic Centre doubles as a theatre, though the formidable local dramatic society, The Company of Ten, has its own Abbey Theatre. There are also frequent concerts and recitals in the cathedral.

Schools are another of St Albans's particular attractions. The local state schools all have good reputations, and there are private schools for those who want them. These include St Albans Abbey School for boys and the Girls' High School.

The really stylish 15th-, 16th- and 17th-century houses are on Fishpool Street, the old London-Holyhead road, where a two- to three-bedroom cottage will fetch between £150,000 and £250,000. The main residential area is Marshalswick. Large detached houses built in the Thirties and Fifties sell for between £250,000 and £350,000. Some of those in Marshal's Drive have tennis courts and likely price tags in the

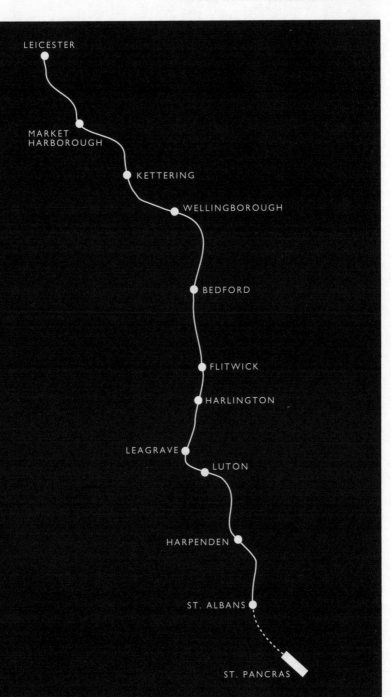

LEICESTER

MARKET
HARBOROUGH

KETTERING

WELLINGBOROUGH

BEDFORD

FLITWICK

HARLINGTON

LEAGRAVE

LUTON

HARPENDEN

ST. ALBANS

ST. PANCRAS

region of £500,000. Marshalswick has its own small shops, library and free car park. Further out of St Albans are roads of semi-detached houses, with prices for three bedrooms in the range of £110,000–£120,000.

For more modern, executive-style houses, the eastern corridor towards Hatfield, around the Hatfield Road, is the place to look. Three- to four-bedroom semis sell for around £130,000 upwards; four- to five-bedroom detached houses may reach £500,000.

Villages in the St Albans catchment include **Chiswell Green** – home of the Royal National Rose Society – **London Colney** and **Shenley**. These are fairly popular with commuters, and look reasonably pleasant at first glance. Locals tend to look down their noses at them, however, because of the volume of ex-council housing.

16th-century town house, St Albans

HARPENDEN

Journey time: *28 min*	Peak trains: *7 per hour*
Season ticket: *£1580*	Off-peak trains: *5 per hour*

Harpenden is, if such a thing is possible, even smarter than St Albans. It has a cricket club, two or three gyms and an outdoor swimming pool. People have to travel to St Albans for the cinema and to London for the professional theatre, though the local amateur dramatic and operatic societies regularly entertain at the civic hall. It has a Sainsbury, supported by plenty of boutiques, gift and speciality shops in the centre of the village. The green runs right through the centre, providing a perfect spot to sit and watch the world go by in summer. Schools for all age ranges – private and state-run – have a particularly high reputation. They include St George's voluntary-aided, part-boarding school for boys and girls; Aldwickbury and Moreton private schools for boys, and St Hilda's for girls.

Some of the most desirable properties are those close to the two golf courses or to the East and West Commons. **East Common** has its own golf course; **West Common** is more purely residential. In the area of the Commons you could pay £120,000 for a two-bedroom terrace; up to £300,000 for a large family house. Properties span various architectural periods from Tudor right through to the present day, and many of them have large gardens with the occasional tennis court and swimming pool. Those with shallower pockets could find a two-bedroom terrace away from the Commons at around £70,000.

There are some extremely pretty villages within reach, any of which might have been lifted straight from the pages of *Country Life* or *Horse and Hound*. **Redbourn**, five miles away and two miles from the M1, is a large village with a population of 5,000, centred around a classic common and picture-book high street. Small shops and a post office provide for day-to-day needs, and there is an infants and junior school. The nicest properties, mainly stylish Victorian houses and older cottages on the common, are expensive – from £200,000 upwards. In the jumble of older cottages in the high street, however, prices are unlikely to exceed £100,000. For Wheathampstead, see page 67.

Kimpton to the north-east also has an attractive high street with small shops, and has good walks nearby in Gustard Wood. Commuters rub shoulders with long-established locals. Prices are slightly lower than nearby Wheathampstead, with two-bedroom terrace cottages starting at £65,000 and four-bedroom modern houses from £110,000. There is a village infants/junior school.

Flamstead, due west, is popular for its charm and active village social life. A thick blanket of green belt gives it a very rural atmosphere, and in the Flamstead Society it has an influential local history group. Newcomers are welcomed as long as they are willing to fit in, though not if they charge around trying to change things. Many of the older-established residents are allotment holders, and the garden show is an important annual event. For the amusement of the young there are a football ground, tennis courts and a table tennis society. Small shops include a good butcher and a post office-cum-greengrocer. The village has its own junior school, and there are two old pubs which attract customers from miles around. The cottages are a picturesque mix of brick and flint. A two-bedroom example will cost around £75,000-plus; a larger 17th-century three-bedroom house £160,000-plus.

LUTON

Journey time: *34 min*	**Peak trains:** *8 per hour*
Season ticket: *£1768*	**Off-peak trains:** *5 per hour*

Luton spreads its mess of modern housing estates, industrial complexes and shopping streets with little grace. It does still have some industrial pride, however, with major local employers including Vauxhall, Electrolux, Whitbread and Luton airport. Shopping is unfussy and run-of-the mill, and includes an Arndale Centre. There is a cinema, three recreation centres, two swimming pools and a polytechnic. Luton Town Football Club play at Kenilworth Road.

There are a few odd enclaves for those who prefer period homes. Along and just off the Old Bedford Road, about half a mile from the centre, are some 19th-century villas which have been so lavishly restored that some of them have two or even three bathrooms. A four-bedroom home here will cost between £130,000 and £170,000, depending on how much has been spent on it. Throughout the town there are plenty of detached Thirties houses selling at between £70,000 and £90,000 for three bedrooms; up to £200,000 for four bedrooms or more.

Kensworth, to the south-west, is a popular commuter village. Cottages line the main road, with a recreation ground and village hall to provide the community focal points. You might get a tiny cottage for as little as £60,000, but the sky's the limit for the large farmhouses in the area. The village has a post office, a general store and a newsagent, and its own junior/infants school. There is also some retirement housing.

To the east and south-east of Luton, just over the border into Hertfordshire, are the small villages of **Breachwood Green**, **Bendish** and **Peter's Green**. Bendish is probably the most stylish, being very tiny with old period cottages. Four- or five-bedroom examples sell for well over £200,000, though you might find a two-bedroom Victorian terrrace for as little as £70,000. Prices at Peter's Green are similar, though the place is so small that you could drive right through before you realise you've reached it. Prices drop by about 15 per cent at Breachwood Green: the village lies directly under the flight path to Luton airport, and the ex-council properties put choosy buyers off.

LEAGRAVE

Journey time: *39 min*	**Peak trains:** *6 per hour*
Season ticket: *£1812*	**Off-peak trains:** *2 per hour*

Leagrave is hardly distinct from Luton. It has its own small precinct of shopping streets, but otherwise can be considered part of the town. In the centre of Leagrave, two- and three-bedroom pre-war terrace houses sell for between £45,000 and £55,000. On the outskirts you find the occasional new development where two-bedroom terraces start at around £45,000.

Dunstable, two miles west at the threshold of the Dunstable Downs, is far more captivating. The old town centre is dotted with timber-framed buildings, old coaching inns (Dunstable was an important coaching stop on Watling Street), and some attractive Victorian terraces. It is full of small designer-shops, good for birthday presents, though for mundane household purchases most people go into Luton. State schools include two middle schools and an upper school which also provides adult evening classes. All have good reputations. There are also two private

Timber-frame
cottages, Dunstable

schools – St George's and Moorland's, for boys and girls. Dunstable has its own sports centre and swimming pool, a nightclub, and the Queensway Hall for local events. The Downs, too, provide plenty of leisure opportunities: they are home to a golf club, the London Gliding Club and Whipsnade Zoo. Victorian terrace homes with two or three bedrooms fetch around £45,000 to £60,000. A two- to three-bedroom semi on a modern estate would cost around £65,000; a three- to four-bedroom detached house up to around £100,000.

Also in the Luton catchment area is **Houghton Regis** – a former village of about two miles square, not quite swallowed up by encroaching development. Modern estates and Thirties semis make up the bulk of the property stock, with prices under £55,000 for three bedrooms. At its heart it has some small quality shops around Bedford Square.

HARLINGTON

Journey time: *41 min*	Peak trains: *6 per hour*
Season ticket: *£1904*	Off-peak trains: *2 per hour*

Harlington, on the very tip of the Chiltern Hills, has an attractive core of timber-framed houses and thatched cottages grouped around the church. They are in a conservation area, and anything with two bedrooms will cost at least £75,000. On the outskirts are two estates built between 20 and 35 years ago. Three-bedroom semis are priced at around £75,000 to £85,000; four-bedroom detached houses at £120,000 upwards. A few local shops and a post office serve a population of approximately 1,000; there is also a good infants school, an upper school and a sixth form college. The nearest middle school is at Toddington (see below), a few miles to the south-west. There is quite a strong sporting tradition in the village.

Toddington, which lies just off the M1, is much larger – really a town with a population of about 10,000 and a range of shops and schools. There are a few elegant houses around the green, and some intriguing old pubs. Toddington Manor is thought once to have been the home of Henrietta Wentworth, mistress of the Duke of Monmouth. The town has grown paunchy with new development, though it is not commuterland – most families seem to have been here for several generations. Property prices are slightly lower than in Harlington, with three-bedroom semis at around £60,000 to £80,000.

Prettier villages in the Harlington area include **Tingrith** and **Milton Bryan**. Both these are hamlets of no more than 40 picture-postcard cottages each, plus the occasional Georgian farmhouse. There are no shops or schools, and both appeal to the more well-heeled sort of commuter. Cottages start at around £70,000; family-sized period houses cost between £200,000 and £500,000.

FLITWICK

Journey time: *48 min*	Peak trains: *6 per hour*
Season ticket: *£1956*	Off-peak trains: *2 per hour*

Little is left of old **Flitwick**, which was just a cluster of timber-framed houses and brick cottages: new development in the last 20 years has entirely changed its character. Much of the new building has been for the benefit of commuters, whose trains come thundering straight through the centre of the town. Apart from the railway, the most noticeable central landmark now is a huge branch of Tesco. The growth is likely to continue, since 2,000 more new houses are planned on the outskirts. Flitwick has four lower schools, but upper-school children have to travel to Ampthill (see below). For those with surplus energy there is a sports centre with swimming pool and squash courts.

Prices in the modern estates range from £65,000 to £70,000 for a three-bedroom semi; £90,000 to £130,000 for a four-bedroom detached house. To the east of the town are some turn-of-the-century houses backing on to Flitwick Wood and open countryside. These cost around £70,000 to £75,000 for three bedrooms; £120,000 and upwards for four.

Ampthill, a small Georgian market town with a population of around 6,000, makes Flitwick look like an ugly sister. Its picturesque centre is set around a market square, dotted with antique and other small specialist shops. It also has a supermarket, schools for children of all ages, and a handsome park of around 150 acres. It is believed that Catherine of Aragon once lived here and received visits from Henry VIII. A small two-to three-bedroom cottage in Ampthill costs around £60,000 to £80,000; a character Georgian town house between £150,000 and £300,000.

Ex-Duke of Bedford cottages, Steppingley

Steppingley, a tiny village a mile to the west of Flitwick, has little more than 40 Duke of Bedford peg-tiled estate cottages, a cricket club, pub and a good restaurant. The atmosphere is up-market and horsy. Prices for two- to three-bedroom cottages are in the region of £70,000 to £110,000. A four-bedroom detached period house will fetch between £170,000 and £300,000. Out of the village along one of the lanes you could expect to pay up to £500,000 for a Georgian farmhouse with a bit of land. Two other villages to consider in this area are Ridgmont and Eversholt (see **Euston to Rugby**, page 116).

BEDFORD

Journey time: *57 min* | Peak trains: *8 per hour*
Season ticket: *£2064* | Off-peak trains: *2 per hour*

Though still a market town, **Bedford** has to a certain extent allowed its individuality to become submerged by its own commercial success. Modern office blocks have appeared in the historic centre, and multinational companies located here include Texas Instruments and Granada TV Rentals. The Harper Centre – a modern shopping mall – is complemented by quality small shops along the high street, plus big-name stores and several supermarkets including two Tescos. The Bunyan Centre is the place for most sports, and there are two swimming pools including the Oasis "beach pool". The Civic Theatre provides a cultural centrepoint, and the Aspects leisure centre has a nightclub, two restaurants, a bowling alley and multi-screen cinema. Bedford has a good mix of state and private schools including Bedford School and Bedford Modern School for boys; Dame Alice Harpur and Bedford High School for girls.

Along the embankment by the River Ouse, where people stroll and sit in summer to watch the waterfowl, are some large, tree-shaded Victorian houses – probably the nicest properties in the town. One of these with five to seven bedrooms would cost between £200,000 and £250,000. There are also some purpose-built flats in the same area. The smallest one-bedroom apartment might cost £35,000; a spacious three-bedroom one might be as much as £180,000. A three-bedroom Victorian terrace house nearby would cost £55,000 to £60,000; a three- to four-bedroom semi up to £130,000. For the rest of the town the general rule is that the houses are more modern the further out you go, but prices do not vary much. You can expect to pay around £65,000 for a three-bedroom semi; £75,000 to £80,000 for a three-bedroom detached.

Most of the sought-after villages in the flat countryside around Bedford are to the north. **Oakley**, just over four miles to the north-west, has in its high street some old brick farmworkers' cottages that once belonged to the Duke of Bedford's estate. You would pay from around £60,000 for one of these with two bedrooms and a long garden. There is also a good deal of modern development where you would pay slightly less than £60,000 for a three-bedroom semi; from £85,000 for a four-bedroom detached. Youngish families mix with the small number of commuters. Village social life revolves around the sports and social club, cricket and football teams, the gardening club and the two pubs. There is a village store, a post office and a primary school.

Bromham, on the Ouse three miles north-west of Bedford, is a large village with a population of 5,000. Many of the local families have lived here for generations and there is a high proportion of elderly people. The limestone cottages in the village centre are surrounded by modern housing, and building is still going on. There are some small shops, a post office, supermarket, newsagent and hairdresser, plus primary and middle schools. Bromham House, an old manor house, is now a hospital for the mentally handicapped. Property prices in Bromham are similar to those in Oakley.

Biddenham, due west of Bedford, is the favourite village for London commuters. It is so close to the town (the station is but a brisk 15-minute walk), yet it feels deliciously remote and is set around a classic village green. All this makes it one of the most expensive villages in the area. Properties range from 17th-century thatched cottages to imposing Thirties houses, plus a few modern developments built with managing directors in mind. Prices range from £85,000 for a one- or two-bedroom cottage to £300,000 for a substantial family house. A new development of 300 houses is planned, and it is hoped that this will provide a shop, a cricket field, tennis courts and a community centre. A cricket club has already been formed, and there are plans to start tennis and football clubs. The village hall is packed at parish council meetings, and everyone gets involved in local events – which includes an annual show in September. Conservation issues are policed by the Biddenham Society.

There are a few small sporting estates in the Bedford area. One with three houses, 500 acres of land, fishing rights and so on recently sold for around £1m.

WELLINGBOROUGH

Journey time: *59 min**	Peak trains: *3 per hour*
Season ticket: *£3104*	Off-peak trains: *1 every 1½ hours*

* Peak time 47 min

Wellingborough is so plain it defies description. There are those who tolerate it and those who are desperate to move out when they can afford to. It has a good range of major chain stores, several supermarkets including Sainsbury and a new Tesco, and a modern shopping mall – the Swangate Centre, formerly the Arndale Centre. Schooling is adequate: there are eight state secondary schools and one private school, Wellingborough School for boys. A night out in Wellingborough probably means going to a pub. There is no theatre but it does have a two-screen cinema, and the nearest sports and leisure centre is in Rushden (see below).

The town has a mix of Victorian terrace houses, smart newish developments and some not-so-nice council estates. New developments around the railway station are particularly popular with commuters. A two-bedroom quad (a quarter of a house split into four) will cost £32,000; a three-bedroom semi £45,000; a four-bedroom detached just over £75,000. There are some pleasant older properties in Northampton Road, where you could expect to pay around £38,000 for a three-bedroom Victorian house; £40,000-plus for four bedrooms. A four-bedroom modern detached house on one of the better developments – the Gleneagles Estate, for instance – would cost between £80,000 and £110,000.

Rushden, a few miles to the east, is about one-third the size of Wellingborough and rather less attractive, with half-completed commercial developments in its centre and some charmless early Seventies architecture. The consolation for housebuyers is some reasonably priced Victorian terraces – ranging from around £37,000 to £39,000 for two or three bedrooms. A four-bedroom detached modern house will cost up to £80,000 or £90,000. Shopping is adequate: there is a Gateway supermarket and a range of smaller shops. The main source of local pride is the sports centre, which includes a swimming pool and sauna complex. There is no cinema since the old picture house was converted into a theatre for amateur dramatics and bingo. Rushden was the birthplace of H.E. Bates, who used Rushden Hall – one of the few historic buildings surviving in the town – as the model for Evensfield in *Love For Lydia*.

Red-brick and stone
cottage, **Wellingborough**

A favourite state school is Chicheley School in **Higham Ferrers**, four and a half miles to the east of Wellingborough. The village has now become a town, hardly separated from Rushden, with an attractive high street lined with period stone properties with new developments fanning out on either side. A four-bedroom stone house here will cost just under £70,000, while a rambling five-bedroom terrace on the market square might cost as much as £225,000. Some of the villages close to it are worth looking at too. **Wymington** has a good mix of stone and thatch with old farmhouses spread down the lanes, while **Podington** has a quality of timelessness that is very attractive. You could find a period three-bedroom stone house for around £70,000.

Wollaston, about seven minutes' drive due south of Wellingborough, is centred around a cluster of old cottages, with modern developments, an industrial estate and council housing on the outskirts. It has small shops, a post office and its own primary and secondary schools. The conservation watchdogs of the Wollaston Society have enjoyed some triumphs, including the arrival in 1985 of a bypass to take the strain off the A509. Property prices start at £44,000 for a three-bedroom semi; £80,000 for a four-bedroom detached; and £100,000 for a 17th-century stone cottage. A four-bedroom, double-garaged detached stone house overlooking the fields might cost £185,000.

For real village atmosphere, however, you should head south to **Grendon**, about five miles from Wellingborough. This pretty village consists of 18th-century cottages gathered around the church, with some Victorian terraces and a few individual modern properties. Villagers get by with one post office/general store and a good primary school. There is no bus service. The population of 500 includes some commuters, and some elderly residents in bungalows. Village life centres around the Church Social Committee, Village Hall Committee, the WI, Scouts, Guides and cricket team. There is an annual church fete and periodic fund-raising ventures which attract considerable support. Expect to pay around £100,000 for a period cottage; upwards of £45,000 for a two-bedroom Victorian terrace.

North-east of Wellingborough is **Raunds** – a small town not to everyone's taste, with a 14th-century manor house and Victorian buildings surrounded by modern estates. Its tightly knit community of about 15,000 is served by two supermarkets, a post office and smaller shops. Little terrace houses can be bought for just under £40,000; three-bedroom Victorian semis £42,000 to £55,000; and modern three-bedroom detached houses for £48,000 upwards.

Also on this side of Wellingborough are **Great** and **Little Addington**. Both are cottagey with some modern development on the wings – mainly four-bedroom detached houses. If your idea of village life includes a post office run from someone's back room, and an infrequent bus service, these are the places for you. The two villages share a vicar, a playing field and WI, though there is still a certain amount of friendly rivalry which brings people out in summer and winter for inter-village sports contests. Another highlight of the social calendar is the annual horticultural society show. There is a youth club, a Church of England primary school, and a playgroup for tots, of which there are a fair number – a third of the population in Great Addington is under 16. You would have to pay around £100,000 for a three-bedroom stone cottage, possibly thatched; between £90,000 and £120,000 for a modern four-bedroom detached house. A five-bedroom stone country house with an acre of land could cost up to £250,000. The area is so seriously horsy that estate agents say that anything with a pony paddock is bound to sell. Green wellies, Land Rovers and waxed jackets are common currency here.

KETTERING

Journey time: *51 min*	**Peak trains:** *3 per hour*
Season ticket: *£3296*	**Off-peak trains:** *1 per hour*

Kettering is one of the prettier East Midlands market towns, well supplied with leisure opportunities and good shopping. All the big-name stores are here, including Tesco, Sainsbury and Marks & Spencer, and the modern Newland Shopping Centre is useful if not actually inspiring. A new leisure centre is being built with ice rink, swimming pool and health club, and the 180-acre Wickstead Park is not far away with its fairground/theme park. Those addicted to more sedentary pleasures, however, will be disappointed by the lack of a cinema or theatre. Another current drawback to life in Kettering is the heavy traffic, though this will soon be relieved by a new M1-A1 link road.

The town has a few Georgian terraces in the centre, larger Victorian houses forming a ring around them, and two modern estates on the outskirts. You might pick up a two-bedroom Victorian terrace for £33,000, or a three-bedroom Victorian house with original features and a good garden for around £55,000 to £60,000.

The countryside here at last begins to pick itself up off the Bedfordshire plains. It is a mellow, slightly rolling, farmland landscape which draws people from Kettering out into frankly villagey little market towns that surround it. Look at **Rothwell** and **Desborough** to the north, and **Burton Latimer** to the south. All are similar, with Victorian market places, small shops, and their own primary and secondary schools. Property prices are similar to those in Kettering. Rothwell is particularly pretty. The centre is a designated conservation area, and it has the benefit of a state secondary school – Montsaye – with a very good academic record. A two-up-two-down terrace house here will cost between £30,000 and £35,000; a three-bedroom terrace £35,000 to £38,000; a three-bedroom semi £45,000 to £50,000; a four-bedroom detached house between £80,000 and £120,000.

One of the more notable smaller villages is **Geddington**, four miles north of Kettering, with a population of around 1,200. A medieval bridge crosses the River Ise here, with a forested hillside providing an attractive green backdrop. It has three pubs, a village hall, two shops, a post office and a primary school. Its heart is a cluster of old cottages, though new housing has forced itself in and there are some Victorian terraces too. For a two-bedroom terrace house or a small cottage you would have to pay upwards of £40,000. Closer to Kettering on this side is the tiny village of **Weekley**. There are possibly no more than 150 people living here altogether, many of them from old farming families, some of them elderly (the old vicarage is now a home for the elderly). There is a post office/ general store but no school – and no pub either, though the village social club is the place to go for an evening drink. It is also the venue for sports club meetings. The village hall, too, rings with the sound of cup on saucer during its frequent coffee mornings. Weekley is a quiet, compact, well-heeled and tight-knit village where a cottage – should you be lucky enough to find one for sale – would cost around £80,000.

MARKET HARBOROUGH

Journey time: *70 min* | **Peak trains:** *1 per hour*
Season ticket: £3636 | **Off-peak trains:** *1 every 1½ hours*

People grow very fond of **Market Harborough**, home of the first liberty bodice, with its distinctive half-timbered Old Grammar School on stilts in the centre, now used for public functions. The population is a manageable 16,000. Georgian offices and shops are still in place in the town centre, and the office blocks of large local employers such as Golden Wonder manage to be not too intrusive. Other companies in the town include HP Foods and a large rubber factory, and there is a large industrial park on the outskirts. A new shopping centre is planned in the old cattle market, and Sainsbury is coming soon. A new leisure centre and swimming pool opened in 1991. There is a 100-seater theatre large enough for local productions, but no cinema.

The M1-A1 link road, which has only just been started and will take at least until 1993 to complete, should siphon off some of the heavy lorries from the centre while at the same time bringing Birmingham and London a little closer. A new bypass opening this year will also relieve the town of traffic from the A6.

Some of the nicest properties are the large Victorian villas along the Northampton Road, where three-bedroom houses start at between £70,000 and £90,000. There are also some rather gracious tree-lined avenues in which mature Thirties semis and detached houses may be bought in the range of £80,000 to £160,000. Victoria Avenue, actually a cul-de-sac, is particularly popular.

North of Market Harborough you enter the wide-open, rolling countryside of the Welland Valley, villages of thatch and stone connected by unhurried roads. This is serious hunting country – Quorn territory. Life in the Langtons – **Church Langton**, **Tur Langton**, **West Langton**, **East Langton** and **Thorpe Langton** – revolves around horses and farming. Church Langton is the largest of this idyllic clutch of villages and West Langton the smallest, though they are all really little more than hamlets, clusters of stone and thatched cottages. All except West Langton have a pub. Tur Langton has a post office/shop and Church Langton the only primary school. Prices vary according to how much land comes with the house and how good the views are, but you could reckon on paying between £70,000 and £80,000 for a three-bedroom stone cottage; up to £190,000 for four bedrooms and an acre of land on a hilltop.

Another gem is **Foxton**. It lies about two and a half miles north-west of Market Harborough on the Grand Union Canal. Its famous series of locks – 10 altogether in two flights rising through 75ft – and the remains of an inclined-plane boat-lift are a great attraction to tourists in the summer. The village itself is pretty too, with old stone and thatched cottages and only a few ex-council houses. Swingbridge Street is possibly the nicest. The population is a friendly mix of young families, commuters and farmers. There is a post office, shop, village hall, infants and junior schools and three pubs. A three-bedroom detached cottage will cost over £90,000, rising to around £140,000 if it has an acre or two of land. Ex-council houses fetch around £60,000 to £70,000. It is worth noting that in the villages to the north of Market Harborough you can still find old manor houses which make very compact, manageable homes. For six or seven bedrooms, a few acres of land and stabling, you would pay between £250,000 and £350,000.

Close to Foxton is **Gumley**, a tiny one-street village on a hill. There is a pub but no shop or school. Many of the villagers own horses and have farming interests. Property rarely comes on the market, but if you were lucky you might buy a two-bedroom Victorian brick cottage for £70,000, or a modern four-bedroom house for £145,000.

LEICESTER

Journey time: *72 min*   **Peak trains:** *3 per hour*
Season ticket: *£4084*   **Off-peak trains:** *2 per hour*

This gutsy, modern Midlands city is not likely to woo the heart of too many London commuters, though it is very conveniently placed close to the M69, the M6 and the M1. Its prosperity was built on hosiery, then on the mass production of boots and shoes, and more recently on engineering and computing. Though it has in recent years been badly hit by the recession. This is the land of steam, antique and agricultural fairs. Leisure here means sport. For participants the city has a mass of bowling rinks, BMX cycle tracks, tennis courts, cricket and football pitches, swimming pools and leisure centres. For spectators there are Leicester City FC and Leicestershire County Cricket Club and the Tigers rugby team.

Highfields, the red light district that has been cleaned up, is generally avoided. So are some of the ugly council estates, though these offer cheap housing – three-bedroom semis at £36,000. Just to the south of the city is the comparative comfort of **Stoneygate**, where there are large Victorian and Edwardian villas, some of which have been converted into flats. A three-bedroom Victorian house here will cost £80,000; a four-bedroom detached £120,000. Prices are similar in **Oadby**, which also has its share of older streets and a gentle mix of new housing.

There are some very pretty villages nearby in the Charnwood Forest and up the Wreake Valley, though perhaps some of the most unspoilt stone villages lie slightly out of reach towards Oakham. To the east is classic hunting country, where the Fernie hunt borders with the Quorn. **Hoby** in the Wreake Valley is particularly charming. In this and any of the villages close by, a four-bedroom detached period house might cost £150,000 to £250,000, while the smaller two-bedroom variety will cost £80,000 to £90,000. In the Charnwood Forest you come close to the coal-mining areas of Coalville and Mountsorrel, but the forest itself is completely unspoilt and fiercely protected. Small cottage prices in **Quorn** are similar to those in the Wreake Valley, but the price of large period properties with six to eight bedrooms and a swag of land can rise into the £300,000–£500,000 bracket.

EUSTON
— TO —
RUGBY

APSLEY

Journey time: *30 min*	**Peak trains:** *3 per hour*
Season ticket: *£1580*	**Off-peak trains:** *2 per hour*

Apsley is mostly Victorian, with three-bedroom terraces ranging in price between £67,000 and £69,000. It is well liked because the houses are within walking distance of the station, and it has a sense of identity. **Boxmoor** is also worth looking at, as a refuge from the modernity of Hemel Hempstead to which it is now annexed. It still has a few little canalside cottages. You can buy older two- to three-bedroom cottages for around £70,000, or spend up to £300,000 on a smart modern house with six or seven bedrooms.

    Bovingdon, to the south-west, is another antidote to Hemel Hempstead. The centre still has a village feel to it, with a well and a green. House prices are 10 per cent higher than in Hemel Hempstead, though there has been a lot of modern development. The market, held on Saturdays on the site of the old Bovingdon airfield, has more than 500 stalls, selling everything from home-made pies to hand-sewn clothes.

HEMEL HEMPSTEAD

Journey time: *28 min*	**Peak trains:** *5 per hour*
Season ticket: *£1612*	**Off-peak trains:** *3 per hour*

Hemel Hempstead may not be to everyone's taste, just pre-dating Stevenage as a New Town, but it is very conveniently placed. The M1 and M25 both pass very close to it; the train to London takes less than half an hour; and Heathrow is but 40 minutes away by car. It also still has rough Hertfordshire meadows on three sides of it. After all, the idea which underpinned the New Town concept was that people could combine the pleasures of the town with the country, and escape the overcrowded conditions of London. The town also has a sports centre, a ski slope and concerts at the Pavilion.

    The old town grew up around the Norman church, with Regency and Victorian villas springing up along Marlowes to take advantage of the distant views to the Chilterns. There is very little in this part for under £65,000. A new shopping centre called The Marlowe Centre has just been opened. To the east you come to Leverstock Green, where the housing is

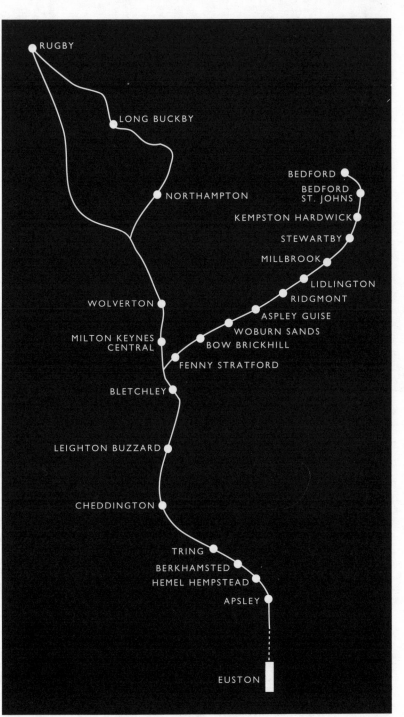

mostly post-Fifties. A one-bedroom starter home would cost about £60,000; a four-bedroom house £200,000. There are also some very large houses set in one-acre plots that fetch between £250,000 and £400,000. Ex-local authority housing tends to sell for up to 10 per cent less than private housing, so a two-bedroom house might be just over £55,000.

The New Town has a brash shopping centre with all the chainstores anyone might need. Large companies located here include Kodak, British Petroleum and Lucas Aerospace. The British Standards Institute also now has its offices in Hemel Hempstead.

Potten End, to the west, is a dispersed Chiltern village with a green, a pond and the Red Lion pub. It borders on beautiful National Trust land that stretches along the spine of the Chilterns from Ivinghoe Beacon to Berkhamsted. You can buy a Thirties detached house with a tile-hung bay window in a quiet suburban road for £225,000 to £275,000. Old cottages, however, are thin on the ground. A substantial house with five bedrooms and an acre of gardens might fetch £400,000.

Chipperfield is expensive too, though the centre has long since been ribboned with new developments built to accommodate escapees from Watford. It is redeemed by its wooded common, and by the old village centre where the green is faced by an inn, the church and some little brick cottages. A four-bedroom modern house (most of the houses are this size or larger) would cost £200,000 to £300,000.

BERKHAMSTED

Journey time: *34 min*	Peak trains: *5 per hour*
Season ticket: *£1696*	Off-peak trains: *3 per hour*

Berkhamsted is a prosperous old market town wedged in the valley bottom, with the railway and canal running through some of the best countryside close to London. A general market is held on Saturdays. The old castle, where Chaucer was clerk of works, is now little more than a few fingers of flint. People are attracted by the thickly wooded common and by the schools – Berkhamsted public school in particular, which can count Graham Greene among its old boys.

On the steep valley slopes to the south are shoals of Victorian and Edwardian houses with large gardens, while the centre of town is packed with Victorian terraces. You can get a double-fronted, bay-windowed, two-bedroom 19th-century house from £80,000. Prices stretch to £200,000 for five or six bedrooms. There are canalside flats right in the centre that sell at between £80,000 and £85,000 for two bedrooms. Detached houses built in the Sixties and Seventies sell for between £150,000 and £195,000. The large, individually designed, secluded houses in private roads fetch £250,000 to £300,000.

At the moment the town is punished by traffic hammering through on the A41, but a new bypass is due to open in 1993. The busy shopping centre has all the chain stores and a shopping mall in the old town hall. Large local employers include the Wellcome Foundation and there is also a business park. A new sports centre is due to open this year (1992) and the local golf course is positioned above the town on the lip of the valley.

Little Gaddesden, to the north, is very desirable, being set on a ridge 600ft up in the Chiltern Hills. Most of the large houses and cottages face directly onto the beechwoods and heathland of the vast Ashridge Estate, which is classified as an Area of Outstanding Natural Beauty. Physically the village is extremely strung out, and socially it is rather cliquey. You would pay £100,000 for a small two-bedroom cottage. There is a Church of England primary school, a church half a mile outside the village, and a village hall that hosts all the usual local activities. The big house has been converted into a college that specialises in management courses. In **Ashridge** itself, which is a discreet enclave of Twenties and Thirties houses with stockbroker-appeal, something with six bedrooms and three-quarters of an acre will cost £750,000 or more.

Three-bedroom cottage, near Tring

Close by is **Aldbury**, a film-set village of thatched and timber-framed cottages that cluster round a large pond with stocks and whipping post. Even the smallest cottage here costs £90,000 and will usually sell by word of mouth. There is a general store and post office, a crafts shop and The Greyhound pub. There are also tourists.

TRING

Journey time: *43 min*	**Peak trains:** *5 per hour*
Season ticket: *£1816*	**Off-peak trains:** *2 per hour*

Tring station is one and a half miles outside the town in a hamlet called

Tring Station. The Rothschilds lived at Tring Park, and their stamp is everywhere. They gave open spaces, provided cottages, and in 1905 built the stockbroker-style, half-timbered Rose & Crown Inn. The Zoological Museum is theirs – unsurprisingly for a family who used to drive around in traps drawn by zebras. Today Tring performs the dual role of commuter dormitory and market town (cattle on Monday, retail on Friday).

There are plenty of Victorian houses and new estates. A two-bedroom flat might cost £50,000; a two-bedroom Victorian cottage £60,000; a three-bedroom semi £80,000; a four-bedroom detached house £250,000 to £300,000. Tring does have a shopping centre, though people tend to use Aylesbury, Hemel Hempstead or Milton Keynes for more serious shopping.

Two and a half miles further north of Tring Station is **Ivinghoe** – a pretty village close to Ivinghoe Beacon from which you can gaze across to the chalkhill white lion of Whipsnade zoo. In the centre of the village the older houses sit sleepily on two sides of the green, and there is a fine watermill.

CHEDDINGTON

Journey time: *48 min*	Peak trains: *4 per hour*
Season ticket: *£1828*	Off-peak trains: *2 per hour*

Cheddington is a quiet little village, best known for the fact that the Great Train Robbery took place at the railway bridge just outside. The farm next to the bridge was being offered for sale last year. It has 378 acres of arable and dairy land, a four-bedroom house and outbuildings, with a magnificent barn. The asking price for the whole was around £920,000. Prices are similar to Tring and slightly more expensive than they are at Leighton Buzzard. You could buy a four-bedroom detached house for around £120,000 or a three-bedroom turn-of-the-century cottage for £105,000.

LEIGHTON BUZZARD

Journey time: *41 min*	Peak trains: *5 per hour*
Season ticket: *£1920*	Off-peak trains: *4 per hour*

Leighton Buzzard now also incorporates **Linslade**, which is where the station is positioned in prime commuter land. Leighton Buzzard proper is an old market town with drunken timber and brick buildings, and a twice-weekly market. The main street is in the process of being pedestrianised. The smartest roads to live in are Plantation Road (known as Bedfordshire's most beautiful mile) and Heath Road, studded with trees and offering a mix of Victorian and modern houses. Prices range between £120,000 and £350,000. You can find older two-bedroom terrace houses for £55,000 in other parts of the town, but the standard price for a modern four-bedroom detached is £125,000. The town is well padded in green belt.

Around the station in Linslade, which is greener than Leighton Buzzard itself, are Victorian terraces where two-bedroom houses sell for between £45,000 and £55,000, and three- to four-bedroom houses up to £85,000. There are two large modern estates, Bideford Green and Knaves Hill, built 15 to 20 years ago. Three-bedroom semis here cost around £60,000; three-bedroom detached houses around £75,000; four-bedroom houses around £90,000.

Soulbury, two miles west, is one of the best examples of an open field village in north Buckinghamshire, and its proximity to the station makes it a favourite with commuters. The half-timbered and thatched houses around the green and church overlook the Ouzel Valley. Other cottages are spread out between fields which are liberally laced with footpaths, and there are a few modern properties at the village margin. You need a car to live here – there is no shop, post office or bus service, though there is a clubroom for the use of local societies. Houses rarely come on the market, and when they do they are expensive. A period two-bedroom cottage would fetch around £75,000; a four-bedroom detached around £250,000.

Further west in the Vale of Aylesbury is **Stewkley** – possibly the longest village in England, stretching a mile either side of St Michael's, its remarkably fine Norman church. Between 1912 and 1914 the suffragette Sylvia Pankhurst and her mother lived here in a 16th-century cottage. The village has a reputation for being rather superior and closed to outsiders whom it decides do not belong. A substantial five-bedroom house would cost between £300,000 and £400,000.

For a less rarified atmosphere you could look southward to **Wing**, a busy, no-frills village with several shops including two general stores, two hairdressers and a bridal shop. Ascott House, bought by the Rothschilds in 1874, is close by, and village employment and activities have tended to revolve around the estate. Apart from the black-and-white estate cottages, there are rows of turn-of-the-century brick terrace cottages, plus the occasional thatched house and the usual modern estates on the fringe. A two-up-two-down Victorian terrace might cost £60,000; a three-bedroom detached house £90,000; a four-bedroom house £115,000.

The village has a junior school and a secondary school, several football teams and an adult education centre (upholstery classes are particularly popular). There is also a large green, with footpaths and swings. The drawback is that the village is beginning to feel hemmed in by Milton Keynes and Leighton Buzzard. It is also used as a rat-run by commuters dashing for the Leighton Buzzard trains, though there is talk of a bypass.

One of the most beautiful villages in the area is **Mentmore** – a charming collection of mock-Tudor houses on top of a hill in old Rothschild country. The large village green is ringed with lime trees and offers breathtaking views in every direction. The big house is Mentmore Towers, which in 1974 was offered to the government, with all its contents and land, for £3m. The offer was rejected, and the contents were later auctioned in what became known as the sale of the century, with the result that many important works of art were taken out of the country. The house itself was sold to a Transcendental Meditation group. A more modest two-bedroom cottage on the crest of the hill in Mentmore village would cost over £90,000; a country house with a few acres up to £1m.

BLETCHLEY

Journey time: *49 min*	**Peak trains:** *4 per hour*
Season ticket: *£2000*	**Off-peak trains:** *4 per hour*

Bletchley is the largest of the three towns gobbled up by Milton Keynes. It has a good shopping centre, and an open-air general market held three times a week. "The funny thing about it is that at the heart of it you will find a 16th-century thatched cottage with an acre of garden selling for around £200,000. Where else can you find an acre of garden in the centre of town?" says a local estate agent. The rest of Bletchley has been developed in waves, reflecting the repeated housing booms during this century and the last. You start with the thatched cottages, then come the grids of Victorian terraces (a large example with a 100ft garden might cost £125,000), and then the classic double bay-fronted Thirties houses, built by Tranfield, some of which still have their sunburst stained glass.

Nearly 40 per cent of the town is council housing, and for this reason it tends to be looked down upon by some of its neighbours. The ex-council houses, however, offer good value for money, with large three-bedroom semis selling for around £50,000. In the last building wave are the houses put up during the Eighties boom – typical mix-and-match styles, with one-bedroom flats, small and large houses all mixed up together. A one-bedroom house costs just over £40,000; a four-bedroom detached house with a garage just under £100,000.

Padbury, to the west, is the classic chocolate-box village with half-timbered and thatched cottages, and a green swathed in leafy trees. It has a butcher and a part-time post office in the garage, but the grocery stores have gone. There are tennis courts, a sports field and pavilion, and a village hall. Despite all this, old villagers complain that it is not the village it used to be: here has been such an influx of commuters and weekenders. Among the attractions for incomers is a highly regarded local school for five- to nine-year-olds. People will wait years to get a house in Padbury, and pay £135,000 for a small semi-detached thatched cottage.

Adstock is slightly closer to Bletchley. Its timber, brick and thatched cottages built along narrow lanes give it a feeling of cosiness and compactness, and there is a popular local pub, the Thatched Inn. A four-bedroom cottage with exposed beams and inglenook fireplace might sell for just under £200,000.

For a vibrant village life, try **Thornborough**. This is a long, thin village with a church, pub and green (with pond), which is the scene of a great number of village events. There are fetes, a donkey derby and a sports day, followed by a barbecue in the evening. There are two football clubs and a cricket team which plays in the evenings as well as at weekends; and a gardening society which has helped with the local landscaping. There is a primary school for children up to eight years old, and a shop which doubles as a post office. When it rains the stream across the road swells and people come out to paddle. There are also ducks, which are somewhat indiscriminate in the matter of where they lay their eggs. Some of the drakes have been known to end up in village freezers. A circular five-mile walk round Thornborough watermill and the old canal is a favourite Sunday afternoon stroll. A five-bedroom detached house here might cost £150,000; a three-bedroom 18th-century stone-and-slate cottage would fetch £180,000.

Branchline to Bedford via Fenny Stratford, Bow Brickhill, Woburn Sands, Aspley Guise, Ridgmont, Lidlington, Millbrook, Stewartby, Kempston Hardwick, Bedford St Johns

No through trains: see below
Season ticket (all stations): £2064

This is the only remaining section of the old Oxford-Cambridge line. It is only 17 miles long but is extremely busy since it serves villages that lack good local bus services and is heavily used by children on the school-run to Bedford. Commuters can change at Bedford for either St Pancras or Kings Cross Thameslink. Or they can go to Bletchley and change for Euston. None of the stations along the line have car parks, nor are they manned. Information is tannoyed from Bletchley to the individual platforms, and tickets are bought from the guard on the train. Season tickets to Euston, St Pancras or Thameslink are available from all stations.

People living in the eastern suburbs of Milton Keynes tend to use the first two stations **Fenny Stratford** and **Bow Brickhill**, rather than drive to Milton Keynes station. Fenny Stratford is mainly Victorian, and you would have to pay around £65,000 for a three-bedroom house here. Bow Brickhill sprawls along a steep hillside reputed to have been one of Dick Turpin's favourite haunts. Old woodland has been cleared to make way for golf courses. It is an old village, with a shop and a pub, but lies on a very busy road. Property is varied, from two-up-two-downs selling at around £55,000, to four-bedroom Sixties houses at around £120,000.

Woburn Sands has its own distinct identity, with a small high street for day-to-day needs, and wonderful walks within five minutes of the centre in the Duke of Bedford's woodlands. There are a couple of dress shops, a delicatessen, a restaurant, wet fish shop, three butchers, doctor's surgery and medical centre, and a lower and middle school. You could buy a small turn-of-the-century house for £50,000, but a four- or five-bedroom Victorian house would be likely to fetch £250,000. Local activities include football teams, bowls and village fairs. **Aspley Heath** (within reach of Woburn Sands station) is where people from Woburn Sands aspire to move, since it has spacious houses set in large gardens with good views. It would be hard to find anything to buy here for less than £250,000.

Woburn itself (also within reach of Woburn Sands station) is a beautifully preserved Georgian town, best known for its proximity to Woburn Abbey, and popular with golfers for the exclusive Woburn Golf and Country Club. Very few houses are freehold since most are tied to the estate, but the occasional four-bedroom modern house might come on the market for around £125,000; or you might find an ex-council three-bedroom semi for around £75,000. It does get cluttered in summer with tourists visiting the Abbey and its Wild Animal Kingdom.

For a sedate, select and expensive village, you would look at **Aspley Guise**. Middle-class Victorians regarded it as an "inland Bournemouth", but modern estate agents like to describe it as "the Darling Buds of May of Milton Keynes". It is very traditional. People smile and say good morning to each other, and they bother to keep the village tidy. There is a shop, post office, butcher, hairdresser and hotel, and the railway station is tiny. People pay a lot to live here and then stay a long time. A two-bedroom Victorian terrace would cost over £60,000; a four-bedroom house would cost between £250,000 and £300,000. People hunt and fish and go to church. The finest house in the village is Aspley House, believed to have been built by an assistant to Wren, or perhaps even by Wren himself.

Eversholt (within reach of Aspley Guise) on the other side of the Woburn Estate, is unusual in that the rows of estate cottages have no front doors. It is said that the Duchess of Bedford didn't like to see people gossiping. A rectory with five or six bedrooms and four acres might cost £600,000.

Ridgmont is a typical Bedfordshire estate village with cottages built in two styles. There are two-up-two-downs with leaded lights that might sell for £70,000; and three-bedroom terraces, built in distinctive red brick in the late 19th century, that might sell for £100,000. But very little ever comes up for sale at all.

Lidlington is another estate village where the Duke of Bedford sought to muzzle the gossips by building houses without front doors. Property prices are similar to those in **Millbrook**, which is little more than an old hamlet built for farm workers, with a pub and a post office. The wooded valley near the church is supposed to have inspired Bunyan's Valley of the Shadow of Death in *Pilgrim's Progress*. A two-bedroom cottage might be bought for £60,000; the odd four-bedroom modern house, built to plug the gaps, might sell for £120,000.

Stewartby is dominated by the local brickworks, which emit fumes the locals say they cannot smell. It was built as a model village in the Twenties by the Stewart family, owners of the brickworks, as a gesture of concern for their employees. The village was extended in the Thirties and Fifties, and a worked-out quarry was flooded to create a lake for watersports within a landscaped country park. A three-bedroom semi here would sell for around £53,000; a two-bedroom house for just under £45,000. **Kempston Hardwick**, the next station along the line, is given mainly to light industry and has very little housing.

At **Bedford St Johns** you have reached a suburb of Bedford and the nursery slopes of the local housing market. Here first-timers can start out with a three-bedroom Victorian terrace at £55,000, or a semi at £60,000 to £80,000. There is some modern Tudoresque development next door to the tiny station, where two-bedroom homes sell for around £45,000. A third bedroom raises the price to £55,000.

MILTON KEYNES CENTRAL

Journey time: *45 min*	**Peak trains:** *4 per hour*
Season ticket: *£2020*	**Off-peak trains:** *4 per hour*

The train service to **Milton Keynes** station is so good that it has a vast catchment area stretching all the way to Daventry. It has some of the newest rolling stock, a better record for punctuality than other lines, and the trains run so frequently that you hardly need bother with the timetable. Passengers are now allowed to travel on the night staff trains, so the station is open all night too; and once the Channel Tunnel is open there will be a Euro train service to Paris. Parking, however, is fairly chaotic, with cars creeping up the side roads to avoid paying for the multi-storey car park.

To enjoy Milton Keynes properly, you need to think American.

The grid pattern of wide boulevards in the centre, with one of the largest covered shopping malls in the country, and the sea of car-parking, can make you feel as if the whole world has been turned into a supermarket. But it is thoughtfully planned and very convenient. The 22,000-acre site, which includes Bletchley, Stony Stratford, Wolverton and 13 old villages, was conceived as a New Town in 1967 and is scheduled to contain a population of 250,000 by the end of the century. This year (1992) the Milton Keynes Development Corporation officially disbands and hands over the reins to the local council.

Housing is arranged in segments, with a mix of starter homes, three- and four-bedroom houses and retirement flats in each one, ensuring a full range of age groups and incomes. There are a large number of commuters, but a lot of people are employed locally too – many major companies, including the Abbey National and Argos, have moved here. Because the town is so young, the population is young with it.

Milton Keynes prides itself on offering cheaper housing combined with a fast commute to couples who cannot afford to live in London but who want to maintain their jobs in the capital. First-time buyers' flats tend to start at £35,000, with prices rising up to £400,000 for a detached six-bedroom house with half an acre of garden. Much emphasis in the design of new housing has been put on energy-saving.

Not all the housing is new, however. There are still places where you can find old thatched cottages (and new thatched houses, too, for that matter).

The sports centres are as new and ambitious as you would expect. The Stantonbury Campus offers a big indoor/outdoor leisure complex, and for watersports there is Willen Lake. Old fields have been retained to give green lungs to the town and provide playgrounds. The Great Ouse

California-style home, Milton Keynes

skirts the northern edge, as do the Ouzel and the Grand Union Canal (along which you can take a cruise). There are also several man-made lakes providing habitats for wildlife. North of the city centre is Linford Wood, a remnant of an ancient forest, now laced with footpaths, bridle-ways and picnic sites, and two wildlife reserves.

Areas are considered up-market or down-market according to how closely together the houses are built, and how spacious they are inside. Perhaps one of the most desirable is **Woughton-on-the-Green**, where the plots are large, houses are traditionally built, and the cheapest four-bedroom detached house would cost £120,000. The **Bancroft** area is nice too, though for different reasons. Houses are built around a cleft in the landscape with an old ruin in it that has been landscaped as a park. A three-storey terrace town house here would cost around £90,000. **Willen** is also popular because it has a lake and a sense of space. Many of the houses have been built by the owners themselves, and one of these might now sell for between £200,000 and £300,000 (though the standard price for a four-bedroom house here would be rather less, at £110,000). In a typically mixed estate like **Bradwell**, a two-bedroom late Victorian cottage would cost just under £60,000; a two-bedroom new house just under £50,000.

One of the nicest villages in the area is **Weston Underwood**, built in greyish Cotswold stone (it lies in the northern section of the same ridge of oolite that gives the Cotswolds its distinctive character) and dating mostly from the 17th and 18th centuries. Ten miles further into Northamptonshire, the stone starts to turn red. Weston Underwood is entered through stone gates topped with pineapples. It remained in the ownership of the Throckmorton family until the 1920s, when it was sold. A small, three-bedroom stone cottage for sale would be a rare find here, and would fetch around £115,000. The green, overlooked by the house once occupied by the poet William Cowper, is decorated with trees and seats and roses, and is the place to buy cream teas during August. There is a small zoological garden which specialises in flamingos.

There are a few new houses but villagers fight tooth-and-nail against new development. Their cause is helped by the water meadows around the Ouse, which are unsuitable for building on anyway. Community spirit is strong, and expressed through the fruit, vegetable and flower shows, and the playgroup. Local agriculture concentrates on cereal crops, but rape and flax are also grown. There are walks through the woods at Salcey Forest. "Village people try to get to know new people, but the big problem is that many of them are mortgaged so heavily that they are both working and we don't see a great deal of them," says one of the older inhabitants.

The local shopping centre is at **Olney**. It is popular because it is as traditional as Newport Pagnell (see below) but more rural. Property prices therefore tend to run at five to 10 per cent higher. In the market square is the red-brick William Cowper museum, in another house that the poet once lived in with his friend Mary Unwin, who cared for him during his lapses from sanity. The town is famous for its pancake race, run every Shrove Tuesday from the market place to the church. The winning housewife gets a silver cup and a kiss from the bellringer.

Ravenstone, three miles west, is as pretty, expensive and exclusive as Weston Underwood. It has a shop-cum-post office and a village green sprouting stone houses. **Stoke Goldington** is the biggest in this clutch of villages, with more new housing stitched in between the old. Another handsome stone village is **Emberton**, with 170 acres of country park and lakes along the River Ouse. Houses in all of these villages sell so easily that the owners often dispose of them privately. This entire belt is very convenient for railway users, and also only a short drive from the M1.

Two and a half miles north is **Castlethorpe**. This is an attractive stone village peppered with modern houses, but it is affected by the railway line running through it. A two- to three-bedroom cottage might be bought for £80,000. A four-bedroom detached house would fetch around £140,000.

North-east is **Newport Pagnell**, on the Rivers Ouse and Lovat. It has changed over the years from a lace-making town to an industrial and commercial one. But it has managed not to become forbidding, and new modern buildings are sandwiched quietly between the old Georgian houses. The cinema has been turned into a shopping mall. A two-bedroom house in a Victorian terrace in the centre of town will cost around £45,000. The most popular road is Lakes Lane, where the houses back onto the common. A three-bedroom semi here will cost around £90,000. There are also some huge six-bedroom houses that could fetch up to £300,000. Green Park is the most popular of the new estates. A modern four-bedroom detached house with a double garage will cost around £125,000.

People living in the villages to the east of Milton Keynes might use Wolverton station as an alternative to Milton Keynes.

WOLVERTON

Journey time: *59 min*	**Peak trains:** *3 per hour*
Season ticket: *£2080*	**Off-peak trains:** *2 per hour*

Stony Stratford is now part of Milton Keynes, but still retains many original 18th-century buildings. As a quaint old market town, with the market square just off the high street, it considers itself to be quite separate from the new upstart town that has swallowed it. The George Hotel presents a wobbly, black-and-white profile among the bakers, butchers and building societies that surround it. Note that there are no superstores here. A Twenties semi with three bedrooms might cost £90,000, but a good Georgian house (one of a pair) would cost £150,000; a detached one would fetch £200,000.

Wolverton has the local station, and is packed with Victorian terraces, some of them reminiscent of *Coronation Street*. A two- to three-bedroom house here would cost between £40,000 and £50,000 – more than 10 per cent less than the equivalent house in Stony Stratford. Three bedrooms would push the price up to £50,000 to £60,000.

To the west of Milton Keynes is **Upper Weald**, a hamlet of brick and stone. There are no shops, but you might find a small period cottage with two bedrooms for just under £100,000. Another worth mentioning is **Wicken**, for its stone houses, church and superb hotel. A 300-year-old stone house might cost just under £170,000. Watch out for **Deanshanger**, which has a chemical factory that pumps out red smoke every day and turns the pigeons pink.

Further afield, on a hilltop in unspoilt countryside, is the county town of **Buckingham**. It is a typical market town, where the stalls still appear on Tuesdays and Saturdays, and it remains a pleasure to walk through its steep narrow streets and look at the old inns and almshouses. You might be able to buy a Victorian detached house with a large garden on Stowe Avenue for £145,000. There are a few modern estates on the edge of the town, of which the most popular is Page Hill. The average price of a four-bedroom detached house here is £110,000 to £115,000. The town is very close to Stowe public school, once the home of the Dukes of Buckingham. The gardens, studded with follies by Vanbrugh, Kent and Gibbs, now belong to the National Trust.

NORTHAMPTON

Journey time: *71 min*
Season ticket: *£2284*
Peak trains: *3 per hour*
Off-peak trains: *2 per hour*

It has to be said that **Northampton** is an unprepossessing town with a rugged commercial and light industrial bustle. Historically its prosperity came from the manufacture of boots and shoes, but in recent years it has widely diversified. There is a large brewing industry (the British headquarters of Carlsberg), and Barclaycard, Express Lifts and Avon cosmetics all have a substantial presence. The market square, where an open-air market is still held, is believed to be the largest in England. The Grosvenor Centre is a huge shopping mall with all the chainstores, while Peacock Place has slightly more up-market shops, such as Next and the Body Shop. Schools include the highly regarded private Northampton High School for Girls.

Northampton has developed over the years in a series of concentric circles. The Victorian workers' terraces at the centre can be picked up for between £35,000 and £45,000. In the next band come the more dignified, tree-lined streets of larger Edwardian terraces and semis, selling for between £50,000 and £60,000. Then come the Twenties and Thirties semis, all pebble-dash and bay-windows, with prices starting at around £85,000. To the north of the town, these are wedged in by an arc of Seventies estates, where prices range between £55,000 and £75,000. The suburbs to the east contain the bulk of the new town development, and those to the south have the most modern estates, on which a detached four-bedroom house might cost just under £120,000. This area is also closest to the M1 (Junction 15).

Northamptonshire has never been as fashionable as other counties north of London because people think of it as being rather plain. There is little in the way of black-and-white building, and the villages close to Northampton tend to be built of dark brown ironstone with roofs of slate rather than thatch. To the north-west you will find some cottages built of cob (clay or earth bonded with straw), which obviously require very careful maintenance. When cob is whitewashed it often looks very much like stone.

Contrasting terrace houses, Northants

To the north-east, towards Kettering and Oundle, you break into a belt of bleached limestone. Being closer to East Anglia, the houses here will sometimes be thatched in Norfolk reed. Or they may have Collyweston slates – which are not slate at all, but rather slivers of very dense, light-coloured limestone.

Due west is **Daventry**, another small market town that has kept its head. It was once a coaching stop on the road to Holyhead. Now it is a commuter haven, not only for London but also for Birmingham and Coventry, especially now that the M40 extension is open. There are plenty of no-frills Sixties estates, where prices are five to 10 per cent lower than they are in Northampton.

Just to the south-west of Daventry is the village of **Badby**, whose 700-year-old woods are famous for their bluebells and beeches. The Knightley Way footpath, which runs for 12 miles to Greens-Norton, touches the western edge of the woods, which have been designated a Site of Special Scientific Interest. The village itself is built in stone and slate, though there is the occasional thatched roof. The local pub, The Windmill, has recently been rethatched and is one of the three buildings in the village that date from before 1500. There is a post office and a general store, a primary school and a village hall where the Brownies, Guides, WI and horticultural society meet. Within a mile you can climb to the highest point in Northamptonshire where, from the top of Arbury Hill, you can see the Malvern Hills. A mile or two in the other direction is the sizeable village of **Weedon Bec**, which has the frustrating disadvantage of having the railway running through it without a station to compensate. It has a similar range of housing and prices to Long Buckby (see below), the next stop down the line.

Harpole is closer to Northampton, and only just off the M1 at Junction 16. A vicarage-sized house here might cost between £250,000 and £300,000, but you might pick up a little Victorian terrace for as little as £50,000. Just down the road, on the south bank of the River Nene, is **Kislingbury**. It is a pretty stone village with some thatched roofs, relatively unspoilt though there is some new housing. A two-bedroom period house might sell for £70,000, but country houses with a couple of acres will reach £500,000.

If you want town life but find Northampton itself too depressing, you might consider looking south to **Towcester**. It isn't as pretty as Buckingham and is therefore cheaper. The central focus is on the square and town hall, and Towcester racecourse and Silverstone motor-racing circuit are nearby. Off the main street, two- to three-bedroom Victorian terrace houses sell for between £40,000 and £50,000; and there are a few large detached Victorian houses that fetch between £110,000 and £170,000. The new four-bedroom detached houses might go for £85,000 if they are pinched for space; up to £130,000 if they are large.

Roade is perhaps plainer still, offering a mix of traditional Northamptonshire stone, Victorian terraces and Sixties estates. It is popular with London commuters because they have a choice of station – Northampton or Milton Keynes – or they could opt to take the car down the M1. Property prices are slightly higher than in Northampton.

East of Northampton you could look at **Earls Barton**, which has a church with a remarkable Saxon tower, thought to be the finest in the country. Built of plaster in four tiers, it has inaccessible doorways on the second tier. The village has blown up into a small town which has a new shoe factory, opened in 1987. The fact that it is a whisker away from the A45 makes it very convenient for people working in Northampton or

Wellingborough, where the boys' public school is. A small Victorian terrace house would sell for over £40,000; a detached house with four bedrooms would fetch £150,000.

LONG BUCKBY

Journey time: *95 min*	Peak trains: *I per hour*
Season ticket: *£2316*	Off-peak trains: *I per hour*

Having grown up around the railway, canal system and A5, the attraction of **Long Buckby** is good communications rather than charm. With a strong Victorian core and a plethora of Seventies estates, it stretches for one and a half miles and contains a population of over 4,000. A four-bedroom detached estate house might be bought for £90,000, but something grander in a landscaped garden could reach £200,000. An old rectory in the area would cost at least another £100,000. The cheapest houses are Victorian cottages selling for under £50,000.

RUGBY

Journey time: *105 min**	Peak trains: *3 per hour (InterCity)*
Season ticket: *£3680*	Off-peak trains: *I per hour†*

* 63 min on InterCity   † Plus I InterCity about every 2 hours

Rugby is a run-down, nondescript town that few people have any affection for. It lacks any architectural flair, and its old industrial base has been replaced with a more commercial one. It is best known for the boys' public school, used as a model for *Tom Brown's Schooldays*, where the eponymous ball game began in 1823 and whose former pupils include Rupert Brooke and Matthew Arnold.

Small houses for first-time buyers are in the centre of town, selling at between £30,000 and £50,000. There is cheap property too in the **Brownsover** area where, if you can overcome the stigma attached to it, you could buy a two-bedroom semi for just over £50,000 or a new detached house for £60,000. The more up-market areas are **Hillmorton** and **Bilton**, where you could find a dignified three-bedroom semi for £55,000 to £65,000, or a larger detached house with four or five bedrooms for £70,000 to £120,000. In Bawnmore Road, Bilton, property becomes more expensive, rising from £50,000 up to £450,000. And in Hillmorton Road, Hillmorton, there are some very substantial houses built in the Twenties, some very close to the town centre, where you could pay up to £200,000.

Living to the south of Rugby is thought to be slightly better than living to the north. Its most salubrious suburb is **Dunchurch**, a village two miles from the centre, where large detached new houses with four bedrooms sell for between £90,000 and £160,000. There are also some period two-up-two-down cottages that fetch around £65,000. Second best is **Clifton upon Dunsmore**, to the north, which again has a villagey feel to it, though the houses here tend to be smaller. A detached Thirties house with three bedrooms would cost just over £100,000; a modernised two-bedroom Twenties house under £50,000.

For a proper village you need to look south-east to **Ashby St Ledgers**, one of the last good Northamptonshire thatch-and-stone villages before the more industrial Midlands takes over. It is remarkable in that it was an estate village, built by Lord Wimbourne in 1912 and designed by Lutyens. Development was then so tightly controlled that there are only 44 houses in all – the tradition was that two new houses were built every time the lord of the manor died. There is an old barn on the green that serves as the village hall. Since the Wimbournes left, the village has changed hands three times. There is a strong community spirit among the old villagers and a pub which strains at the seams. The half-timbered gatehouse next to the church is where Robert Catesby, one of the ringleaders of the Gunpowder Plot, is supposed to have met the other conspirators. Houses rarely come on the market, and you could expect to pay £20,000 above local market values for the privilege of living here.

Birdingbury, south-west of Rugby, is another sought-after village. It has only about 100 houses, most of which are now occupied by commuters rather than the agricultural workers for whom they were built. Houses tend to be a bit more expensive because it is so close to Leamington Spa (see page 148). A two-bedroom period cottage might cost around £125,000. The River Leam meanders through the village, and there is a fishing club. There is a post office and a village store but no pub, though villagers tend to use the Birdingbury Men's Club for meetings. Cricket and football are played at **Marton**, a mile away. There are too few young people in Birdingbury itself to make up full teams. The nearest school is at **Leamington Hastings**, the next village south.

Sheer convenience make **Kilsby** and **Barby** commuter havens. Both are beside Junction 17 on the M1, and close to Rugby. Kilsby is unremarkable, but has a supply of four-bedroom modern detached houses selling for around £85,000. Some are more lavish, built in stone with five bedrooms, and sell for around £187,000. Barby is smaller, with a stronger sense of village about it, and has a few old cob houses among the 19th-century and modern brick. A four-bedroom detached house here might sell for around £160,000. There are a few shops, a village hall, a school, and a claim to fame in that the MacLaren baby buggy was designed here in the Sixties by Owen Maclaren.

MARYLEBONE — TO — AYLESBURY

(via Chorleywood)

CHORLEYWOOD

Journey time: *27 min* | **Peak trains:** *8 per hour**
Season ticket: *£1164* | **Off-peak trains:** *4 per hour**

* Includes Metropolitan Line service to Baker Street

The Victorian development of the railways created **Chorleywood** by making the lovely Chess Valley accessible from London. The M25 has done its best to make it inaccessible from anywhere. In theory it is possible to get to Heathrow in 15 minutes. In practice the motorway is often blocked, and locals are not at all happy at the idea of widening it. Their fear is that this would simply increase the number of cars passing through the village on their way to the M1 a few miles to the north.

Nevertheless, people enjoy the large common with its nine-hole golf course and the wonderful views across the valley – so much so that they are willing to pay £95,000 for a two-bedroom cottage, up to £190,000 for a four-bedroom detached house in what is known as the station estate, a ring of Victorian and Edwardian houses built to take advantage of the first rail link with London. Berks Hill, South Road, Haddon Road and Hillside Road are all highly prized. Then comes a later ring of Thirties and Fifties houses, then a final ring of Seventies and Eighties. Grovewood Close and Old Shire Lane have three- and four-bedroom detached houses for £170,000 and £190,000 upwards; in Chalfont Lane, where large houses are set in a couple of acres, the prices are closer to £1m. There are a few small flats from £65,000 – a price which in Watford would buy a two-bedroom house – but first-time buyers in Chorleywood are young city types who can afford to start at £100,000. Whatever the price range, the emphasis is on individuality – very rarely are two houses exactly the same.

In addition to the advantage of a half-hour journey into London, Chorleywood offers a lively community which makes good use of the public and club tennis courts and the football and cricket facilities. The district beyond the village centre is very scattered, with houses trailing up either side of the valley leaving the shops behind in the valley bottom. This is inconvenient for elderly pedestrians, though there is a bus service which shuttles from one side to the other. Big shopping is done in Amersham,

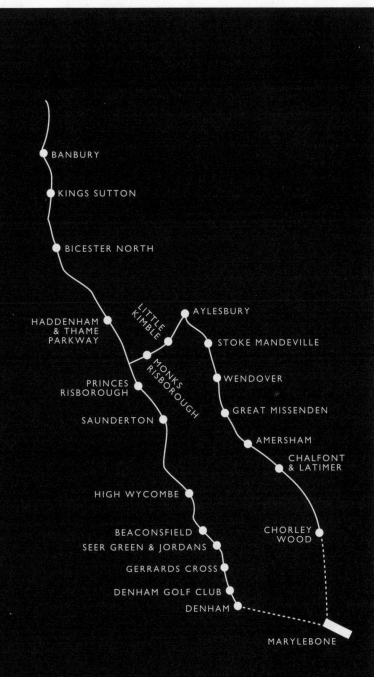

BANBURY

KINGS SUTTON

BICESTER NORTH

LITTLE KIMBLE

AYLESBURY

HADDENHAM & THAME PARKWAY

STOKE MANDEVILLE

MONKS RISBOROUGH

WENDOVER

PRINCES RISBOROUGH

GREAT MISSENDEN

SAUNDERTON

AMERSHAM

CHALFONT & LATIMER

HIGH WYCOMBE

BEACONSFIELD

SEER GREEN & JORDANS

CHORLEY WOOD

GERRARDS CROSS

DENHAM GOLF CLUB

DENHAM

MARYLEBONE

Northwood and Beaconsfield, and at the three-times-weekly market in Watford. Parents bemoan the passing of the schools into Hertfordshire control as this has taken them out of the grammar school system still practised by Buckinghamshire. Nevertheless, local schools retain a very high standard and reputation.

CHALFONT & LATIMER

Journey time: *31 min*   **Peak trains:** *8 per hour**
Season ticket: *£1164*   **Off-peak trains:** *4 per hour**

* Includes Metropolitan Line service to Baker Street

Little Chalfont consists of the station, a strip of shops, a mini roundabout, a library and a number of very expensive houses in large grounds. "Too spread out to be matey," said one resident. **Latimer**, with one shop but, unusually for a village, no pub, is much prettier with timbered cottages around a triangular green. The River Chess, flowing past Latimer House, offers trout fishing. **Chenies**, equally picturesque, was a typically feudal village owned by the Dukes of Bedford for 400 years until 1954. Be prepared to pay £100,000 in either village for even the smallest cottage. A couple of miles north-west of the station is **Ley Hill**, a particularly lively and friendly community with golf and cricket on the common, a couple of nice old pubs, a post office and village shop, and an infant and junior school. There are lots of local activities, including a flower club and two or three dog clubs. The wooded countryside which surrounds all these villages contains the only local hazard – being run down by backpackers enjoying the many spectacular walks.

AMERSHAM

Journey time: *35 min*   **Peak trains:** *7 per hour**
Season ticket: *£1280*   **Off-peak trains:** *4 per hour**

* Includes Metropolitan Line service to Baker Street

The old town of **Amersham** is centred on a 17th-century market hall, and its high street, lanes and little courtyards offer a picturesque variety of architectural styles from timber-framed houses to Georgian brick, sometimes just facades on much older buildings. A plethora of old pubs recalls the town's history as a staging post on the coach road from London to Aylesbury, and traffic still comes to a halt in September when the annual fair is held in the high street. The smallest period cottage will cost from £100,000, with substantial houses up to £500,000. The new part of the town, Amersham-on-the-Hill, was developed in the 1920s when the Metropolitan Railway Company brought city merchants and West End traders from Aldgate and Baker Street. As the last stop on the Underground, Amersham was considered the end of commuterland until motorways made more distant villages accessible. The more modern housing includes ex-council flats from £50,000, three-bedroom semis from £90,000, and Twenties four-bedroom family houses at £200,000. There are cricket, football and hockey clubs, a swimming pool, a film society, an arts club and several riding stables and pony clubs. People often move here to take advantage of the local grammar schools – Dr Challoner's for boys in Amersham, and the high school for girls in Little Chalfont. **Chesham Bois** (from the Boyes family who owned the manor in 1276, and not to do with the surrounding woods) is no longer a separate village but merges into Amersham-on-the-Hill. It has a village school and a common but little sense of community as the houses stand well apart from each other, some in an acre of land. Prices range between £200,000 and £400,000.

Chesham is only a short drive away and is also on the Metropolitan line. The town is utterly charming, cupped by the Chiltern Hills, with the River Chess flowing through it, attended by a riverside walk that takes you out through beechwoods, past watercress beds and a trout farm. It provides good shopping because it not only has the standard supermarkets and multiple stores, but also has speciality shops including a saddler, French baker and a music shop. Many of the shops front ancient buildings, some half-timbered 16th-century, others brick and plaster.

GREAT MISSENDEN

Journey time: *43 min*	**Peak trains:** *3 per hour*
Season ticket: *£1764*	**Off-peak trains:** *2 per hour*

The narrow main street lined with houses and shops from the 15th to 19th centuries gives **Great Missenden** an intimate air and makes it an attractive small centre within easy commuting distance of central London. It is also within easy walking distance of the surrounding woods. High street shops provide day-to-day needs, otherwise the main shopping is done in Amersham. A good private school, The Gateway, plus Misbourne secondary school and a sixth-form college add to the attractions, but apart from a private tennis club there is little entertainment for the young. ''No youth club, no cinema, no transport. If you are under drinking age, forget it,'' said one. A few born-and-bred residents live in the centre, where 19th-century cottage conversions with two or three bedrooms cost between £94,000 and £148,000. There is a good deal of later development within walking distance of the centre from £115,000 for a three-bedroom semi and £175,000 for a newly built three-bedroom detached. There are also some handsome Edwardian houses set in mature grounds at around £219,000. For a Thirties four-bedroom house in a couple of acres you might expect to pay £375,000.

The surrounding villages have a pecking order headed by **The Lee**, a secluded community in the leafy uplands above Great Missenden. It has some of the grandest houses ever set around a tiny village green, and a picturesque pub. The rambling manor house is owned by the Liberty family, who have had a great deal to do with the preservation of the village. No new development is allowed except on the sites of existing buildings, so there are several handsome conversions. There is "a little new money, but they keep the properties as they should". The area is favoured by captains of industry, writers and actors distinguished enough to need shelter from the public gaze. There is nothing under £190,000 here, and the average is £250,000 for a four-bedroom cottage.

Next in line is **Lee Common**. It belies its name by having no common, but the cluster of streets has pretty rural surroundings and some attractive period houses; and it has the further benefit of a village shop and local primary school. A four-bedroom, semi-detached 19th-century cottage would cost around £185,000. For Thirties houses overlooking green belt farmland, look at **South Heath**. It has a sub post office-cum-stores, and a likely price tag of £185,000 for a four-bedroom detached.

WENDOVER

Journey time: *50 min*	**Peak trains:** *3 per hour*
Season ticket: *£1820*	**Off-peak trains:** *2 per hour*

The beautiful National Trust countryside of the Chilterns attracts a lot of walkers to **Wendover**. The street tables outside the bistro cafés make a picturesque setting for a refreshment stop. Part of the Icknield Way, Europe's oldest highway, runs through the broad high street, which is cobbled and tree-lined and offers a good variety of shops, plus post office, banks and library. There are many period houses, from Georgian back to the enchanting thatch-and-timber row of Coldharbour Cottages, said to have been a gift from Henry VIII to Anne Boleyn. Infilling has been carefully done and blends well with the mature buildings. A two-bedroom cottage costs around £69,000. Three-bedroom Victorian houses are in the region of £126,000. There is a first, middle and secondary school in the town and three golf courses in the neighbourhood, plus tennis, bowls and squash clubs, church societies and handsome old inns which allow plenty of opportunities to be companionable. Yet the town safeguards privacy by being too big for everyone to know everyone else's business.

At the turn of the century **Weston Turville**, north-west of Wendover, was breeding Aylesbury ducks for the London market and making straw plait for the Luton hat industry. Its older properties are on the eastern edge of the village, but they are well outnumbered by the modern development. Family houses range from three-bedroom semis to four-bedroom detached at prices of £69,950 to £115,000. There is a

Early 19-century
cottage, Bucks

convenient post office and small parade of shops, several pubs, tennis
courts and golf and squash clubs. The village has a combined first and
middle school; older children go to grammar and secondary schools in
Wendover or Aylesbury.

STOKE MANDEVILLE

Journey time: *55 min*	**Peak trains:** *3 per hour*
Season ticket: *£1828*	**Off-peak trains:** *2 per hour*

Stoke Mandeville now is little more than a suburb of Aylesbury. It has a
general store, several pubs and a combined first and middle school but is
largely dominated by the world-famous hospital and a lot of Thirties
houses. These sell from £90,000 for a three-bedroom semi to £180,000
for a four-bedroom detached house in ample grounds.

AYLESBURY

Journey time: *60 min*	**Peak trains:** *3 per hour*
Season ticket: *£1856*	**Off-peak trains:** *2 per hour*

Commercial development has overshadowed a good deal of **Aylesbury's**
ancient past. Its heart was cut out in the Sixties to make way for office
blocks, and large council estates were built on the north side to
accommodate London overspill. Shoppers flock in to the pedestrianised
malls of multiples but, although there are some 17th- and 18th-century
terraces and almshouses – and despite the inconvenience of having to

drive into town and try to park – commuters prefer to live in the surrounding villages. Farmhouses are the popular choice – there is no equivalent of the Surrey stockbroker house here. For those who want something more modern, a three-bedroom semi goes for £70,000, a two-bedroom mid-terrace for £55,000, a studio flat for £40,000. Aylesbury grammar school for boys and high school for girls, and Sir Henry Floyd High School, have excellent reputations; and there is an unusually good selection of hospitals in the area. Aylesbury has a cinema, but otherwise not a lot of excitement.

Most of the surrounding villages have had their share of new developments but **Bishopstone** is still a quiet retreat. A timber-framed farmhouse costs around £200,000. **Dinton**, too, is peaceful and still has buildings made of witchert. Dinton Hall, where Cromwell's sword was once kept, has recently created a furore by obtaining planning consent to turn itself into a hotel with two golf courses. Some locals welcome this as an added attraction; others deplore it as a loss not only of the village fete but of a sense of tradition and continuity.

To the north-west of Aylesbury, **Quainton** has all the ingredients of the chocolate-box rural idyll – pretty thatched cottages, a broad village green and a ruined medieval market cross, a restored windmill and a group of 17th-century almshouses with dormers and Dutch gables. Discriminating buyers will pay a premium to live here. Prices range from £150,000 for a two-bedroom cottage to £170,000 for a modern four-bedroom detached. It is a horsy area, and the stud farm five miles away at **Whitchurch** has recently been bought by Pat Eddery.

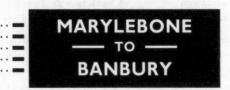

MARYLEBONE TO BANBURY

DENHAM AND DENHAM GOLF CLUB

Journey time: *28 min*	Peak trains: *3 per hour*
Season ticket: *£1132*	Off-peak trains: *1 per hour*

If **Denham** had come straight out of the scenery department of the old Denham studios it couldn't be more picturesque. It is a patch of rural peace only 18 miles from London with a village hall, a small green and a stream winding past wisteria-clad old brick. It would be perfect but for the pub visitors whose motors clog the lanes, accounting for the village's sobriquet as "the prettiest car park in Buckinghamshire". Several of the houses are well hidden behind high walls and wooded gardens, so the area is perfect ambassadorial territory and a retreat for distinguished participants of courtroom and courtroom drama. A two-up-two-down cottage will command £160,000 to £200,000 and the larger houses go for £750,000 to £1m. The other Denhams – **Higher**, **New** and **Denham Green** – are simply a few streets of Thirties semis and bungalows and Fifties houses. Denham Golf Club is little more than a railway halt for the club.

GERRARDS CROSS

Journey time: *27 min* | **Peak trains:** *4 per hour*
Season ticket: *£1236* | **Off-peak trains:** *2 per hour*

Because of its easy access to London by rail and road – M40, M25 and M4 all within spitting distance – the area around **Gerrards Cross** has the reputation of being one of the most expensive in the country. Definitely not for the first-time buyer, this is classic stockbroker belt with tree-lined roads, and grand Victorian and Edwardian houses in half an acre or so for £350,000 to £1.6m. There are some modern infills but these, too, are big and luxurious. Five-bedroom detached houses go for £300,000 to £400,000. Smaller Victorian terraces with two or three bedrooms are from £100,000. The population of commuters takes off early, leaving the centre to its small-town trading and the common to dog-walkers treading the tracks once haunted by highwaymen. Properties south-east of the town should be visited several times at different times of day, as noise from the motorways can be a problem in some roads. Golf and tennis are the main sports. Both private and secondary schools have high standards and are well liked.

South of Gerrards Cross is the neat and tidy village of **Fulmer**, with its little green, post office and well-kept gardens. Small, two-bedroom mid-19th-century cottages cost from £150,000. Further west is **Hedgerley**, which is short on facilities but strong on rural remoteness. The lanes are lined with three- to four-bedroom detached houses with large gardens, selling at around £250,000. Despite the lack of schools and shops, the average age is thirtysomething.

SEER GREEN & JORDANS

Journey time: *38 min* | **Peak trains:** *2 per hour*
Season ticket: *£1360* | **Off-peak trains:** *1 per hour*

Seer Green is a small rural community with a station and a modern estate in the middle where a two-bedroom cottage will cost £77,000. Its neighbours are more famous. **Penn**, to the west, is a long straggling village with a green surrounded by Georgian houses and 17th-century cottages in timber and flint stone or brick. Views over the surrounding beechwoods are magnificent. Tourists come to see the brasses, portraits and monuments to the family of William Penn, who founded the Quaker Society of Friends in neighbouring **Jordans** where he is buried. This is *the* place to live in the area. Houses, which range from the 16th century to the 1940s, are at a premium. A four-bedroom detached which would sell in Beaconsfield, the next stop along the line, for £250,000, will command £300,000 in Jordans and hopeful buyers need to be in the know to hear about a sale. Agents count themselves lucky to get hold of them. Included in the price is a charming village centre designed by Fred Rowntree in 1919, with gabled brick houses set well back from a central green planted with silver birch and poplar. There is also the bonus of a good nursery school.

BEACONSFIELD

Journey time: *33 min*	**Peak trains:** *3 per hour*
Season ticket: *£1396*	**Off-peak trains:** *2 per hour*

Beaconsfield has a dual personality and a dual population. The old town grew at the crossroads of the coaching routes to Windsor and Oxford and is centred on a broad square and a pleasant green. Local people house-hunt in the old town for 17th- and 18th-century cottages at £90,000 to £110,000 for a one-up-one-down terrace. Commuters and the many incomers who have arrived as a result of the several company relocations prefer the convenience of the new town which has developed near the station since the 1920s. The average cost of a four-bedroom detached 1930s house is £225,000 to £273,000, bought by middle management and young city strivers who move on up the scale to houses costing up to £2m. A good private school and state schools with high reputations add to the attractions, but what used to be a strong community spirit is

Part 16th-century property, Beaconsfield

struggling to stay alive. It revives most energetically on 11 May for the annual fair. Old town shops include delis and boutiques which draw visitors who have come to see Bekonscot, the model village and railway, but locals bemoan the lack of a local butcher and trundle off to High Wycombe for their major shopping.

HIGH WYCOMBE

Journey time: *39 min*
Season ticket: *£1568*

Peak trains: *5 per hour*
Off-peak trains: *2 per hour*

High Wycombe has had strong connections with craftspeople since the 17th century, when it was an important wool centre and its famous furniture industry was founded. Modern industries also include papermaking and engineering, and the result is a wide variety of housing from the large Victorian piles lining the main roads to the Thirties and more modern houses that spread upwards on either side of the valley. One- and two-bedroom maisonettes start at £46,000, and there are plenty of starter homes for first-time buyers in the £35,000 bracket. At the upper end of the price scale a four-bedroom detached will cost £250,000. The smart places to be are on the fringes of the town in **Downley**, **Booker** and **Loudwater**. There is a variety of schools with excellent reputations – Wycombe High and Lady Verney for girls, John Hampden and the Royal Grammar for boys, plus the famous Wycombe Abbey public school for girls. A new arts complex is being built in the centre, to be opened by 1993, but otherwise entertainment is thin.

Sought-after villages are to the west and include **Lane End**, which has a pretty, cottagey high street with a pond, and **Beacon's Bottom**, where 18th-century brick-and-flint houses start at £100,000 for two bedrooms. Both villages have basic shops and post office and a range of modern housing from £50,000 for one-bedroom cottages to £250,000 for a family detached. Farms and smallholdings in this area sell for upwards of £500,000.

SAUNDERTON

Journey time: *55 min*
Season ticket: *£1692*

Peak trains: *1 per hour*
Off-peak trains: *1 every 4 hours*

Saunderton itself is little more than a station surrounded by small industrial units, but, for those who do not want to drive into High Wycombe for a more frequent train service, it is the most convenient station for some of the prettiest villages in the area. To the west is **Bledlow**, an area of outstanding natural beauty. It lies peacefully beneath Wain Hill, site of one of the two huge turf-cut crosses in the county, and has a variety of properties from thatched cottages to a few modern houses. No further building is allowed at present because of its conservation status. There is a village hall and a pub but no post office or shop. Despite this the average age has gone down, and the young residents take their children a mile down the road to Longwick junior or to secondary school in Princes Risborough. Nearby **Lacey Green** is a sprawling village with a school, a post office/shop, a couple of pubs and an active community which has won an award for its well-run village hall. A lot of new housing overshadows the few cottages, and the whole area is less cottagey than you might expect. When you can find something small with two bedrooms it will cost £90,000 or so. Often the houses are large and detached in ample grounds. One with a generous paddock would cost from £300,000. Many houses round these villages have superb views over the Vale of Aylesbury, and unlike other areas, where houses tend to cost more in outlying districts than they do in town centres, prices in remote villages vary very little from those in Princes Risborough.

PRINCES RISBOROUGH

Journey time: *50 min*   **Peak trains:** *2 per hour*
Season ticket: *£1748*   **Off-peak trains:** *1 per hour*

A pleasant market town with the relaxed feel of an overgrown village, **Princes Risborough** has a semi-pedestrianised high street with a small market house in the centre – an attractive place to shop and stroll but one that is abandoned for the city each day by at least half of its population. Human-scale architecture is here in plenty – no large modern estates but a few mellow 16th- and 17th-century houses set along little roads and cul-de-sacs. There are some Victorian terraces, not always in the best locations but costing from £80,000; and Thirties to Seventies detached

Converted barn, near Princes Risborough

family houses up to £180,000 for four bedrooms. There is a good range of schools from nursery to secondary, and several local clubs including tennis and bowls. The most prestigious area is **Whiteleaf**, right on the flank of the Chilterns. It has a few cottages and a pub but mainly contains very expensive houses with large grounds and paddocks. These are owned by the stockbroker set, who belong to the local golf and cricket clubs.

LINE TO AYLESBURY (see map)

MONKS RISBOROUGH

Journey time: *53 min*	**Peak trains:** *1 per hour*
Season ticket: *£1800*	**Off-peak trains:** *nil*

No longer separated from Princes Risborough but rather a suburb of it, **Monks Risborough** has a few relics of its medieval past and some pretty cottages, but now mainly consists of Sixties and Seventies semis and a good many bungalows which attract retired people. A two-bedroom maisonette costs around £57,000, and a reasonably sized three-bedroom semi around £90,000 to £100,000.

LITTLE KIMBLE

Journey time: *57 min*	**Peak trains:** *1 per hour*
Season ticket: *£1800*	**Off-peak trains:** *nil*

Many of the villages in this area are sprawling rather than focused, and **Little Kimble** is typical. Its straggling lanes contain a mix of properties from a few listed 17th- and 18th-century cottages to 1900s and modern houses. The station house itself is a private dwelling. Prices are very similar to those in Princes Risborough for average-sized houses, but there are also a few around £500,000 with large grounds and paddocks (Kimble races is an annual event). Although there is no focal point there are a couple of pubs, a post office-cum-stores and a village hall. With only 900 on the electoral roll, most locals would be able to call "I spy strangers" when prospective buyers come calling. Local activities include the WI and a horticultural society which knows where to look for the wild orchids that bloom on what used to be a rifle range. There is also the British Legion and a youth club. Walks in the area take in Chequers and Ellesborough church, where successive Prime Ministers offer photo opportunities from time to time.

AYLESBURY

See **Marylebone to Aylesbury** (page 131).

CONTINUATION OF MAIN LINE TO BANBURY

HADDENHAM & THAME PARKWAY

Journey time: *57 min*	Peak trains: *2 per hour*
Season ticket: *£1864*	Off-peak trains: *1 per hour*

Whichever way you look at it **Haddenham** is a pretty big village or a big, pretty village, now split into two, the old and the new. The Sheerstock estate of two-, three-, four- and five-bedroom houses, priced from £60,000 to £180,000, is the new. The southern end is the old. Here the green with its duckpond is an acknowledged beauty spot popular with television crews filming *Inspector Morse* and Agatha Christie series. Here and there are walls made of witchert (the Saxon word for white earth) topped rather surprisingly with Spanish tiles and forming little lanes leading to attractive Georgian and Victorian houses. The smaller cottages cost between £80,000 and £100,000. This is a great place for people to retire to, and within the past 15 years the streets have been pedalled by a clutch of titled residents known locally as the five bicycling knights. Otherwise social life is divided into an energetic squash-playing set who live on the new side, and the old Haddenham agricultural and arts set. Lots of residents commute to London on the M40. There are plenty of local sports, arts and activity clubs, and a village hall where it all happens.

Thame is distinguished by an unusually wide high street, which the annual fair turns into a medieval parade ground against a backdrop of houses from the 15th century to the present. There are plenty of three- and four-bedroom houses at around £100,000 – many with rooms let out to students from Rycote Wood college of woodwork and furniture. There are three primary schools and good sporting facilities – football, rugby, squash and snooker – and a sports and arts centre. Some commuters prefer to drive to Princes Risborough for the better choice of early and late trains into London.

West of the A418 between Thame and Aylesbury are three sought-after villages. **Cuddington**, which for the last two years has been voted the best-kept village in Buckinghamshire, has a green and lots of old thatch. Two-bedroom cottages start at £91,000. **Chearsley** has a green, pub, shop and church, but no longer a local school. A three-bedroom house here costs £120,000, a detached bungalow £185,000. **Long Crendon** is considered to be the *crème de la crème* of the area. Once the centre of the needle-making industry, it has a picturesque high street running off the market square, an attractive green, a primary school and several pleasant pubs. It is the sort of place that everyone dreams of calling home, and properties here attract a 10 per cent price premium. The majority of people who live here work in Oxford.

BICESTER NORTH

Journey time: *70 min* | Peak trains: *2 per hour*
Season ticket: *£2008* | Off-peak trains: *I per hour*

Bicester has a long history and a famous hunt dating back to the 1700s. But despite an old market square (triangle, rather) and some 16th-century gabled houses, it stopped being a period piece when the army depot, now one of the largest in the country, was established in 1941. The town is mainly regarded as a modern, cheapish area of very large housing estates. One-bed starter homes are priced at around £42,000; two-bedroom houses around £53,000.

Villages to the west of Bicester – Steeple Aston (see page 147) and the **Bartons** (**Middle** and **Steeple**) – have suffered from the noise of F111s and Tornados from the USAF base at Upper Heyford, and everyone is eagerly awaiting the promised run-down of the base so that they can return to rural tranquillity. Meanwhile the stone-built village of **Kirtlington**, where Christopher Wren's father is buried, has retained its popularity because of its polo park and stud farm. It has a village green with a pond, a post office stores, a couple of pubs and a junior school. New developments here are stone-built in cottage style to blend with the older houses. The larger four-bedroom detached properties cost £200,000. Small houses start at £56,000. An 18th-century cottage with two bedrooms would be likely to fetch £100,000, and a 16th-century four-bedroom cottage in stone and thatch would be in the region of £200,000.

Villages north of Bicester are good value. For the price of a three-bedroom house closer to Oxford you will get four bedrooms in **Stratton Audley** – Stratton meaning enclosure on a Roman road, and Audley from the family who built the 14th-century moated castle. It is a tiny village where the houses around the central green are occupied by families who have lived there all their lives, despite the lack of facilities and schools. Two-bedroom houses are from £52,000, three-bedroom from £60,000. For £250,000 you could buy a substantial four-bedroom stone period house with spacious rooms and large gardens. Prices are about the same in **Stoke Lyne**, a similarly quiet Chiltern village set in undulating countryside where people are said to keep to themselves.

Just over the county border is **Marsh Gibbon**, with houses built of local stone rather than the brick and timber more usual in Buckinghamshire. A sprinkling of low-cost housing has been built here for sale to local families. The result is a busy little place with a village pond, a primary school and a younger than average age profile. A three-bedroom detached house can be found for £85,000.

Launton, back in Oxfordshire, is growing rapidly into a dormitory of Bicester, though the intervening railway and bypass will prevent its being swallowed completely. It has a mix of old and young in both population and property. There are quite a few modern bungalows and new estates where a two-bedroom semi would cost around £60,000. Young children go to the local primary. Their older brothers and sisters, in common with those from all the surrounding villages, attend secondary school or sixth form college in Bicester.

KING'S SUTTON

Journey time: *86 min*	**Peak trains:** *1 per hour*
Season ticket: *£2240*	**Off-peak trains:** *1 every 2 hours*

A few London commuters travel regularly from **King's Sutton**. Others prefer to drive to Bicester, which has a more frequent service. The majority of local residents work in Banbury or Oxford. Apart from the village green, which is set with thatched cottages and 18th-century stone houses, the property mix is almost exactly 50 per cent old stone houses, 50 per cent council brick, which residents say makes for a good community. They take advantage of the opportunities to get together through the Playing Fields Association, small tennis club and three churches, all with their own social activities. The local baker who called three times a week to bake fresh loaves for the village has been closed by Eurobureaucracy but there are still four village shops, one incorporating a post office, and four pubs. Children go to the local primary school, then to Middleton Cheney Secondary. The local hunt meets in King's Sutton and there is a strong farming community, despite the fact that several farms and barns have been sold off for conversion. A Georgian five-bedroom house with a staff bungalow and paddock costs £340,000; a two-bedroom cottage £100,000.

Neighbouring **Charlton** is a one-street village with the best-liked pub in the area and pleasant stone houses costing from £60,000 for a small two-bedroom cottage. **Aynho** has pretty cottages too, plus one or two Georgian houses priced at around £160,000 for four bedrooms. It has a shop but no village green. Both Aynho and **Souldern** have been badly affected by noise from the M40, but those who don't mind say the A41 was bad enough anyway. There are big properties around here, hidden away in a couple of acres, and for £300,000 you could find something quite special.

Deddington, a couple of miles south-west of King's Sutton, was equal in importance to Banbury until the canals and railways bypassed it. It is officially a town, but its atmosphere is villagey. Attractive houses and small shops are grouped around a spacious market place, with side roads lined with honey-coloured stone houses and cottages, many of them Grade II listed. There is plenty of local life based on the primary school, the church, a variety of clubs from football, bowls and badminton to yoga and nature conservation, and there are more than a hundred cottage businesses ranging from jewellery-making to publishing. Residents work locally as surveyors, accountants and solicitors and the area is also popular with pilots flying from Heathrow and Birmingham. "They put a pin in the map between the two and seem to hit Deddington," says one local. Commuters have tended to drive to Milton Keynes, half an hour's train journey from London, rather than suffer the slower Banbury line. Otherwise the M40 is close enough for convenience and has unclogged the A423 between Oxford and Banbury. Prices range from £65,000 for a two-bedroom Victorian brick cottage to £73,000 for a Grade II listed 17th-century cottage of similar size. More modern stone houses with four or five bedrooms range from £135,000 to £189,000.

Local stone, ex-weaver's cottage, Deddington

BANBURY

Journey time: *90 min*	**Peak trains:** *2 per hour*
Season ticket: *£2240*	**Off-peak trains:** *1 per hour*

See also **Paddington to Leamington Spa** (page 148).

Banbury has spent a lot of time burying its past in order to make way for a bright new future which hasn't happened yet. House prices shot up to Oxford and Home Counties levels when the M40 was agreed, but since it opened they have halved. Eighty acres to the east of the town have been scheduled for commercial business parks and light industry. This will mean increased housing demand, but so far the progress is just potential. The older part of the town is late Victorian, early Edwardian, but most properties are post war. Small semis sell well from £40,000, but on the western, prestigious side large Sixties houses in well laid out gardens command £350,000. Parking at the station is easy enough but there have been many noisy grumbles about the infrequency of the train service.

The M40 has also had a mixed effect on the villages within five miles of Banbury. To the north-west, **Warmington**, which is very picturesque, **Shotteswell** and **Mollington** have all been adversely affected by noise; but **Wroxton**, a charming village with winding lanes, thatched cottages, grassy verges and a duckpond, has been made more accessible without suffering any serious damage. Just off the A422 to Stratford-upon-Avon, it preserves its tranquillity and yet is only a few minutes' drive from the motorway. It has a school and a couple of pubs but no shop – people nip over to Horley or do their main supermarket shopping in Banbury. A small, semi-detached, stone-and-thatch cottage with two bedrooms will cost about £80,000; a three-bedroom detached house £120,000; a four-bedroom detached £135,000 to £150,000.

On the whole, though, commuting professionals tend to prefer **Bloxham**, so prices here are slightly higher than in the neighbouring villages – £120,000 for a three-bedroom cottage. There are several 16th-

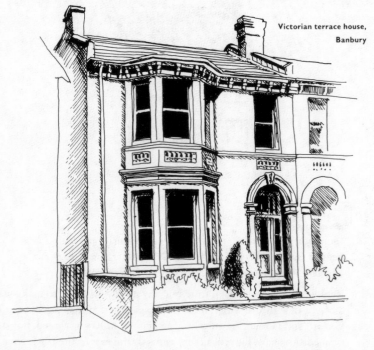

Victorian terrace house,
Banbury

and 17th-century ones built in the local ironstone and tucked away down pretty lanes. There is a parade of shops, a public school and a good girls' school. A couple of small estates of modern houses have brought more cars which clog the centre.

Shenington, too, is a popular and pretty village, full of lovely old golden stone houses. The presence of a rubbish tip not far away does deter some househunters, although most residents feel it isn't a problem. There is also a neighbouring airfield where noisy go-karting is held, but this happens only a few times a year. There is a pub with seats outside on the verge of the green. The charming cottages nearby fetch around £100,000 for three bedrooms, while larger five-bedroom houses go for between £120,000 and £150,000.

Sibford Ferris, a little further south, has delightful mullioned houses with broad grass verges and a mellow blend of stone and thatch. It also has a village shop and post office and a well-respected Quaker school. Two-bedroom cottages here start at £85,000, and the average price for a four-bedroom period house is £250,000. A large seven- or eight-bedroom Queen Anne or Georgian house with stables and three or four acres commands £600,000.

The Chiltern line stops at Banbury where there are connections for Leamington Spa, which also has a direct InterCity link to Paddington (see page 148).

PADDINGTON
— TO —
LEAMINGTON SPA/EVESHAM

For stations between Paddington and Reading, see page 156. See map (page 154).

Tilehurst, Pangbourne, Goring & Streatley, and Cholsey

For commuters who can rely on regular office hours these are worth considering, since there are some through trains to Paddington each morning and evening. If you miss them, however, you are left to get a fast train and change at Reading.

Off-peak trains to Reading: 2 per hour
Season tickets (all stations): £2028

For **Tilehurst**, see Reading (page 164). **Pangbourne**, just five miles off the M4, is a riverside commuter haven where the Thames meets the Pang; where Kenneth Grahame, author of *Wind In The Willows* lived; and where the buffoons in Jerome K. Jerome's *Three Men In A Boat* stopped off. Its discreet Georgian charm, with its square, weir and meadow, has now developed a certain bustle as the original village population has swollen to 2,500. Estate agents and bad planning have intruded among the old-fashioned shops which help give the place its character. "You can ask for a four-inch nail with a hook on the end, and the chap'll go to a box he last looked into in 1923," says one local resident. Pangbourne College, the boys' public school, stands on Pang Hill. Prices are high. A modern semi in Kennedy Drive would cost £95,000; a Victorian terrace £100,000; a detached house £175,000, and flats with river views just under £100,000. Much larger houses go for anything between £400,000 and £1m.

People who live in **Goring** and **Streatley** often prefer to travel from Reading rather than from their own local station. The two villages sandwich the Thames, and both are expensive and pretty with enough shops – one famous for its cheeses – to make life manageable. There is a diverse range of properties, and anything with three bedrooms will cost £130,000 upwards. Streatley doesn't have the frill of modern housing on its outskirts that Goring has, and it has the Swan Inn on the towpath, which is now a conference centre. **Cholsey** is sprawly, so the prices here are lower. Its main feature, a pretty village green edged with listed cottages, is ruined by a parade of ugly shops on the other side. The shops and post office are useful, though, and the place has attracted large numbers of commuters in the last two decades. Any early resentment of them was resolved long ago. It has a busy horticultural society and the Cholsey Silver Band which is acquiring quite a reputation. The primary school currently has a headmaster who favours the more traditional methods of teaching. Agatha Christie is buried here.

DIDCOT

Journey time: *50 min*	**Peak trains:** *5 per hour*
Season ticket: *£2400*	**Off-peak trains:** *1 per hour*

Though the off-peak trains average 50 minutes, the evening peak has a train that does the journey in 33 minutes – one of Britain's fastest commuter trains, averaging 98mph from Paddington to **Didcot**.

Didcot itself lacks any romance, though its train service might be the envy of the west. It has about 19,000 residents and is scheduled to expand even more. As a shopping centre it is adequate – with all the usual chain stores – but it is uninspired and has no theatre or cinema. After a long planning wrangle Tesco has finally gained permission to develop in the town centre, so it may become a bit more lively. The most attractive part of it is **Northbourne**, which is old Didcot and still very beautiful. **East Hagbourne**, just outside, is distinctly special, displaying all the architectural eclecticism of the area – timber frame, thatch, zig-zag brickwork – clustered around the old village cross by the church. **West Hagbourne** is similar but quieter, with a village pond. Both are popular among those employed at the Atomic Research station at Harwell who can afford the £250,000 or more for a three-bedroom 15th-century cottage.

Perhaps the village with the most charm and vigour is **Blewbury**, set against the Downs. Blewburton Hill to the east is crowned with an

16th-century
thatched cottage,
Blewbury

extraordinary prehistoric camp. The village has pretty old inns, a football club, a cricket green, local wine-makers, a church choir, and once you get off the B4017 the prices are high. An early 16th-century cottage with four bedrooms and inglenook fireplace might fetch around £300,000, though you could pick up a four-bedroom modern house on a small new development for £200,000. **East Hendred**, to the west, is a typical Downland village peppered with thatch and timber, close to the ancient Ridgeway, where you can walk at a giddy height for miles in either direction. "It's very horsy and a bit arty crafty. Lots of Volvos with stickers saying Slow Down For Horses," is how one local resident describes it. **Harwell**, by comparison, is plainer with plenty of workman-like Victorian houses. An old three-bedroom farmer's cottage here can be had for £75,000 upwards, with four-bedroom modern houses at £160,000 to £180,000.

The combination of riverside with proximity to London makes some of these villages obvious film-star territory (Michael Caine lives nearby). **Shillingford**, on a bridge over the Thames, and **Warborough** both reek of money. **Wallingford** has a pretty shopping centre with a notable bookshop, but houses around the square are probably too noisy to consider. On the river front they cost from £250,000 into the millions, though purchasers should make sure that if they buy a bit of river bank they are prepared for the sometimes crippling cost of maintaining it.

Appleford, Culham and Radley
There is one peak-hour through train, otherwise you have to change at Didcot or Reading to get to Paddington.
Season ticket (all stations): £2400

Appleford is little more than a halt with a string of bungalows threaded to the railway line. **Long Wittenham** is a village in two halves, old and new, and is convenient for those who want to use The European School at **Culham**, which was established for the children of people working at the research station there. **Radley** has more trains serving it than the other two halts, but it is a bit betwixt and between any distinct area to be really sought after. Its main feature is Radley College, the boys' public school.

OXFORD

Journey time: *52 min*	Peak trains: *2 per hour*
Season ticket: *£2400*	Off-peak trains: *1 per hour*

Oxford can seem insufferably cliquey to some, but if you belong in some way to the publishing, university, hospital or industrial scenes then it is not too much of a problem. Travelling on the Oxford train can be a bit like attending a literary tea-party. As well as the city's obvious beauty, its schools are a great attraction to outsiders. Public schools abound – Magdalen College School, St Edward's, Radley College just outside, and the Oxford High and Headington School for girls.

The nicer bread-and-butter houses for those making a start in Oxford lie in **Osney** or **Jericho**, both within walking distance of the station. Osney is almost moated by a combination of the Thames and the canal, and two-bedroom Victorian houses here sell for between £80,000 and £90,000. Three bedrooms will take you up to around £120,000. Prices in Jericho are slightly higher, though the houses are small. Another area to consider is **Grand Pont**, where a Victorian house with three bedrooms would sell for £170,000.

For many, the *only* area to live is North Oxford, which is peppered with academics and the most successful professionals. It mushroomed in the 19th century after it was suddenly decided that dons should be allowed to marry. Huge Victorian houses on wide, tree-lined roads provided them with new homes, which now sell at between £300,000 and £500,000. There are just not enough of them to meet demand. Houses get smaller and slightly cheaper towards **Summertown**, where Cherwell comprehensive is a much-respected school – as is the St Phillip and St James primary. **Wolvercote** village, a little further out, is particularly lovely, with The Trout Inn backing onto Port Meadow. Cheaper little brick-and-tile houses here sell at around £80,000.

Headington is popular with staff working at the hospital there, but it is the wrong side of Oxford for the station. Coaches heading for London, Victoria, stop there and many commuters use these instead. **Old Headington** and **Old Marston** are both charming old villages with crooked lanes and stone cottages that have been absorbed by the suburbs. Inhabitants tend to be rather rarefied. Pretty cottages in either might sell for over £300,000. The equivalent of Oxford's stockbroker belts – large detached houses with the occasional tennis court or pony paddock – lie outside at **Hinksey, Cumnor** and **Boars Hill**. A 1930s house with five bedrooms, three bathrooms, lofts, outbuildings, swimming pool and over two acres of formal gardens in a woodland setting, could be bought for around £430,000 on Boars Hill.

LINE FROM OXFORD TO LEAMINGTON SPA (see map)

Tackley and Heyford

No through trains: *change at Oxford*
Season ticket: £2400

Since Oxford is so strangled by traffic and efforts to drive to the station are likely to be stressful, **Tackley** and **Heyford** come into their own with their local trains. **Steeple Aston**, a grey stone-walled village above the

Cherwell, is definitely worth looking at. It has a village shop and post office, a choral society, history society, Scouts, young wives group, and the Steeple Aston Players who put on productions of plays written by local people. Commuters generally try to join in. This area is also seriously horsy, and there is a large riding school with livery stables. **Hopcroft's Halt** nearby is where the French highwayman Claude Duval clattered about on his horse. The American Air Force Base at **Upper Heyford** can be a bit of a nuisance, though apparently you become oblivious to the jets after a while. The once large American presence has dwindled, however, and there are now only a few families living in the area.

Then there are the **Tews** (**Great**, **Little** and **Duns**). Great Tew is particularly prized because it remained in a time-warp for so long and attracted a great deal of national publicity. This village of stone and thatch, punctuated by greens and clumps of ornamental trees, has now been tidied up with such care that even the telephone kiosk is painted grey in case the traditional red might strike a discordant 20th-century note. A tiny two-bedroom cottage will cost £100,000.

BANBURY

Journey time: *95 min* | **Peak trains:** *1 per hour*
Season ticket: *£2400* | **Off-peak trains:** *nil*

See **Marylebone to Banbury** (page 141).

LEAMINGTON SPA

Journey time: *115 min* | **Peak trains:** *1 in 2 hours*
Season ticket: *£3440* | **Off-peak trains:** *nil*

Despite a relatively painless, less-than-two-hours' InterCity service into London, **Leamington Spa** has fewer commuters than it had five years ago. The people who choose to live in this spacious spa town, with its many Georgian and Victorian houses and attractive riverside walks, have often come because of the development of light industry between Leamington and Warwick. One of the most prestigious parts of the town is the tree-lined Beverley Road, offering a mix of Fifties and Sixties detached houses which sell from around £130,000 unmodernised up to £300,000. Northumberland Avenue is another sought-after road, in which the minimum price for a good-sized Victorian or Edwardian house is £200,000, rising to £400,000 for the best.

Those who are willing to drive across five miles of farming landscape to Leamington station settle in **Harbury**, a lively village with a good mixed age community and a cosy, clustered centre near the church, and with a variety of modern housing on the outskirts. Small modern houses here start at £55,000; cottages and terraces go up to £250,000.

Neighbouring **Bishop's Itchington** is known in estate agency terms as Harbury's poor relation – a two-bedroom terrace here goes for £50,000; a detached house for £150,000. **Bishop's Tachbrook** has a small chatty post office stores and a little row of shops, but the few thatched houses are well outnumbered by Sixties and Seventies red-brick estates. A two-bedroom terrace is in the region of £52,000, and a family detached with four or five bedrooms will fetch about £170,000. The higher price reflects the new bonus of easy access to the extended M40, which tends to attract young professionals.

Terrace cottages, Broadway

LINE FROM OXFORD TO EVESHAM (see map)

This takes you to what many people consider is the most beautiful side of Oxford to live, where villages of golden stone rise up from the fields. It is worth remembering that British Rail runs a skip-stop service. **Charlbury**, **Kingham** and **Moreton-in-Marsh** are better served than **Handborough**, **Combe**, **Finstock**, **Ascott-under-Wychwood** and **Shipton**, which are sandwiched in between them. There are a couple of through trains, designed specially for the morning and evening commuters, that run from Evesham to Paddington and stop at these three stations. Otherwise you have to get the local train into Oxford and change there. On the way to London it is a same-platform change and therefore not so stressful; but on the way home it is necessary to change platforms.

CHARLBURY

Journey time: *64 min*	Peak trains: *I per hour*
Season ticket: *£3112*	Off-peak trains: *nil*

This area is a tapestry of extraordinarily lovely villages. You have to watch for those which are under the Oxford influence, which means they are more expensive than those further afield. **Charlbury** itself has doubled its original size and is on the mains gas supply. Modern three-bedroom houses can be bought for £65,000, or three-bedroom period cottages for £85,000. The larger house with four bedrooms would start at £120,000 to £150,000. It is just too far from Oxford to be really expensive, or to appeal to the young who say there is nothing to do there.

Woodstock, once the Elizabethan glove-making capital of the area, is slightly more expensive because its old stone houses lie closer to Oxford and it is only two miles from **Combe** station. It does, however, swarm with visitors in summer, who browse through it on their way to Blenheim Palace. **Bladon**, just apart from it, where Sir Winston Churchill is buried, is more remarkable still. Its collection of ancient cottages is crowned by the elegant, 15th-century chimneys of the old malthouse, and it is scarcely a mile from **Handborough** station.

One of the best-liked small towns west of Oxford is **Witney**, which is rather less rarefied than some of the villages that surround it. Its fortunes were built on the blanket industry, which used the waters of the Windrush and the wool from the local sheep. It is a refreshing mix of old and new property, with greens at either end, raised pavements studded with limes, and modern shopfronts elbowing between their Georgian counterparts. The central market place and the old covered butter cross give it a strong heart. Though it is only three miles from **Finstock** station, a lot of commuters from here choose to drive. The town is just off the A40 which now links easily to the M40. There are long rows of old blanket workers' cottages that sell for around £70,000 each. A huge new housing estate is going up on the outskirts and will eventually provide thousands of new houses, with a new school and shops.

KINGHAM

Journey time: *74 min*	Peak trains: *I per hour*
Season ticket: *£3292*	Off-peak trains: *nil*

The winding lanes, banked by streams and meadows looking down into the woodlands of the Evenlode Valley, can make you feel quite isolated here. **Kingham** and all the villages around it are cut in fudge-coloured stone, with the occasional trimming of council houses at the edge. People tolerate the longer commute to London from here because it is just out of reach of the Oxford influence and therefore cheaper. A handsome four-bedroom stone house could be bought for around £150,000, three bedrooms for £120,000 and a smaller terrace for around £85,000.

The **Wychwoods** (**Milton-under**, **Shipton-under**, and **Ascott-under**), being closer to Oxford, are slightly more expensive. **Ascott-under-Wychwood** has its own station, served by regional trains running from Evesham to Oxford. Many people moving to the area will aim for the catchment area of **Burford** comprehensive school, which has a formidable reputation. A stone house with beamed ceilings, stone mullioned windows with leaded lights, Tudor fireplaces and five to six bedrooms might sell for around £285,000.

Cotswold house, near
Moreton-in-Marsh

Bourton-on-the-Water, though a model Cotswold village with its own miniature model village as a permanent exhibition, pushes commuter tolerance a little since it is about 10 miles from Kingham station. But with it come the **Slaughters** (**Lower** and **Upper**), the Lower set upon a stream that wriggles through little stone bridges, and the Upper being right on the banks of the Windrush. Locals tend to be farmers, retired couples or craftsmen who don't mind being miles from anywhere. A five-bedroom 18th-century stone farmhouse with outbuildings will cost just under £300,000 in this area. The nearest local shopping centre is **Chipping Norton**, an old market town where the huge old Bliss tweed mill is being restored and sold as flats. It is dubbed wet and windy by locals who say it qualified for extra coal rations in the war because it was the coldest place in the region.

MORETON-IN-MARSH

Journey time: *80 min*	**Peak trains:** *1 per hour*
Season ticket: *£3756*	**Off-peak trains:** *nil*

The perfection of villages such as **Moreton-in-Marsh** and **Stow-on-the-Wold** has meant torture by tourism. They seethe in summer and become totally deserted in winter. "The only people who live there are old dears in unmodernised houses who freeze every winter, or those involved in the tourist industry, or the very rich who can spend the hundreds of thousands necessary to buy one of the lovely big country houses," says one local resident. A little mid-17th-century thatched cottage with three bedrooms and a garage would go on the market with an asking price of around £250,000, and a large country house can run into millions.

Stow-on-the-Wold is also full of second homes so local activities are thin on the ground. Antique dealers dominate but there are two butchers, a bakery and two small supermarkets too. A lot of people buy second homes here rather than commute daily and consequently even a two-bedroom cottage could cost up to £100,000.

Broadway and **Chipping Campden** are both beautiful towns, built mainly of stone. Chipping Campden attracts elderly people retiring from Birmingham, and it brims with local activities. The Chipping Campden Society looks after the historic buildings, and there are drama, hockey and football clubs as well as dance bands that play regularly for teenagers at the British Legion. It has two primary schools and a comprehensive which gathers children in from surrounding villages by the coachload. The 14th-century Woolstaplers Hall is an interesting little local museum with displays of mantraps, mangles and military uniforms as well as a tiny cinema.

EVESHAM

Journey time: *95 min*	**Peak trains:** *1 per hour*
Season ticket: *£4036*	**Off-peak trains:** *nil*

Though not a great many people would choose to commute daily from **Evesham**, many might consider part-time commuting. Its tree-lined walks, lawns along the Avon, and some wonderful old buildings, give it obvious charm. It also has a golf club, and another course is being built at Fishampton. Property prices are lower here than up in the Cotswolds. A three-bedroom Victorian terrace house might sell for £60,000, while a three-bedroom modern detached house on an estate could fetch £70,000. Two-bedroom cottages can be found in the surrounding villages for £65,000 to £70,000, with three-bedroom versions in the range of £80,000 to £100,000.

The Pershore side is particularly pretty, with picturesque black-and-white villages such as **Charlton**, **Cropthorne**, and **Fladbury** (where the canoe club is run by a British national coach and sends members to the Olympics). Fladbury is not a particularly horsy village, and it tends to attract Birmingham rather than London commuters. The three new housing developments draw a constant flow of new people. It has a village shop, butcher and florist, though most people use the Tesco at Evesham. It also has a church primary school for five- to eight-year-olds. The middle school is in the neighbouring village of Pinvin, and the secondary is in Evesham. Further north of Evesham is another black-and-white village, **Norton**, which at the moment is ruined by the traffic thundering along the A435, but is about to be saved with a bypass. The **Lench's** (**Church** and **Atch**) are also popular on this northern flank.

For truly grand landscape, however, you should look to the west, in the villages beneath Bredon Hill. The **Combertons** (**Little** and **Great**) are especially lovely. **Great Comberton** has a heady mixture of half-timbered farmhouses and thatched cottages, and a village dovecote that has walls over three feet thick and more than 500 nesting holes. Another, red-brick, dovecote in the village is even bigger, with 1,425.

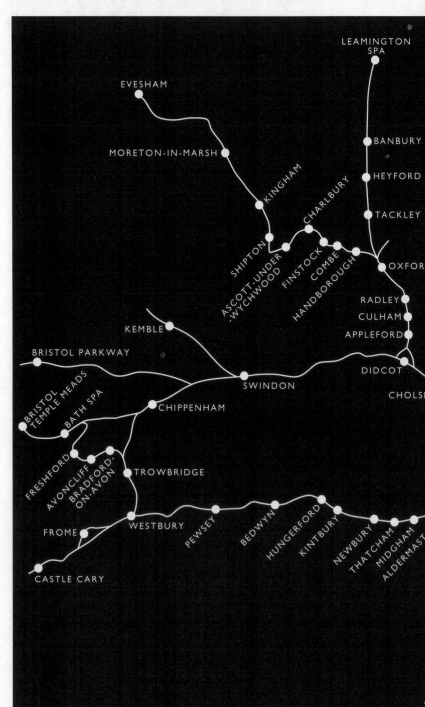

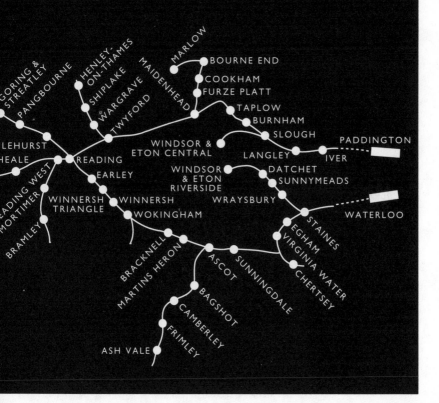

GORING &
STREATLEY
PANGBOURNE
HENLEY-
ON-THAMES
SHIPLAKE
WARGRAVE
MAIDENHEAD
TWYFORD
MARLOW
BOURNE END
COOKHAM
FURZE PLATT
TAPLOW
BURNHAM
SLOUGH
PADDINGTON
LEHURST
HEALE
READING
WINDSOR &
ETON CENTRAL
LANGLEY
IVER
EARLEY
READING WEST
MORTIMER
WINNERSH
TRIANGLE
WINNERSH
WINDSOR
& ETON
RIVERSIDE
DATCHET
SUNNYMEADS
WRAYSBURY
WATERLOO
BRAMLEY
WOKINGHAM
STAINES
BRACKNELL
MARTINS HERON
ASCOT
SUNNINGDALE
EGHAM
VIRGINIA WATER
CHERTSEY
BAGSHOT
CAMBERLEY
ASH VALE
FRIMLEY

PADDINGTON
— TO —
READING/BRISTOL

See map (page 154)

IVER

Journey time: *33 min*	**Peak trains:** *3 per hour*
Season ticket: *£1092*	**Off-peak trains:** *1 per hour*

This village is a bit betwixt and between, being neither Slough nor Windsor. It has some 16th- and 17th-century cottages clustered around the church, with tree-covered lanes around, and **Iver Heath** nearby. House prices start at £250,000 and rise depending on the amount of land. There are one or two blocks of exclusive flats where you will pay around £80,000 for two bedrooms.

LANGLEY

Journey time: *34 min*	**Peak trains:** *4 per hour*
Season ticket: *£1192*	**Off-peak trains:** *2 per hour*

Langley is really an extension of Slough, with lots of new housing developments. The big Ford plant is closing down, so unemployment is likely to rise. Ex-council houses with three bedrooms could be bought for £65,000. One of the few three-bedroom Victorian semis in the high street would fetch just over £70,000.

SLOUGH

Journey time: *22 min*	**Peak trains:** *4 per hour*
Season ticket: *£1284*	**Off-peak trains:** *4 per hour*

The huge trading estate – supposedly the largest in Europe – is the backbone to **Slough**, but it doesn't make it pretty to look at. It offers a reasonable shopping centre with an Asda superstore, and all the main multiples have outlets here. There is also a leisure centre and a sports centre, a 10-screen cinema and an ice rink, but many people don't consider it a terribly safe place to walk around in alone at night. There is a mix of council housing and private modern estates. Windsor Meadows is particularly sought after by airline staff because it is ideal for the M4 motorway and Heathrow. A one-bedroom studio starts at around £42,000. A four-bedroom house comes at around £130,000. On the whole, Slough vies with Reading to provide the cheapest properties in

Berkshire. A small Victorian two-bedroom terrace house would cost £65,000, and a larger four-storey town house might fetch £90,000 to £100,000. Slough has a large Asian population which has settled in certain areas, particularly Chalvey.

The train service to Paddington is astonishingly good – one fast non-stopping train an hour, and a handful of stopping ones. The station has a pavilioned roof reminiscent of a French château, and there is good parking.

The thing to watch out for in this area is how close you are to a Heathrow flight path. **Colnbrook**, a village two miles to the east, is affected by low-flying planes, but you can pick up a listed, detached four-bedroom house in a quarter of an acre for £200,000. Or, at the bottom end of the market, you could get a studio flat for £42,000. Two miles north, the landscape becomes suddenly rural and a village like **Stoke Poges** feels very out-of-the-way. The poet Thomas Gray is supposed to have written his famous *Elegy* in the garden graveyard to St Giles Church, where he is buried. Stoke Poges is a cheaper version of Gerrards Cross, with a small parade of shops and a population peppered with both elderly and young stockbroker types. You might pay £400,000 for a large detached turn-of-the-century house in one of its tree-lined avenues. At the lower end of the market you could buy a three-bedroom house on one of the small Sixties estates for £80,000 to £90,000. It's the kind of place where a decade or more ago you could have built a new house in your garden and still have had an acre to spare. Sunday afternoon walks are taken at Langley Park and Black Park.

Modern estate houses,
south Bucks

Branchline to Windsor & Eton Central

Trains to Slough: 3 per hour (peak)/2 per hour (off-peak)
Change at Slough at all times
Journey time: 36 min
Season ticket: £1448

See **Windsor & Eton Riverside** on the **Waterloo to Reading** line (page 179).

BURNHAM

Journey time: *34 min*	Peak trains: *4 per hour*
Season ticket: *£1372*	Off-peak trains: *2 per hour*

Burnham has quite a few modern shops, but still manages to cling on to some of its 15th- and 16th-century charm. The centre is quaint and busy. Just off the main street, a 17th-century black-and-white beamed house could be had for under £220,000. **North Burnham** is the place to be. It leads to Burnham Beeches with its huge pollarded beeches and winding lanes – a 600-acre remnant of a forest that once covered the Chilterns. Here a house with five bedrooms in an acre of land will cost well over £500,000. The area attracts successful stockbrokers, bankers and the odd television presenter.

The northern flank offers some classic Buckinghamshire villages. **Farnham Royal** and **Farnham Common** are strung between Maidenhead and Slough. Huge houses set in several acres cost at least £500,000. Horse-riding is the popular pastime for wives left at home while their husbands are in the City. Both these little villages are right on top of Burnham Beeches.

For less expensive housing you have to look at somewhere like **Cippenham**, where Lovell Homes has built a new community of about 5,000 homes. It has an Asda superstore and everything from one-bedroom starter homes for £45,000 to executive homes for £150,000.

The station is used by those who work on the Slough Trading Estate as well as commuters to London. It has only a small car park.

TAPLOW

Journey time: *37 min*	Peak trains: *4 per hour*
Season ticket: *£1448*	Off-peak trains: *2 per hour*

This is where you start to find wonderful riverside villages with modest-sized yachts moored to the banks and anglers hunched beneath their green umbrellas. **Taplow** has lots of old cottages and a modern church with a distinctive copper spire. You can see Cliveden House, formerly the home of Lady Astor, in the distance on the cliffs above the river. There are enormous houses with gardens running down to the Thames that go for over £1m, though in the village itself there are two-up-two-down Victorian cottages for around £100,000. There are also a lot of flats. A one-bedroom converted flat in a large Edwardian house will fetch £75,000. People who live here might prefer to go to Maidenhead or Slough to pick up the faster train service and park the car more easily.

MAIDENHEAD

Journey time: *41 min*	**Peak trains:** *4 per hour*
Season ticket: *£1544*	**Off-peak trains:** *3 per hour*

Maidenhead is an old Thameside town with an ancient heart, small shops and a high street that is now mainly pedestrianised. Just outside the centre you will find grids of reasonably pleasant turn-of-the-century terrace houses. The ones with two bedrooms sell for just over £70,000. The modern developments are on the south-western outskirts, where two-bedroom flats or maisonettes cost £60,000 to £70,000 and three-bedroom semis are just under £90,000. The most sought-after areas, such as Maidenhead Bridge and Boulter's Lock, are close to the river. Here the houses are large, detached late Victorian, with big gardens and wealthy owners who can afford to pay £250,000 for four bedrooms. A short walk along the Thames is Brunel's Sounding Arch, a remarkably long brick viaduct built in 1838. Maidenhead station has three car parks but still the space runs out. Trains are fast and frequent.

Bray, scarcely two miles out of Maidenhead, is a tiny picturesque village on the lip of the Thames and one of the most expensive places to live even in this expensive area. It combines closeness to London with a good train service, and has narrow irregular streets with timber-framed and Georgian houses. The Roux brothers have their famous Waterside Inn restaurant here, and there is a clutch of resident television stars, including Ernie Wise and Michael Parkinson, who brings his own cricket team to play at the local club.

The Fisheries offers huge mansions in a woodland setting with a river frontage – and prices running into millions. One of the things to watch for is the very occasional river flood. Just outside the village is Bray Studios, where the Hammer House of Horror films were made. Today it is a recording studio for rock bands. Bray has a post office, general shop, estate agents and small dress shop, plus a hockey club and tennis court. Tourist coaches tend to drive straight through because there is no tearoom. There are a few modern estates but they are hidden away. It is a conservation area, and if you want to build anything new, or change the exterior of your house, you can expect heavy opposition.

Heading south you come to **Holyport** – an attractive village set around a large green. This has a pond and two pubs on it, and a village fair is held here every year. Cricket on the green has been stopped because too many windows got broken, but the rounders matches still continue. Holyport has some huge Tudor and Georgian houses, and small former estate cottages. A house with half an acre might cost £300,000. The village is too spread out to have a strong sense of community, but there is a preservation society. It has some council housing and new private estates, a small handful of shops, a primary school and a special school for mentally handicapped children.

Restyled Edwardian house,
near Maidenhead

To the west is **Littlewick Green**, where the houses are built around the cricket pitch and the pub is called The Cricketers. This and neighbouring villages attract a lot of commuters – people running private businesses and staff from Heathrow. Another pretty village, still within the two- to three-mile belt around Maidenhead, is **Pinkneys Green**. It has some huge old houses that sell for between £200,000 and £500,000, and the National Trust's Maidenhead Thicket. The first Girl Guide troop was formed here by Olave Baden-Powell in 1910. Another village worth considering is **White Waltham**. It is very rural, and has a thriving primary school but no shops. Then there is **Hurley**, on the Thames, where cottages cost around £170,000.

Branchline to Marlow via Furze Platt, Cookham, and Bourne End

No through trains
Trains to Maidenhead: 2 per hour (peak)/1 per hour (off-peak)
Journey time: 70 min (from Marlow)
Season ticket from Marlow: £1720

The service that connects these stations to Maidenhead is nicknamed the Marlow Donkey. It is very short and slow. The line follows the river and rises out of the valleys to give good views. The area is close enough to London for people to commute by car, either on the M40 or on the M4.

Furze Platt station was built in 1937 to serve north Maidenhead, which had been taken over by light industrial development. A spread of new housing has followed in its wake over the last 20 years. At **Cookham** you are in prize countryside now grazed by commuters and television celebrities. The Queen's Swan Keeper also lives here. The snob address is Cookham Dean, up on the common, where house prices start at £250,000 and go on upwards. Cookham Village is old and lovely, but the butcher and baker have long been replaced by chic little restaurants. Stanley Spencer lived here, and the Spencer Gallery shows some of his works. The Cookham Rise area was added in the Fifties, close to the brick and flint station building. A three-bedroom semi here costs around £100,000; or you might find a small cottage at around £90,000. The river towpath provides walks and rides for ponies. The nearest leisure centre is at Maidenhead.

The river village of **Bourne End** is just as expensive, though much of the social life revolves around sailing. The Upper Thames Sailing Club is here, and at Spade Oak Reach there is a marina with timber chalet holiday homes. These cost around £110,000, including a mooring. A more substantial, secluded riverside home, typical of the area, with six bedrooms, a boathouse and half an acre running down to the river, would sell for around £750,000. A large proportion of the population commute, but they tend to drive to Beaconsfield and get the train to Marylebone rather than suffer the Marlow Donkey.

Marlow is also prime commuter country. It has an ancient high street (with a proper butcher and fishmonger) that stretches down to the river, and an open-air Wednesday market. A two-bedroom Victorian cottage would fetch around £90,000; a three-bedroom terrace about £105,000; an Edwardian house of similar size about £150,000. Large houses on the river rarely come up for sale and cost at least £600,000. The west side of town is considered better than the east. At Marlow Bottom, two miles from the centre, is a huge modern estate with houses selling at between £105,000 and £160,000. Since it is on the Berkshire, Buckinghamshire, Oxfordshire borders, parents can choose the local education policy that suits them. At **Bisham** nearby is the famous Compleat Angler restaurant and the Marlow Rowing Club, together with some very pretty Tudor cottages, but it is rather spoilt by the heavy through traffic into Marlow. Bisham Abbey is a national sports training centre – both the English football team and national tennis players train there.

TWYFORD

Journey time: *50 min*	Peak trains: *3 per hour*
Season ticket: *£1820*	Off-peak trains: *2 per hour*

Twyford is a typical small town surrounded by countryside. It has all the essential shops, though for major shopping expeditions people travel to Reading or Maidenhead. There are rows of Victorian terrace houses close to the station. Two-bedroom ones sell for £70,000, with three-bedroom versions going for around £95,000. There is a huge, tightly packed new estate, with a range of properties from starter homes at £60,000 to four-bedroom detached houses at £160,000. The older, more established and expensive part of the town is Ruscombe, with prices ranging up to £700,000.

Waltham St Lawrence is two miles away and, like the rest of this area, combines a rural atmosphere with very high prices. Houses are detached, with land, and fetch at least £300,000. There are also some black-and-white cottages and a few modern houses. The village has a general store and a post office combined with a picture-framers. There is a good primary school within walking distance, plus Brownies, playgroups, and a football team with its own pitch. The cricket team has its pitch at **Shurlock Row**, which is rather smaller. It has a post office and general store, a much-respected butcher and a garage. It is also pretty, with a pond at the end of the main street. Villagers are currently fighting an appeal against plans to extract gravel from a site nearby, and local people are also worried about plans to widen the M4.

For cheaper properties you have to look at the dense modern housing at **Woodley**, built on the aerodrome used by Douglas Bader. Here a three-bedroom detached house might cost over £90,000. At **Charvil**, a modern three-bedroom terrace could be had for £72,000.

Branchline to Henley via Wargrave and Shiplake

No through trains. Trains to Twyford: 1 per hour
Journey time: 70 min (from Henley)
Season ticket from Henley: £1852

Wargrave lies on a charming stretch of the Thames, and its narrow streets, trees and Georgian timber-framed houses on the river make it a rather prestigious place to live. You could get something with three bedrooms on a modern estate for between £110,000 and £135,000, but good secluded houses start at £250,000 and go up over the million mark. **Shiplake** is similarly expensive and exclusive. It has a number of new developments where four- to five-bedroom detached houses cost around £260,000.

The rowing regatta, held during the first week in July, has put **Henley** on the map. The first inter-university boat race was held there in 1829, and by 1839 it had become a recognised annual event. The hordes of people who now come to drink Pimms in the pink-and-white marquees give the town an annual seizure. Though it remains pretty and rural, straddling the river by means of a lovely stone bridge, it has been affected by the influx of money. Small shops are closing and big supermarkets are moving in. There is a battle to keep open the old cinema (which has an organ that rises up out of the floor). Two-bedroom Victorian cottages sell for around £85,000; larger terrace houses with no parking sell for around £150,000 to £200,000. Anything large with a river frontage would have a starting price of over half a million. Commuters often opt for flats with views of the river – two bedrooms might cost £190,000.

Hambleden, four miles away, is also worth looking at, if only to admire the cluster of houses around the huge chestnut tree with the village pump underneath. The village has a church, general store and

Riverside residence, Henley

post office, cobbled pavements and a pretty little stream running through. Properties rarely come on the market. A small cottage with no rear garden or parking might be picked up for £170,000.

READING

Journey time: *28 min*
Season ticket: *£2028*

Peak trains: *9 per hour*
Off-peak trains: *5 per hour*

Reading is a significant shopping and business centre, and a university town. Its prosperity used to be based on beer (Courage), bulbs (Suttons) and biscuits (Huntley & Palmer), but now it has a much higher profile, fast and busy, and traffic can be a problem. The train service to London is superb as it is one of the busiest rail interchanges in the country (see also **Waterloo to Reading**, page 191). Reading is also the terminus of the Kennet and Avon canal, which was reopened in 1990 and offers some marvellous walks to the west.

Different areas offer different things. **Caversham Heights**, on the Thames, has a mix of detached houses, flat conversions and modern flats, and is very residential. The most expensive address is The Warren, up on a hill with river views. A three-bedroom flat in an Edwardian conversion with a mooring and garden sloping down to the river would sell for around £120,000. A modern four- to five-bedroom bungalow would fetch £375,000. **Lower Caversham** offers mainly Victorian terrace housing with some modern infilling. A three-bedroom terrace would cost £67,000; a modern flat on the river £50,000 to £60,000. **Caversham Park** village is made up of town houses built a couple of decades ago, where prices range from £67,000 to £75,000 and attract young families and first-time buyers. **Emmer Green** is very Thirties, with a lot of open land and golf courses. A four-bedroom house here would cost around £180,000.

West and east Reading are cosmopolitan, and prices are slightly lower. A one-bedroom flat would cost just over £40,000; a three-bedroom Victorian house might fetch around £55,000. To the south is Lower Earley (see page 190). **Tilehurst** is a suburb with its own railway station (see page 144); a three-bedroom semi costs around £66,000. Whiteknights Park, where the university is, has large Edwardian houses that sell at around the £150,000 mark.

The popular villages nearby include Pangbourne, Goring and Streatley (see page 144). **Sonning Common**, just inside Oxfordshire, is very sleepy and countrified. It has a few small shops but lacks a central focus. A two-bedroom detached bungalow could be bought for just under £90,000. Most of the villages to the south of Reading are not particularly outstanding in any way. **Burghfield** has suffered a huge population boom, and extensive new building and more new houses are planned here.

DIDCOT

Journey time: *50 min*   Peak trains: *5 per hour*
Season ticket: *£2400*   Off-peak trains: *1 per hour*

See **Paddington to Leamington Spa/Evesham** (page 145).

SWINDON

Journey time: *53 min*   Peak trains: *5 per hour*
Season ticket: *£3756*   Off-peak trains: *2 per hour*

Swindon itself is architecturally brutal though wonderfully convenient for commuting, since the InterCity trains stop here before pelting on to the West Country. Professionals, bank managers and the wealthier shopkeepers huddle together in the **Old Town**, in Victorian and Edwardian houses on the south side of Bath Road. A three-bedroom terrace at the cheaper end of the market here would cost £90,000, while four bedrooms in a more expensive road would fetch £250,000 to £280,000. **The Lawns**, near the lake and nature walks of Coate Water Park, is also sought after. Five-bedroom detached houses with gardens here cost £195,000 to £225,000. Or there is **Broome Manor**, with its golf course and a mix of modern Georgian, Regency and ranch-style houses selling at over £200,000 and evoking the atmosphere of Dallas.

On the whole, people tend to flee Swindon for the chalk villages of the Marlborough Downs or the Vale of the White Horse. The east is more popular, with villages such as **Liddington**, **Wanborough**, **Bishopstone** (which still has its watercress beds) and **Aldbourne**. These are cohesive, and tend to have primary schools and huge churches and pubs that are still free houses. A four-bedroom house could be bought for around £200,000 here, with ex-council properties in the range of £50,000 to £60,000. Although they are only just off the M4, they have some prime hacking country right on the doorstep and are seriously horsy. The Berkshire Downs combine a sense of history with wonderful riding country. The white horse is at **Uffington**, with Dragon Hill nearby where St George is supposed to have killed the dragon. It is worth remembering that the further you go from Swindon, and the nearer you get to Hungerford or Faringdon, the more attractive the villages are, and the higher the prices. You can reckon on a premium of up to £20,000.

The National Trust owns much of the land to the north of Swindon, including the villages of **Coleshill** and **Buscot**. Here the infant Thames is hardly more than a stream running beneath the willows. Though **Lechlade** is idyllically pretty with a good collection of Georgian houses, it fills with boating people in the summer and, being 10 miles from Swindon, is a bit of a slog to reach at the end of a hard day. The stone for St Paul's Cathedral was loaded here. **Fairford** is worth considering. The

Country house,
Swindon area

American air base has been reduced to a skeleton staff and is no longer the blight that it used to be. A small Cotswold stone manor house with six bedrooms might sell for £295,000.

Villagers driving in from the west of Swindon have to cope with a traffic problem on their way into the town centre. **Wootton Bassett** has a good range of local shops with a delicatessen, and Hackpen Hill nearby has a white horse on its flank. The weekly market used to be so disorganised that an early photograph shows a large cow emerging from a solicitor's office. You can get studio apartments for £30,000, and ordinary little three-bedroom houses for £65,000. The **Somerfords** (**Little** and **Great**), divided by the River Avon, both have a shop and post office, and are popular because they border the Cotswolds and are closer to the prettiness of **Malmesbury** than to the dead weight of Swindon. They have lots of local societies, from under-fives to the Somerford Stagers amateur dramatic group. Great Somerford also has a primary school. An interest in horses is a useful social passport. The Vale of the White Horse hunt provides good hunting; there is polo at Cirencester Park, and endless bridle-ways and footpaths criss-crossing the Cotswolds. The price of a new detached house with four bedrooms, two bathrooms and a double garage hovers around the £159,000 mark. **Brinkworth** is worth looking at, too. It is notable for its extraordinary length – stretching to about five miles. A former Methodist manse with four bedrooms went on the market here with an asking price of £189,000. Slightly to the west is **Lydiard Millicent**, typically north Wiltshire, with a local pub, post office and green belt buffer zone to insulate it from Swindon. A four-bedroom, two-bathroom new detached house with a double garage might cost £165,000. **Purton Stoke**, which has a pub and a village street that tapers into open countryside, is much nicer than **Purton**, which has sprawled to encompass a population of around 4,000. A restored Queen Anne house with six bedrooms in half an acre at Purton Stoke might have a price tag of just under £300,000. A three-bedroom reconstituted stone cottage would cost around £125,000.

To the south there are a very few villages scattered in the sweeping chalk hills between Swindon and Marlborough, which actually lies closer to Pewsey station (page 199).

LINE TO KEMBLE (see map)

KEMBLE

Journey time: *75 min*	Peak trains: *1 per hour*
Season ticket: *£3968*	Off-peak trains: *1 per hour**

* Change at Swindon

Kemble is a very pretty Cotswold village, often commended in best-kept-village competitions in Gloucestershire. Planning controls are tight, so that even the council houses are built in local stone. The village has a school and a general store-cum-post office, though most people do their major shopping in Cirencester. The abiding local interest is reflected in the biannual flower and vegetable shows. Three-bedroomed former estate-workers' cottages sell for around £72,000; Victorian railway cottages for around £85,000 to £90,000; four-bedroom modern houses for £120,000 to £130,000. Larger farmhouses run into several hundred thousand pounds.

To the east is a belt of very desirable small villages and hamlets. **Poole Keynes**, the nearest, was little more than a farming hamlet with a medieval priory until the Sixties imposed a modern housing development on it. **Somerford Keynes** also has a lot of modern development but is socially very active. It has a thriving WI, plus bridge clubs, mothers and toddlers, and other groups. There is no shop, but the pub sells coffee and sugar, and bread is delivered three times a week. **Ashton Keynes** has a primary school, a petrol station, two shops and some lovely period houses close to the river. As you approach from South Cerney, you will see some beautiful 17th-century cottages on the other side of the bridge. A large farmhouse with a couple of cottages in the countryside nearby would cost around £485,000, while smaller houses are on a par with the rest of the area. **South Cerney**, which has the local secondary school, is close to the Cotswold Water Park – a collection of flooded gravel pits with water-skiing, sailing and fishing. A converted barn with four bedrooms in this area would cost around £165,000. The village is marred slightly by the large quarry with its constant lorry traffic. At least six miles from Kemble but well worth the journey is **Down Ampney**, the most charming of the Ampneys (the others being **Ampney St Peter**, **Ampney Crucis**, and **Ampney St Mary**), famous as the birthplace of Ralph Vaughan Williams and much admired for its beautiful gabled manor house, Down Ampney Hall. Little here sells for under £100,000. A four-bedroom detached house could cost £135,000, and the larger secluded country houses sell for £200,000 to £500,000.

CHIPPENHAM

Journey time: *70 min*	Peak trains: *3 per hour*
Season ticket: *£4140*	Off-peak trains: *1 per hour*

Chippenham thankfully has no serious traffic problem. It has plenty of car parking, and all the basic shops anyone would need – though no Marks & Spencer or department store. It is a place for small family businesses, with a new business park on the western outskirts. In 1962 the set-piece village of **Castle Combe**, five miles away, was declared the prettiest village in England. The arched bridge over the Bye brook, and little stone cottages with their steeply pitched roofs, were then transformed to serve as a seaport for the film of *Dr Dolittle*. It is a bit of a goldfish bowl to live in because of the tourists, but at least the visitors are expected to leave their cars at the top of the village and conduct their inspections on foot. Residents become very attached to the place, and properties rarely come on the market. A three-bedroom terrace cottage would cost around £80,000.

Far quieter and just as pretty is **Biddestone**, slightly closer to Chippenham, which has the classic village centre with stone houses, a duck pond, pubs and a recreation ground for football and cricket. Prices are high. A modern detached house in an acre with a double garage will cost around £275,000. To the north-east is **East Tytherton**, which is very small, has a village shop and attractive stone houses, and is close enough to the M4 to be favoured by those who prefer the car to the train. **Bremhill** is charming too. A former resident, the vicar and poet Canon Bowles, kept the bells around the necks of his sheep tuned to thirds and fifths, and was a favourite visitor at Bowood House a few miles to the south. Bremhill has a post office-cum-general store, and a pub. A three-bedroom brick-and-tile modern house here would cost around £125,000.

People much prefer **Corsham** as a small local shopping centre, which contains a delicatessen specialising in local produce. A handsome stone double-fronted house with four double bedrooms and double garage sells for around £120,000 here. A restored Grade II listed house with five bedrooms, two garages, workshops and walled garden would fetch around £225,000. Further towards Bath on the A4 is **Box**. At one time it housed the workers building the Great Western Railway for Brunel; now it harbours the occasional rock star and is considered ideal by those who want to be within easy reach of Bath but also close to Chippenham railway station. Peter Gabriel has his Real World Studios here. The village has a general store, a home-made quiche and pie shop, a greengrocer, a chemist and a hairdresser, and two primary schools. There are lots of local activities and the village fete, known as the Box Revels, usually lasts for a week. House prices are reasonable at the moment, with three-bedroom stone cottages selling at about £70,000 – though larger houses will top the £200,000 mark. Local interests manage to be both horsy and cultural, and also sporting. Here you are in rugby country – thanks to the proliferation of boys' public schools and the huge success of the Bath Rugby Club.

Marshfield, west of Chippenham on the A420, is slightly more expensive. A three-bedroom terrace house, in what was once the last staging post to Bath, would cost around £90,000. The long grey-stone main street is dominated by the church tower and has some remarkable little almshouses dating from 1625.

Very few local sons and daughters can afford to buy homes in the villages they have grown up in. First-time buyers are eased out into small towns such as **Calne** – a pleasant Georgian town with the site of an old Victorian bacon factory put down to grass in the centre. Flats can be bought for less than £40,000. One-bedroom houses start at £40,000, with three-bedroom ex-council houses a few thousand more. Another possibility is **Compton Basset**. It has been made a conservation area because of its delightful chalk-stone cottages and 12th- and 13th-century church, but it also has a stock of surplus Ministry of Defence houses that are eagerly snapped up by younger buyers.

Other villages worth looking at include **Cherhill** (pronounced Cheryl), towards Marlborough, which stands beside a huge Iron Age camp and white horse, and has its own primary school. A 250-year-old whitewashed house with four bedrooms here would cost around £170,000. Then there is **Heddington** – a small village with its own shop, infant and primary schools. It is very up-market: a three-bedroom family house with large garden would sell for around £127,000. Another very sought-after cluster of properties is at **Charlcutt**. The place doesn't have any real sense of community, but the houses all have breathtaking views of the countryside for 20 miles in all directions. Something with five bedrooms and a double garage will cost around £265,000. Although **Sandy Lane** straddles the A342, it is very beautiful and has some very lovely thatched houses. A two-bedroom cottage here might go for £185,000. Its population is mainly retired, and the residents tend to grow high beech hedges to guard their privacy. It is short of local activity but contains a great deal of wealth. One London commuter from here prefers to travel by helicopter rather than by train. Unfortunately the village is used as a short cut by motorists heading off the M4 for Southampton.

South of Chippenham the showcase village is **Lacock**, but the jumble of timbered houses in its gorgeous twisted streets around the Abbey are all in the hands of the National Trust. The fringe offers the occasional find. A late-Victorian country house, with formal gardens, paddock, stabling, coach house and just under three acres, is priced at £318,000.

Part-time commuters might choose to live in some of the wonderful villages further south in the Avon Valley, which are also served by the Trowbridge, Bradford-on-Avon, Avoncliff and Freshford branch line to Bath (see below).

Line via Trowbridge, Bradford-on-Avon, Avoncliff and Freshford

There are no through trains to Paddington. You must either go to Bath and change, or Westbury and change.

Bradford-on-Avon is so expensive that it vies with Bath. Indeed, it is built of the same limestone as Bath, on hills falling so steeply towards the Avon that the winding paths between the houses give one the feeling of being in a Greek village. Across the arched stone bridge, and open to the public, is one of the biggest tithe barns in the country. Bradford attracts many tourists who come in summer to wander the river and old shopping streets, and to buy from the craft shops. It has a good swimming pool, rowing and sailing clubs, and an annual festival. There are also marvellous walks to be had along the Kennet and Avon Canal.

The attraction of owning a house overlooking the tessellated rooftops of weavers' cottages, miniature 18th-century homes and narrow gardens bulging with hollyhocks, is difficult to quantify. There is a definite ex-military and ex-naval presence here. Larger houses sell for hundreds of thousands of pounds. But it is occasionally possible to find a period three-bedroom terrace house on four floors, with a tiny garden, at around £108,000. On the outer roads, three-bedroom ex-council houses in reconstructed stone will sell for around £43,000. Towards the higher end of the market on the edge of town you could get a four-bedroom Victorian stone semi, with outbuildings in over half an acre, for £290,000.

Broughton Gifford is much quieter, set in deep countryside with a village green faced by Gifford Hall, a 1688 village house. **Steeple Ashton**, like Bradford-on-Avon, was built on the profits of the wool industry. It has its own pub and post office, and also a swag of new housing. A four-bedroom detached house could be bought for around £100,000. Just next to it is **Keevil**, a collection of rather exclusive cottages with a stone manor house. It has a sub post office-cum-general store, and a primary school. But the pub, which was not always popular, was recently closed. A tasteful modern three-bedroom semi with a small garden would sell for around £62,000.

Freshford is favoured greatly by retiring Bathonians. It is a strong little community, with its own shop and local railway station. Nipper trains drop you quickly into Bath, so there is no problem with parking the car.

BATH

Journey time: *80 min*	Peak trains: *3 per hour*
Season ticket: *£4280*	Off-peak trains: *1 per hour*

People have been known to move to **Bath** and move out again within a couple of years because they haven't been able to break into any of the social circles that revolve around its elegant 18th-century squares and crescents. Its attractions are manifold: beautiful parks, specialist shops, some of them rather rarefied, and restaurants where the prices compete with Mayfair. The beauty of commuting from Bath, though, apart from its obvious physical splendour, is that you can live within walking distance of the station. Indeed you have to, otherwise the combined traffic and parking problems would sour your temper before the day even began.

The social hubs include the much-acclaimed international festival in June; the Theatre Royal, which is the starting point for many West End plays; the Royal Photographic Society; the Bath Rugby Club; and of course the Pump Rooms, where balls are regularly held. Various hotels, clubs and pubs rise and fall in the firmament as the right places to be seen at, or as the favoured watering holes for cliques of businessmen. Old Bathonians are extremely tight-knit. Public schools include King Edward's School, Kingswood School for boys and girls, Monkton Combe for boys and girls, and Prior Park College, which is a Catholic school for both sexes.

The sought-after areas are the two hills to the north and south of the river. **Sion Hill** to the north is a sudden slope looking south over the city. This is where all the major crescents were built, including the Royal, for prominent figures in elegant 18th-century society. Very few of these are left intact: most have been split into flats. A first-floor, two-bedroom flat in Royal Crescent, converted in the Sixties, would go on the market at around £158,000. Between the roads full of architectural gems you find a mixed bag of houses, though nowhere are prices cheap. A four-bedroom Victorian bay-fronted semi in a quiet road might sell for £300,000.

To the south of the river is **Bathwick Hill**, with Widcombe and Lyncombe Hills, where a sister spa to the famous central spa was found in the late 18th century. The architecture is equally fine, but the views from the houses are rather more rural than those from Sion Hill. Both attract businessmen, professionals and culture vultures, but people attach fiercely to their particular hill and would never swap.

Living in the centre of Bath only became fashionable again in the early Eighties. For decades previously the Georgian architecture was not cherished, and the buildings had blackened and become gloomy. In the late Seventies, for instance, you could buy a complete Georgian town

Georgian town house, Bath

house in The Circus for £7,000. Now it would fetch £600,000. There is a tendency for the houses to have tiny gardens because they were designed in the belief that people would take their recreation in the parks. If you own a house in a square, you will often have the right to buy a key to the central garden.

For £150,000 you could shop for a house in any area – even near Sion Hill – but you would have to settle for smaller rooms (12ft by 16ft instead of 18ft square) and lower ceilings (10ft instead of 13ft) with plain rather than ornate cornices. Two-bedroom houses start at £50,000. A modest little house close to the canal with a little garden, two reception rooms and two bedrooms might be found for £79,000.

It is possible to live outside the city in one of the villages, but driving into Bath is a problem. Parking adds an expensive premium to the season ticket, and traffic wardens are vigilant. To the south is the old Somerset coalmining area, still with the occasional slag heap on the horizon. **Peasedown St John**, an early mining town, is now being carefully redeveloped, but people say it is not a place to wander about in after dark.

Norton St Philip, however, has conservation status. It was built in local stone from the profits of the wool industry, and has some small modern cul-de-sacs stitched unobtrusively into the whole. It has a shop, but is best known for its pub, The George, which is one of the best preserved medieval inns in the country. Pepys paid a visit with his wife in 1668, dined on 10 shillings and noted a plaque in the church to twin ladies who had only one stomach between them. **Hinton Charterhouse** is similarly unspoilt but less self-sufficient, with the 13th-century ruins of Hinton Priory close by. The countryside is full of similar villages that you chance upon as you dip in and out of the valleys. **Wellow**, for instance, offers up the kind of perfection that looks as though it might have escaped from the Cotswolds. A local farmer herds his cattle through the village at dawn and dusk. It no longer has a post office, but the postmaster from Hinton Charterhouse comes to the village hall once a week to hand out the pensions. Its population is largely of retired people, but it also has a very popular primary school that attracts children from surrounding villages. Many people own horses, and there is a Trekking Centre that caters mostly for weekenders.

To the west are the villages served by the Bradford-on-Avon branchline (see above). To the north is another magical stretch of countryside where time seems to have frozen. **Charlcombe, Swainswick** and **Woolley** lie in a U-shaped valley in a landscape which is almost Welsh, and which at its northern end becomes positively austere. It is expensive. In Woolley even a two-bedroom converted stable in need of redecoration would sell for £130,000, and a three-bedroom end-of-terrace with integral garage might fetch £165,000. To the east of the A46 is another stretch of villages that have that haphazard, ancient quality, including **St Catherine**, and **Northend**. **Batheaston** is a favourite retire-ment village, since it has a few old people's homes but manages also to be a working village with a butcher, greengrocer, newsagent, florist and grocery shop, and a large council estate. It has 142 listed buildings altogether, and the Batheaston Society does its best to preserve them. Although the village is bisected brutally by the A4, it may be rescued by a bypass fairly soon. For breathtaking views you could look at **Bathford**, where a bungalow on the hill will give you a splendid look-out across the water meadows to the city. Again the old Bathonians like to retire here. Further north towards the M4, in villages like **Upper Wraxhall** and **North Wraxhall**, prices drop considerably but you become a little separated from the spirit, social life and interests of Bath.

BRISTOL TEMPLE MEADS

Journey time: *90 min*	Peak trains: *3 per hour*
Season ticket: *£5044*	Off-peak trains: *1 per hour*

Commuting from **Bristol** is never easy. Parking is difficult, and the station is hard to get at, being surrounded by rows of houses that have escaped from *Coronation Street*. There are huge traffic problems. The M32 regularly clogs into four-mile tailbacks, and there is no integrated public transport system to relieve the pressure in a city where a lot of major companies – British Aerospace and NatWest, for example – have their headquarters.

Culturally, however, it is rich, with the Bristol Old Vic, the theatre school and various pubs providing fringe theatre. The Hippodrome attracts the ballet and opera companies. Colston Hall is the venue for rock bands and symphony orchestras, and the Watershed arts and media centre in the docks shows the arty films. Another big local interest is expressed through Bristol Rugby Club. The well-known public schools include Bristol Cathedral School, Bristol Grammar School, Clifton College, Colston's School and Queen Elizabeth's Hospital.

Clifton and **Cliftonville** are Bristol's Olympian heights, where the mix of Georgian, Regency and Victorian is very special and very expensive. Some of the houses are so large, with eight or nine bedrooms, that they have been divided into flats for upwardly mobile couples who will pay over £100,000 for something stylish with two bedrooms, marble fireplaces, balcony, ceiling mouldings and a drawing room with shutters. Most of these huge old places have coach houses at the back to serve as garages. In Cliftonville, many of the 10-bedroom Victorian mansions overlooking The Downs have been converted into offices. It has good schools – Clifton High for girls and Clifton College (public school) for boys. A four-storey Victorian house here would cost around £145,000. A Bath-stone house with four bedrooms and ornate cornicing in the ground floor rooms would fetch £175,000.

More affordable but no less sought after is the **Redland** area, offering a mix of Georgian, Victorian and Thirties in a distinctly bohemian atmosphere. The closer to the city centre you get, the more you feel the presence of students from Bristol University. A one-bedroom first-floor flat in a Regency terrace in Redland, close to Clifton Downs, would be priced at around £55,000. A mid-terrace three-bedroom Edwardian house, or a charming four-bedroom town house, could be had for £135,000. The problems of getting to Temple Meads station are so acute, however, that people might prefer to drive out to Bristol Parkway station (see below).

Another area worth considering, if you haven't got a family, is the Bristol **Docklands**. Huge new purpose-built legoland developments are interspersed between old warehouse conversions. The idea is that if you live in Baltic Wharf or Merchant's Wharf, you can get a river-taxi to Bristol Temple Meads station. One-bedroom flats cost around £50,000. Three-bedroom town houses with meagre gardens are £120,000.

Waterfront apartments,
Bristol

BRISTOL PARKWAY

Journey time: *78 min*	**Peak trains:** *3 per hour*
Season ticket: *£5044*	**Off-peak trains:** *1 per hour*

The villages near here are perfect for commuters because the station is easy to reach and parking is plentiful. It also lies at the centre of a motorway network that can speed you north, south, east or west and link you with the major commercial centres of Wales as well as with Birmingham, Swindon and London. It is possible for a couple to live here and for one partner to work in Exeter and the other in London. It offers countryside, yet Bristol is on the doorstep. The station is on a spur that goes direct from

Swindon, so you can be whisked to London in very little over an hour.

Only six minutes from the station are the pricey villages of **Almondsbury** and **Awkley**. They are out of earshot of all the motorways, and an old stone house with four bedrooms might typically cost £170,000 to £180,000. Though they are out of the way, there is some worry that these villages may be affected by the building of the second Severn crossing, which will link to Junction 17 of the M5 motorway, but some effort is being made to ensure this doesn't happen. **Hambrook** is also a village with instant appeal. It has a much-loved bakery, a couple of pubs, a hotel and Hambrook Common at its centre. Four-bedroom houses easily creep up into the £220,000 to £250,000 range.

Also within six minutes of the station is **Stoke Gifford** – a village in three parts which contains a Sainsbury, a doctor, dentist, hairdresser, chemist and dry cleaners. The village-proper is packed with old cottages, with those in Mead Road tending to be more expensive than the rest. A one-bedroom cottage without garden or parking will sell at around £38,000. A four-bedroom Sixties house in a discreet infill will fetch £170,000. The other two parts of the village are a pair of Bovis housing estates, one being newer and much more popular than the other. The most sought-after roads are Touchstone and Fabian. Prices range from £40,000 for a one-bedroom house or two-bedroom flat, up to £115,000 for three bedrooms.

It is impossible to ignore the ever-mushrooming site of **Bradley Stoke** on its doorstep, billed as the largest development in Western Europe. Builders have been working on it for five years already, and when it is finished in eight or nine years' time it will contain about 11,000 houses with primary schools, sports centres, pubs and supermarkets. The housing is pick-and-mix, with one-bedroom flats being sold for £38,000, three-bedroom houses at £50,000 to £100,000 depending on size, and four bedrooms at £75,000 to £150,000.

Much care is being taken at Bradley Stoke to try and avoid the mistakes that were made at **Yate**, an earlier modern development grafted on to **Chipping Sodbury** that offered unrelieved monotony. Chipping Sodbury itself, providing you pick the right part, remains a lovely old Cotswold town with a typically wide main street flanked with houses in Georgian brick and Cotswold stone. Prices here are similar to those in the nearby villages of **Winterbourne**, **Frampton Cotterell** and **Coalpit Heath**. These blend one into the other, offering a mixture of old and new with a few working farms in the outlying areas. At the bottom of the market you could buy a three-bedroom ex-council house for £50,000. At the top end you could pay £200,000 for a five- to six-bedroom Georgian mansion. **Iron Acton** is also very pretty, with a village green featuring Maypole dancing in the spring, and two pubs, one of which does a delicious oak-smoked steak.

If you are looking for a house around here it is worth remembering that in the area between Bristol and Wooton-under-Edge, prices are affected by people who commute into Bristol. As you proceed beyond **Thornbury**, prices start to drop. On a bad day from this part, the journey to Bristol Parkway station could take 15 minutes, which many might consider too much.

WATERLOO —— TO —— READING

STAINES

Journey time: *28 min*	**Peak trains:** *6 per hour*
Season ticket: *£1268*	**Off-peak trains:** *4 per hour*

Staines has been an important communications point ever since the Romans had a river crossing here on their way from London to the West. Not all subsequent bridges have been successful – three had collapsed (including a stone one designed by the Professor of Architecture at the Royal College) by the end of the 18th century, but the present one, opened by William IV in 1832, survives despite the heavy traffic from the A30 and M25. A surprisingly small station car park for only 50 or so cars means that the surrounding roads are clogged by all-day parkers, and commuters in outlying areas prefer to travel from other stations if they can. There is a wide range of housing, from large developments of flats and houses from £45,000 for a studio, £60,000 for a two-bedroom flat to £80,000 for a three-bedroom semi and £150,000 to £200,000 for a four-bedroom detached. The river is a big attraction and the small roads leading off Laleham Road to the water are very popular. Shopping is in the usual high street-cum-shopping complex with a cinema and lively pubs. There is a sailing and a rowing club as well as indoor water sports at the big leisure centre.

Laleham, on the way to Shepperton, is the most favoured village with its long stretch of riverside and annual regatta. It has its own cricket club and a few basics – a small grocery, a clothes shop and three pubs – and what one local called a "cliquey atmosphere but a nice clique. Everyone gets on well". There are a couple of small estates of three-bedroom terraces from £90,000, but most of the properties here are large four-bedroom detached houses from £190,000.

Branchline to Windsor & Eton Riverside via Wraysbury, Sunnymeads and Datchet

WRAYSBURY	SUNNYMEADS
Journey time: *41 min*	Journey time: *43 min*
Season ticket: *£1332*	Season ticket: *£1368*
Peak trains: *2 per hour*	Peak trains: *2 per hour*
Off-peak trains: *2 per hour*	Off-peak trains: *2 per hour*

Wraysbury is a spread-out village with several unusual assets. It has two stations – Sunnymeads, only a mile away, still counts as Wraysbury – and three miles of water frontage. It is surrounded by gravel pits which have been landscaped into lakes, providing sanctuaries for wildlife and magnets for serious birdwatchers. A further plus-factor is that the village is not on mains drainage. This has prevented major new developments, so 80 per cent of the houses are detached and individually built. Most roads are privately maintained by the residents, many of whom work at Heathrow airport. The M25 skirts the village without spoiling it, and counts as a convenience rather than a drawback. Wraysbury at one time was a weekend retreat for Londoners and there were many riverside shanties. These have since been replaced by houses in the £150,000 to £250,000 bracket, plus a dozen or so in two-acre plots at £350,000 to £650,000. There is a sprinkling of pre-Georgian cottages, a few Edwardian and Victorian terraces and some substantial Thirties houses. Modern houses include two-bedroom terraces from £75,000; detached bungalows from £120,000 to £200,000. There is a handful of local shops with a post office, a village green and a junior school which has a high percentage of grammar school entrants. One of the major features of life in Wraysbury is the number and quality of the local societies. These offer every option from cricket and fishing to history, drama, country & western and jazz – all well attended and well organised. Opposite the village is Runnymede where King John signed the Magna Carta.

Sunnymeads, Wraysbury's second station, is on the boundary between Wraysbury and **Horton**, which is a rural village with a green, one shop and two pubs, both listed. It has proud historical connections with John Milton, who wrote some of his poems here, and with the Bowes-Lyon family who lived here. The local forge built the equestrian statue of George III, known as the Copper Horse, which stands on Snow Hill in Windsor Great Park. The mix of properties ranges from a handful of listed houses to council semis. Prices are between £80,000 for a three-bedroom semi and £500,000 for a four- to five-bedroom Thirties detached.

DATCHET

Journey time: *46 min*	Peak trains: *2 per hour*
Season ticket: *£1404*	Off-peak trains: *2 per hour*

Only a mile from Windsor, **Datchet** has avoided being overshadowed and retains a village personality. Physically it is compact and shaped like a letter H with two cross-bars. The left of the H is on the river (one of the ports of call in Jerome K. Jerome's *Three Men In A Boat*); the right is on the village green and the two cross-bars are High Street and Queens Road. The railway runs up the middle, regularly halting road traffic at the level crossing. Until recently, most of the houses here were in the upper price bracket. In the last 10 years, however, new estates aimed at first-time buyers have appeared. Studios and one-bedroom terraces cost between £55,000 and £66,000. Elsewhere three-bedroom semis are from £150,000; detached houses with 150ft gardens and 45ft frontages £200,000. Southlea Road is one of the most desirable and has some large 18th-century houses at £300,000-plus. Expensive properties are often interspersed with cul-de-sacs of less distinguished houses. Datchet has always attracted London commuters and there is a large station car park. The other strong connection is with Heathrow: both ground staff and aircrew favour the village for its pleasant atmosphere and easy access to the airport. Datchet's charms have also attracted its share of past and present celebrities, including Sir William Herschel, the astronomer, Sir Robert Watson-Watt, the inventor of radar, and now a clutch of showbiz personalities. A few local shops, a post office and a bank that opens two hours a day serve basic needs, and there are good local primary and secondary schools. There is a local golf club with a long waiting list, a dry ski slope, cricket and sailing.

WINDSOR & ETON RIVERSIDE

Journey time: *49 min*	Peak trains: *2 per hour*
Season ticket: *£1404*	Off-peak trains: *2 per hour*

Windsor & Eton Riverside is **Windsor**'s second station, a slightly slower route to London than the shuttle from Windsor & Eton Central to Slough to pick up the 125 from Reading to Paddington (see page 158). Commuters from either station benefit from Windsor's attractive mix of quaint old streets at the foot of the castle and smart new shops – everything from old family businesses to chain and department stores. It also has all the pleasures of the 4,800 acres of Windsor Great Park close by. Apart from a few Georgian houses on Castle Hill, the centre of the town is composed mainly of Victorian terraces. A small cottage in need of improvement will cost £60,000;

a three-bedroom house £90,000 to £130,000. The west and south of Windsor evolved in the Thirties and Fifties – semis from £100,000 to £130,000. As development is restricted because of the Crown lands, only small infills have been built since the Sixties.

The most fashionable locations are St Leonard's Hill, King's Road, Adelaide Square and Bolton Avenue, all of which have a mix of properties including modern five-bedroom detached houses at £500,000. Nothing here has been purpose-built for first-time buyers, who gravitate to Bracknell or Slough. There is a deceptive bit of architecture on the Old Town Hall in the high street. On seeing Christopher Wren's plans in 1687, the councillors are said to have demanded more columns to support the upper floor (and their own combined weight). Wren obliged – up to a point. The new columns all ended slightly short of the ceiling.

Old Windsor, south-east of the town, was described in the Domesday Book as the third largest town in Berkshire. It had a wooden Saxon palace which deteriorated once William built his castle, and it was reduced to the status of a village. Today it is more like a small town with parades of shops, a post office and a bank. There is a bus service into Windsor for major shopping. A good deal of modern building has gone up since the Fifties, and there is a good selection of detached houses, some with river frontages. The Friary is the road to aim for – Victorian houses in good-sized grounds at £350,000. The main road is fringed with Twenties-built houses from £150,000, and there are one or two houses large enough to satisfy those who want a private estate close to London. These only rarely

Dutch-style family house, near Egham

come on to the market, but would probably fetch £500,000–£750,000 if they did. Two large housing estates provide less expensive homes, generally priced slightly lower than their equivalents in Windsor where communications are better. Those who choose Old Windsor do so for its more rural atmosphere and its lively community with plenty of sporting and social opportunities.

Eton is full of antique shops, restaurants and schoolboys in wing collars and tailcoats who occasionally escape from the boys' public school. There is, inevitably, something of an us-and-them atmosphere. A three-bedroom Victorian house on the high street could cost just over £200,000; a modern town house with three or four bedrooms down by the river £200,000; and down one of the side roads off the high street you can find two-up-two-down Victorian houses with small gardens at £110,000.

EGHAM

Journey time: *35 min*	Peak trains: *4 per hour*
Season ticket: *£1332*	Off-peak trains: *2 per hour*

Although **Egham** technically is a small town it retains an unhurried atmosphere from its village past. While Staines across the river is still bustling after dark, Egham shuts at 5.30pm and puts its feet up. There is a 17th-century coaching inn but most of the building is Victorian, some of it rather neglected. There are some new estates suitable for first-time buyers, however, where one-bedroom flats cost from £50,000. In the town centre, two-bedroom Victorian semis cost between £73,000 and £80,000. Thirties mock-Tudor semis in Manor Way fetch around £145,000. The town has a good mix of local shopping, including a butcher and a baker whose families have been serving the community for more than 100 years. There are plenty of sports and social clubs, and an active conservation society.

To the west, **Englefield Green** has a rustic atmosphere and a footnote in history as the site of the last fatal duel fought in England.

VIRGINIA WATER

Journey time: *38 min*	Peak trains: *5 per hour*
Season ticket: *£1404*	Off-peak trains: *2 per hour*

Virginia Water may have slipped a little in the exclusivity league since the opening of the M25, but the Wentworth Estate, built by C.W. Tarrant, the speculative builder of the early 1900s who created the first golf-course development here and at St George's Hill, is still a highly prized address. A five-bedroom family house here will command upwards of £650,000. Similar houses in half an acre in Lower Wentworth, which does not overlook the golf course, will fetch £400,000. The atmosphere is quiet and rural – the first breath of real countryside outside London – but there is little sign of rural hardship. There are two parades of specialist shops, including an excellent bookshop owned by the writer and film director Bryan Forbes, very cheap station parking (currently 50p per day) and several excellent preparatory schools. Less expensive houses are few in number. For a two-bedroom Thirties semi you would pay around £120,000 – which represents a small premium over the next most prestigious area, Sunningdale. The stretch of water which gives the area its name is a great ornamental lake created in the 18th century by the Duke of Cumberland. He also built the nearby Fort Belvedere, later the home of Edward VIII and where the abdication was signed.

To the north-east is **Thorpe**, a village bisected by the M25. Despite this apparent handicap, houses here are 15 per cent or so more expensive than their equivalents in Egham. The smallest two-bedroom Victorian semi will cost around £90,000, and there is a preponderance of large houses in spacious plots. A four-bedroom detached house built in the Thirties or Fifties will fetch between £250,000 and £300,000; a 17th-century five-bedroom house in five acres will be £400,000-plus. There is a theme park and water centre just outside the village but the traffic to it does not pass through the village itself.

Two other sought-after villages are **Lyne** and **Longcross**, but they lack properties of real character. There are some Victorian semis and modern bungalows at £100,000 to £200,000, but the agricultural smells and lack of a bus service are still enough to make country-lovers feel at home.

LINE TO CHERTSEY (see map)

CHERTSEY

Journey time: *50 min*	**Peak trains:** *4 per hour*
Season ticket: *£1404*	**Off-peak trains:** *2 per hour**

* I via Staines, I via Weybridge. Peak hours it is faster to travel via Staines; off-peak via Weybridge

A mature town with little space left for development, **Chertsey** is reaping the commercial benefit of lying just inside the M25 – an arbitrary boundary chosen by many London companies relocating their head offices. Very little remains of the famous Benedictine abbey founded in 666 – Henry VIII ordered the stones to be used in the rebuilding of his palace at Oatlands Park. But the handsome, seven-arched 18th-century bridge is still a landmark, and there is a good selection of period properties which, foot for foot, offer better value than up-market Weybridge. A three-bedroom Georgian town house would cost less than £200,000 in Chertsey. Abbey Road is popular – a Victorian three-bedroom semi here will sell for £95,000 – and Abbey Gardens offers well-proportioned between-the-wars houses in good gardens for around £220,000 for three bedrooms. First-time buyers can find turn-of-the-century two-bedroom cottages in the town centre for £60,000. Good schools include Sir William Perkins' girls' grammar, and there is a very highly regarded hospital, St Peter's.

SUNNINGDALE

Journey time: *43 min*	**Peak trains:** *3 per hour*
Season ticket: *£1568*	**Off-peak trains:** *2 per hour*

The development of the Southern Railway at the turn of the century made **Sunningdale** accessible to London businessmen who wanted to build country mansions with golf and racing on their doorsteps. Several of these minor palaces still survive intact, but many were demolished in the Thirties and Sixties to make way for new development; others have been converted into flats. It is a village of two parts – the old village around the church, and the busier shopping area near the station. Part of it lay within Surrey until 1991, when the whole was switched into Berkshire. The most sought-after houses are in Titlarks Hill, leading to the golf course, and in Ridgemount and Priory Roads. Large houses in half to one acre sell for between £300,000 and £800,000. Sunningdale is not exclusively a playground for the rich, however. In the old village there are three-bedroom Victorian semis for between £90,000 and £120,000. Think twice before buying a house too close to the A30. When the M25 gets blocked the traffic pours on to the other through roads and jams those too. Schools include an excellent comprehensive, a Church of England primary, and several private schools. Sport is plentiful but rather exclusive. There are two top polo clubs, and golf at Wentworth and Sunningdale, which has the oldest golf club for women in the country. As one resident put it, "You've got to have the odd penny or two to enjoy living here".

Sunninghill to the west is a large parish covering several communities, none of which has retained its original atmosphere. The area known as Cheapside comes closest to a traditional village feel. It has a pub, a shop, and a population of about 500. The centre of Sunninghill has a busy high street with 50 or so shops, but its identity problem is not helped by the fact that Ascot station (see below) is actually in Sunninghill, and most people prefer it to Sunningdale station. All east-west trains stop at Ascot, and the car park has been considerably extended in the past couple of years. A good deal of the housing was built around the turn of the century and sells to London commuters or to those with jobs or businesses in

Camberley or Heathrow. You would pay between £95,000 and £120,000 for a two- or three-bedroom semi. There are a number of thriving social groups based on church activities, and a keen dramatic society.

A couple of miles south of Sunninghill is **Windlesham**, which is still a village but with urban overtones. Housing here is strictly for high fliers. A five- or six-bedroom Thirties house standing in one or two acres in Westwood Road will fetch up to £1m.

ASCOT

Journey time: *45 min*	**Peak trains:** *5 per hour*
Season ticket: *£1668*	**Off-peak trains:** *2 per hour*

Because of its high racing and fashion profile, strangers expect **Ascot** to be a glamorous place to live. They are often surprised by its lack of real character. Its main attraction obviously is the racecourse, which was laid out in 1711 for Queen Anne. As a shopping centre it offers little more than a row of minor retailers. The level of wealth, however, can almost be measured by the height of the hedges and they are lofty here. Racehorse owners pay a premium for four- to five-bedroom detached houses in the quiet cul-de-sacs, Coronation Road and Brockenhurst Road. They buy into a rich man's playground close to Windsor and Heathrow airport, with golf at Hawthorn Hill and Wentworth, racing at Ascot and Windsor, polo at Smiths Lawn and the Royal Berkshire Polo Club, and boating and sailing on the nearby Thames. For the very rich there are some sizeable mansions. Not more than a mile away is Ascot Place and its several hundred acres which is believed to have changed hands for £20m, thought to be the highest price ever paid for a house in England. There are slightly smaller fry though. You could get a small Georgian manor house – that is to say it would have 11 bedrooms and around 10 acres of land, staff quarters and stabling – for £850,000.

North Ascot is quite different in character to the Ascot that surrounds the racecourse. Concentrated building began here in the 1880s and has been spreading north and west of the racecourse ever since. A Victorian semi in North Ascot will cost £85,000 to £90,000; a detached family house up to £120,000. Small houses on the 25-year-old infill developments start at around £75,000. A five-bedroom modern detached house in a third of an acre will fetch around £275,000. Royal Ascot golf club is in the centre of the racecourse. There are also opportunities for squash, tennis and cricket.

Parts of Ascot are in the parish of **Winkfield**, the largest in the county. It covers nearly 10,000 acres and contains several communities which are described as settlements rather than villages with traditional focal points. Winkfield itself is semi-rural, with some listed buildings and small terraces with modern infill. It has several parks and recreation areas but no village green, though it still has an annual festival. A small parade of shops serves everyday needs. A small terrace house sells for around £100,000, or £70,000 if it needs renovating. A wing in a Georgian-style 1860s house in ample grounds is priced at around £265,000.

Most of the small communities in this area have their own local societies and, as this is metropolitan green belt, the strongest voices belong to the residents' associations and conservation societies fighting against new development. Golf and polo are the favourite outdoor activities and there are numerous riding establishments. To avoid frightening the horses in the Cranbourne area you need to drive around almost permanently in bottom gear.

Branchline to Ash Vale via Bagshot, Camberley and Frimley

BAGSHOT

Journey time: *56 min*

Season ticket: *£1712*

Peak trains: *3 per hour*

Off-peak trains: *2 per hour**

* Change at Ascot

Once a wild heathland where Dick Turpin rode, **Bagshot** developed in the mid-19th century and is carefully maintaining its Victorian atmosphere. Lamp-posts are period-style, and new developments and refurbishments have to be in keeping. The area thrives because of the many London companies which have relocated in nearby Fleet. There is convenient day-to-day shopping, good schools and plenty of opportunities for leisure. Connaught Park, a four-year-old development on the outskirts, is often known as Terminal 5 because of the high concentration of airport personnel who live there – and also as Little Australia since several of the houses have been sold to Australian golfers. Three-bedroom semis here sell for £90,000; four-bedroom detached houses for £200,000. College Ride is highly prized for its gardens backing on to Windsor Forest and a tract of land just made available by the Crown for public use, although it is reported to be "pretty overgrown and strictly for hearty walkers". Victorian and Edwardian houses start at around £90,000 for two bedrooms. Commuters would be more likely to drive to Farnborough station and pick up the fast trains coming in to Waterloo from Salisbury and Southampton, than use this smaller line (see page 208).

CAMBERLEY

Journey time: *62 min*

Season ticket: *£1764*

Peak trains: *3 per hour*

Off-peak trains: *2 per hour**

* Change at Ascot

Before the mid-19th century when the Royal Military Academy was established at Sandhurst, **Camberley** simply did not exist. Large houses with between six and 12 bedrooms were built for officers, with more modest developments and shops following between 1880 and 1910. At first there were two areas named Cambridge Town and York Town after the two Dukes who had been heads of the academy. But when the mail kept going to the university town instead of the military one, the whole area was united under the single name, Camberley. The largest old houses have now gone – demolished to make way for new cul-de-sacs. A neo-Georgian detached house in one of these would cost around £200,000. There are also some Victorian terraces and new developments of smaller houses. One disadvantage of living in Camberley is traffic noise from the A30 and M3. Attractions include good high street shopping, which includes a large Marks & Spencer/Tesco complex, and excellent schools. All three local comprehensives have good reputations.

For something more rural you need to look west of Sandhurst to **Eversley**, where £180,000 will buy a thatched cottage with three bedrooms, or a wing of a Georgian house.

Modern two
-up-two-down,
near Bracknell

FRIMLEY

Journey time: *66 min*   **Peak trains:** *3 per hour*
Season ticket: £1764   **Off-peak trains:** *2 per hour**

* Change at Ascot

Frimley is too modern to have the character of a village. It is a one-high-street sort of a place, with all the basics and some good schools within walking distance. Most of the housing is contained on three large estates. Paddock Hill, for example, was built seven years ago and offers one-bedroom maisonettes at £58,000, three-bedroom semis at £75,000 and Tudor-style four- and five-bedroom houses at £200,000. A lively young population entertains itself at Bagshot's nightclub or at Basingstoke's bowling alley, ice rink and cinema, 20 minutes' drive down the M3. Five minutes from the centre is Frimley Green, where there are some small terraces and a few shops. The roads off the green have a mix of houses built in the Thirties, Seventies and Eighties. The oldest of these with two or three bedrooms sell for £80,000 and may be in good need of attention. Commuter parking is limited, but most people either walk to the station or drive instead to Farnborough, whence the direct line to Waterloo takes only half an hour.

ASH VALE

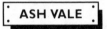

See the line to Alton (page 206).

MARTIN'S HERON

Journey time: *50 min*
Season ticket: *£1692*
Peak trains: *3 per hour*
Off-peak trains: *2 per hour*

BRACKNELL

Journey time: *54 min*
Season ticket: *£1712*
Peak trains: *3 per hour*
Off-peak trains: *2 per hour*

Nothing in **Bracknell** today suggests that in the early 19th century it might have been described as "a small thoroughfare hamlet adorned with many genteel residences and delightful villas". In 1948 it was incorporated as Berkshire's only New Town, planned for a London overspill of 25,000. It now has more than 50,000 inhabitants, all of whom must have chosen it for convenience rather than charm, with an increase in commuter traffic sufficient to require the building of a second station, Martin's Heron, three years ago. Property prices are relatively modest given that the journey to London takes less than an hour. One-bedroom flats can be found for £50,000; three-bedroom ex-council terraces fetch between £58,000 and £65,000; modern semis and four-bedroom detached houses between £100,000 and £170,000, with a few new Bovis homes near the town centre at £185,000 to £245,000. Unkind critics attach the "concrete jungle" tag, but there is plenty of high-tech industry to keep a large proportion of the young population busy locally, with good sports facilities, including swimming, dry skiing and ice skating, to fill their leisure hours.

Three miles west of Bracknell is **Binfield**, which in the last four years has almost outgrown its status as a village. Historically it is notable chiefly for its connection with Alexander Pope, who lived here as a boy in the early 1700s. There are several green areas, rather than a focused, maypole-dancing village green, and shopping is limited. There is a post office, a couple of grocers and bakers, a flower shop and two well-patronised takeaways.

Binfield offers a variety of modern and ex-council housing, with three large new estates providing commuters with one-bedroom flats at £57,500, three-bedroom houses at £87,000 to £129,000, and detached family houses rising to £300,000. A community spirit still survives, however, and young mothers as well as the established older residents are involved in the two community centres, drama club and several Scout, Brownie and Guide groups. The local primary school has a good reputation, with secondary age children moving on to Bracknell.

WOKINGHAM

Journey time: *60 min*   **Peak trains:** *3 per hour*
Season ticket: *£1780*   **Off-peak trains:** *2 per hour*

Despite centuries of doffing the collective cap to nearby royals in Windsor Forest, **Wokingham** was not granted a coat of arms until Coronation Year, 1953. A relic of the royal hunt still survives in Nine Mile Ride, which was cut through the forest to enable ladies to follow the chase from their carriages.

The town has expanded rapidly during the last two decades, and its population has swelled from 9,000 to around 30,000. Strategically it is extremely well placed, served by the A329 London to Reading road and by the M4 which links it to Heathrow airport, the West of England and South Wales. Bus services provide links to Reading and Bracknell. The town centre is surrounded by modern residential streets, many of which are still lined with old oaks and other forest trees. On the west side stands the Woosehill development, containing more than 2,000 houses plus shops, schools and community and health centres. Most of it went up in the Seventies and Eighties. The mixed estate offers flats and one-, two-, three- and four-bedroom houses at prices ranging from £55,000 to £150,000. Heading west out of town you come to a number of council developments – Barrett Crescent, for example – where many of the houses are now privately owned and have been nicely upgraded.

A few handsome older buildings survive in the town centre. The best of them is perhaps Lucas Hospital in Luckley Road, which was built in 1665 to provide a home for 16 old men. The hospital is arranged around three sides of a quadrangle, with a chapel filling the right wing. Visitors are admitted by appointment. Elsewhere there are some attractive old houses – particularly in Rose Street and Shute End. An 18th-century three-bedroom house in Rose Street with no garden could cost £76,000.

The most expensive parts of town are in Murdoch, Sturges and Denton Roads, all just to the south-east of the centre. Most of the properties here are large Edwardian houses, often with four or five bedrooms and large gardens. Prices range from £200,000 to £300,000. Cheaper properties built in the Sixties are clustered around the Mulberry Business Park, with more along the Finchampstead and Luckley Roads. A three-bedroom semi here will cost around £75,000. There are also some large family houses built in the Seventies, now priced at around £200,000.

In the north the large Emmbrook development was begun in the Thirties, with additions in the Sixties, Seventies and Eighties. Modest estate-type housing predominates, with prices starting at around £65,000 rising to £110,000 for a four-bedroom detached house. The area is popular because of the Emmbrook School – a secondary with such an excellent reputation that people from more expensive parts of the town often send their children here.

Wokingham has public playing fields, a sports centre, indoor and outdoor swimming pools, a small theatre and a cinema. There are two public golf courses nearby – one in Hurst, the other at Easthampstead Park – and three miles away is the East Berkshire golf club with its own 18-hole course. Shops include Tesco, Waitrose and W.H.Smith, but there is no major department store. Wokingham people tend to work and shop in Reading or Bracknell.

WINNERSH

Journey time: *65 min*
Season ticket: *£1812*
Peak trains: *3 per hour*
Off-peak trains: *2 per hour*

WINNERSH TRIANGLE

Journey time: *67 min*
Season ticket: *£1844*
Peak trains: *3 per hour*
Off-peak trains: *2 per hour*

Winnersh is gradually being absorbed into Wokingham. The Winnersh Triangle sounds dangerously exotic, but it's not a place where boats disappear without trace – rather it's a large business park, some of it vacant in the recession. Traffic-hum from the adjacent A329M and M4 is a constant reminder of the quality of the road communications.

The most famous former resident of Winnersh was John Walter II, son of the founder of *The Times*. He built a Georgian mansion called Bearwood, which his son replaced with the present mansion, now a boys' private school. Walter also built the "model" estate of Sindlesham with its church, pub, school, dower house, cottages and farm. The rhododendron drive which he planted to the next village of Barkham still largely survives, though it has been hacked about a bit by new development. The model estate itself is now part of Winnersh and rather swamped, but Sindlesham is still fairly rural and attractive. Along the Reading Road are some good-value late Sixties and Seventies houses. The village is generally cheaper than Wokingham. A 20-year-old three-bedroom town house will cost £68,000. There are also some half-timbered houses.

To the north lies **Hurst**, a "proper" village with a duckpond and green, much the nicest on this side of Reading. The most desirable four-bedroom cottages here sell for around £245,000, but there are cheaper properties too.

EARLEY

Journey time: *70 min*
Season ticket: *£2028*

Peak trains: *3 per hour*
Off-peak trains: *2 per hour*

Despite the name – **Earley** derives from the Anglo-Saxon words for eagle and wood – there is nothing at all rural on the horizon here. There are four parts to Earley – **Maiden Earleigh, Lower Earley, Old Earley** and Earley proper. By some calculations Lower Earley is the biggest housing estate in Europe, clamped to the southern underbelly of Reading, right beside the M4. Many of the ex-council houses here are now privately owned and being offered for sale at prices ranging upwards from £50,000. Old Earley has the oldest and most expensive properties – older in this context meaning turn-of-the-century. Prices range from £57,500 for a two- or three-bedroom terrace to £85,000 for a three-bedroom semi and £110,000 for a four-bedroom house. The houses in Maiden Earleigh were

17th-century thatched cottage, Earley

built mainly in the Sixties and Seventies. Those with three bedrooms sell for around £75,000.

The area is nicer than the less appealing parts of Reading but still rather a suburban sprawl. You might find the occasional 17th-century thatched cottage, for which you would probably have to pay something in the region of £215,000. The centre of Reading is about 15 minutes away by car, and the "village" – a misnomer if ever there was one – is enlivened by a large hall of residence for students of Reading University.

READING

Journey time: *73 min*
Season ticket: *£2028*
Peak trains: *3 per hour*
Off-peak trains: *2 per hour*

See **Paddington to Bristol** (page 164).

PADDINGTON — TO — CASTLE CARY

For stations between Paddington and Reading, see page 156. See map (page 154).

READING WEST

Journey time: *40 min*
Season ticket: *£2028*
   * Change at Reading

Peak trains: *4 per hour**
Off-peak trains: *2 per hour**

See Reading on the **Paddington to Bristol** line (page 164).

Branchline to Mortimer and Bramley

No through trains. Trains to Reading: 2 per hour
Journey time: 55 min (from Bramley)
Season ticket from Bramley: £2028
It is possible to go via Basingstoke to Waterloo in the other direction.
Season tickets are valid both ways.

Mortimer is the smaller and more rural of the two villages, with little in the way of new development. Prices are quite high: £90,000 for a two-bedroom period cottage, £200,000 for a family house. **Bramley** is a linear dormitory village which grew up around the railway in the mid-1890s. It has a green, a pond and a church, but expanded rapidly eastwards during the Thatcher years. A one-bedroom flat with garage on a new development will cost around £50,000; a larger detached house between £150,000 and £200,000.

THEALE

Journey time: *42 min*
Season ticket: *£2028*

Peak trains: *3 per hour*
Off-peak trains: *3 every 2 hours*

Since getting into Reading is a nightmare, many people prefer to use **Theale** station instead. It marks the beginning of the Berkshire farming belt beyond Reading, yet is more accessible and gets some fast trains. The county council has just spent a large amount of money on restoring the town's Victorian image, reinstating cobbles and period lamp-posts. Most of the main street, which has a butcher, baker, greengrocer and a few offices, is included within a conservation area.

    Theale has accumulated large modern housing estates and an

industrial area to the south, but environmentalists are thick on the ground and are fending off the considerable pressure for more development. British Rail has been trying to build a leisure park, and a large business park is being built behind the station to accommodate major companies moving out of London, including Smiths Crisps and Panasonic. Some people expect this to cause a small local property boom. Currently a new two-bedroom house is likely to cost around £60,000; three bedrooms £90,000. A turn-of-the-century, three-bedroom semi backing on to fields might cost £85,000. Four-bedroom houses are in short supply.

ALDERMASTON

Journey time: *55 min* | Peak trains: *2 per hour**
Season ticket: *£2028* | Off-peak trains: *1 per hour**
  * Change at Reading

Aldermaston is a very pretty village on the Kennet and Avon Canal, with a main street of red-brick and timber houses sandwiched between Elizabethan cottages. To outsiders, however, it is best remembered as the starting point for the Ban the Bomb marches, chosen by protesters because of its proximity to the Atomic Weapons Research Establishment nearby. Despite the traffic that thunders through it on the A340 to Basingstoke, the village has been well preserved. Until recently it was an estate village, and every third year on 13 December a candle auction is still held to determine the rent charged for a small piece of land called Church Acre – the end of the bidding is signalled by the extinction of a candle flame. The big house, Aldermaston Court, that stands at one end of the main street, is now converted into offices. There is also a parish hall, a village green, a store and post office.

The station itself is useful only for shuttle services into Reading, whence fast trains to Paddington are plentiful. The proximity of the Atomic Weapons Research Establishment drags property prices down by about five to 10 per cent. An inglenooked period cottage could be bought for around £90,000 to £100,000.

MIDGHAM

Journey time: *59 min* | Peak trains: *2 per hour**
Season ticket: *£2028* | Off-peak trains: *1 per hour**
  * Change at Reading

Like Aldermaston, **Midgham** is not served by the early morning London trains and commuters have to shuttle into Reading and change. It is a straggly linear village with no shops but a good pub, the Coach & Horses. You could buy a large detached farmhouse with six bedrooms and a couple of acres for £350,000.

THATCHAM

Journey time: *51 min*
Season ticket: *£2028*

Peak trains: *3 per hour*
Off-peak trains: *3 every 2 hours*

The old village of **Thatcham**, with the green at its centre, has been vastly swollen by new development in the last couple of decades. It is good for secondary shopping but Reading or Newbury (only two miles away) offer much more. The most sought-after new developments are Siege Cross and Kennetlea, both of which are within walking distance of the station and are established stamping grounds for professional couples and young families. Prices range from just over £50,000 for a one-bedroom flat to £130,000 for four bedrooms. South Thatcham is less popular and sometimes less savoury (being close to the sewage works), so prices are lower. The average price for a three-bedroom house is around £65,000.

Thatcham station is favoured by visits from the few through trains to London in the early morning. The snag is that you have to negotiate the level crossing before you can park the car. "If you are not careful, you can be stuck in your car at the crossing waiting for your own train to whoosh by," says one exasperated commuter.

Cold Ash, a little over a mile away, is particularly popular. Though it straggles a bit, and has no central focus, it is attractively positioned on the hill sloping down to the Kennet Valley. It has about 1,500 residents, a community hall, a few shops and some modern infilling. Property here sells quickly. You could expect to pay between £110,000 and £120,000 for a three-bedroom bungalow; between £300,000 and £400,000 for a large five- to six-bedroom detached house in a couple of acres.

The village of **Bucklebury** nearby has some pretty cottages and a large common, and is close to Bradfield, the boys' public school. A small cottage here might be had for as little as £125,000, but anything larger with land attached will run into hundreds of thousands. There is a curious little 17th-century painting of a fly in the local church, with the body and legs on one side of the glass and the wings on the other.

NEWBURY

Journey time: *55 min**
Season ticket: *£2068*

Peak trains: *3 per hour*
Off-peak trains: *3 every 2 hours*

* 45 min on occasional InterCity

Newbury is a prosperous former market town with a good train service to London, and is hugely popular. It has a mass of pretty downland villages (*Watership Down* country) within reach and is positioned on the edge of the so-called Silicon Valley. The centre is mostly 17th- and 18th-century with a good range of shops, including an old-fashioned pork butcher and pie-maker, and has the Kennet and Avon canal running through it. Many people feel, however, that new buildings have erased all sense of its being a brick-and-tile traditional country town. "Forty or 50 years ago I can remember cattle and sheep being driven in, and the circus arriving by train and walking from it through the town. It's hard to imagine any of that now," says one old resident.

A great mix of people are attracted to Newbury. Computer companies have brought in the upwardly mobiles; the racecourse (which has its own weatherboarded station) attracts the experts on horseflesh. There is a shortage of two-bedroom houses for first-time buyers. Close to the centre you could find a two- or three-bedroom restored Victorian house for around £60,000. Standard executive houses in Speen Lane are priced between £160,000 and £500,000. In Garden Close or Tydehams there are large houses built earlier this century in large private grounds, selling for £250,000 upwards.

The young tend to say that there isn't a lot to do in Newbury, though there is a recreation centre, a swimming pool and a cinema, half of which is now a bingo hall. A new golf course and hotel have been built at Donnington just outside. Local conservationists are extremely exercised by plans to build a ring road across Enborne Chase, a beautiful unspoilt belt of land south of the town.

Chalet-style house, Newbury

Villagers as far to the north-west as **Lambourn**, and as far south as Hurstbourne Tarrant, will come in to use Newbury station. The National Hunt racecourse training centre is at Lambourn, so there are about 1,000 horses in Lambourn and **Upper Lambourn** together, making them both busy working villages. Most of the stable hands work from about seven in the morning until the middle of the day, when they rush to the village to do their shopping, and then start work again at about four o'clock. Lambourn itself has a few general stores, a farm shop, butcher, delicatessen, post office and saddler. Upper Lambourn has very little other than a pub. You need a car if you live here because buses to Newbury and Swindon are few. Strings of 20 to 30 horses, exercising in the narrow lanes across the rolling chalk hills, can frustrate commuters driving to the station to catch the early morning trains.

Eastbury, two miles closer to Newbury, is also picturesque. It is on the River Lambourn, and houses are built on the river banks which are cleverly planted with shrubs and bulbs. It is a popular place to retire to. An old three-bedroom thatched house on the river would sell for around £140,000. Just next door in the village of **East Garston**, a four-bedroom Thirties house standing in an acre of garden would sell for around £250,000.

Further east are two more good chalk villages, **West** and **East Ilsley**, just off the A34. East Ilsley has a central square with a pond, and has allowed very little new building apart from some new sheltered housing for the elderly. Village life has changed dramatically over the years. This used to be the site of a twice-yearly sheep fair (the greatest sheep market in England after Smithfield, they say) and there were 13 pubs. Today only three pubs remain and the place is largely inhabited by commuters who also happen to be keen conservationists. It has a shop-cum-post office, and all the walks that the nearby Downs can offer, including the Ridgeway, along which Neolithic and Bronze Age man once commuted. West Ilsley is pretty too, with a church at its heart, a village green, cricket pitch and pavilion, and a good collection of cottages. It has one shop, a post office and a pub. Its social life tends to be dominated by the horse-racing fraternity. A four-bedroom period house set in half an acre would sell for between £230,000 and £250,000.

Stanford Dingley, set in the valley of the River Pang a good six miles to the north-east, is thought to be one of Berkshire's most beautiful villages. It has a classic mellow red-brick Georgian rectory, a 13th-century church screened by chestnuts, and two old inns called The Bull and The Boot. At The Bull a game called Ring The Bull is played, in which a ring dangling from the ceiling has to be swung on to a horn. "We're an active village," says the parish clerk. "We have barn dancing and play boules on the little green opposite The Bull. We hold summer fetes, usually in someone's garden. The River Pang runs through some of the gardens and at the fetes we hold a tug of war over it, so that the losers fall in. We also have a mini-agricultural show at the rectory with produce and flower-arranging." The village has an antique shop and a post office open only for a few hours a week, but no school. Houses rarely come on the market because people tend to stay put. A typical early Victorian brick house with three or four bedrooms might be bought for under £250,000. An extra bedroom would put the price up to £275,000, and with a couple of acres it could go up again to £325,000.

Yattendon, just north of the M4, has a picture-book village square with black-and-white 17th-century houses surrounding it. The partly moated manor house, the church, rectory and malt house, all look immaculately cared for. Robert Graves's ashes are in the churchyard. Yattendon has a general store and post office, butcher, hairdresser and a smithy, and socially it remains fairly feudal. Keep-fit and badminton take place in the village hall, and there are tennis courts and a cricket pitch. The village fete is the main annual event. Property prices here are so high that an affordable housing scheme has been set up to provide 12 houses at lower prices for native villagers. On the open market, apartments in a converted manor house sell at around £200,000 for three bedrooms. A house with six bedrooms in two acres will fetch £400,000.

Much closer to Newbury, two miles north, is the village of **Bagnor**. It is scattered around a tributary of the Lambourn and remains fairly unspoilt, with a pretty green and a pub called The Blackbird. **Leckhampstead** also has a stunningly beautiful setting, high above the Wantage to Newbury road, with a gathering of thatched cottages on a small green.

Heading south you come to **Highclere**, on the main Andover road, with a selection of properties ranging from a four-bedroom detached house at £180,000 to a three-bedroom period cottage in half an acre for £170,000. **Ecchinswell** nearby is an attractive village where a period four-bedroom cottage will cost around £180,000.

KINTBURY

Journey time: *80 min*
Season ticket: *£2140*
  * Change at Reading

Peak trains: *2 per hour**
Off-peak trains: *1 every 2 hours**

Kintbury is an unremarkable and yet endearingly compact and likeable village. It sits on the Kennet and Avon canal deep in agricultural Berkshire, and its position attracts an element of tourism. There is a full range of house types and prices, from new developments for first-time buyers to executive detached houses. A rectory-sized old house with three acres beside the canal is priced at around £450,000. A six-bedroom Georgian house with two acres is about £500,000.

Two miles away is **Inkpen**, a village strung out so thinly that you can't locate its centre. It is worth looking at, however, because of its position in the shadow of the Berkshire Downs. Steep winding lanes carry you hundreds of feet up to magical windy walks, and panoramic views from the gibbet on Walbury Hill.

HUNGERFORD

Journey time: *85 min*
Season ticket: *£2196*
  * Change at Reading

Peak trains: *2 per hour**
Off-peak trains: *1 every 2 hours**

Being just off the M4, **Hungerford** is a favourite starting place for househunters in the area. It is on the twee side of pretty, with a pleasant wide high street stretching down to the Kennet and Avon Canal and the River Kennet. It combines the tea and trinket shops of tourism with up-market interior design shops and a delicatessen. It is the local antiques capital, and has an antiques arcade which is open on Sundays. Sheep graze the huge 180-acre common – originally given by John of Gaunt in the 14th century – which gives way to chalk downs and wooded hills beyond.

The community is close and tightly knit. As the mayor says: "We have a cracking cricket team, a football team, choir, theatre club, band, good nursery school and so on. People get involved here. All the time something is happening, making it all tick." Ancient rituals are still

Black-and-white period house, Hungerford area

observed. On the first Tuesday after Easter the Tutti men tour the town extracting kisses from all the women in return for oranges.

Off the high street you can buy older two-bedroom terrace houses for around £65,000. On the high street a four-bedroom Georgian house would fetch around £200,000. A four-bedroom detached house on a modern development could be had for between £110,000 and £150,000. But pressure on housing is a controversial issue here. The area has been earmarked for growth by Berkshire County Council and there are plans to build 500 new houses, starting in 1995 and spread over a period of seven years. This will swell the current population of 5,500 by a third. At a public meeting last year every single person present voted against the plan.

Within easy reach of Hungerford is the village of **Chilton Foliat**, a picturesque combination of brick, slate and thatch, with one shop and a pub. A three-bedroom thatched cottage on the main street is priced at about £140,000. **Little Bedwyn**, on the Kennet and Avon canal, is lovely too. It has an outstanding 18th-century farmhouse in chequered brick-work, with a rare octagonal game larder. The farmyard, with timber and brick barns, is right in the village centre.

BEDWYN

Journey time: *90 min*	Peak trains: *2 per hour**
Season ticket: *£2260*	Off-peak trains: *1 every 2 hours**

* Change at Reading

This is the last station along the line that is properly served by Network SouthEast. Beyond this point the number of trains is much reduced. By the Kennet and Avon canal towpath is the Crofton Pumping Station, which houses the two oldest steam engines in the world that are still in working order. They are used to raise the water level in the canal. A large four-bedroom Victorian house with a good garden in **Great Bedwyn** will cost around £215,000.

PEWSEY

Journey time: *65 min*	Peak trains: *1 per hour*
Season ticket: *£2924*	Off-peak trains: *nil*

Daily commuters become rather thin on the ground here because it is beyond the reach of Network SouthEast. The trains that serve it are mostly InterCity services from the West, which are relatively infrequent. There is one special commuter express each morning and evening, but this hardly makes for commuter flexibility. It is always possible to get a train to Newbury and change.

Pewsey is a pretty agricultural town between Salisbury Plain and the Marlborough Downs. Some of the shops are still roofed in thatch, and a statue of Alfred the Great stands in the centre, overlooking the young River Avon and its resident ducks. It has a few supermarkets, estate agents, banks, bakery and so on, and its own comprehensive school, playing fields and swimming pool. It also has one of Wiltshire's six white horses, cut into the chalk hillside in 1785.

A three-bedroom thatched cottage here could be bought for £100,000; a four-bedroom detached Victorian house for £130,000. Just outside the town is a Charles Church development where little two-bedroom houses are priced at £54,000; four-bedroom detached at £126,000.

The pretty villages around include **Manningford Bruce**, two miles away, where thatched cottages cluster around the village church. A small house here could be bought for around £150,000. The whole of this area is classified as an Area of Outstanding Natural Beauty. A few miles to the north-west you come to **Stanton St Bernard**. The Pewsey Vale Riding Centre is here, and there are lots of weekend cottages and larger country houses. A four-bedroom detached Victorian house will cost around £150,000; a thatched house with four bedrooms would be nearer the £200,000 mark.

Urchfont, though a little far from the station (nearly 10 miles west), is also extremely popular. It contains all the essential ingredients of the ideal village – thatched cottages, a couple of good pubs, 16th- and 17th-century houses around the greens, one of which is next to the church and has a charming little duckpond. There is also a William and Mary manor house. Something with four bedrooms and a sense of history will cost around £200,000.

One of the advantages of living to the west is that you are within reach of **Devizes**, which is so attractive that it is a treat to go shopping there. The market square is surrounded by houses which are older than their Georgian facades. The town has good small butchers and bakers, as well as a large Safeway on the outskirts. A small period terrace house will cost around £40,000; a Thirties bow-fronted three-bedroom house £70,000; a modern four-bedroom house £100,000. The Kennet and Avon Canal here offers a flight of locks, 29 over a two-mile stretch, as the water rises 237ft on the way up to the town.

Less than three miles to the east of Pewsey is **Wootton Rivers**, where you pay a premium for the prettiness. A three-bedroom thatched cottage here is about £135,000 to £140,000. There is only one street, running up from the bridge over the Kennet and Avon Canal. Along the towpath you will find the lock and lock-house, both of which have recently been restored. The character of the place is so rural that even the churchyard seems merely an interruption in the farming landscape. The church itself is distinguished by a wooden belfry containing an unusual clock with a broomstick for a pendulum. Just to the north, for those in search of sylvan solitude, are the 2,300 acres of the Savernake Forest.

East Grafton, a few miles further east towards Hungerford, offers slightly larger houses than some of the other villages. A thatched house with five bedrooms, stables and a few acres would cost around £300,000. It has the A338 running through it, but it keeps away from the village proper, where there is a large green and a Victorian church edged with old thatched cottages.

To the north is **Marlborough**, the old halt for 18th-century stagecoaches on the run down from London to Bath. Today the town is rather more dominated by the boys' public school, which now takes some girls, and the tearooms where they buy their sticky buns. Marlborough is an extremely popular place in which to live because it is close enough to the M4 at Swindon, it has a good range of small specialist shops and is surrounded by spectacular countryside.

Thatch is noticeably absent. Terrible fires in the 17th century resulted in its being banned. The town has a Georgian feel, though there are plenty of half-timbered houses hidden down the small back lanes off the broad open high street. A four-bedroom detached Georgian house might be had for £160,000, though a similar house on the main A4 would cost considerably less – around £120,000. Two-bedroom Victorian terrace cottages tend to sell at around £50,000.

Apart from the indoor swimming pool, there is very little for the young in Marlborough. The church is strong. There is a Church of England Society, a choral society, civic society and railway society that has restored the old railway track to Swindon as a cycle path. The Scouts and Cubs have taken it upon themselves to clean the chalk outlines of the white horses in the area.

WESTBURY

Journey time: *78 min*   **Peak trains:** *1 per hour*
Season ticket: *£4280*   **Off-peak trains:** *1 every 2 hours*

Westbury was once a charming small town, with Georgian houses grouped around the market place and church, but it has been swamped by new housing. There are a few shops to meet basic needs: butcher, greengrocers, bank and post office. Two-bedroom starter homes can be bought for £45,000; and three-bedroom semis for £53,000, though they tend to be small. High above Westbury stands the oldest white horse in Wiltshire, believed to have commemorated King Alfred's victory over the Danes in the ninth century.

Bratton, a couple of miles to the east, offers sleepy lanes where a small stream runs past some of the old cottages tucked into the hedgerows. The village has a post office, a store and a school. A 200-year-old three-bedroom cottage here would sell for around £80,000; a modern three-bedroom bungalow with three acres for around £180,000. **Edington** is similar, though more remote. This area is rather far from any large town so prices tend to be lower and commuting is rigorous. The number of daily commuters probably totals no more than a dozen.

FROME

No through trains. Trains to Westbury: *1 every 2 hours*
Season ticket: *£4348*

Frome is neither quite in the best countryside close to Bath nor in the most beautiful part of Somerset. But it has a distinct character with lots of stone buildings set on the steep hillside on the eastern flank of the Mendips. The old market place is still there, though the cattle market moved out a few years ago. Its shopping centre is unimaginative, but it does have a sports centre to serve the needs of the surrounding villages. The narrow, twisted streets are worth walking through just to admire. The most famous of these is Cheap Street, which is cobbled and has a water course running down the centre.

An old terrace cottage with three bedrooms will cost between

£50,000 and £60,000 in the conservation area just off the centre. Larger houses will sell for £200,000 to £300,000. A Regency house right in the centre, with six bedrooms and a garden, will fetch £240,000. There are modern estate homes on the outskirts too, ranging from one-bedroom units at £40,000 to four- or five-bedroom detached houses at £130,000 to £160,000. Trains are not frequent from Frome. The station is on the loop served by trains from Weymouth.

To the west and south-west are several villages that teeter on the edges of the old stone quarries. When you look, bear in mind that there are plans to expand the quarries at Whatley and Leigh upon Mendip. Three miles north is **Lullington**, a very pretty little hamlet with a green and a church but no shops, where an old stone house with three bedrooms might be had for just under £100,000.

Late Victorian house, near Frome

CASTLE CARY

Peak through trains: *1 per hour*
Off-peak trains to Westbury: *1 every 2 hours*
Season ticket: *£4592*

This is long-haul commuting, but people do it. Parking at the station is easy, and you can pick up the occasional train pelting back and forth to the Devon seaside resorts. **Castle Cary** sits on the last few ripples of the Mendips before the relentless flatland of the Somerset Levels. The town owes much of its prosperity to agriculture, and also to the horse-hair weaving trade. There is still a weaver in the town, though the hair he uses now is imported from China. The remains of the old motte-and-bailey castle that gave the town its name are still here, and a rather desultory market is still held on a couple of days each week.

The mellow, golden local stone is what makes people fall in love with the place. There are a few traditional shops, a thatched hotel called The George, and a notable rectory just outside at **Ansford**, which was once the home of the Reverend James Woodforde, author of *Diary of A Country Parson*. A two-bedroom period cottage would cost around £55,000 to £65,000. Larger houses lie on the edge of the town where something with three to four bedrooms, a paddock and views across the fields would cost between £125,000 and £145,000. A period farmhouse would reach into the £150,000 to £175,000 range. There are some modern estates on the outskirts, where a retirement bungalow costs around £75,000 to £85,000 and a modern detached house with four bedrooms £145,000 to £165,000.

Commuters necessarily have to live very close in to the station because of the length of the journey. A clutch of villages within the five-mile belt include the stone villages of **North** and **South Cadbury**, and **Yarlington**, which is a good agricultural working village with a mix of modern and old houses, priced very similarly to those in Castle Cary. To the north-west is **Ditcheat**, also a good working village. This is dairy country – rich, green and undulating – where much of the milk goes to butter and cheese-making factories.

WATERLOO
—— TO ——
SALISBURY/SOUTHAMPTON

WEST BYFLEET

Journey time: *30 min*   **Peak trains:** *5 per hour*
Season ticket: *£1368*   **Off-peak trains:** *3 per hour*

West Byfleet is a large village that has expanded over the years to become inseparable from Woking. Property prices are high because of its closeness to London. A modern three-storey town house will be unlikely to cost less than £90,000; an older house with three or four bedrooms will be at least £200,000.

WOKING

Journey time: *27 min*   **Peak trains:** *10 per hour*
Season ticket: *£1532*   **Off-peak trains:** *7 per hour*

Woking is a busy but unremarkable commercial town, popular with commuters. The rail service is very frequent, even if available seats may be few, and it is conveniently placed for access to the A3, the M3 and even the M25. The north side of the town is mostly given over to council houses and the south tends to be more sought after. A one-bedroom flat in a large converted Victorian or Edwardian house would cost £56,000; a neo-Georgian three-bedroom house on a small development would sell for around £80,000; a new four-bedroom detached house would cost £200,000. Hook Heath is where the wealthy gather, in mini-mansions on large plots, which sell for over £300,000. For lower prices but a vast range of choice, you could look at Goldsworth Park, where 6,000 homes have been built over the last two decades. You could buy a two-bedroom terrace house for under £65,000; a large, four-bedroom detached house for £150,000–£160,000.

    Horsell, on the outskirts, tends to be slightly more expensive than Woking proper. H.G. Wells lived in Woking for a time, and in *The War of the Worlds* he described the Martians landing on Horsell Common. A Thirties detached house with three bedrooms would cost around £115,000.

    For a vintage Home Counties village there is **Chobham**, two miles to the north-west, no weakling in the Best Kept Village stakes. Lorries have been banned from the high street, which is very much a conservation area – full of antique shops, with a pretty hump-backed bridge over the

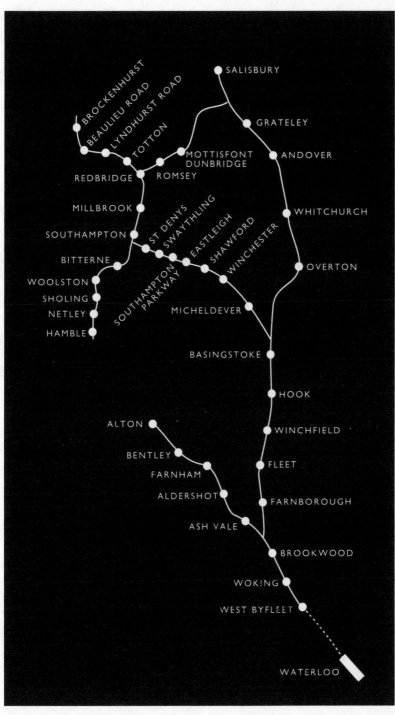

Bourne brook. Chobham Common is a precious green lung in this part of Surrey, providing wooded bridle-ways for pony lovers. People from outside the village run the football, tennis and cricket, but the Brownies, Guides and WI are domestic affairs. It claims to have the biggest Venture Scout troop in Surrey. The village is very sought after, so a small period cottage will cost at least £75,000. For a larger period house you must expect to pay anything from £250,000 to £500,000.

BROOKWOOD

Journey time: *37 min*	Peak trains: *4 per hour*
Season ticket: *£1620*	Off-peak trains: *4 per hour*

Brookwood has the edge on Woking because people prefer the idea of living in a village, no matter how built up it has become. The strangest fact about the station is that it was built originally to serve the enormous cemetery, not for the convenience of commuters. Small cul-de-sacs of fairly new houses abound. A three-bedroom Thirties detached house would cost around £110,000.

LINE TO ALTON (see map)

ASH VALE

Journey time: *38 min*	Peak trains: *4 per hour*
Season ticket: *£1716*	Off-peak trains: *2 per hour*

Ash Vale is usually considered a rather unfashionable address, though it has the attraction of affordable prices for first-time buyers. It consists mainly of Victorian terraces arranged in grids around the railway station. You could buy one of these terrace houses for less than £60,000.

ALDERSHOT

Journey time: *42 min*	Peak trains: *4 per hour*
Season ticket: *£1780*	Off-peak trains: *2 per hour*

Aldershot is an Army town with a pretty rough feel to it. There are 14,000 military personnel here, against 22,000 civilians. Victorian terraces went up in Aldershot like mushrooms in a cow pasture. You could buy one now for just over £50,000. They will be surrounded by lots of Army married quarters, built in the Thirties and Sixties. Prices rise a little on the Farnham side of town, where a three-bedroom detached house will cost around £110,000.

FARNHAM

Journey time: *49 min*
Season ticket: *£1828*

Peak trains: *4 per hour*
Off-peak trains: *2 per hour*

Farnham is something of a refuge from Aldershot, having a Georgian town centre and some expensive commuter housing. People living anywhere between the two towns will always say they live in Farnham. The south side is more up-market than the north: it has more of a country feel, even though it is very well connected to London by train and the A3. A three-bedroom detached Thirties house in a quiet road will cost £130,000; a more spacious five-bedroom house £230,000. There are some modern apartments on the south side, where a three-bedroom unit will cost around £120,000.

BENTLEY

Journey time: *55 min*
Season ticket: *£1844*

Peak trains: *2 per hour*
Off-peak trains: *1 per hour*

Bentley is an older village of attractive cottages and houses, with one or two discreet modern estates. These include a small Charles Church development of large four-bedroom houses with double garages, selling at around £145,000. The smaller three-bedroom period cottages may be bought for around £72,000. Jane Austen's brother was once curate of Bentley; Robert Baden-Powell lived in Pax Hill House; and a director of the White Star shipping line, owners of the *Titanic*, lived at the big house, Jenkyn Place, whose gardens are now open to the public. The station is some distance from the village near Alice Holt Forest.

ALTON

Journey time: *61 min*
Season ticket: *£1912*

Peak trains: *2 per hour*
Off-peak trains: *1 per hour*

Alton is a handsome little market town whose square still fills with stalls every Tuesday. The station building is painted in the old Southern Railway livery of green and cream. The community of 10,000 is essentially a rural one, though there are quite a number of commuters who have been attracted by the lovely countryside that surrounds it. At the lower end of the market you might find a Grade II listed house with two bedrooms, beams and an inglenook fireplace dating from 1800, all for around £68,000. Newer three-storey town houses with three bedrooms start at £85,000. A new development is going up on the fringe of the town, with five-bedroom houses priced in the region of £170,000.

Period five-bedroom thatched houses in the local lanes will cost from around £300,000 up to £500,000. One of the most sought-after villages is **Chawton**, two miles away, though the stone-and-thatch cottages only rarely come up for sale.

Chawton's main claim to fame is that Jane Austen lived in a small cottage with her parents and wrote most of her novels here. Her nephew, Edward Knight, lived in the manor house. The cottage is now open to the public. **East Worldham**, high on Worldham Hill, is the place to live if you want dramatic views over the countryside. A number of barns have been converted into houses that sell for just under £400,000 each. Some have been divided into flats, at £100,000 to £150,000.

Old manor house, Alton area

CONTINUATION OF MAIN LINE TO BASINGSTOKE

FARNBOROUGH

Journey time: *43 min*	Peak trains: *4 per hour*
Season ticket: *£1780*	Off-peak trains: *2 per hour*

It is socially advantageous to have some connection with flying if you live in **Farnborough**. This is where the Royal Aircraft Establishment is, and where the Farnborough Air Show is held. The heart of the town has been fairly unceremoniously ripped out. What remains is a shopping arcade and some small Victorian terraces – suitably priced for first-time buyers at around £56,000 to £60,000 each. Further out, the housing is of Sixties vintage: three-bedroom semis at £70,000 to £75,000; four-bedroom detached houses at between £100,000 and £130,000.

FLEET

Journey time: *48 min*	Peak trains: *4 per hour*
Season ticket: *£1824*	Off-peak trains: *2 per hour*

The Army is to **Fleet** what the Air Force is to Farnborough: there is a huge camp here. The train service to London is good, and it is popular with commuters. Another great attraction nearby is Fleet Pond, with 133 acres of freshwater lake, woodland, heath and reedbed, all fiercely protected by the Fleet Pond Society. Fleet itself divides neatly into quarters, each one conveniently date-stamped. If you have a taste for the Twenties, you'll find a good selection of Arts and Crafts houses with three-bedroom semis in the £80,000–£90,000 range. If you prefer the architecture of the Fifties and Sixties, closely packed in leafy roads, then you'll find a range of choice at between £70,000 and £80,000. The other two quarters are modern, built in the last two decades, with many of the three- or four-bedroom houses aimed squarely at that archetypal creature of the Eighties, the yuppy. You could pay £140,000 for four bedrooms; £200,000 for a house with five bedrooms and three or four reception rooms.

WINCHFIELD

Journey time: *53 min*	Peak trains: *4 per hour*
Season ticket: *£1832*	Off-peak trains: *2 per hour*

Around the station there is scarcely a village to speak of. Little more than a mile away, however, is **Hartley Wintney**, practically two centuries removed from Fleet. It has old coaching inns with archways leading into cobbled yards; five village ponds and five village greens with ancient oaks; and the second oldest cricket club in England. The centre is full of antique shops, but there are two butchers (one with a fishmonger and game counter), a bakery and a coffee shop. Social highlights include productions by the local dramatic society, and there are all the usual clubs and societies – WI, Scouts, Brownies and so on. As usual, high prices follow the 17th- and 18th-century architecture. Council houses are tucked out of sight. A classic three- or four-bedroom 18th-century town house in the centre might cost £100,000, but a four-bedroom house with half an acre on the common would be in the range of £200,000. In a small new development on the outskirts, a three-bedroom semi might be had for £80,000–£85,000, but even an ex-council house will fetch up to £70,000.

HOOK

Journey time: *57 min*	Peak trains: *4 per hour*
Season ticket: *£1872*	Off-peak trains: *2 per hour*

Hook is modern-day Commuterland as opposed to Metroland, with hundreds of new houses arranged in estates. The London-bound trains are frequent, and it is very close to Junction 5 of the M3. A four-bedroom detached house will cost between £170,000 and £180,000, rising to £200,000 for one from the up-market builders Charles Church. There is a big helicopter base a couple of miles away at RAF Odiham. Thomas Burberry, of raincoat fame, had a house here called Crossways, the site of which is liberally covered with modern developments.

BASINGSTOKE

Journey time: *47 min*
Season ticket: *£2028**

Peak trains: *5 per hour*
Off-peak trains: *3 per hour*

* Also valid to Paddington via Reading

The station car park is capacious and there is a good selection of fast trains. Some actually start from here; others come through from Bournemouth and Weymouth. Thirty years ago **Basingstoke** was a comparatively sleepy market town with a few local engineering firms and a population of 25,000. Now it is a London overspill town with a population of 90,000 and more than 400 companies, including the AA, Digital, Sony Broadcast and Sun Life of Canada. The shopping centre, refurbished and pedestrianised, has all the usual chain stores. Basingstoke Leisure Park has a 10-screen cinema, 26-lane tenpin bowling rink, swimming pool, championship-size ice rink and golf driving range. The old town is the place for wine bars, pubs and restaurants. It is also the place for two-up-two-down Victorian terraces, priced at around £60,000, and four-bedroom Thirties houses at £120,000–£200,000. In the quiet of Cliddesdon Road, large detached five-bedroom Victorian and Edwardian houses sell for around £170,000. Further out you come to the council estates and more sedate private bungalows: one of these with three bedrooms would cost between £80,000 and £90,000. The modern estates are on the outskirts. North Chineham is one of the most popular ones because it has matured over a decade and has a shopping centre with a Tesco superstore. There are also plans for a new station here. One-bedroom studio flats cost £40,000; three-bedroom semis £70,000; five-bedroom detached houses £190,000. Hatch Warren is very similar, but it is only three years old and not quite so well established.

Watercress beds are a particular feature of the local countryside. Old Basing, Mapledurwell, St Mary Bourne and Whitchurch all have them. One of the best-known villages, only four miles to the south-west, is **Dummer** – a small linear village that found itself besieged by the world's press at the time of Prince Andrew's wedding, being the home of his new parents-in-law. A two-bedroom period cottage will cost at least £90,000 and a larger Georgian pile will cost at least £200,000. It has a permanent gypsy site on the edge.

Very close to Basingstoke's eastern flank is **Old Basing**, where old brick cottages are prettily arranged around the church, the River Lodden, and what remains of Basing House. The house was a glamorous Tudor mansion which became the focus of a two-year siege by the Roundheads during the Civil War and was eventually destroyed. Some of the stone was salvaged and used to build houses in the village. A two-up-two-down period cottage would cost at least £80,000. Two hamlets nearby, **Mapledurwell** and **Upton Grey**, are the stuff of an adman's dream, with Range Rovers carelessly parked outside idyllic thatched cottages. Upton Grey has a duck pond, willow trees and some 17th-century cottages. Prices vary from over £100,000 for a small cottage to £350,000 for a new four-bedroom house.

MAIN LINE FROM BASINGSTOKE TO SALISBURY (see map)

OVERTON

Journey time: *60 min*	Peak trains: *2 per hour*
Season ticket: *£2032*	Off-peak trains: *1 every 2 hours*

Overton used to be rather pretty and had a defined role as a venue for sheep fairs and silk mills. It still retains a certain appeal, though it has become extremely corpulent with new housing estates tugging at its seams. There are some thatched cottages, shops, pubs and restaurants, and a gun shop. A 17th-century, four-bedroom former pub in the centre was priced at around £135,000. Family houses on the new developments cost up to £200,000; large individual houses around £400,000.

WHITCHURCH

Journey time: *65 min*	Peak trains: *2 per hour*
Season ticket: *£2092*	Off-peak trains: *1 every 2 hours*

Whitchurch is another old silk-mill village on the River Test. The mill on Frog Island is now restored and sells extremely expensive silk-lengths. But Whitchurch, too, has grown fleshy with huge council estates and private developments purpose-built for those who made money in the Eighties. At Lynch Hill, for instance, are huge mock-Tudor and mock-Georgian houses selling in the £215,000 to £230,000 bracket. At the lower end of the market are two-bedroom terrace houses at around £62,000, and to the west of the village are densely built four-bedroom houses at around £110,000. On the village doorstep is the wonderful rolling chalk downland that envelops the River Test, the landscape used by Richard Adams in *Watership Down*. An 18th-century brick-and-flint farmhouse in this area would cost around £215,000.

ANDOVER

Journey time: *70 min*	Peak trains: *2 per hour*
Season ticket: *£2204*	Off-peak trains: *1 per hour*

Andover had the stuffing knocked out of it in the Sixties and is now a town of shopping malls and modern housing. Huge new estates were built to accommodate Londoners moving out, many of them – especially in the north and east – council estates. Not even Andover's best friend would call it a cultural oasis, but there is the Cricklade Theatre, and there are drama and music societies. One of the most prominent new shopping centres is the Chantry, which takes up much of the old upper high street. The tapering market place has survived the onslaught, however, and there is a general street market on Thursdays and Saturdays.

In the few Victorian streets that remain, you might buy a three-bedroom terrace for around £56,000. Some of the most popular properties are the Twenties and Thirties houses which sell at around £65,000 for three bedrooms. The west of the town is where the newest housing is to be found. At Weyhill, for example, you could buy a four-bedroom detached family house for £100,000.

The villages in the chalk hills around Andover are some of the loveliest in the country and all those along the Bourne Valley, from Hurstbourne Tarrant down to Longparish, have a definite social cachet. **Hurstbourne Tarrant** sits in the valley bottom with Hurstbourne Hill casting a steep green shadow in the background. Stagecoaches used to change horses here before tackling its merciless incline. William Cobbett visited on his *Rural Rides*, and his initials are on a brick in the garden wall of Rookery Farm where a former owner used to put out plates of food for hungry travellers. To live here now you have to pay through the nose. A two-bedroom period cottage could cost £70,000; a four-bedroom period house £200,000.

St Mary Bourne, south-east of Hurstbourne Tarrant, is along the sparkling chalk River Bourne which is often called the Swift by locals here, especially when it is in full spate. The village is a wonderful muddle of brick-and-flint, oak beams, wattle-and-daub and thatch. It has 15 listed buildings and a lovely Norman church with a black marble font. There is a general store and a very traditional Victorian village school, and in addition to all the usual village societies there are now an aerobics group and a youth club. Some of the local families have lived here for centuries, as an 1842 tithe map has proved. "Our main worry," said the parish clerk, "is that new people moving in want to throw a glass dome over the place and don't want it to change, even though the demands of the village are changing." A two-bedroom thatched cottage will cost around £80,000; a modern four-bedroom house around £200,000.

Longparish, at the lower end of this exclusive corridor, is indeed a very long parish, threading along three and a half miles of winding lane and the meandering River Test. Some of the field walls and the thatched cottages are built of clunch (chalk stone), with some modern estates sandwiched in between. The big flints in the fields are known as "Hampshire diamonds"; the other white specks are sheep. Property prices are similar to those in St Mary Bourne.

Ludgershall, to the north-west, offers housing cheaper than Andover – if you can bear the development going on all around you. A three-bedroom terrace house built in the Twenties will cost around £46,000; a two-bedroom terrace house around £54,000. Further west are **North Tidworth** and **South Tidworth**, both of which offer outstanding value for money. The Army, which has a strong presence in the area, has been shedding staff, with the result that you might pick up a two-bedroom flat for £30,000, or a three-bedroom house for £40,000. **Shipton Bellinger** is very ordinary and again dominated by the Army. Three-bedroom semis fetch around £40,000 to £50,000. Closer to Andover itself is **Penton Mewsey**, where you might buy a four-bedroom period house for £150,000 – £50,000 less than it would fetch in the Bourne Valley.

To the south-west is **Monxton**, with the Pill Hill brook gambolling through it under a small bridge. It is a very compact village with some timber-frame and thatched cottages and a small green, but no shops. It is popular with retired people, but there are also some young families with children at the local playschool. Village barbecues are a regular social event. A small thatched terrace cottage would be likely to cost between £80,000 and £100,000; a four-bedroom modern house £160,000. **Abbotts Ann**, close by, is also pretty though it doesn't have Test or Bourne Valley status. You could buy a thatched cottage with three or four bedrooms for £160,000; a four-bedroom detached modern house for about the same.

Stockbridge, to the south, does however have enormous cachet. It lies in breathtakingly lovely countryside and is a great angling centre for some of the best and most expensive fishing in England along the River Test. The Grosvenor Hotel, with its huge overhanging porch, might as well be an exclusive club for fishermen. The wide main street, edged with Tudor and Georgian houses, belies the village's size for there are very few back streets. Stockbridge Down, a mile away, is dotted with ancient earthworks, and up in the hills are the Iron Age forts of Woolbury Camp and Danebury Ring. A two-bedroom period terrace house with a small garden in Stockbridge will cost £115,000; a more substantial Georgian terrace £150,000 to £160,000. Half a dozen six-bedroom detached houses have recently been added, at prices around £250,000 to £275,000. An oddity close to Stockbridge is **Leckford** – an estate village of tied thatched cottages owned since 1928 by John Lewis. All the properties are occupied by retired former employees of the John Lewis Partnership, and all the gables and woodwork are painted John Lewis green.

GRATELEY

Journey time: *80 min*	Peak trains: *2 per hour*
Season ticket: *£2312*	Off-peak trains: *I every 2 hours*

Grateley proper is an old-fashioned farming village. Many of the old period properties have been in the same families for years and few come on to the market. The range of property is wide, however. You could pay just under £80,000 for a two-bedroom Victorian slate-roofed terrace house; up to around £200,000 for a four-bedroom period house if you were lucky. The Andover side of the village is best. There is a newer area of development around the station, where there are starter homes and council houses. **Over**, **Middle** and **Nether Wallop** are attractive villages with some nice period properties, but surrounded by a sea of post-war council estates. A four-bedroom pink-washed thatched cottage at Over Wallop sold recently for £200,000.

SALISBURY

Journey time: *83 min*	Peak trains: *2 per hour*
Season ticket: *£2508*	Off-peak trains: *I per hour*

The city of **Salisbury** is full of visual treats, architectural nooks and crannies, gabled houses, half-timbering and Chilmark stone. Unlike Winchester, which grew out of medieval clutter, it was built on a grid pattern and so has a greater sense of space and order. At the heart of it is the confluence of the Rivers Avon and Nadder, spanned by time-forgotten medieval bridges. Another remnant of medieval life is the open-air market on Tuesdays and Saturdays. Shops in the city centre tend to be small and specialised, with Sainsbury and Tesco kept out of sight. The Salisbury Playhouse is the main theatrical venue, with the Salberg providing productions on the fringe. The Arts Centre has celebrity lectures and book fairs.

The top of the property pyramid in Salisbury is the Cathedral Close – once home to the novelist Henry Fielding and now to Edward Heath – right beside the river. It is regarded as one of the most beautiful closes in England, dating from the late 18th century when graves were pushed to one side and some remarkable houses built for the city's more important residents. One of them, Mompesson House, is now in the hands of the National Trust. The close is perfectly quiet, shut away behind locked gates at night and as expensive as Chelsea or Westminster. A 10-year lease here will cost £150,000; a freehold could well top £500,000. There are some other good streets near the cathedral, overlooking Queen

Elizabeth Gardens. In this area you might pick up a four-bedroom turn-of-the-century terrace house with a 60ft garden for around £150,000. A short distance away is Fisherton Island, a small group of detached houses built in the Sixties which also command high prices – around £135,000 for four bedrooms. It is also possible to buy into one of the oldest streets in Salisbury, Guilder Street, where an old brick-and-timber cottage with two bedrooms might cost £75,000. Popular schools include the Cathedral School, the Godolphin, Westwood St Thomas comprehensive and Bishop Wordsworth, an old grammar school.

At the lower end of the market are hundreds of turn-of-the-century terraces fronting directly on to the pavements – but beware the terrible parking problem. You might get a two-bedroom terrace house for just over £50,000. But in the gentrified streets – identifiable by the hanging baskets – you could pay up to £70,000, and in St Anne's Street over £80,000. On the city outskirts, areas like Shady Bower offer retirement flats at around £85,000; modern three-bedroom houses at £125,000. For a more villagey feel, look to the leafy lanes of Milford, where four-bedroom detached houses fetch around £150,000.

Outside Salisbury, the Wiltshire chalk downlands and the five valleys of the Avon, Wylye, Nadder, Ebble/Chalke and Bourne, provide the setting for some very attractive, unspoilt villages. Those to the south tend to be more popular. Those to the north are on the edge of Salisbury Plain, where there is a massive military presence and the magic of a country walk might be exploded by a training exercise.

Penetrating quite deeply into the south you come to **Fording-bridge**. This is rather far for regular London commuters, but people's fondness for it is such that it acts as a magnet for the villages between it and Salisbury. Its best asset is the River Avon, crossed by a seven-arched medieval bridge and overlooked by a statue of Augustus John, who once lived here. It has shops good enough to meet day-to-day needs, as well as a bookshop, antique shop and china shop. It is ideally placed for people who like to hack across the New Forest and for anglers with rods on the Avon. Inevitably, it is also popular with retired people. There is a real mix of housing, from the often flimsily built but very sought-after houses of the New Forest, for which you could pay £150,000 for two bedrooms, to huge Twenties set-pieces in 20 acres of ground at £750,000. Pony paddocks are very expensive here. On one of the several modern developments you would pay £65,000 for a three-bedroom detached house; £74,000 for four bedrooms.

Nearby is **Breamore**, a typical Wiltshire brick village. Breamore House, the home of the Hulse family, is an Elizabethan manor overlooking the Avon Valley, open to the public. There is a good choice of period houses, with three-bedroom brick-and-tile cottages at around £145,000 and larger, thatched brick cottages at around £185,000. Villages slightly to the west within this group – **Rockbourne** and **Martin**, for example – are also very rural and pretty, with properties selling at similar prices. Rockbourne shares with Damerham one of the first federated primary schools in the country, sharing teachers and facilities. Its reputation is good.

Closer to Salisbury's southern edge, yet with the advantage of being close to Fordingbridge, is **Downton**, a village that once depended on lace-making, flour-milling and paper-making, and which still has a working tannery. It has an authentically ancient atmosphere, especially in the lovely main street, The Borough, where you would pay over £100,000 for a 16th- or 17th-century house. It is a large village, with a population of around 2,500, so it has better amenities than most, including shops, a medical centre, a couple of banks and a library.

Even closer in beside the city's water meadows is **Britford**, a pretty village of brick cottages and farmhouses on the River Avon. It has a school and a common, but there are no shops and it has to share its vicar with other villages. Residents have a reputation for being rather reclusive and rarefied – particularly those who occupy the large houses on the lower road along the river bank. A good period house with four bedrooms would cost well over £200,000. Nearby are **Odstock** and its neighbours **Nunton** and **Bodenham**, where the social life is rather more robust. People who have moved away find themselves drawn back for the annual fete, to join in the river raft races and dance the night away. Odstock has a school, and a pub popular with doctors from the nearby hospital. Prices are similar to Britford's.

Thatched cottage,
Chalke Valley

The Ebble Valley to the west is also a good hunting ground. **Bowerchalke**, though very much a one-road village, occupies a beautiful position surrounded by the downs, just before the countryside tips over into Dorset. It has a mix of brick-and-flint, cob and grey Chilmark stone, and with some modern houses too. Everyone knows everyone else. There is no pub, but it does have a general store, a playgroup and upholstery classes. There is a trout farm and a small stream running through, and endless walks. Houses here and in the neighbouring village of **Broad Chalke** are usually easy to sell. A 19th-century two-bedroom cottage will fetch £80,000; a modern four-bedroom house in vernacular style £250,000. Broad Chalke is right on the Ebble where it meets the Chalke, and it regards itself as the capital of the Chalke Valley. It lies between two chalk ridges, Here Path and Ox Drove Road, which both provide challenging walks. There is an ancient pub, shops including a butcher who makes his own faggots, and a teashop. The village school is still going strong, and there is a doctor's surgery. One of the most successful of its many clubs and societies is the youth silver band. South Street is particularly pretty because of its thatched cottages. The house that was once Cecil Beaton's is now occupied by Toyah Wilcox.

The town of **Wilton**, three miles west of Salisbury, is spoilt by its position on the A30 and A36, though it has a good market square and some nice old houses. A two-bedroom cottage could be picked up for around £50,000. This is where the Royal Wilton carpets are made. Much of the town is owned by the Pembroke estate. The nearby Wilton House, built by the Earl of Pembroke, is open to the public.

The next spoke in the wheel of valleys around Salisbury is the Wylye Valley. The villages here both retain their sense of rural remoteness and yet have easy access to the city along the A36. **Codford St Mary** and **Codford St Peter** are rather strung out along the road and have plenty of modern houses. A four-bedroom house would cost around £120,000; a three-bedroom Thirties semi around £58,000.

To the north of Salisbury, the Woodford Valley is given particular charm by the River Avon. There is a dearth of smaller cottages, however, so this is not first-timer country. A four-bedroom period family house, possibly with a paddock, is likely to fetch over £200,000. There are people here whose families have lived in the area for centuries; many of the newer arrivals have military connections. **Lower Woodford**, **Middle Woodford** and **Upper Woodford** are all very strung out, so there is no very strong sense of community. There is no shop or post office, though there is a pub, a church and a football team (the cricket team has died out) at Middle Woodford. Heal House, where Charles II sheltered after the Battle of Worcester in 1651, opens its gardens to the public. Lower Woodford also has a pub, beside some old thatched chalk cottages. **Great Durnford** also lies in this exclusive belt and is similarly expensive.

The last spoke of the wheel is the Bourne Valley where the villages are pleasant but unremarkable.

Further north, a couple of miles from Stonehenge is **Amesbury**. This is in the neighbourhood of three army camps – Larkhill, Tidworth and Bulford – and the 4,000 army personnel help keep the first-time-buyer market ticking over. A mass of new developments has sprung up in the last two decades alongside the older brick-and-flint cottages. On the new estates you would pay around £45,000 for a one-bedroom house, £65,000 for a three-bedroom semi, and £110,000 for a four-bedroom house. Older three-bedroom cottages fetch around £75,000. There are a handful of select roads such as Countess, London and especially Ratfyn, where large detached houses built in the early part of this century sell for close to £200,000.

Just to the east of Salisbury is **Laverstock**, which has really been absorbed as a suburb. Large riverside houses appeal to the local bank-manager class, and there are one primary and three secondary schools which have a good reputation. A modern detached house with four bedrooms will cost around £150,000.

MAIN LINE FROM BASINGSTOKE TO SOUTHAMPTON
(see map)

MICHELDEVER

Journey time: *76 min* | Peak trains: *3 per hour*
Season ticket: *£2124* | Off-peak trains: *1 per hour*

The countryside really takes over here. **Micheldever** has a good collection of old thatched cottages arranged haphazardly by the Dever brook and around a triangle of grass, with a seat and a tree on it, known locally as the Crease. Duke Street is perhaps the prettiest for terrace cottages: two bedrooms will cost around £100,000. There is an old-fashioned village school, a store and a pub. The station is a couple of miles from the old village, but has had a whole new community spring up around it. There are Fifties and Sixties estates and bungalows, where a family-sized house could cost £100,000. The area has been earmarked for new town development. The main road at one end of Micheldever does tend to impinge on the rural dream, but most people hear the A33 and M3 only as a low purr on quiet nights.

WINCHESTER

Journey time: *65 min* | Peak trains: *4 per hour*
Season ticket: *£2316* | Off-peak trains: *3 per hour*

Its beautifully simple Norman cathedral, boys' public school and streets lifted straight from Jane Austen give **Winchester** a compelling appeal. Winchester society is a force to be reckoned with. Much of it revolves around a tightly-knit farming set, for whom the sporting weekend is essential. There are several fashionable hunts and shooting estates, and the Houghton Club on the River Test provides some of the best trout fishing in the country. The shopping centre is much as you would expect, rather up-market, with pricey toy shops – the kind that sell hand-made rocking horses – and Jaeger and Laura Ashley, plus an antiques market in King's Walk. There are lots of pubs and restaurants which have kept busy in spite of the recession. Art exhibitions are held at the Guildhall Gallery, the Winchester Gallery and the Heritage Centre; concerts at the Guildhall and in the cathedral. Chesil Theatre and John Stripe Theatre are busy with amateur theatrical productions, while the recently restored Theatre Royal attracts national and international stars and shows newly released films.

Little Minster and Great Minster, right by the cathedral and close to Winchester College, are two of the best addresses in the country outside London. Tourists are the main drawback. Flocking through to see where William the Conqueror claimed his crown, and where King Canute and Jane Austen are buried, they can't help pausing to look at the beautiful 18th-century houses too. Small terrace houses in Cannon and Colebrook Streets are also extremely sought after, though life here can be inconvienced not only by the seriously difficult parking problem but also by film units seeking period backdrops. A tiny flat-fronted terrace house could cost between £85,000 and £110,000; a larger imposing Georgian house £250,000. At the cheaper end of the market, two-bedroom Victorian terrace houses fetch between £73,000 and £75,000, rising to £130,000 for three- to four-bedroom semis. The area down by the water meadows in **St Cross** is popular with young professional families. Here you can buy two-bedroom Victorian terrace houses, or single-bedroom flats in converted houses at around £46,000. Two more areas that are within walking distance of the city centre and are coming up are **Hyde**, where you would have to pay £94,000 for a three-bedroom Victorian terrace, and **Fulflood**, which is slightly cheaper.

Some people prefer the comparative peace of some of the avenues, such as Chilbolton Avenue and Bereweeke Avenue away from the city centre, where a four-bedroom detached house could be bought for £200,000. These houses range from Victorian through to Sixties. Just outside Winchester is a large modern development called Badger Farm. One-bedroom flats cost £45,000; two-bedroom terraces £55,000; small three-bedroom houses £78,000.

The neighbouring villages compete to be the most beautiful and socially spirited. The particularly desirable area to the north-east contains **Itchen Abbas**, a village described by Charles Kingsley in *The Water Babies*. The Pilgrims' Way runs through it, as does the River Itchen. There is no shop, but the village does have a school, the usual local societies and a football pitch used by the Plough Inn team. For cricket you must follow the river down to **Easton**, another pretty village with a mix of thatch and half-timber, Victorian and modern, with the dim drone of the M3 in the distance. **Avington** is also in this select group. Most of its old brick-and-flint cottages are protected within a conservation area. Its flagship is Avington Park, a fine Carolean mansion set in ancient parkland with a lake, which is open to the public. You could expect to pay £110,000 for a two-bedroom thatched cottage in any of these villages.

Alresford attracts day trippers because of the Watercress Line, an eccentric railway which offers a half-hour return journey through Hampshire farmland, chalk cuttings and hills. Antique and curio shops have sprung up as a result. Nevertheless, small two- and three-bedroom Victorian terrace houses around the centre can be bought for under £60,000. To the south is New Alresford, which is so new that many of the houses haven't yet been sold. A four-bedroom detached family house costs £165,000.

To the north-west is **Crawley**, where there are some picturesque thatched cottages by the village duckpond. It has the kind of star quality that earns it regular appearances on scenic calendars. As an old estate village it was planned as a whole, and some of the architecture is flamboyant. You could pay well over £190,000 for a three-bedroom house, and perhaps £220,000 to £260,000 for four bedrooms with half an acre of land. A larger detached house with grounds could reach £500,000.

Sparsholt is rural and convivial, and provides the opportunity of walks from the back door into the 1,000 acres of hills and woodland in Farley Mount Park. The village is particularly proud of its Church-controlled primary school. There is also a village shop and a new hall, funded partly through the efforts of the local community, where country dancing is a regular event. Property prices are similar in most of the villages throughout this area. Due south of Winchester a controversial extension of the M3 is planned to cross Twyford Down and join the M27, but the European Commission has put it on hold for further assessment of its environmental impact.

SHAWFORD

Journey time: *90 min* | **Peak trains:** *2 per hour*
Season ticket: *£2316* | **Off-peak trains:** *1 per hour*

Shawford is bisected by the A33, due to become the M3, so one of the major factors governing prices here is whether or not properties are on the main road. For example, you would pay just over £80,000 for a two-bedroom Victorian or Edwardian terrace away from the main road; 10 per cent less if it's in the traffic zone. Towards Compton there are some huge individual houses, built on large plots, that sell for £250,000 to £500,000.

EASTLEIGH

Journey time: *74 min*	Peak trains: *3 per hour*
Season ticket: *£2400*	Off-peak trains: *3 per hour*

Eastleigh is quite a comedown after Winchester. It was built around the railway and still has a large railway works, though it is now trying to attract new companies and has had a facelift in the form of a new shopping centre. In the early days the distinct social divisions between railway employees were underlined by their choice of address. Drivers and inspectors lived in the north; everyone else in the south. Today the north is still the better side of town, and properties here sell for slightly more. Its basic stock in trade is a mass of late Victorian terrace housing, fronting the pavement, selling at between £47,000 and £55,000 apiece.

Modern development, Chandler's Ford

Bishopstoke and **Fair Oak** were once older villages but they now behave more like comparatively prosperous suburbs of Eastleigh. Bishopstoke has new estates where you might buy a three-bedroom house for less than £65,000, or a four-bedroom detached house with two *en suite* bathrooms and double garage for £130,000. Fair Oak is slightly more up-market, with its old village square still intact.

The stockbroker belt is at **Chandler's Ford**, parts of which consider themselves to be more Winchester than Eastleigh. Much of it is modern. The Hiltingbury area, developed in the Sixties, has three-bedroom semis at between £60,000 and £65,000; three-bedroom detached houses at £75,000; and chalet-style houses at just under £80,000. The Oakmount area followed in the late Sixties and early Seventies, with two-bedroom maisonettes now costing around £42,000 and three-bedroom terraces between £48,000 and £56,000. A lot of them are very close to the A33. In the Eighties came Valley Park. You could buy a five-bedroom house for £150,000 here, though you might think they were rather tightly packed. The expensive side of Chandler's Ford is Hocombe, built in the Thirties when little heed was paid to land values. Large four-bedroom houses with spacious sitting and dining rooms spread themselves over large gardens, and change hands at £200,000 to £250,000. This is where the IBM executives from Hursley tend to congregate. Also on the northern side are two good comprehensive schools, Toynbee and Thornden, which themselves are an attraction to the area.

SOUTHAMPTON PARKWAY

Journey time: _60 min_	**Peak trains: _3 per hour_**
Season ticket: £2600	**Off-peak trains: _2 per hour_**

This station is really here for the convenience of Southampton airport. The train service as a result is fast and frequent, but the station car park is rather expensive. Many of the houses are close to the railway line. A three-bedroom Victorian terrace would cost between £48,000 and £55,000.

SWAYTHLING

Journey time: _68 min*/101 min†_	**Peak trains: _1 per hour_**
Season ticket: £2600	**Off-peak trains: _1 per hour_**

* **Change at Southampton Parkway**   † **Through train**

Swaythling is an area of Victorian terraces with prices lower than those in Eastleigh. A two-bedroom house might cost £45,000. Many workers from the nearby Ford factory have their homes here, and students from Southampton University are a strong presence in the rental market.

ST DENYS

Journey time: _72 min*/104 min†_	**Peak trains: _1 per hour_**
Season ticket: £2600	**Off-peak trains: _1 per hour_**

* **Change at Southampton Parkway**   † **Through train**

This is one of the older parts of Southampton, and a happy hunting ground for first-time buyers. Turn-of-the-century terraces and semis sell for between £40,000 and £50,000.

Branchline to Hamble via Bitterne, Woolston, Sholing and Netley

No through trains. Trains to St Denys/Southampton: 1 per hour
Journey time: 125 min (from Hamble)
Season ticket from Hamble: £2600

Bitterne, **Woolston** and **Sholing** float on the skyline like a sea of chimney pots. This is probably the cheapest part of Southampton, composed mainly of turn-of-the-century terraces but with some Thirties housing stitched in too. It lies on the east side of the Itchen River, crossed by a tollbridge which can seem a bit of a bother. A three-bedroom terrace would cost around £46,000; a three-bedroom Thirties house about £50,000, possibly with good views thrown in. Houses backing on to the river cost rather more. They might once have set you back up to £90,000, but the recession has pulled them back closer to £60,000.

Netley is given a certain status by its pebbly shoreline on Southampton Water. It leads to the Royal Victoria Country Park – a marvellous place for picnics, and a vantage point for watching the ferries and tankers chugging across to the Fawley oil refinery on the other side of Southampton Water. Netley also has the remains of the Royal Victoria Hospital, where Florence Nightingale nursed casualties from the Crimea. Large four-bedroom family houses, built in the early Eighties in three-quarters of an acre, might cost around £170,000. A small, two-bedroom terrace house would fetch around £52,000. Part of the old military hospital has been converted into flats, at around £150,000 for two or three bedrooms.

Hamble (together with the village of Warsash on the other side of the Hamble River) was used as the setting for the television series *Howard's Way*. It is one of the most concentrated yachting centres in the country, positively bristling with marinas and boats for hire. It is very smart, though in spite of all the visible wealth it still retains the atmosphere of a village. There is a green and a church, and a huge common that leads down to the water. It was a working fishing village until 1914. Some pioneering aviation work was also carried out here, and in World War Two the Americans used it as a base to prepare for the D-Day landings. Property prices can break the £500,000 barrier, but you could find an ordinary three-bedroom semi for around £72,000.

SOUTHAMPTON

Journey time: *68 min* | **Peak trains:** *3 per hour*
Season ticket: *£2600* | **Off-peak trains:** *2 per hour*

Southampton is a busy modern city that has managed to attract some sizeable companies to relocate. Price Waterhouse and Skandia Life are here already, and Meridian Television and the Department of Transport's Marine Directorate are due in 1993. Its increasingly aggressive commercial face, excellent shopping centres and proximity to the sea and the New Forest are all major assets. It can also offer five museums, four cinemas, nightclubs and discos, an art gallery, the Mayflower Theatre, the Gantry arts centre, and Southampton University, which has its own gallery, theatre and concert hall. The Dell is the home of Southampton Football Club; there is first class cricket at the Hampshire county ground and races at Goodwood. Participation sports include golf (four courses in the area), plenty of tennis (especially now the new Europa Tennis Centre has opened), athletics (there is a floodlit synthetic track), and swimming (an international standard pool). There is also a choice of health and fitness clubs. Southampton airport provides flying lessons for those with strong stomachs and the money to match. But the principal leisure activity is still probably sailing. There are clubs, moorings and dinghy schools all around the coast here.

The biggest new development locally is **Ocean Village**, a mixture of docklands architecture, frivolous shopping, bars and restaurants – the Port Grimaud of southern England, where a lot of the early property buyers turned out to be interested in investment only. A two-bedroom apartment with a berth for the boat costs £80,000 to £90,000; a town house might cost £140,000 to £145,000, rising towards £175,000 if it has a berth.

Old Southampton is also thought to be rather special. The old town stretches from Bargate in the north to Town Quay in the south – a good vantage point from which to watch the *QE2* or *Canberra* sail into port. The old medieval town wall is another reminder of the city's long maritime history. One of the most popular old/new developments is a listed warehouse which has been converted into luxury apartments overlooking the old pier. The price is around £175,000 for four bedrooms. There is a restaurant on the ground floor. Inner Avenue is one of the best places to look for older town houses. A two- or three-bedroom house within walking distance of the city centre would cost between £50,000 and £60,000. For cheaper housing you could look at Shirley, where a two-bedroom turn-of-the-century terrace would fetch just over £40,000.

Further out from the town centre is **Bassett**. This has become rather chic because of its proximity to Southampton Common, the university and two good schools – the King Edward VI independent school for boys (girls admitted to the sixth form), and Atherley independent school for girls. A three-bedroom Thirties semi here might cost £75,000; a three-bedroom detached house around £100,000. There are some larger, rather distinctive, four-bedroom houses which sell for up to £130,000.

North of Southampton is **Chilworth**, which is considered irredeemably smart. Wealthy businessmen are attracted to the individually built large houses with anything from half an acre to two acres of ground. Smaller three- or four-bedroom houses start at around £180,000, with prices rising inexorably towards the £400,000 mark as you enter the mini-mansion market.

Line to Romsey and Mottisfont Dunbridge (see map)

No through trains. Trains to Southampton: 3 every 2 hours (Romsey); 1 every 2 hours (Mottisfont Dunbridge)
Journey time: 110 min (from Mottisfont Dunbridge)
Season ticket (both stations): £2608

Romsey scores high marks for quality of life. It is a classic English market town with a strong agricultural base, and a general market is still held once a week in the market square (overlooked by the statue of Lord Palmerston). The silent simplicity of the abbey, which is essentially Norman, gives the centre of the town a tremendous architectural and spiritual uplift. It has a lavish leisure centre and small specialist shops, with Southampton near enough for major purchases. It also has its own newspaper and a local theatre, The Plaza, bought by the amateur dramatic society and used by the Romsey Art Group. In the centre of town a restored two-bedroom Victorian terrace house would cost around £65,000. The small farms and older country houses dotted along the Test Valley start at over £100,000 and run up into hundreds of thousands. Broadlands, once the home of Lord Mountbatten and now occupied by his grandson Lord Romsey, is nearby. Some commuters prefer to drive to Winchester and pick up a train for London from there.

Michelmersh, where David Frost has a house, is a rather sought-after village which spreads itself out through the lanes like the fingers of a hand. Part of it is a designated conservation area. Its exclusivity is guaranteed by some of the country's best – and most expensive – trout fishing on the Test nearby. It also contains a brickworks that still produces hand-made bricks. You could buy a four-bedroom house for around £170,000, but prices vary enormously depending on position and age.

Mottisfont is another of the area's wonderful surprises. Few people who move here will ever move again. You will need at least £200,000 to be in the market for a four-bedroom period house. The post office is known for its superior cream teas, and is a stop-off point for ramblers on a trail that runs from Totton, close to Southampton, along the chalk downs to Inkpen Beacon. Mottisfont Abbey, with its gardens of old-fashioned roses beside the River Test, belongs to the National Trust.

LINE TO BROCKENHURST (see map)

Millbrook, Redbridge, Totton, Lyndhurst Road, Beaulieu Road

All these have 1 off-peak train per hour, change at Southampton. Totton and Lyndhurst Road also have an occasional peak service to Waterloo.

New Forest Thirties-style house

At **Millbrook** you are still in the Southampton suburbs, where late 19th-century terrace houses can be picked up for around £42,000. By **Redbridge** you are hitting the new modern estates, where a one-bedroom flat might cost around £36,000 and a two- to three-bedroom semi around £56,000. **Totton** likewise is part of the Southampton sprawl, being joined to the city by a causeway across the River Test. It offers a wide variety of new estates, with four-bedroom, double-garaged detached houses priced at over £100,000. The Woodlands side of Totton, which faces on to the New Forest, is distinctly more up-market. Here you could pay £150,000 for a three-bedroom house with a paddock; £155,000 for a modern bungalow with two double-bedrooms.

Lyndhurst Road station is actually at Ashurst, for this is the closest to **Lyndhurst** that the powerful local landowners would allow the railway to come. Lyndhurst, known as the "capital" of the New Forest, is exquisitely pretty but handicapped in summer by its tourist appeal. Its one-way system clogs up with traffic. People come to visit the church, with its stained glass by William Morris and Burne-Jones, and to admire Swan Green with its cordon of thatched cottages. The Forestry Commission has its headquarters here in the Queen's House, a former royal hunting lodge. It has proper shops, including a butcher who makes his own venison sausages, and a fruit and veg shop that does home deliveries.

Property prices in the New Forest are high, despite the fact that the scarcity of building materials means that the quality of the older houses is often rather poor. Prices start at around £200,000 and rise pretty effortlessly to the £400,000 mark. A new development in the centre provides cheaper property, with three-bedroom detached houses at around £85,000 and four-bedroom versions around £110,000. The New Forest Butterfly Farm, set in 2,000 acres of woodland, is nearby.

At **Beaulieu Road** you come to a rather isolated part of this ancient bog-and-bracken landscape, where there is little more than a handful of cottages and a hotel. This is where the New Forest ponies are sometimes rounded up and sold.

BROCKENHURST

Journey time: *83 min*	**Peak trains:** *3 per hour*
Season ticket: *£2784*	**Off-peak trains:** *2 per hour*

Brockenhurst is blessed because it receives the fast trains from Weymouth. They stop here, then at Southampton and Southampton Parkway, then go non-stop to Waterloo. This is a pretty, vibrant village with some gracious old houses set in half an acre or so, for which you might pay £350,000; and some new estates within walking distance of the centre where you could pay £150,000 for four bedrooms. Brockenhurst teems with tourists in the summer: the nearby Beaulieu Motor Museum is a great attraction. **Beaulieu**, four miles east, is the most exclusive village in the area, where people compete for invitations to Lord Montagu's drinks parties. A three-bedroom thatched cottage costs at least £200,000; a six-bedroom house with a couple of acres on the Beaulieu River, fit for the occasional stray pop star, sells for around £1.5m. The whole of this area is very close to the sea, and in particular to **Lymington** – an extremely expensive but rather quaint yachtsman's playground. A former shipbuilder's cottage with a glimpse of the water and three bedrooms will cost £150,000 here. A fast shuttle train links it to Brockenhurst.

WATERLOO — TO — PORTSMOUTH

WORPLESDON

Journey time: *50 min* | Peak trains: *4 per hour*
Season ticket: *£1564* | Off-peak trains: *1 per hour*

Worplesdon, sandwiched between Woking and Guildford, is a main-road village with the A322 cutting straight through it. The station is at least a mile from the centre but is close to some rather nice private roads running off Goose Rye Road. Large Twenties and Thirties detached houses here sell for £250,000 upwards. A four- or five-bedroom gabled and dormered house with a detached granny-annexe will fetch around £450,000.

    Sutton Green, a mile south-east of the station, is semi-rural, with Sutton Place, one of the finest Tudor houses in the country, once the home of Paul Getty. A two-up-two-down turn-of-the-century cottage will cost around £80,000; a four-bedroom detached house of the same period will be over £200,000.

GUILDFORD

Journey time: *30 min* | Peak trains: *5 per hour*
Season ticket: *£1704* | Off-peak trains: *2 per hour*

See also line via London Road (Guildford), page 243.

Even though it is so close to London, **Guildford** offers rich pickings for shoppers and culture vultures alike. The steep, cobbled, pedestrianised high street has a wide variety of boutiques and specialist shops, and the Friary shopping mall has all the major chainstores. Its top floor is a kind of global restaurant selling foods from all over the world. Architectural highlights include the 1683 Guildhall with its famous projecting clock, and one of the country's few modern cathedrals, designed by Sir Edward Maufe with a very plain interior. The Yvonne Arnaud Theatre has a very good reputation and attracts London-bound shows on their way to the West End. The Guildford Harmonic Orchestra is also widely respected. For those in search of more vigorous pursuits, the sports centre offers a competition-size swimming pool with water chute, health and fitness studio, squash, judo, football, cricket and so on.

    It is possible to live right in the centre of the town. A one-bedroom flat over the high street shops will cost around £50,000; a purpose-built, three-bedroom, two-bathroom flat just off the high street around

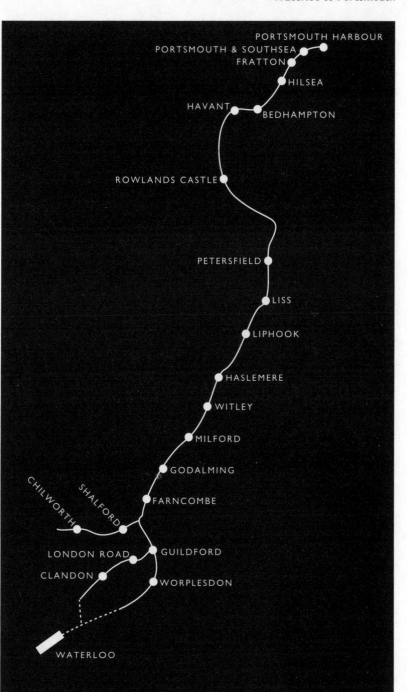

£120,000. There are some streets of old houses around Guildford Museum and the remains of the 12th-century castle at the bottom of the high street. Most have been converted to business use, but the occasional three-bedroom terrace comes up for around £70,000.

Small modern estate house,
Guildford area

On the north side of town, in the **Woodbridge Hill** area, are the typical bay-fronted, net-curtained, respectable mind-your-own-business streets of provincial England. The houses are solid, with good-sized rooms, but – even though it is convenient for the hospital, the cathedral and the university – nobody rushes to live here. A three-bedroom detached house will cost around £90,000; a three-bedroom semi £75,000 to £85,000. Cornhill Insurance has its headquarters here. Much more popular is **Fairlands**, where housing of the Sixties and Seventies has bedded down and matured nicely, and where a good community spirit has evolved around the school, the doctor's surgery and so on. It even has its own free newspaper, *The Fairlands News*, and residents are trying to upgrade the name of the place to Fairlands Village. It is a good place to look for a bungalow: three bedrooms for £100,000. A three-bedroom semi-detached house will cost only slightly more.

On the north-eastern fringe is **Burpham** – no longer a village but a sea of modern houses, designed with enough breathing space to make them palatable. There are three developments – Weybrook Park, Weyley Farm and Merrow Park. A tiny studio costs just under £40,000; a three-bedroom semi £85,000 to £90,000; a large four- or five-bedroom house between £170,000 and £200,000. There are also some large early 20th-century houses with five bedrooms and four reception rooms that sell in the range of £230,000–£300,000. Nearby **Merrow** is now also a suburb of Guildford. It has a golf course and leafy private roads where houses built in the Thirties now have the occasional bungalow wedged between them. Both bungalows and houses, with four to five bedrooms, tend to sell in the £250,000 range.

The south of the town is particularly well-heeled, and attracts successful local professionals. In White Lane are some large houses, built in the Twenties and later, with big gardens and views across to the North Downs. The likely price for one of these would be in the region of £400,000. Further to the south-west is Loseley Park, an Elizabethan country house which is open to the public and whose farm produces the well-known dairy products that bear the Loseley name.

A very popular village to the south-east is Cranleigh (see under Ockley, page 275). Closer to Guildford's southern flank is **Bramley** – well liked and rather expensive. Its exclusivity is well expressed by the presence of a busy Ferrari dealer and well-subscribed golf club. Another attraction is the girls' private school, St Catherine's, which is the sister school to Cranleigh School for boys. A three-bedroom semi here will cost £95,000. A four-bedroom detached with a large garden and driveway could cost £320,000.

To the west of Guildford is **Wood Street**, a large linear village surrounded by farmland, with a large village green, a church and a post office. The council housing is discreetly tucked away and there is quite a lot of property built between the Thirties and the Sixties. For £95,000 you might pick up a three-bedroom Edwardian semi, or a more modern three-bedroom detached house with a large garden backing on to fields.

North Downs Line east to Shalford and Chilworth

No through trains. Trains to Guildford: *1 every 3 hours*

Shalford is a one-street village of period houses and cottages with a green. Two-bedroom Victorian terrace houses start at £75,000; five- or six-bedroom houses can cost £200,000 or more. Shalford Mill, an 18th-century tile-hung watermill on the River Tillingbourne, is now in the hands of the National Trust.

Chilworth spreads itself rather uneasily along the A248, a bland mix of houses and bungalows built in the Thirties and Fifties. Cars tend to park along both sides of the road as few of the houses have garages. Chilworth has its own primary and middle school, and an old gunpowder factory on the banks of the Tillingbourne. A three-bedroom Thirties semi will cost £115,000 at the better end of the village; £80,000 at the other.

FARNCOMBE

Journey time: *43 min*

Season ticket: *£1748*

Peak trains: *3 per hour*

Off-peak trains: *2 per hour*

Farncombe is the poor man's Godalming (see below), of which it is really now a suburb. It does have its own recognisable centre, however, graced by the presence opposite the playing field of 10 early 17th-century red-brick almshouses, still administered by the Worshipful Company of Carpenters. A four-bedroom Victorian terrace house in Farncombe will sell for around £130,000; a Twenties detached three-bedroom house for just under £100,000; a modern two-bedroom terrace for £70,000 or slightly less.

GODALMING

Journey time: *45 min*

Season ticket: *£1764*

Peak trains: *4 per hour*

Off-peak trains: *2 per hour*

Forever prosperous, **Godalming** thrived first on the wool trade, then as a coaching stop on the London to Portsmouth road, and since the 1870s as the home of Charterhouse, the private school for boys and girls. The high street contains a wonderful collection of 16th-, 17th- and 18th-century buildings, and in the centre is The Pepperpot, a distinctive colonnaded building with a clock tower, which houses a local history collection. Godalming was further distinguished by being the first town to replace gas street lighting with electric. Its shopping is typically small-town, with one or two specialist shops and a Sainsbury on the edge. There are good walks along the River Wey and Godalming Navigations, complete with locks and weirs that run from Godalming Wharf to the Thames at Weybridge.

The two most fashionable areas of Godalming are **Busbridge** and **Charterhouse**. Busbridge has quiet leafy streets lined with properties spanning every period from Victorian to the Thirties. Most of the houses here, regardless of age, sell in the range of £115,000 to £120,000, though you could pay up to £350,000 for a large house with half a dozen bedrooms and a capacious garden. Charterhouse is similar, though the houses tend to be larger. Mark Way is a private road where some of the older houses were built in such enormous acreages that strips of garden were sold off for building plots in the Fifties. A four- or five-bedroom house set in a third of an acre will cost at least £250,000. At the lower end of the market are some two-bedroom terraces on small modern developments that sell for around £80,000.

The nearby village of **Dunsfold** is lovely if you can afford it. The houses, some of them dating from the 15th and 16th centuries, are gathered around an open common, with the church picturesquely set apart on a mound next to a 1,000-year-old yew tree. Even a tiny two-bedroom period farmworker's cottage here will fetch £120,000 to £130,000. Larger houses go for up to £1m.

MILFORD

Journey time: *48 min*	Peak trains: *3 per hour*
Season ticket: *£1800*	Off-peak trains: *I per hour*

Milford has been rather carved up by main roads (including the A3), but there are compensations in the pretty rambling-and-riding countryside that surrounds it. The village sprawls around the shops and church, and provides a broad range of properties. You might pay just under £70,000 for a two- or three-bedroom ex-council house; £80,000 for a modern three-bedroom semi; £90,000 for a Thirties semi; £250,000 to £275,000 for a four- to five-bedroom Victorian or Edwardian family home.

Elstead, three miles to the west, is more rural, with some bracken-covered Surrey commons within walking distance. Sir Edwin Lutyens spent the early part of his career working in the area, which contains a large number of his houses – there is a borough car trail to 24 of them. Elstead itself has one good example – Fulbrook, built in 1896. The village also has a pretty watermill, the only survivor from six, plus a green and a couple of pubs. A one-bedroom flat in a converted Edwardian house will cost just over £50,000; a Victorian two-up-two-down terrace just over £70,000; a Thirties semi £85,000. A large detached house, built in the early part of this century and backing onto the commons, will cost £200,000 upwards.

WITLEY

Journey time: *52 min*	Peak trains: *3 per hour*
Season ticket: *£1828*	Off-peak trains: *I per hour*

Witley is spread out over several miles, with housing estates from the various 20th-century building booms linking arms around the half-timbered and tile cottages of the old village centre. You would pay anything from £70,000 for a two-bedroom terrace up to £250,000 or £300,000 for an early 20th-century detached house with five bedrooms. Witley Common, 500 acres of National Trust land, is a great local asset.

The station, however, is a mile to the south at **Wormley**. It is a quiet residential area where a detached house built in the Twenties, shielded from the road by a bank of trees and a long driveway, is likely to cost between £150,000 and £250,000. The National Institute of Oceanography is here; so, on a hilltop eminence, is King Edward's private school for boys and girls.

Hambledon, a mile to the east, is a more conventional village. It lies in a hollow surrounded by hills and woods, with good views of the Hog's Back. The village has a pretty green with a cricket pavilion and duckpond.

The annual fete is held here and usually has a fancy-dress theme – Alice in Wonderland, for example. Just off the green, one of the oldest houses, Oakhurst Cottage, is kept by the National Trust as a 17th-century museum. Facilities otherwise are fairly minimal. The village school is now a nursery, the shop has closed down and so has the WI. Houses rarely come on the market here, and the tiniest of cottages would be likely to fetch £100,000. A 17th-century Grade II listed house with three bedrooms set in half an acre might cost £275,000; grander houses would fetch £350,000–£500,000.

Chiddingfold, two miles south of Witley station, is also tailored to the traditional image of a perfect English village. The green in the centre hosts a massive and spectacular Bonfire Night party every November with 400 torchbearers. It is overlooked by the oldest pub in Surrey, the Crown Inn, and by an 11th-century church. Other events on the green include an annual festival and vintage-car rally. Shops include a newsagent, chemist, greengrocer and delicatessen that also sells bread. Outside the general store is an ancient thorn tree, supposedly 1,000 years old, which is now held together with hoops. The wealth of the village was built on glass-making: in the reign of Elizabeth I there were around a dozen glassworks on the green, the profitability of which can be seen in the lovely half-timbered houses of the same period. The church is notable both for its Chiddingfold glass windows, and for the huge collection of lichens in the churchyard which attracts botany students from all over the country. The large 16th- and 17th-century houses on the green would sell for £200,000 upwards if they ever came on the market. There are a couple of small modern developments where you might buy a four-bedroom modern detached house for £150,000.

HASLEMERE

Journey time: *44 min*	**Peak trains:** *5 per hour*
Season ticket: *£1912*	**Off-peak trains:** *2 per hour*

Repossessions have hardly been heard of in **Haslemere**. This is rich commuter territory, surrounded by National Trust land and with a pretty high street stiff with half-timbered 16th-century buildings. The shops are intimate and intriguing. One of the town's best-known features is the Dolmetsch Workshops, founded by the Swiss Arnold Dolmetsch, who helped revive an interest in early musical instruments including the recorder. Replicas are still made, and the public can visit the workshops by appointment. There is a festival of early music every July. Another attraction is the Haslemere Educational Museum, which contains displays of British birds, geology, zoology, local history and so on.

There are very few houses in the centre. In Lower Street you might find an artisan's Victorian two-bedroom cottage for just over £60,000.

Or in Petworth Road you might get a large detached Victorian house with walled gardens for £500,000. There are the ubiquitous Thirties semis too spreading outwards from the centre, selling for £150,000 and upwards depending on the street.

A lovely address to aspire to is Lord Tennyson Lane, named for the poet who lived here. The huge Victorian and Edwardian mansions have large grounds with views of Blackdown Hill (National Trust), and are within 15 minutes' walk of the centre. The larger ones sell for well over £1m, though some of the smaller interlopers, slipped on to remnants of garden, might be had for £200,000. Scotlands Lane is similar, though the houses are later (Twenties and Thirties) and the road itself is not so quiet.

On the Wey Hill side of town you find the Victorian terraces, with banks and building societies, small supermarkets and chip shops conveniently to hand. A two-bedroom terrace house here will sell for just over £60,000. There is some new development too. On the Deepdene estate you might buy a two-bedroom terrace for just over £60,000; a three-bedroom semi for just over £90,000; a four-bedroom detached house with a garage for £150,000.

Just to the north of Haslemere is the 900ft Gibbet Hill which, if you are up to the climb, gives lofty views over the Weald and the South Downs. Just to the west is the open heathland of Frensham Common with Frensham Great and Little Ponds. Both have sandy beaches and were created in the 13th century to supply fish to, among others, the Bishop of Winchester. Between these two beauty spots lies **Hindhead**, which was once rather fashionable – both Sir Arthur Conan Doyle and George Bernard Shaw lived here – but which has had its nose put out of joint by the A3 and accompanying Happy Eater. There are still some huge houses that sit snugly behind their shields of greenery, but there's little point considering them unless you have upwards of £400,000 to spend. Hindhead Common, 1,100 acres of heath and woodland, is a major local attraction.

Though it has a proper little shopping centre, **Grayshott** is still at heart a village where those who can afford it retire for peace and quiet. A two-bedroom Victorian house will cost £65,000 to £75,000; a large Thirties-built house with several acres of land and a pony paddock could fetch £350,000. **Grayswood** nearby is less exclusive. There are plenty of Twenties and Thirties detached houses priced from £100,000 for three bedrooms; and three-bedroom Victorian cottages for just over £70,000.

Seven miles south, beyond the Blackdown Hill, is **Midhurst** – a market town on the River Rother whose attractions include the Cowdray Park polo ground. It is in many respects a rather plain town, but at least the shops have not been completely homogenised and there are some very attractive houses. Next to the church, for example, is a Queen Anne terrace with likely price tags close to £300,000. The parklands of some of the largest houses in the town – Heatherwood, Elmleigh, Guillards Oak and Heathfield Park – have been developed as small housing estates. The average price for a four-bedroom detached house (of which there is a great number) is £150,000. Heathfield Park also has some pseudo-Georgian three-bedroom terraces, priced at around £115,000. Another good area is Close Walks Wood. A dozen or so houses have encroached into the woodland and would fetch around £400,000 for four bedrooms. Elsewhere in the town you could find an ordinary three-bedroom turn-of-the-century terrace for around £70,000.

LIPHOOK

Journey time: **58 min**	Peak trains: **3 per hour**
Season ticket: **£1924**	Off-peak trains: **2 per hour**

The Surrey/Hampshire boundary looms large in people's minds because there is intense rivalry between the two counties. **Liphook** is very Hampshire. It is cheaper than Haslemere because it is further south, and it doesn't have the same character. It badly needs the planned bypass to relieve it of the A3. The Square, where six roads converge, is a designated conservation area dominated by the 17th-century Royal Anchor Hotel. Otherwise there is quite a lot of post-war development. Loseley Park, built roughly a decade ago, is a network of terraces and small developments of detached houses. A three-bedroom semi will cost £75,000; a four-bedroom detached £135,000. Victorian three-bedroom semis in Liphook fetch between £80,000 and £90,000.

LISS

Journey time: **65 min**	Peak trains: **3 per hour**
Season ticket: **£1988**	Off-peak trains: **2 per hour**

Liss is sliced in two by the railway and River Rother. It is very mixed and not greatly sought after, though it does provide a good range of houses. One-bedroom modern flats start at £40,000; two-bedroom Victorian terraces cost £60,000; three-bedroom modern detached houses £120,000. There are some large Victorian properties at Liss Forest, which is an extension of the village, where a four-bedroom house will cost £130,000. On the outskirts, a four- or five-bedroom period house with a few acres can fetch as much as £345,000.

Four miles north-west is **Selbourne** – an idyllically pretty village slightly handicapped by a main street too narrow for the volume of traffic. The Wakes, the home of the naturalist Gilbert White, is an attraction to tourists, as are the beech hanger and meadows (now owned by the National Trust) which he described in his classic book *Natural History and Antiquities of Selbourne*. The high street is lined with picturesque brick-

and-flint cottages, some thatched, some early Victorian. A small late 19th-century stone cottage here will sell for around £85,000. A larger four-bedroom cottage on the hillside, with large grounds and lovely views, could fetch £275,000. There is a small amount of modern housing. The price for four bedrooms and a double garage is around £160,000.

PETERSFIELD

Journey time: *56 min*
Season ticket: *£2056*

Peak trains: *3 per hour*
Off-peak trains: *2 per hour*

The countryside to the west of **Petersfield** is a designated Area of Outstanding Natural Beauty which is often referred to as Little Switzerland or the Hampshire Alps. A line of hangers, or hanging beechwoods, follows a meandering escarpment from Binstead, just to the west of Alton, down to Petersfield where it connects with the South Downs and rises to a 900ft peak at Butser Hill. Butser is within the Queen Elizabeth Country Park, four miles south of the town, which is the place for picnics, pony rides and even grass skiing.

Fifties detached house,
Petersfield

With this remarkable landscape to hand, and with Winchester and Chichester only half an hour by car, it is not surprising that Petersfield is a very desirable, and hence expensive, place to live. (Beyond Butser Hill to the south, property prices drop rapidly as you move outside commuting range.) Petersfield owed its initial prosperity to wool, leather, and its usefulness as a coaching stop on the road to Portsmouth. Its charm comes from the grouping of ancient buildings around The Square, a former market place. Running off it is Sheep Street, lined with 16th- and 17th-century houses. A small two-bedroom house here would cost around £80,000. The Spain is a kind of unexplained opening in the original street plan, now containing some good Georgian houses. Petersfield was once a predominantly agricultural town, but is now popular with retired couples as well as with commuters to London and Portsmouth. The proximity of the HMS *Mercury* Royal Naval station near Clanfield means there is a naval presence too.

Just a short walk from the high street is a pond and 69 acres of heath. Here there are boats for hire, a cricket pitch and golf course, as well as lonelier spots where you come across Bronze Age burial mounds. The Heath every October is the scene of the Taro Fair – once a horse fair but now a thing of roundabouts and stalls. The best addresses in town are on The Heath. Imposing Victorian or Edwardian detached houses, with possibly eight bedrooms, several reception rooms and a billiards room, sell for between £350,000 and £500,000. Typical residents are successful local solicitors and retired naval officers.

On the outskirts are some substantial houses built in the Twenties. Four bedrooms could cost as much as £380,000. A few major new developments have appeared during the past two decades. Herne Farm is still under construction and offers everything from one-bedroom flats at £40,000 to five-bedroom detached houses at £200,000. The Village, built in the centre of the town, is of "olde worlde" design and colourfully painted. A two-bedroom house here costs just under £80,000; four bedrooms around £200,000. Stoneham Park, built in the Seventies, has two-bedroom houses at under £60,000; four bedrooms at £120,000. The Gallifords is slightly cheaper.

Surrounding Petersfield are some beautiful villages. Two miles north is **Steep**, a trickle of houses across a hillside which they share with the co-educational private school Bedales. There are dramatic views of the beechwoods, to which you can walk by taking a route across the common, past the children's primary school and up into the hangers. There is one village store-cum-post office. Two notable features of village life are the New Year's Day soup-and-cheese lunch, to which everyone is invited, and the social events at Bedales, which include concerts and talks. There is also an art gallery open to the public. You could buy a small period cottage in Steep for around £70,000; a three-bedroom Victorian semi for £100,000; a four- or five-bedroom detached Victorian house for up to £180,000. A one-off five-bedroom detached modern house with an acre of garden might cost £295,000. Villagers are hoping that the new Petersfield bypass won't come within earshot.

Sheet, one mile north-east of Petersfield, exudes an historic charm. An ancient horse chestnut tree stands on the village green close to the Queen's Head pub, with the church and a terrace of old cottages nearby. Two former mills set off some of the larger houses very nicely. Sheet has its own post office and a well-patronised shop, plus a large primary school which also serves the extensive Thirties housing estate on the other side of the A3. A two-bedroom period cottage will cost around £70,000; a three-bedroom Thirties detached bungalow £120,000 to £130,000. A four-bedroom Georgian house might come on the market at around £220,000.

To the south-east of Petersfield is **South Harting**, recognisable from a distance for its octagonal copper church spire seen against the backdrop of Linch Down. The main street, running uphill to the church, has thatched and timber-framed cottages, a village store, hairdresser, post office and art shop. A half-timbered cottage in South Harting will cost just over £80,000; a three-storey Georgian house with four bedrooms around £205,000. The village hall is the meeting place for all the local clubs and societies, including WI, the Harting Society and a four-days-a-week playschool. There is football and cricket on the recreation ground. Uppark, the National Trust house being restored after a fire, is a mile away up the hill.

To the west is **West Meon**, which suffers from traffic on the A32, and its sister village **East Meon**, both lying in the shadow of the Downs. West Meon has a primary school, a post office-cum-store and a police station, plus all the usual clubs and societies. A 16th-century four-bedroom thatched cottage in need of modernisation might cost a little under £180,000; a Seventies-built three-bedroom semi around £85,000. East Meon is the prettier of the two, with the River Meon flowing beneath a sequence of little bridges. There are one or two 14th-century houses, plus some Tudor and Georgian. A four-bedroom Georgian house with two or three reception rooms would be likely to cost over £200,000; a modern four-bedroom detached house with a garage and flint-walled garden would be a little less.

ROWLANDS CASTLE

Journey time: *85 min*	**Peak trains:** *3 per hour*
Season ticket: *£2168*	**Off-peak trains:** *1 per hour*

Rowlands Castle has all the appearances of a traditional English village – a crescent of green at the centre, flanked by terrace cottages, Georgian and Victorian houses. A large country house, Deerleap, stands behind a flint wall opposite, and has in its grounds the remains of the castle which gave the village its name. The whole place is stiff with money. "This is a village for IBM executive types, where you need a really new Volvo estate and a headscarf to pick up the children from school," is how one local observer put it. There is a long waiting-list of people eager to pay the not inconsiderable fee to join the golf club. The village has its own primary school, a few shops, football and cricket pitches, and a tennis club with courts open to the public. Huge detached houses built in the Twenties and

Thirties with an acre of garden, sell for around £300,000 in Links Lane, which is the smartest address. Bowes Hill is also smart, with four- and five-bedroom houses of the same period priced between £150,000 and £200,000. Nearby is Ditcham Park, the private school for boys and girls, which has a liberal tradition but is not as fashionable as Bedales. Rowlands Castle is strung between the ancient Forest of Bere and Stansted Park, the family seat of the Earl and Countess of Bessborough which is open to the public.

HAVANT

Journey time: *68 min*	Peak trains: *3 per hour*
Season ticket: *£2272*	Off-peak trains: *2 per hour*

Havant, too, is fairly sedate. It lies inland from Langstone Harbour, which is a popular sailing and watersports centre with good moorings and a sailing club. The town is also well placed to take advantage of the cultural riches offered by Chichester, 10 miles to the east. Another major attraction is the old shore path to Warblington and Emsworth, running past Hayling Island and a much-prized area of marsh and mudflats designated as a Site of Special Scientific Interest. The older part of Havant is now masked by modernity, notably by the Meridian shopping centre, with library and multi-storey car park *en suite*. A short walk away is The Parchment, so called because the new flats and mews houses here are built on the site of an old parchment-making works. A two-bedroom flat will cost £40,000; a four-bedroom house with two bathrooms £100,000. More up-market areas are Meadowlands and Wade Court, both within half a mile of the town centre. Individually designed detached houses with four and five bedrooms, built in the Twenties and Thirties with plush gardens, sell for around £350,000. They attract successful accountants and executives from IBM, which has a production plant here and a headquarters at Portsmouth.

A mile to the east is **Denvilles**, a comforting Thirties suburb where detached houses with large gardens sell for around £75,000 and humble three-bedroom semis can come as cheap as £50,000. A four-bedroom detached house on a Seventies estate would fetch between £75,000 and £90,000. There is also a huge council estate, reputed to be the third largest in Europe, built in the Fifties to house Portsmouth overspill.

BEDHAMPTON

Journey time: *87 min*	Peak trains: *2 per hour*
Season ticket: *£2272*	Off-peak trains: *2 per hour*

Bedhampton is, with Denvilles (see above), one of the prime residential areas of Havant, catering mainly for the retired. It was developed in the

Fifties as a series of bungalow estates where something with three bedrooms will cost £75,000 to £90,000. There are three-bedroom semis for between £60,000 and £70,000 and detached houses too for £80,000 to £100,000.

Housing developments hang on to Havant for several miles around, and to the north they don't let go until you get beyond Clanfield. Within this built-up area are former villages such as **Cowplain**, where there are 20- and 30-year-old estates and bungalows. A three-bedroom detached house on a Sixties development might cost £85,000; a bungalow of the same size £75,000 to £80,000. **Denmead** village proper is very sought after. It has shops, pubs and a village green, and a turn-of-the-century cottage with two bedrooms and a bit of land could fetch £150,000. There are also plenty of small new developments, popular with young families because of the school and swimming pool. Prices are similar to those in Waterlooville (see below).

Waterlooville is a very modern quiet suburb, around 80 per cent of which was built during the last decade. Off Tempest Avenue, which runs from one end to the other, is a run of cul-de-sacs with mixed housing in each. A studio apartment will cost £29,000; a three-bedroom semi £65,000; a four-bedroom detached house £85,000 to £100,000. **Purbrook** has an air of retirement about it. The streets are quiet, the population is older, and there are some turn-of-the-century houses between the bungalows. A two-bedroom bungalow will cost £60,000.

HILSEA	**FRATTON**
Journey time: *98 min*	Journey time: *95 min*
Season ticket: *£2400*	Season ticket: *£2400*
Peak trains: *2 per hour*	Peak trains: *2 per hour*
Off-peak trains: *1 per hour*	Off-peak trains: *2 per hour*

Hilsea is really north Portsmouth (see below). Streets of houses built in the Thirties fan out around the station. A three-bedroom semi will cost between £60,000 and £70,000. **Fratton** is the home of Portsmouth Football Club, known to friend and foe alike as Pompey. For the rest it is very *Coronation Street*, like much of Portsmouth. Flat-fronted two- to three-bedroom terrace houses sell for £40,000 to £43,000.

PORTSMOUTH & SOUTHSEA	**PORTSMOUTH HARBOUR**
Journey time: *79 min*	Journey time: *83 min*
Season ticket: *£2400*	Season ticket: *£2400*
Peak trains: *3 per hour*	Peak trains: *3 per hour*
Off-peak trains: *2 per hour*	Off-peak trains: *2 per hour*

The Navy dominates **Portsmouth**. Not only is it the biggest local employer but it can sometimes create a them-and-us feeling in the city – particularly when hordes of Americans land and head straight for the nightlife in Southsea. The dockyard has been home to the Royal Navy for 500 years, and the fleet is still serviced here. It is not only a good place for spotting modern warships: there is also an impressive collection of historic ships, including HMS *Victory* and the *Mary Rose*, which attract tourists all year round. On top of the naval traffic, of course, is the constant coming and going of the Cherbourg, Le Havre, Caen and St Malo ferries in and out of Albert Johnson dock. In the Mountbatten Centre, the city has one of the best leisure centres in southern England, which also doubles as a conference and trade show venue. Portsmouth Grammar School is the local private school that takes both boys and girls.

Portsmouth Harbour station is close to the ferry terminal for the

Edwardian family
home, Portsmouth

Isle of Wight and Gosport and to **Old Portsmouth**. An 18th-century four- or five-bedroom house in this area would cost around £200,000. Quaint little cottages of the same period, built along cobbled streets, cost between £70,000 and £100,000. The Hard, right beside the ferry terminal, is the red light district. North of Portsmouth Harbour is **Port Solent**, a product of the high-earning, fast-living Thatcherite years. The marina is the centrepiece, with the surrounding houses, shops, restaurants and sailing school offering "the ultimate maritime lifestyle". A two-bedroom flat will cost around £110,000; a three-bedroom town house £150,000.

Throughout the city, first-time buyers have a plentiful supply of two-bedroom Victorian and Edwardian houses, priced at around £42,000. A third bedroom puts the price up to around £46,000. Those who are looking for their second or third purchase on the housing ladder, and who are attracted to modern property, could look in **Anchorage Park**. This is a huge development north of the city, built in the last decade, where one-bedroom flats cost £30,000; four-bedroom detached houses £100,000. Fogeys might prefer to browse among the bay-fronted Victoriana of **North End**, an area undergoing gradual gentrification. A three-bedroom terrace here would cost around £65,000.

Southsea has more the feel of a seaside resort, with two piers, a shingle beach, permanent funfair, ballroom and the King's Theatre. It is packed with shops, restaurants and pubs. The Pyramids leisure centre is a wonderland of fun pools, water chutes and so on. Running back from the sea-front are plenty of Victorian and Edwardian houses. You would pay around £50,000 for three bedrooms; up to £80,000 for a double-fronted example with cellars.

WATERLOO TO LONDON ROAD (GUILDFORD) VIA CLANDON

CLANDON

Journey time: *46 min*	Peak trains: *3 per hour*
Season ticket: *£1508*	Off-peak trains: *2 per hour*

West Clandon and **East Clandon** both command very high house prices. The station is at West Clandon, a linear village, part of which is protected as a conservation area, and includes the National Trust property, Clandon Park. East Clandon was an estate village until 1900, attached to Hatchlands, another National Trust house with splendid Robert Adam interiors and gardens by Repton and Gertrude Jekyll. A terrace period cottage in either village could cost between £100,000 and £200,000.

LONDON ROAD (Guildford)

Journey time: *52 min*	Peak trains: *3 per hour*
Season ticket: *£1608*	Off-peak trains: *2 per hour*

See **Guildford** (page 228).

VICTORIA/LONDON BRIDGE
— TO —
ARUNDEL/BRIGHTON

(and on to Eastbourne, Lewes and Worthing)

REDHILL

To Victoria	To London Bridge
Journey time: *30 min*	Journey time: *27 min*
Season ticket: *£1368*	Season ticket: *£1368*
Peak trains: *3 per hour*	Peak trains: *2 per hour*
Off-peak trains: *3 per hour*	Off-peak trains: *1 per hour*

Redhill has now outstripped its older neighbour Reigate (see below), though it only began to sprout in about 1841 when the railway arrived. It is now heavily commercialised, and Redland Bricks are large local employers. A huge new shopping centre called The Belfry is opening, anchored around a large Marks & Spencer. There is also a multicultural centre where you can see everything from flamenco dancing to wrestling, from local community theatre to Sooty and Sweep. The Donyngs is the local sports centre for saunas, jacuzzis, swimming and gym.

Redhill is slightly cheaper than Reigate. There is an abundance of good old Thirties semis and detached houses with bay windows and steep cottage-style rooftops. Studio flats start at £45,000, one-bedroom flats at £52,000 and two-bedroom flats at almost £60,000. Then you can get little two-bedroom cottages for around £66,000, three-bedroom terrace houses for £85,000 and three-bedroom semi-detached houses for £90,000 up to £120,000. Something more sumptuous, with a third of an acre and a heated swimming pool in the garden and a playroom in the loft, could be bought for £265,000.

North Downs Line east to Nutfield

No through trains. Trains to Redhill: *1 per hour*

Nutfield is little more than a ribbon town which has grown up along the A25, though the local pub is thought to be good. You can buy two-bedroom maisonettes in converted Victorian houses for around £75,000 to £80,000. But a substantial house with five or six bedrooms in this area could cost £300,000. **South Nutfield** has a school, a grocer, a butcher and a petrol pump. A turn-of-the-century terrace house here might cost £80,000 to £90,000; but again there are

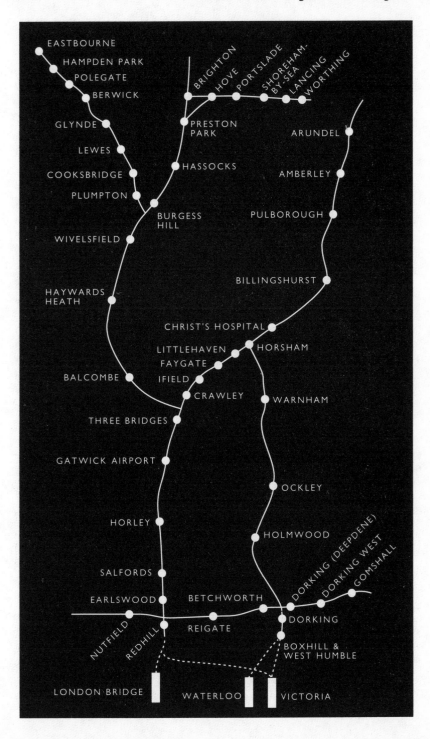

some very exclusive properties, particularly in The Avenue, which sell for over £300,000.

North Downs Line west to Reigate

Peak trains: *1 per hour to London Bridge*
Off-peak trains: *2 per hour to Redhill*

Reigate is Redhill's older brother, tucked under the North Downs, with rows of quiet residential streets and a shopping centre that is being redeveloped. Sunday afternoon walks are taken on Reigate Heath, 130 acres of open space on the edge of the town, where there is a restored windmill that is used as a church. Education is shared with Redhill. Primary education is based on the Plowden system. Children go to their first school from five to eight; then to middle school from eight to 12, before moving on to secondary school. There is a Roman Catholic/Church of England co-ed comprehensive called St Bede's that prepares students for 'S' levels and Oxbridge entrance. East Surrey College is strong on art, design, science and computing.

Properties are probably one per cent more expensive than in Redhill (see above). A large family home in a private road with two thirds of an acre, garaging for three cars and four double bedrooms would cost £365,000. But a little detached Victorian house with three double bedrooms, close to the high street, could be bought for rather less, at just under £130,000.

EARLSWOOD

To Victoria
Journey time: *37 min*
Season ticket: *£1404*

Peak trains: *2 per hour**
Off-peak trains: *1 per hour*

* Plus 2 per hour to London Bridge

It is hard to find a dividing line between **Earlswood** and Redhill. Many of the people who live here work at the nearby hospitals – the Royal Earlswood Hospital for the mentally handicapped (where *The Sun* claimed a member of the Royal Family had been quietly kept for many years); and the new East Surrey Hospital which recently replaced the old Redhill General. There are also plenty of commuters, travelling to both Croydon and London. Earlswood is not as sought after as Redhill, but it does have a beautiful common and two lakes for boating and fishing. A purpose-built two-bedroom flat would cost £50,000; a three-bedroom turn-of-the-century semi around £75,000.

SALFORDS

To Victoria

Journey time: *40 min*	Peak trains: *3 per hour**
Season ticket: *£1584*	Off-peak trains: *nil*

* Plus 1 per hour to London Bridge

Salfords is nice in parts but has the disadvantage of straddling the A23. It has a village shop-cum-post office, a chemist and a newsagent, but people tend to aim for Redhill, Horley or Hookwood for their major shopping. It has a first school and a middle school, but older children have to bus to Horley or Redhill for secondary schools. Long-suffering parents spend a lot of time chauffeuring their children about because there is not much for them to do in the village itself. The nearby aerodrome is a thorn in the side. Night-flight training programmes for light aircraft and helicopters are a regular irritation. A three-bedroom semi with a long garden here might cost just under £110,000 and a bungalow with two double bedrooms wouldn't cost much less at £95,000.

HORLEY

To Victoria

Journey time: *42 min*	Peak trains: *2 per hour**
Season ticket: *£1572*	Off-peak trains: *2 per hour*

* Plus 2 per hour to London Bridge

Compared to the two commercial bullies, Reigate and Crawley, that lie on either side of it, **Horley** is a mute backwater. "A lot of people think it is too quiet," says one resident. There is no leisure centre or cinema, though it does have a swimming pool, plus cricket, hockey, squash, bowling and football clubs. Gatwick airport is a big local employer. The two main thoroughfares are the A23 and a modest high street. The two senior schools have now merged to improve the choice of sixth form subjects, and the redundant school building has been turned into an adult education institute. In the sea of Thirties semis you could pay anything between £74,000 and £95,000 for three bedrooms. There are also some Victorian terraces where three-bedroom houses sell for around £70,000. And there is a huge new estate, with over 2,000 houses on it, that has won awards for landscaping and design. A five-bedroom detached house with two acres would cost £250,000.

The village of **Charlwood** struggles admirably to hang onto its rural image, in spite of the fact that Gatwick airport is only a few miles away and is constantly wanting to expand towards it. A formidably active parish council keeps a watchful eye on all planning applications and development proposals. Villagers lovingly nurse the large number of listed buildings, which include a Grade I listed Norman church. The village also has a hardware shop, a newsagent which also sells fruit and groceries, a cobbler, a post office, a soft furnishing shop and a builders' merchants. There is a school for the under-sevens. People living here have the choice of commuting either from Horley or from Gatwick, where the service is fast and frequent. A brick-built two-bedroom cottage might be bought for £70,000; a third bedroom puts the price up to around £137,000.

Grade II listed house, Charlwood

Smallfield, to the east, has been greatly affected by the development of Gatwick. Aircraft noise is a problem, and the very presence of an airport has allowed more industrial development than there would otherwise have been. It has a population of about 4,000, with a good mix of young and old, yet it is straggly and has no real centre. People hope that the village spirit may be revived if a new village hall is built. There is an annual flower show, a carnival each July, and dinner-dances in the church and school hall. Prices are similar to those in Horley. A Victorian semi-detached cottage sells at £80,000 and the detached version at between £90,000 and £110,000. Four-bedroom detached houses cost around £180,000.

GATWICK AIRPORT

To Victoria	To London Bridge
Journey time: *30 min*	Journey time: *33 min*
Season ticket: *£1652**	Season ticket: *£1652*
Peak trains: *5 per hour*	Peak trains: *2 per hour*
Off-peak trains: *6 per hour*	Off-peak trains: *2 per hour*

* *£2008 if valid for Gatwick Express*

Gatwick Express trains whistle into London from here at a frequency of one every 15 minutes, in addition to the ordinary service, making it a popular choice for commuters in a hurry. People living in villages to the west, for example, might prefer it to stations on the nearer, but much slower, **Victoria/Waterloo to Horsham** line (page 271).

THREE BRIDGES

To Victoria	To London Bridge
Journey time: *38 min*	Journey time: *40 min*
Season ticket: *£1652**	Season ticket: *£1652*
Peak trains: *4 per hour*	Peak trains: *3 per hour*
Off-peak trains: *3 per hour*	Off-peak trains: *2 per hour*

* £2008 if valid for Gatwick Express

Some of the better parts of Crawley such as **Pound Hill** and **Copthorne** are close to this station. One-bedroom flats cost about £53,000; three-bedroom detached houses about £90,000. **Three Bridges**, so-called because of the bridges that cross the River Mole nearby, was a village in its own right before Crawley was first thought of. It contains some Victorian terraces that sprang up around the railway station, but the bulk of it was built in the early Fifties when more than 2,000 houses were put up for 4,800 newcomers. Prices are similar to those in Crawley (see below).

MAIN LINE FROM THREE BRIDGES TO ARUNDEL
(see map)

CRAWLEY

To Victoria	
Journey time: *42 min*	Peak trains: *2 per hour**
Season ticket: *£1668†*	Off-peak trains: *3 per hour*

* Plus 2 per hour to London Bridge   † £2008 if valid for Gatwick Express

Crawley is not much loved by anyone – least of all by the young, who complain that it has nothing to offer except for one nightclub for over 24-year-olds. They are lucky in one respect, however, in that unemployment is not such a problem in Crawley. There are jobs at Gatwick airport, and the factory estates and business parks that have grown up around it include every kind of industry from light manufacturing to pharmaceuticals and foodstuffs.

It was developed as a New Town after the war – the only one in the south of England. Ironically it was meant to provide some of the best living conditions for people moving out of London. It was designed originally as nine neighbourhoods (now there are 14), each with a population of 6,000. Each would have its own shopping parade, primary school, church, pub, community hall and playing fields. A 250-acre industrial estate was placed to the north of the town so that the prevailing winds would carry the noise and smells away from the houses. The first new-towners moved in during 1949, when Gatwick airport was no more than a wartime runway on boggy ground on the town's outskirts.

People moving to the area would probably choose to live in one of the neighbouring villages, or closer to Three Bridges station, and go into Crawley only to take advantage of the shops (the biggest covered shopping centre in the south-east is opening this year, 1992), the two leisure centres, multi-purpose arts centre, and the 18-hole municipal golf course.

For £80,000 it is possible to get one of the original three-bedroom semis put up at the beginning of the new town. Studio flats cost around £38,000 and one-bedroom flats between £45,000 and £48,000. The original neighbourhoods are still identifiable. West Green, for instance, was one of the first, and it still has rows of brick terraces and some older labourers' cottages. The less popular and less successful neighbourhoods are Broadfield, which has a lot of council housing, Bewbush, which was hastily put up to accommodate second generation Crawley families, and Langley Green.

IFIELD

To Victoria

Journey time: *57 min*	Peak trains: *1 per hour**
Season ticket: *£1692†*	Off-peak trains: *2 per hour*

* Plus 2 per hour to London Bridge (j/t: 44 min)   † £2008 if valid for Gatwick Express

Ifield is on the outskirts of Crawley, but at least there is a conservation area which contains the old village green, a mill with a millpond, St Margaret's Church and the Plough Inn. A larding of new houses was added in 1956, and by 1990 the population had risen to nearly 9,000. You can get three-bedroom semis at £80,000 to £83,000 and two-bedroom cottages at £55,000 to £58,000.

FAYGATE

To Victoria

Journey time: *60 min*	Peak trains: *nil**
Season ticket: *£1748†*	Off-peak trains: *1 per hour*

* Plus 1 per hour to London Bridge   † £2008 if valid for Gatwick Express

Property is more expensive in **Faygate** than in Crawley because people like the intimacy of scale offered by the village. Something with four bedrooms might cost around £260,000.

LITTLEHAVEN

To Victoria

Journey time: *63 min*	Peak trains: *1 per hour**
Season ticket: *£1828†*	Off-peak trains: *2 per hour*

* Plus 2 per hour to London Bridge (j/t: 50 min)   † £2008 if valid for Gatwick Express

Littlehaven was once a separate village but is now essentially a part of Horsham, with modern estates providing the putty between the two. The older houses are in Rusper Road, but much of the property for sale is modern, with three-bedroom semis sensibly priced at around £70,000.

HORSHAM

To Victoria

Journey time: *52 min*	Peak trains: *2 per hour**
Season ticket: *£1828†*	Off-peak trains: *3 per hour*

* Plus 2 per hour to London Bridge   † £2008 if valid for Gatwick Express

Horsham is a busy little Sussex town which manages to combine its old character as a smugglers' haunt and late 18th-century garrison town with plenty of interesting little shops and local businesses. It has a population of 27,000. It is in a marvellous position with a good train service to London, but with house prices lower than they are across the border in Surrey. Chichester and Guildford are close enough for theatres, and the sea is 20 miles away over the South Downs. You can go to the races at Goodwood, show jumping at Hickstead, hunt with the Crawley and Horsham Pack, and there are golf clubs at Pulborough, Mannings Heath, Pease Pottage and Ockley. It also has Christ's Hospital public school for boys and girls, where there is a separate railway station (see below).

Some of the houses in the town are collectors' items. Walk down Pump Alley and into the Causeway, for example, and you find a street that is much as it was 300 years ago. These houses with bulging walls and uneven roofs very rarely come on the market, and could fetch around £300,000. For something more ordinary – a detached Thirties house with three bedrooms, within walking distance of the town – you could pay £145,000. A small modern two-bedroom house would cost just under £60,000. There are council estates to the east and west of the town.

Local villages also maintain strong links with the past. **Slinfold**, to the east, has a good collection of Georgian houses hemmed in by tall hedges and walls, strung out along a very pretty winding lane. It still has a village shop. A classic Sussex tile-hung house with four bedrooms, two bathrooms and large gardens backing on to fields would cost just under £300,000. Closer to Horsham, separated from it by the A24, is **Broadbridge Heath**, which has a sports centre with athletics, football, badminton and table tennis. It also has a Tesco, and is the site of the West

Sussex County Council highways depot.

Further south is **Itchingfield**, which has an intriguing priest's house attached to the church; and **Southwater**, which is little more than a dormitory to Horsham. Moving east you come to **Nuthurst**, where there are 16th-century houses and a timber-framed inn. **Lower Beeding** is small and pretty too, and has a small post office-cum-shop. An old gardener's cottage with three bedrooms and outbuildings in three-quarters of an acre might fetch just under £200,000. The big house, Leonardslee, has rhododendron gardens that are occasionally open to the public. The countryside lapses back into heathland here in St Leonard's Forest – 12,000 acres of old Royal hunting ground that was once thought to have harboured dragons. To the south is **Cowfold**, which has lost much of its character and suffers through being on the junction of the A272 and the A281. Flats here start at £50,000, but a country house in the area with six bedrooms, three bathrooms and three acres would cost £400,000.

North of the forest is **Rusper**, an enchanting village with an ancient church (origins in the 13th century), a high street full of black-and-white timber buildings and two pubs, The Plough and The Star, which are centuries old. On this side of Horsham you have to beware the noise of aircraft from Gatwick.

CHRIST'S HOSPITAL

To Victoria

Journey time: *56 min*	Peak trains: *2 per hour**
Season ticket: *£1844†*	Off-peak trains: *1 per hour*

* Plus 1 single train to London Bridge   † £2008 if valid for Gatwick Express

Christ's Hospital, hardly distinct from Horsham, is dominated by the public school, fondly known as C.H. by local people, which disgorges pupils in their distinctive blue and bright yellow uniform. Around it has grown a low-level brick settlement, largely 20th-century, which is not technically a village though it has a chapel, a shop and a disproportionately large railway station. It is a very expensive area, much sought after, and houses sell quickly. There are modern bungalows that sell for between £110,000 and £115,000, three-bedroom semis at £110,000 and £115,000, and four-bedroom red-brick turn-of-the-century cottages that sell at £130,000.

BILLINGSHURST

To Victoria

Journey time: *63 min*	Peak trains: *2 per hour**
Season ticket: *£1900†*	Off-peak trains: *1 per hour*

* Plus 1 per hour to London Bridge   † £2008 if valid for Gatwick Express

Billingshurst feels more like a small town than a large village, with some fine 15th-century houses beached on a shore of modern developments. It is very much divided by the A29, which follows the route of the old Roman road, Stane Street. It is very popular with commuters because it is more intimate than Horsham or Crawley yet has the fast rail links. A two-bedroom turn-of-the-century cottage will cost £70,000. **Wisborough Green**, two miles away, is literally a film-set village, regularly used by film directors as a backdrop. It has a cricket green that borders the A272, a few village shops, a garage and two inns. A Grade II listed period tile-hung cottage with four bedrooms, two bathrooms, gardens and 10 acres of paddock would cost around £300,000. You need to remember that stations south of Horsham are much less well served by trains to London.

PULBOROUGH

To Victoria

Journey time: *70 min*	
Season ticket: *£1960†*	

Peak trains: *2 per hour**	
Off-peak trains: *1 per hour*	

* Plus 1 per hour to London Bridge   † £2008 if valid for Gatwick Express

This is where the Arun Valley becomes spellbindingly beautiful, and houses backing onto it are extremely sought after. "The wetlands, the bird sanctuary, the downland walks, make it an absolutely glorious place to live, full of sunny corners," says one happy local resident. This rather belies the fact that **Pulborough** is under a lot of development pressure, and community spirit is a little battered. Local societies do not play a large role (though the allotments are well patronised) and the shops are also struggling for survival. The village has two butchers, a baker and a good supermarket, but it has lost its delicatessen. In the jumble of brick, flint and thatch you could pick up a little three-bedroom detached house for £90,000.

Many of the villages on the felted slopes of the South Downs are very lovely. **West Burton** and **Sutton**, for instance, are very small and rural, no more than a handful of cottages and a pub. A three-bedroom cottage might cost between £180,000 and £260,000; a four-bedroom house £250,000 to over £300,000.

Nutbourne, just to the north-east, is another little hamlet with a pub, where a two-bedroom cottage might be bought for £100,000. It also has a vineyard with a much higher price on its head. It was rumoured to have sold last year for over £1m. Further east you come to what local people tend rather dismissively to call the Surrey part of Sussex – meaning that it is more suburban in character than the wilder countryside to the west. A three- to four-bedroom bungalow in comparatively manicured **West Chiltington** will cost £200,000 to £250,000. It is close to the shops at **Storrington**, a village that long ago burst its boundaries with new houses but which offers a reasonable range of shops.

The star in the west is **Petworth**, the village that stands at the gates of Petworth House, with hundreds of acres of National Trust land and a house begun by the Duke of Somerset at the end of the 17th century. The old timber-frame houses in the tangle of narrow streets around the square attract lots of tourists in the summer. The large local car park is full by breakfast-time, much to the annoyance of the local shoppers. Petworth is also an antiques centre, with more than 30 antiques shops. There aren't a lot of other shops, though there is a gunsmith for the sporting fraternity. Villagers feel oppressed by the traffic coming through on the A285 and the A272; a bypass has been talked of since 1935. A brick-and-tile house with four bedrooms, a garage and garden, would cost around £145,000. Commuters have the choice of using the faster line into Waterloo from Haslemere, which is some 10 miles away – see **Waterloo to Portsmouth** (page 234).

Fittleworth, closer to Pulborough, is a more mixed kind of village. It has its own shop, church and inn, and is close to marvellous riding country in Bedham Woods and on the Downs. A four-bedroom Sussex tile-hung house set in one acre would cost just under £250,000.

Period town house,
Petworth

AMBERLEY

To Victoria

| Journey time: *76 min* | Peak trains: *1 per hour* |
| Season ticket: *£2040* | Off-peak trains: *1 per hour* |

Amberley is another of the many villages in this area that have hung on to their character. It is protected from heavy traffic on a side road off the B2139. Old flint-and-thatch cottages with old-fashioned cottage gardens cluster around Amberley Castle, once the residence of the Bishops of Chichester and dismantled by Parliamentarians during the Civil War. A footpath to one side leads to Amberley Wild Brooks, protected water meadows visited by migrating birds. The village has a shop and a post office. A four-bedroom cottage could be bought for £215,000. Villages further from the station would be significantly cheaper, with similar cottages selling for as little as £115,000.

ARUNDEL

To Victoria

| Journey time: *81 min* | Peak trains: *2 per hour** |
| Season ticket: *£2088* | Off-peak trains: *1 per hour* |

* Plus 1 per hour to London Bridge

Arundel is a busy old town on the River Arun, dominated by its castle which is often described as Windsor in miniature. The high street, winding steeply between the river and the castle, has plenty of antique shops but few of the standard chainstores. There are butchers and bakers, general stores, a walking-stick shop and a Toy and Military Museum. Chichester is only 10 miles away with its attractions for yachtsmen and theatregoers (though Arundel has its own Priory Playhouse for smaller-scale productions); Goodwood racecourse is a mere three miles, and there are plenty of golf courses. The sea is three miles away, and there is a good beach at Climping. The River Arun has to be watched. It is tidal, and one of the fastest flowing rivers in the country after the Severn.

You could buy a two-bedroom cottage now for £60,000: two years ago it would have cost £20,000 more. For a building in traditional brick-and-flint, you will have to pay a premium of around £5,000. For three-bedroom houses the price jumps to £100,000 – though you might be lucky and find a three-bedroom terrace for around £86,000. People either opt for old Arundel, which climbs steeply up the hill, layer upon layer towards the castle, or they look at the larger Fifties houses on the Chichester side. These have large gardens and garages, are within walking distance of the town and are rather more suburban. A four-bedroom house in this neighbourhood will cost around £160,000. The Arundel Wildfowl Trust, founded by Sir Peter Scott, runs special events for children during the school holidays.

The villages of **Burpham** and **Wepham** lie to the east, on the way up to the top of Harrow Hill where the views are wonderful. Both are popular, and a thatched two-bedroom semi with small garden would cost just over £100,000. **Slindon**, to the west, is the kind of village people wait years for a chance to move into. Not only because of its beauty but because the involvement of the National Trust means that very few houses are still freehold. A period house with three to four bedrooms could cost £300,000. The village has its cheaper end where two-bedroom bungalows sell for around £90,000.

MAIN LINE FROM THREE BRIDGES TO BRIGHTON
(see map)

BALCOMBE

To Victoria
Journey time: *43 min* | Peak trains: *2 per hour**
Season ticket: *£1736†* | Off-peak trains: *nil**

   * Plus I per hour to London Bridge   † £2008 if valid for Gatwick Express

Its position on a railway line set deep in an Area of Outstanding Natural Beauty has gilded house prices in **Balcombe**. Commuters now have quite a strong presence there, most of them high earners. They usually begin by sending their children to the local school, but switch them into the private system soon after. The village has an old quarter and a modern quarter, and its great good luck is that the new estates have been planned well enough to avoid any feeling of claustrophobia. Just off the village centre in the old quarter, Victorian semis with three bedrooms, three reception rooms and a garden sell briskly in the £125,000 range.

The village is described by the parish clerk as "happy, friendly and caring". Amongst the myriad clubs and activities is a Care Group which arranges to take people to hospital, collect prescriptions and so on; and a Christmas Tree club to aid the needy. There are societies to cover the needs of every age group from Brownies to old age pensioners, plus tennis, cricket, football and badminton clubs. The actor Paul Scofield lives here.

It is close to Ardingly (the last syllable rhymes with eye) Reservoir where people sail, windsurf and fish at weekends. Mostly it is used by students from Ardingly College, the independent school for boys and girls which sits on the bank. The hill-ridge village of **Ardingly** is best known for the National Trust's Wakehurst Gardens. These are leased by the Royal Botanical Gardens at Kew and for the South of England Showground. The three-day agricultural show every June makes it the agricultural capital of Sussex. The grounds are also used for antique shows and Pony Club displays. Ardingly's village hall is heavily booked with ballet and dog-training classes, mothers and toddlers, playgroups and horticultural society meetings. A Thirties semi with three bedrooms in a quiet cul-de-sac within walking distance of all these activities sells at around £110,000.

HAYWARDS HEATH

To Victoria	To London Bridge
Journey time: *46 min*	Journey time: *52 min*
Season ticket: *£1856**	Season ticket: *£1856*
Peak trains: *5 per hour*	Peak trains: *4 per hour*
Off-peak trains: *3 per hour*	Off-peak trains: *1 per hour*

* *£2008 if valid for Gatwick Express*

This is prime commuter country, close to the M23 and the M25, fed by fast trains to London yet close enough for trips to the sea. Successful local businessmen and airline pilots from Gatwick also help put prices up. The town feels hugely superior to Burgess Hill, which is three miles away and probably has slightly better shops, though **Haywards Heath** has recently hoisted itself up a notch in the shopping stakes by acquiring both a Marks & Spencer and a Sainsbury. Property prices are high. A simple one-bedroom flat will cost around £45,000, rising to between £50,000 and £60,000 for a two-bedroom flat and £60,000 to £65,000 for a two-bedroom house. A detached four-bedroom house with two bathrooms is likely to cost around £130,000. Better parts of town are in the conservation areas at Franklands Village, Lucastes, The Heath and Lewes Road. Also popular is Muster Green, where the large Victorian and Edwardian houses have ample gardens around an open space that has much of the character of a village green. You can throw money at houses in the Haywards Heath area. A 15th-century house with five bedrooms, swimming pool, seven garages, two cottages and 70 acres could cost around £900,000.

Villages close to Haywards Heath are also very popular. **Lindfield**, just to the north, has all the ingredients of the perfect village – a high street with tile-hung Sussex houses, a pond with ducks and swans, a large open common and a historic parish church. It is in two halves. One half remains Elizabethan, with property prices possibly five to 10 per cent higher than those in Haywards Heath. The other half consists of ex-council housing. Stockbrokers' houses are slipped into the lanes round about. A Tudor house with six main bedrooms, three further bedrooms and five bathrooms might sell for around £700,000. Ordinary four-bedroom town houses can be bought rather more cheaply at around £275,000.

Further north still, **Horsted Keynes** is another village that mutated during the Fifties. You drive through the centre thinking how lovely the village green is, then turn a corner and confront a mass of cheap housing. The pretty bit is still very popular and commands higher prices than

Haywards Heath. A two-bedroom bungalow with views over the countryside would cost around £110,000. About a mile away is the privately run Bluebell Railway, a great delight for steam-train enthusiasts. **Paxhill Park** is popular for its golf course but lacks a real village spirit. A Tudor house with seven acres of land, six main bedrooms and three further bedrooms is the classic stockbroker buy here at £700,000.

To the east is **Scayne's Hill**. It has been sliced in two by the A272 but has some dignified Victorian houses, with prices starting at £65,000 for two bedrooms. Fletching is tiny but has a lovely collection of 16th-century houses and a couple of pubs (see page 283).

Less than two miles to the west of Haywards Heath is the tall spire of **Cuckfield** parish church, which German bombers used as a landmark during the Second World War. Beyond it you negotiate a tortuous bend, then climb the beautiful 15th-century high street, lined with medieval cottages. At the brow of the hill the spell is broken and medieval England dissolves into Victorian and modern. A tiny Grade II listed cottage with one bedroom sells at £75,000.

Since the village was once a staging post it is well endowed with pubs – six altogether, for a population of 2,000. Cuckfield is extremely active and shows its independence in eccentric ways. A fight with the district council over the ownership of the green (where donkey race meetings are held) resulted in the village declaring independence and producing its own passports, currency and stamps. It still holds mock elections for a mayor every year, and residents pay one penny to vote. The Independent State of Cuckfield, which is the local pressure group, also fought off plans to place a rubbish tip in the valley and hung the village in bunting to celebrate their victory. Cuckfield has its own museum, library and local beauty spot, New England Wood.

To the west are the more remote hamlets of **Bolney** and **Warninglid**. Both had strong connections with the medieval iron industry, and are now very quiet and beautiful, and kept scrupulously tidy by elderly inhabitants. A four-bedroom chalet bungalow in Bolney with three-quarters of an acre would cost around £160,000.

WIVELSFIELD

To Victoria	To London Bridge
Journey time: *51 min*	Journey time: *57 min*
Season ticket: *£1872**	Season ticket: *£1872*
Peak trains: *3 per hour*	Peak trains: *3 per hour*
Off-peak trains: *2 per hour*	Off-peak trains: *1 per hour*

* £2008 if valid for Gatwick Express

Wivelsfield is not particularly sought after, and property prices are similar to those in Burgess Hill (see below). People tend to pass through it on their way to Haywards Heath or Lewes. The influx of London and Brighton commuters since the war has doubled the population to 1,200, but the old village families are still involved in agriculture and Young Farmers' events are well attended. It has a post office-cum-village store which stretches to delicatessen food and French bread, and there are two garages. The primary school is popular. Older children move on to Haywards Heath comprehensive and a tertiary college at Chailey. There are lovely old tiled cottages in some of the older roads, such as Church Lane. A modernised, tile-hung terrace house with three bedrooms and a 150ft garden backing onto open countryside sells at around £85,000.

Unusual tile-hung cottage,
Wivelsfield

This was where the first donkey derby was held in 1951, organised by a local farmer, Jim Dinnage. He had begun by soft-heartedly buying a forlorn-looking male donkey from a rag-and-bone man. The animal's anti-social midnight braying then persuaded him to provide a harem of 13 females. Other donkey charity work followed, and celebrities including

Laurel and Hardy and Charlie Chaplin took an interest. Dinnage died in 1963, and his widow turned Lone Farm Barn into a donkey hospice.

BURGESS HILL

To Victoria	**To London Bridge**
Journey time: *62 min*	Journey time: *59 min*
Season ticket: *£1872**	Season ticket: *£1872*
Peak trains: *3 per hour*	Peak trains: *2 per hour*
Off-peak trains: *1 per hour*	Off-peak trains: *1 per hour*

* £2008 if valid for Gatwick Express

Burgess Hill was an intimate little place until a few decades ago. In 1951 its population was just 8,000. Since then it has been overwhelmed by new estates built to accommodate London overspill, and the population has shot up to 26,000. The area to the west is still growing, with a new relief road planned that will unlock new pockets of building land for thousands more new houses. The old Sixties shopping centre, The Martletts, has been redeveloped in a new Nineties mould. There is a Waitrose and Tesco, but otherwise the shopping is unimaginative. It has its own comprehensive school, which is oversubscribed, and the private Burgess Hill School for Girls.

The town is down-market of Haywards Heath and probably offers the lowest property prices to be found in this expensive mid-Sussex belt, though still higher than south Sussex. A bottom-of-the-market flat, for example, might cost £45,000 in Burgess Hill and only £30,000 in Brighton. Two-bedroom houses start at around £55,000; three-bedroom houses at £62,000; four-bedroom detached houses at £100,000. Silverdale Road, Keymer Road and Folders Lane are where you find the most expensive older houses, with company directors and airline pilots settling at around £200,000 to £300,000. A few very old farmhouses still survive on the former commons. Grove Farm House, for example, just south of Station Road, is thought to be 16th century.

The town hall provides the setting for productions from the local dramatic, operatic and choral societies, and from the local primary schools. There is also a two-screen cinema.

HASSOCKS

To Victoria	**To London Bridge**
Journey time: *66 min*	Journey time: *63 min*
Season ticket: *£1880**	Season ticket: *£1880*
Peak trains: *4 per hour*	Peak trains: *2 per hour*
Off-peak trains: *1 per hour*	Off-peak trains: *1 per hour*

* £2008 if valid for Gatwick Express

Hassocks likes to think of itself as a village, but it is actually town-size with a population of 9,000 containing quite a high proportion of retired people. It is really an amalgamation of **Hurstpierpoint** and **Keymer**, though the people of Hurstpierpoint do not regard themselves as part of it. The small shopping parade meets basic needs, but for serious food shopping people go to the Waitrose or Tesco at Burgess Hill. Hassocks is not architecturally distinguished. It grew up around the railway in the 19th century, with new developments appearing in the Thirties and Fifties. But it does sit under the wing of the South Downs, so there are magnificent views and it is good for riding or walking.

You would pay around £120,000 for a three-bedroom modern detached house, but older properties go for much more. A four-bedroom wing of a country house might cost £170,000; a four-bedroom Edwardian semi around £130,000. People are still asking more for their houses than they are likely to get, so advertised prices might be misleadingly high. Hassocks has primary and secondary schools which are thought to be good. There is a Beacon Club for the mid-teens, but not much for older teenagers to do. The old Sussex game of stoolball is still played here, kept alive by the Stoolball Association. It is a form of rounders, invented by milkmaids who wanted a recreational use for their three-legged milking stools. There is an amenity association which looks after conservation, plus drama and horticultural societies.

Ditchling, just to the east, is one of the most rarefied villages in this part of Sussex. Outsiders call it plain snobby. To live in this superb setting with its backdrop of hills, you'll need to spend 20 per cent more than you would pay anywhere else in the county. A gracious, four-bedroom Thirties house in an acre of garden would cost around £240,000. On the outskirts, where a council estate seems to have approached almost by stealth, a three-bedroom semi might be picked up for around £75,000. The strange thing is that houses at the bottom end of the market sometimes tend to stick because people moving to Ditchling want something rather more special. Over the years it has attracted many famous inhabitants, including the actress Dame Ellen Terry and currently Dame Vera Lynn. It has a few basic shops, teashops, an art gallery, a good primary school and a Museum of Local Life. It is particularly proud of its choral society. Nearby is Ditchling Common, offering nearly 200 acres of walks; and Ditchling Beacon, over 800ft high, where a fire was lit to warn of the approach of the Spanish Armada.

The illustrator Raymond Briggs lives in the nearby hamlet of **Westmeston**, which is also a beautiful quiet retreat at the foot of the Downs. There is no shop or post office but it does have a public telephone box. There is a private nursery school, but the nearest primary school is in Ditchling. The secondary schools are in Lewes, Chailey and Hassocks. To outsiders, Westmeston might seem a little stuffy.

PRESTON PARK

To Victoria	To London Bridge
Journey time: *73 min*	Journey time: *70 min*
Season ticket: *£2016*	Season ticket: *£2016*
Peak trains: *3 per hour*	Peak trains: *2 per hour*
Off-peak trains: *1 per hour*	Off-peak trains: *1 per hour*

Preston Park is a part of Brighton that particularly attracts commuters because of its railway station. Small Victorian and Edwardian houses with two bedrooms sell for between £50,000 and £60,000. It is very similar in character to North Laines and Westhill, which are both close to the station in Brighton proper.

BRIGHTON

To Victoria	To London Bridge
Journey time: *51 min*	Journey time: *73 min*
Season ticket: *£2016*	Season ticket: *£2016*
Peak trains: *4 per hour*	Peak trains: *2 per hour*
Off-peak trains: *2 per hour*	Off-peak trains: *1 per hour*

Brighton is busy trying to become a mini-London, developing an increasingly sophisticated and cosmopolitan air, playing up its strengths as a conference centre and weekend retreat. It is short on domestic gardens and garages, but the frivolity of the Royal Pavilion, the beautifully landscaped parks and the backdrop of the Sussex Downs make it an enviable place to live. It has an annual music festival, film festival, a plethora of restaurants and the Theatre Royal which attracts many plays on their pre-London tours. There has always been a theatrical crowd in Brighton – Lord Olivier once lived there – attracted by the Regency terrace houses of Montpelier with their canopied bow fronts and panelled drawing rooms. Brighton has always been the place to have a flat, and the various building booms of the last few decades have provided plenty of them, both in purpose-built blocks and in large houses that have been converted. There is also now a boating crowd, drawn by the marina.

Commuters tend to live within walking distance of the railway station, which is very central and within half a mile of the sea-front. The shops, sea-front and residential areas are so closely knit that many people don't have cars at all. There are various interlocking conservation areas which househunters might aim for. **North Laines**, **Westhill** and **Clifton** are close to the station, all now rather gentrified with little boutiques and antique shops. In Clifton Terrace there are huge houses with self-contained basement flats selling for around £250,000 to £300,000.

Millionaires' row is at **Rodean**, just beside the girls' private school and opposite the marina. Vast houses with indoor swimming pools sell here for anything up to £1m. If you think about buying anything facing the sea, however, do think of the havoc wrought by salt-laden winds on your exterior paintwork and the extra decorating bills you'll have to face as a result.

Georgian terrace house, Brighton

MAIN LINE FROM PLUMPTON TO EASTBOURNE (see map)

PLUMPTON

To Victoria
Journey time: *57 min*   **Peak trains:** *1 per hour*
Season ticket: *£1900**   **Off-peak trains:** *nil*
  * £2008 if valid for Gatwick Express

The railway line divides **Plumpton** into two parts, Plumpton proper and **Plumpton Green**. The latter is a mass of modern housing close to the railway station, with the National Hunt racecourse to the south. A good five-bedroom modern family house with a double garage will cost £215,000. The old village is anchored to Plumpton Place, a 16th-century moated manor. It has a general store-cum-post office, a couple of garages and a primary school, and is the home of the East Sussex Agricultural

College. There are no public riding stables, but there is wonderful riding over the Downs if you have your own horse. **East Chiltington** is very close by. Here you could pay £265,000 for a family house with four double bedrooms, double garage and half an acre.

COOKSBRIDGE

To Victoria

Journey time: *62 min*	**Peak trains:** *1 per hour*
Season ticket: *£1936**	**Off-peak trains:** *nil*

* £2008 if valid for Gatwick Express

The desirability of **Cooksbridge** is reduced because it sits both on the main road to Lewes and on the railway line, both of which can be noisy. A two-bedroom flat could be bought for £45,000; a three-bedroom end-of-terrace house for £55,000. Ex-railway workers' cottages with three bedrooms come on the market at around £80,000.

LEWES

To Victoria

Journey time: *63 min*	**Peak trains:** *1 per hour**
Season ticket: *£1960†*	**Off-peak trains:** *1 per hour*

* Plus 1 per hour to London Bridge   † £2008 if valid for Gatwick Express

Large parts of **Lewes** are still medieval – particularly along the main street, which follows the route of an ancient causeway. The passages winding away from it are an irresistible invitation for shoppers to explore. Bookshops, antique shops and 15th-century timbered cottages lean against colour-washed houses. The old Bloomsbury connection (Vanessa Bell and Duncan Grant used to live nearby, and Virginia Woolf lived at Rodmell two miles away) has left an arty-crafty atmosphere. It is the county town of East Sussex and is always alive with exhibitions and craft shows, and displays of pottery and paintings for sale. It has its own coterie of resident artists, several of whom work at the Star Brewery where there are five small studios.

Property is more expensive than in the surrounding areas. A four-bedroom Edwardian terrace costs just under £140,000. It would be likely to have a mean garden or a small courtyard since the town is tight for space, and this means that parking is difficult too. The tiny cobbled streets just off the high street – Grange Road and Rotten Row, for example – have a particular cachet, and houses here don't often come on the market. There is a high proportion of council housing too – the highest per capita in East Sussex. And there are some modern private estates where you might buy a two-bedroom terrace for £56,000, or three bedrooms for £63,000.

Shopping is adequate. Lewes has its own Boots, Safeway, Iceland and Next; and Eastbourne and Brighton are not far away. The local private school is The Old Grammar School. The great social occasion of the year is the huge Bonfire Night party which celebrates the burning, not of Guy Fawkes, but of a batch of Protestant martyrs.

There are some extraordinarily lovely Downland villages around Lewes. **Kingston**, in the south, has a street of distinguished old houses and a modern estate where four-bedroom houses sell for around £200,000. And there is **Rodmell**, which seduced the Bloomsbury Group with its mix of flint-and-thatch and tile-hung cottages. A two-bedroom cottage will cost almost £100,000; a four-bedroom house backing onto fields is likely to reach £250,000. Neither of these villages has shops.

To the north is **Barcombe**, which has prices to match its beauty. A modest four-bedroom detached house with a garden and double garage would cost £140,000; a more lavish four-bedroom house with a large garden might fetch £225,000. It is really a village of three parts. There is Barcombe Cross, which has tile-hung houses and shops, plus a pub and the 16th-century Forge House. Then there is Barcombe Mills, on the River Ouse, where people go for picnics. And then Old Barcombe, by St Mary's Church, which was largely abandoned during the plague. **Ringmer** is more of a dormitory to Lewes, where houses sell briskly. Three-bedroom semis fetch about £90,000; four-bedroom detached houses around £140,000. The centrepiece is the village green, fringed with old cottages, and with the parish church standing by, where cricket is played in the summer.

GLYNDE

To Victoria

Journey time: *89 min*	Peak trains: *nil**
Season ticket: £2028	Off-peak trains: *1 per hour†*

* Plus 1 per hour to London Bridge (j/t: 72 min)   † Change at Lewes

Glynde consists of little more than the big house, Glynde Place, an 18th-century church, and a grassy bank that becomes a cloud of daffodils in spring. The Glyndbourne Opera House, which draws the dinner jackets with their picnic hampers between May and August, is on the parish boundary with Ringmer. Much of the property which sits at the foot of the awe-inspiring Mount Caburn is in private ownership and leased to villagers.

BERWICK

To Victoria

Journey time: *95 min*	Peak trains: *nil**
Season ticket: £2068	Off-peak trains: *1 per hour†*

* Plus 1 per hour to London Bridge (j/t: 78 min)   † Change at Lewes

Berwick is best known for having a church decorated with murals by Duncan Grant and Vanessa Bell which were so vivid that they caused an outcry when they were painted in the Forties. Most of the houses were built during the Thirties, and many of them offer good views of the Downs and Arlington Reservoir. A three-bedroom semi sells at around £75,000 to £80,000; a four-bedroom detached house around £145,000.

POLEGATE

To Victoria
Journey time: *76 min*
Season ticket: *£2144*

Peak trains: *1 per hour**
Off-peak trains: *1 per hour*

* Plus 1 per hour to London Bridge (j/t: 84 min)

Polegate is really the outer rim of Eastbourne. It is a village that billowed during the Thirties, and again during the Eighties. The single high street has everything from a greengrocer to a hairdresser. Victorian two-up-two-down workers' cottages sell at about £50,000; Thirties and Fifties semis at between £65,000 and £70,000. The smarter roads are St John's Road, Wannock Road and Wannock Lane, where you would pay £145,000 for three bedrooms and clipped lawns. Polegate sprawls towards Hampden Park and there is no distinct division between the two.

HAMPDEN PARK

To Victoria
Journey time: *93 min*
Season ticket: *£2248*

Peak trains: *1 per hour**
Off-peak trains: *1 per hour*

* Plus 1 per hour to London Bridge (j/t: 88 min)

There are expensive and cheap sides to **Hampden Park**, which glories in all the variations on the suburban mock-Tudor style that you could imagine. Three-bedroom terrace houses sell for little over £40,000; detached houses tend to fetch around £180,000. There is nothing in the Victorian department. This is where Eastbourne has its industrial estate, and all the aircraft hangar-sized stores such as B&Q, Payless and Tesco have been put here too.

EASTBOURNE

To Victoria
Journey time: *83 min*
Season ticket: *£2248*

Peak trains: *1 per hour**
Off-peak trains: *1 per hour*

* Plus 1 per hour to London Bridge (j/t: 91 min)

Eastbourne is still very much a holiday resort and retirement town. Attractions such as Fort Fun and the Treasure Island theme park resound in summer to the shrieks of holidaying children, who then make for the beautiful Victorian pier to gorge themselves on ice cream. For more adult amusements there are the huge theatre/entertainment hall called The Congress, the Winter Gardens, the Devonshire Park Theatre and the Royal Hippodrome Theatre. There are also nightclubs and cinemas. Healthier pursuits include stupendous cliff walks over Beachy Head and those vast switchbacks of chalk, the Seven Sisters.

To live within walking distance of the station you have a choice of Edwardian and Victorian houses, or some Thirties detached. Prices vary enormously depending on size. You could pay £135,000 for three bedrooms; up to £315,000 for a mock-Tudor house with 10 bedrooms. The cheaper flats start at over £30,000. One of the most prestigious addresses is The Meades, a conservation area that attracts professionals and couples who have retired early. A modest semi here might cost £130,000, while a detached house with six bedrooms, six bathrooms and a jacuzzi might fetch all of £500,000. You can also expect to pay a premium price if you want to live near any of the three golf courses – the Royal, the Downs or the Willingdon.

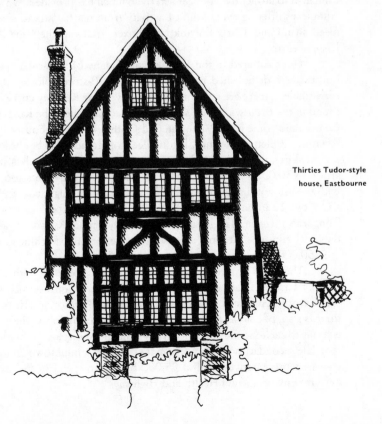

Thirties Tudor-style
house, Eastbourne

MAIN LINE FROM PRESTON PARK TO WORTHING
(see map)

There are other seaside stations along the route, but the London trains don't stop at them.

HOVE

To Victoria

Journey time: *61 min*	Peak trains: *2 per hour**
Season ticket: *£2016*	Off-peak trains: *1 per hour*

* Plus 1 per hour to London Bridge

Hove is much more sedate and "respectable" than its neighbour Brighton. Its image has been that of a haven for the elderly, and indeed it does have plenty of sheltered housing and low-level flats, but it is now making strenuous efforts to change its spots. The town has adopted as its marketing slogan the apologetic remark that people often make when they admit to not quite living in Brighton – "Hove, actually". As part of its campaign to attract the younger set, the council has provided two sports complexes offering every kind of activity from martial arts to synchronised swimming. Chris Eubank, the boxer, trains at the King Alfred leisure centre.

Hove suffered in the Thirties when many of its most important houses were demolished and replaced with 10-storey blocks of flats. Nevertheless, there are still some classic, sweeping Regency curves to be found in the Brunswick area; some Sussex cottages near the King Alfred Centre; and some good Victorian and Gothic Victorian houses in The Avenues, Willett Estate and Cliftonville. Property tends to be cheaper on the outskirts, where the modern estates are. Two-bedroom flats start at around £50,000. There are plenty of Thirties developments too, built with the ubiquitous shopping parade, where a semi might cost £75,000 and a two-bedroom bungalow £65,000. The most expensive roads are Tongdean Avenue, Tongdean Road and Dykeroad Avenue. Sea-front flats with film-star interiors are also hugely expensive, fetching as much as £250,000.

The town is strong on sport, being the home of both Sussex County Cricket Club and Brighton and Hove Albion Football Club. There are two golf clubs – the West Hove and the Brighton and Hove. And there is also, of course, the beach. As part of its youth policy, the council is trying to excite an interest in local government among local schoolchildren. The secondary schools were invited to elect a mini town council of teenage representatives, with a £5,000 budget to spend in the areas of Leisure, Environmental Health and Highways.

PORTSLADE

To Victoria

Journey time: *67 min*	Peak trains: *2 per hour**
Season ticket: *£2016*	Off-peak trains: *nil*

* Plus 1 per hour to London Bridge

Just as Hove has had something of a complex about Brighton, so **Portslade** has one about Hove. It might not look particularly impressive as you drive through, but if you turn off the main road you will find some 16th-century flint cottages and the old church of St Nicolas, which dates back to 1100. Its recent history is not very distinguished. Two decades ago it was know locally as "Nappy Valley" because it offered a mass of housing cheap enough for young couples to buy and breed in. Housing is still relatively inexpensive. Two-bedroom terrace houses sell for around £50,000; three-bedroom terraces for £55,000; three-bedroom semis for £55,000 to £65,000. Estate agents' books have been swollen by repossessions, and the bulk of the properties for sale are likely to be priced at under £65,000.

Villagers have succeeded in protecting from development an old field in the centre, so there is a green of sorts for people to walk on. More recently the local council at Hove has spent some money on restoring Portslade's main streets. They have re-paved, installed Victorian-style street lamps, and renovated the Victorian red-brick water tower which used to supply an isolation hospital. American Express has sponsored the installation of a camera obscura which gives a wonderful panoramic view of the South Downs.

SHOREHAM-BY-SEA

To Victoria

Journey time: *68 min*	Peak trains: *2 per hour**
Season ticket: *£2068*	Off-peak trains: *1 per hour*

* Plus 1 per hour to London Bridge

Shoreham is a Victorian seaport through which wood, gravel, wine and cars are brought in. The high street, which has the River Adur running along the bottom of it, has basic shops for day-to-day needs, but clothes shopping has to be done in Brighton or Worthing. It is free from hotels and B-and-Bs and does not feel like a seaside resort. It does have a sandy beach, however, and a popular pit-stop for wildfowl in the Widewater, a lagoon formed behind a man-made shingle bank. Shoreham airport (whence the first commercial flight was made in this country) still has flights to the Channel Islands, and is the base for several flying schools. Across the river on the shingle spit is the site of what was once Bungalow Town – a colony of wooden huts, made largely from disused railway carriages, which were once occupied by the London Music Hall fraternity. Some early films were made there, but most of it was destroyed in the Second World War to prevent its being used as a possible beachhead.

Modern, three-bedroom terrace houses sell at around £55,000. A two-bedroom seaside bungalow with a sunroom would fetch around

Bay-fronted bungalow,
Shoreham-by-Sea

£75,000; a third bedroom would put the price up to nearer £100,000. For a Marbella-style seaside hacienda, with a garage for every bedroom, you would have to pay upwards of £150,000. There are two secondary schools, the most popular being on the border of Shoreham and Southwick; and the boys' public school at Lancing is nearby.

LANCING

To Victoria
Journey time: *76 min*
Season ticket: *£2068*

Peak trains: *2 per hour* *
Off-peak trains: *nil*

* Plus I per hour to London Bridge

Old north and south Lancing have now blended into one and the once pretty high street has been spoilt by tasteless development. Many people commute to Gatwick and Brighton from here but few to London. There is still a smattering of thatch-and-flint in the north and fishermen's cottages in the south. A two-bedroom flat will cost £30,000 but the price of a period cottage or a newer substantial detached house is likely to be nearer £250,000. The boys' public school Lancing College, which takes girls in the sixth form, stands in 550 acres on a spur of the Downs overlooking the sea. There are several state primary schools here too which feed the state secondary school, Boundstone Community College.

WORTHING

To Victoria
Journey time: *75 min*
Season ticket: *£2132*

Peak trains: *2 per hour**
Off-peak trains: *1 per hour*

* Plus 1 per hour to London Bridge

Worthing has been increasingly popular with commuters over the last decade, absorbing housebuyers displaced by high prices from Surrey. To be within walking distance of the station you would need to live in one of the Edwardian terraces in the town centre, though the price you pay for being conveniently close to shops and station is that it is difficult to find parking spaces. Mid-terrace houses near the Promenade sell for between £60,000 and £80,000. B-and-Bs are concentrated in the centre, near the four large hotels, nightclubs, theatres and cinemas. The shopping centre is surprisingly varied, with specialist shops – one selling dolls' houses and dolls' furniture – and an art gallery called The Terrace. So don't imagine a town full of little old ladies in fluffy hats: the largest segment of the population is the 18–24 group, and the adult education centre is very well subscribed. Big businesses have settled here too. International Automobile Design, Nissan (now AFG) and Beecham's Pharmaceutical all have their offices here. Worthing is proud of the fact that it is the home of bowls. The world bowls championships are being held here this year (1992). One small warning: the sea-front can get rather smelly when the seaweed is churned up from the Bognor Regis beds.

VICTORIA/WATERLOO
—— TO ——
HORSHAM

BOXHILL & WEST HUMBLE

To Victoria
Journey time: *49 min*
Season ticket: *£1332*
Peak trains: *1 per hour*
Off-peak trains: *1 per hour*

To Waterloo
Journey time: *42 min*
Season ticket: *£1332*
Peak trains: *3 per hour*
Off-peak trains: *nil*

Just beyond the necklace of the M25, London suddenly lets go and gives way to one of the best-known beauty spots in the south-east. The hill itself rises to nearly 400ft above the River Mole, and affords panoramic views of the surrounding chalk downland and glimpses of the South Downs. But this does not necessarily make it a good place to live. The approaches to it are given over to caravan sites, and estate agents tend to say that **Box Hill** is more a place to look at, and look from, than to live in.

DORKING

To Victoria	To Waterloo
Journey time: *41 min*	Journey time: *44 min*
Season ticket: *£1368*	Season ticket: *£1368*
Peak trains: *2 per hour*	Peak trains: *3 per hour*
Off-peak trains: *2 per hour*	Off-peak trains: *nil*

Dorking is an ancient market town shot through with new buildings, antique shops and a couple of delicatessens. It prides itself on the variety of restaurants it provides, from Thai to French. Reigate Grammar School and St John's School at Leatherhead are the two popular local public schools, and Guildford is close enough for smart shops and the theatre. Most trains terminate here during the daytime, and you have to change if you want to travel further out of London. This makes it one of the most convenient stations on the line, and the web of villages that surround it have much to offer. In and around Dorking, prices are much the same with a three-bedroom semi with work to be done on it selling for around £90,000. One in better condition will cost around £120,000. There are also one-bedroom flats that sell for between £50,000 and £60,000.

Five miles west is **Shere** – a village so pretty, with a stream bubbling through it, that British Gas used it to illustrate the rural idyll in an advertising campaign. The square is picturesquely framed with old houses; it has a 12th-century church, several shops, a post office, tearooms, a couple of antique shops and a craft shop. Social activities abound – gardening club, youth and old folks' organisations – and for the moment it still retains its village school. The dramatic society is shared with **Peaselake**, which backs on to Hurtwood Common, one of the many Surrey commons that are covered in golden brooms and gorse, with shelter-belts of pine. The village has a green with a war memorial, and is very leafy.

Another very popular village is **Abinger Hammer**, which has a green and an insatiable passion for cricket. The Australian touring team was invited to play here, and the villagers managed to make the return match Down Under too. There is also an annual celebrity match. Opposite the pub is a clock tower from which a little man emerges every hour to bang the bell with a hammer – hence the name of the village.

Nearby is **Holmbury St Mary**, which has a green and a post office but has lost its school. This was once considered to be one of the most remote places in Surrey. The poor soil made it unsuitable for farming, so it became a refuge for smugglers and squatters and only began to be recognised as a village in the 1850s. Then it became popular with weekenders who built the first large Victorian houses up on Holmbury Hill, from which there are magnificent views over the Weald. By far the most remote spot here now is **Coldharbour**. Designated an Area of Outstanding Natural Beauty, it clings to the side of the 960ft Leith Hill, from which, on a clear day, you can see the Channel. It is a mountain in the middle of Surrey. The narrow winding roads that lead up to Coldharbour are often cut off in winter. There is no school, though it has a pub, a church, and a much-valued post bus that takes elderly villagers into Dorking.

To the east is **Brockham**, with 18th-century houses overlooking the green, pubs, and 16th-century church. You can easily spend £200,000 to £500,000 on a large house, but there are also some superb smaller ones which go for around £100,000. The main event of the year is the bonfire on Guy Fawkes Night, which draws thousands of people from miles around. **Newdigate** is another extremely popular village tucked right away from the main roads, though it has no green or village shop.

North Downs Line west to Gomshall

No through trains. Change at Dorking (Deepdene) – footpath link to Dorking station
Trains to Dorking (Deepdene): *2 per hour (peak)*

Dorking Deepdene is a good-quality residential area, close to the station yet set in beautiful woodland. It takes its name from the Deepdene Estate, which was owned by the Howard family. Large detached houses sell for around £300,000; smaller, three-bedroom detached houses for around £180,000; three-bedroom semis for around £120,000. **Dorking West** is partly residential, partly commercial, with new business parks springing up. A small terrace house would cost around £60,000; a semi between £100,000 and £120,000. **Gomshall** is an expensive village in which a Victorian two-bedroom semi would cost just under £100,000.

North Downs Line east to Betchworth

No through trains. Change at Dorking (Deepdene) – footpath link to Dorking station
Trains to Dorking (Deepdene): *2 per hour (peak)*

Betchworth sits on the banks of the River Mole surrounded by the North Downs and is something of a local beauty spot. It has some 17th-century houses, and there is a golf course in Betchworth Park. A three-bedroom detached house is likely to cost £220,000.

HOLMWOOD

Journey time: *51 min*	**Peak trains:** *2 per hour**
Season ticket: *£1600*	**Off-peak trains:** *1 per hour†*

* **Victoria only   † Victoria or Waterloo (change at Dorking)**

Note that after Dorking the train service is not as good, and it stops altogether after 2030. Some villages have been badly affected by the A24 cutting south. **Beare Green** straddles it, and now consists mainly of houses built during the Seventies and Eighties. They sell for less than those in Dorking, of which it is effectively a dormitory. The **Holmwoods** (**North** and **South**) are also staked out along the A24. North Holmwood still retains its green and pond, but has been submerged by new houses. The surrounding countryside is lovely, however, with 600 acres of common, pony treks and long walks. Just to the north is a memorial to Alfred Gwynne Vanderbilt, a member of the American millionaire family, who sacrificed himself by giving his lifejacket to a woman passenger when the *Titanic* sank.

OCKLEY

Journey time: *55 min*	**Peak trains:** *2 per hour**
Season ticket: *£1628*	**Off-peak trains:** *1 per hour†*

* **Victoria only   † Victoria or Waterloo (change at Dorking)**

Ockley's prettiness is being spoilt by the traffic on the A29, but it has some strong points: its own cricket pitch (visible from the main road), a conventional green with old houses set round it, and its own school. This whole area lies close enough to Guildford for commuters to take advantage of the fast trains into Waterloo (see page 228) as well as the local

Modern family house,
Horsham area

theatre and shops. Other commuters choose to jump a station by driving to Clandon (see page 243), where it is easier to park the car.

Cranleigh, strung between Ockley and Guildford, would meet many people's idea of the perfect small town. This is where the first cottage hospital was established. The main street has a story-book intimacy. The town still thinks of itself as a village, though the population runs to 12,000 people. It has a cricket green and a cinema, food shops, gift shops, shoe shops, delicatessens and a gun shop for the green wellington fraternity which has a strong presence here. A three-bedroom period cottage might cost around £200,000; a larger old house with three acres and a tennis court could fetch £400,000. Modern houses sell for less: five bedrooms for around £275,000. The area is wealthy – popular with executives in insurance, banking and oil (Esso recently moved its offices to Leatherhead), and those who own successful local companies. Jim Davidson, Eric Clapton and Phil Collins live nearby. Cranleigh School is the local boys' public school; the sister school, St Catherine's, is at Bramley near Guildford (page 231).

WARNHAM

Journey time: *68 min*	Peak trains: *2 per hour**
Season ticket: £1740	Off-peak trains: *1 per hour*†

* Victoria only   † Victoria or Waterloo (change at Dorking)

A sign warning that deer may cross the road is the first thing you see as you approach **Warnham** and its deer park. The old farming community has now been largely replaced by commuters to Guildford, London or Horsham, who are attracted by the green, pubs and old houses. A small semi in Bell Road in need of modernisation might sell for £90,000. Larger detached houses start at around £200,000.

HORSHAM

See line to Arundel (page 251) – it is by far the faster route into London from Horsham.

VICTORIA/LONDON BRIDGE
—— TO ——
UCKFIELD/EAST GRINSTEAD

OXTED

Journey time: *38 min*   **Peak trains:** *2 per hour**
Season ticket: *£1376*   **Off-peak trains:** *2 per hour*

* Plus 3 per hour to London Bridge

Oxted represents everything that most people would want a small town to be. It is safe for children and pleasant to live in, but not so pretty that it suffers invasion by tourists. It has a population of between 12,000 and 14,000, and all its vital organs are centralised within walking distance of each other – station, cinema, swimming pool and shops. There is still an old-fashioned cinema, privately owned, where the lady who sells the tickets also holds the ice-cream tray. It gets all the new releases, yet the atmosphere is cosy enough for parents to allow their children to go there unaccompanied. The town is also reasonably safe to walk around in after nightfall.

There are two main shopping streets – Station Road West, which is lined with mock-Tudor shops, and Station Road East. There is already a Sainsbury and a Gateway, and the town is divided by a controversy over plans for a new superstore. Some welcome the idea; others fear it will destroy the character of the place. Old Oxted is the prettiest part of the town, with 14th- to 16th-century cottages with pleasantly weathered pantiled roofs. Much of the rest is classic Thirties development.

A huge number of people commute to London or Croydon; otherwise people work in local shops or in the factories at Hurst Green. The wealthier residents live in the private wooded roads of Rockfield Road and Icehouse Wood, where large detached houses cost at least £400,000. Nearly all gardens in the town are large by London standards, some extending to over an acre or an acre and a half. Even the few modest two-bedroom Victorian terraces, selling at £80,000 to £90,000, have 100ft gardens. There are plenty of Thirties houses, with a five-bedroom detached costing around £270,000.

Teenagers looking for a good night out head for East Grinstead or Croydon, where there are nightclubs. Older funsters go into London for theatres, or to the country restaurants in the area. There are a couple of golf courses nearby, including one at Limpsfield.

Limpsfield and **Limpsfield Chart** are five minutes away by road. Both villages are occupied almost exclusively by newcomers, and both are

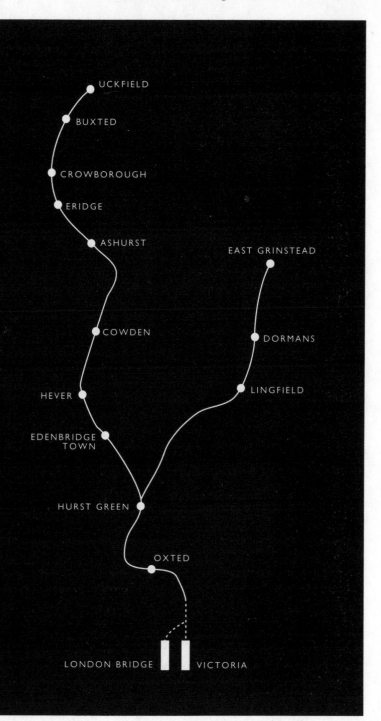

split by the A25. A car is essential for living here. Limpsfield is olde worlde and expensive. Its main street is eye-catching because of its old stone cottages. There are a few shops, a pub, and a highly rated expensive restaurant called The Lodge. Limpsfield Chart is also attractively set in a National Trust landscape. The Chart is the name of a stretch of common land which tumbles over the edge of the Weald, offering superb views as you head south and where you can see remnants of the old Roman road. In spring the woods sprout carpets of bluebells. A grand four-bedroom house on the common overlooking the North Downs, with tennis court and two acres of garden, could sell for £450,000.

16th-century cottage, Oxted

The village of **Tandridge** is less expensive, with Sixties and modern housing added to the mix. Three-bedroom Victorian houses and artisans' cottages cost around £160,000. Tandridge has shops, pubs and a school, but it is most definitely a commuter village. Unlike the Limpsfields, however, it is not near a main road and has much more the feel of a proper village. The north is the nicest part, with a lovely church and steeple standing on a little hill.

HURST GREEN

Journey time: *41 min*	**Peak trains:** *2 per hour**
Season ticket: *£1408*	**Off-peak trains:** *2 per hour*

* Plus 3 per hour to London Bridge

Hurst Green is more mundane and sprawly than Oxted, and cheaper. But it is a popular choice for people moving out of London looking for varied house types at low prices. On the 1960s Home Park estate, for instance, you could buy a two-bedroom house for £80,000; three-bedroom for £110,000. There is also a Wates estate, built about seven years ago, where one-bedroom starter homes on Barnfield Way cost around £55,000 to £60,000, and a couple of council estates with some former council houses for sale. The town is very segmented, and some of the segments are much nicer than others. The Green itself is picturesque. It is surrounded by older houses in the £200,000 range which have the advantage of being only a short walk from a splendid shop called Hobbs Stores, purveyor of fresh French bread and other goodies. It would be possible to do your entire weekly shop at Hobbs. Other parts of Hurst Green harbour the odd factory or two. All the segments have infants and junior schools, churches, post office and shops. Between Hurst Green and Edenbridge lies Staffhurst Wood, famous for its bluebells.

MAIN LINE FROM HURST GREEN TO UCKFIELD
(see map)

EDENBRIDGE TOWN

Journey time: *56 min*	**Peak trains:** *1 per hour*
Season ticket: *£1564*	**Off-peak trains:** *1 per hour**

* Change at Oxted

Edenbridge has two stations, the other one being Edenbridge on the North Downs line. The stations are a mile apart, and the two railway lines hold the worst bit of town in a pincer-grip between them, a depository for factories and council estates (though many of the former council houses are now privately owned). The best parts of town are in the north and south. First-time starter flats cost around £55,000 to £65,000; or for the same price you could buy an attractive one-bedroom terrace cottage. Four-bedroom houses on a well-kept estate like The Ridgeway, built in 1959, cost about £150,000, including a 200ft garden.

Although Edenbridge is not one of the gems of Kent, it does have its attractions. It is an hour from London and the same from the coast. Gatwick is only half an hour away, but not so close that aircraft noise is a worry. The town has a seemingly endless high street, with houses and the odd factory and then more shops. The south-eastern portion of the town, towards Hever, is more pleasing. The south-west end of town, towards **Haxted**, is also nice. It is small-scale with some attractive properties, antique shops and a large working watermill which is now a museum. On the northern flank is a mini-industrial estate and a very large, sprawling London overspill council estate called Spittals Cross, where the houses have thin slit windows and flat roofs. Wits say that Edenbridge is a tale of two towns, offering a spectrum of urban blight to rural delight within one and a half miles. The river Eden meanders through the southern tip, and keeps anglers happy. There are all the other usual leisure pursuits too: cricket, football, tennis, badminton, rugby, hockey, bowls and golf clubs.

The villages surrounding Edenbridge are much more scenic than the town itself. They have a number of fine timber-framed houses from the 16th century, built on the proceeds of the iron industry which collapsed in about 1700.

HEVER

Journey time: *58 min*	**Peak trains:** *1 per hour*
Season ticket: £1600	**Off-peak trains:** *1 per hour**

* Change at Oxted

Hever is one of the area's tourist attractions, popular with visitors en route to Hever Castle, where Henry VIII courted Anne Boleyn. The village is unspoilt, and is an extraordinarily small place to command its own railway station. A house here in consequence will cost around £50,000 more than a similar property in Edenbridge. For a four-bedroom house you will have to pay in the region of £200,000. There is no cheap property in Hever, but the least expensive are the former labourers' cottages from the Astor estate. These have been sold and, as the locals put it, "tweed up" by their new owners. The village has a church, a few houses and the Henry VIII pub. This lost its licence some years ago, to the horror of the villagers, but has now been restored. Beyond a massive stone gateway you enter the drive to Hever Castle and its strange mock-Tudor village, which is hired out for conferences etc. In high summer, plays and concerts are held in the Italian gardens.

The village has a Church of England primary school which reverses the usual demographic trend. Instead of children being bussed from village to town, children from Edenbridge are brought to Hever, so high is the reputation of the school. There are no shops in the village, and the nearest post office is three miles away in Four Elms. Horticultural shows are held in the village hall. Although Hever proper is small, the parish has 800 on the electoral roll and is quite far flung. There is a village rota to help ferry pensioners to the shops. As there is absolutely nothing for teenagers to do, it is probably just as well that the population consists of solicitors, commuters, retired people and minor landed gentry.

COWDEN

Journey time: *61 min*	**Peak trains:** *1 per hour*
Season ticket: £1652	**Off-peak trains:** *1 per hour**

* Change at Oxted

Cowden is a very pretty village cushioned amid the quiet leafy lanes that wind through the Weald. Its strikingly wide main street has a curious symmetry, with a pub and a housing estate at each end, and it contains the village's oldest houses – many of them 400 years old. Buses do exist here but you would be seriously inconvenienced without a car, for there are no shops. It pays to get on with the neighbours because the same people are likely to belong to all the same societies and to turn up at all the same events – the horticultural society, British Legion and WI. There is no school, and teenagers have little to do except gatepost-hang. A modern four-bedroom house designed in the Kentish-farmhouse style, with a small garden and double garage, was recently offered for sale at £185,000.

ASHURST

Journey time: *67 min*	**Peak trains:** *1 per hour*
Season ticket: *£1692*	**Off-peak trains:** *1 per hour**

* Change at Oxted

Ashurst is very rural and slightly stand-offish in its attitude to newcomers. You may have to spend six months standing on the platform with the other six passengers at Ashurst station before they get round to noticing you. The village is very small but it manages to cram in a village hall, a church, a post office-cum-shop, and a pub called the Bald Faced Stag. It is more expensive than nearby Eridge (see below), but properties in both villages rarely come up for sale and you'll have to move quickly if you want to buy. There is a bus service of sorts but, as ever in this area, car ownership is practically essential.

The larger villages of Langton Green (see page 291) and **Groombridge** are also close to Ashurst. Groombridge straddles the county boundary with the new, modern dormitory village forging into Sussex and lovely Old Groombridge lingering in Kent. The old part is currently feeling rather threatened because the owner, Rosemary Newton, died recently and much of it is up for sale. She owned the 16th-century terrace cottages, the pub called the Crown Inn which faces the triangular village green, the 17th-century moated manor house, Groombridge Place, and its 200-acre estate. The whole lot has been priced at £3.25m. Groombridge Place was used by the director Peter Greenaway for the film of *The Draughtsman's Contract*.

ERIDGE

Journey time: *72 min*	**Peak trains:** *1 per hour**
Season ticket: *£1740*	**Off-peak trains:** *1 per hour†*

* Plus 1 per hour to London Bridge   † Change at Oxted

Eridge is a very small village, best known for its huge park which is scored with footpaths. It has a church and a store, though the post office closed recently. Much of it was once part of the Abergavenny estate and some of the old estate cottages still come onto the open market sometimes.

CROWBOROUGH

Journey time: *77 min* | **Peak trains:** *1 per hour**
Season ticket: *£1824* | **Off-peak trains:** *1 per hour†*

* Plus 1 per hour to London Bridge   † Change at Oxted

Crowborough is one of those strange areas that are sedate and suburban to the core, yet lack a proper focus or a shopping centre. It began as a series of big hilltop hotels built around a golf course and later became a popular retirement haven and then, in the early Fifties, came an explosion of housing estates which turned it into a commuter dormitory with a population of 27,000 people. The only cinema closed down a few years ago, but there is a leisure centre with swimming pool, badminton and squash, and there are two supermarkets.

The Warren is the smartest part of town, built to the north and looking down over Ashdown Forest. Homes in The Warren are mainly in the £200,000 to £250,000 bracket, detached houses with four or five bedrooms. Most of the larger houses, which once stood in extensive grounds, have now had smaller houses or flats built around them. This infilling has spoiled the previously rather gracious character of the area.

On the newest estates a one-bedroom starter home costs £50,000 and a three-bedroom house £85,000. Much of the building in and around the town centre is Victorian, and the least attractive streets are those near the station and the industrial estate. Further out are a number of former 16th- and 17th-century farmhouses. Sir Arthur Conan Doyle lived at Hurtis Hill, and when he died in 1930 he was buried in his back garden overlooking Crowborough Common and the golf course. His body was later exhumed and re-buried in Minstead Churchyard in the New Forest. The house has since been turned into a hotel called Windlesham Manor.

Rotherfield nearby offers Edwardian and Victorian houses, and is very much an adjunct to Crowborough. A small cottage costs around £85,000.

BUXTED

Journey time: *86 min* | **Peak trains:** *1 per hour**
Season ticket: *£1896* | **Off-peak trains:** *1 per hour†*

* Plus 1 per hour to London Bridge   † Change at Oxted

Buxted is mostly modern but nevertheless quite attractive. It has a population of around 4,000, and real shops that sell clothes and food rather than antiques. Property prices are about the same as those in Uckfield, which is only a brisk walk down the road.

UCKFIELD

Journey time: *91 min*
Season ticket: *£1904*

Peak trains: *1 per hour**
Off-peak trains: *1 per hour†*

* Plus 1 per hour to London Bridge † Change at Oxted

Uckfield is a rapidly expanding "strip" town. The population currently stands at around 15,000, but new houses are going up all the time. Older properties are mainly Victorian, and a semi of this period will cost around £100,000 to £110,000. Locals describe the rail service as abominable, and suggest that it would be quicker to travel by pram. For a smallish town there are a lot of facilities – leisure centre, cinema, library, bowling green, and the nearby Piltdown golf club. It is also surrounded by lovely countryside, ideal for walking or cycling. To the north-west, the country lanes wind into the Ashdown Forest. Here there are also some rather grand houses which have been dropping their prices. A five-bedroom house with a paddock and enormous garden could be bought for between £300,000 and £450,000 depending on the urgency of the sale. Repossessions offer the best opportunities for relatively cheap buys.

Because of the shortcomings of the local rail service, many London commuters prefer to drive the 12 miles to Haywards Heath (page 257) and use the faster service from there. Uckfield is now bypassed but used to be a notorious bottleneck on the A22 to Eastbourne. Fortunately all public car parks in the town are free – a mercy for people from the surrounding villages, who have very few shops of their own.

The beautiful villages nearby are **Fletching** and **Nutley**. Fletching is the most desirable. It has no new estates and is set in the Ashdown Forest which is ideal for walks and pony rides. This is a village like villages used to be, with a close-knit community, a good village centre and beamed pubs. Many of the houses are picture-postcard trim. Three-bedroom houses, some with half an acre of land, sell for around £140,000 to £150,000.

Little Horstead, to the south, is popular with golfers because of its proximity to Horstead Place, a large country estate with hotel and golf complex.

MAIN LINE FROM HURST GREEN TO EAST GRINSTEAD (see map)

LINGFIELD

Journey time: *48 min*
Season ticket: *£1600*

Peak trains: *1 per hour**
Off-peak trains: *2 per hour*

* Plus 3 per hour to London Bridge

Lingfield and Dormansland (see below) are merged as one, glued in the middle by the squash club which is the villages' social pivot. The club also has snooker and a gym, where there are special workout sessions for women.

Lingfield is the larger and older of the two villages, with a population that now reaches over 4,000. There has been very little new development, so the marvellous collection of 15th-century, Tudor, Jacobean and Georgian properties has been kept intact, and many of the buildings are scheduled as ancient monuments. Modern interlopers include the occasional Thirties house and a small Eighties estate.

The area is very popular with people who need to be close to Gatwick airport. Pilots, air hostesses and ground staff live here; so do many business travellers. There are excellent communications, with the M25 only eight minutes' drive away and the M23 also close by. Lingfield has a typical range of village shops including two small supermarkets, a butcher and a baker. Next to the pond at the heart of the village is a strange stone structure roofed with iron bars. This is the so-called "cage", built in 1473 and thought to have been used as a lock-up for poachers and drunkards.

House prices cover an enormous range, from £60,000 to £600,000 – perhaps even more for a major property fronting the common. Houses at the top end of the market might come with their own equestrian facilities; one even has an indoor riding school. There is no such thing as a "typical" Lingfield house to extrapolate average prices from, but a three-bedroom terrace might go for £70,000; a three-bedroom detached for as much as £250,000.

Lingfield racecourse nearby is one of two in Britain to have an all-weather surface, but few trainers or jockeys live in the area. The style is more pony-club and conspicuous wealth. The village has a first and second school, but older children are bussed to Oxted.

DORMANS

Journey time: *51 min*	Peak trains: *1 per hour**
Season ticket: *£1616*	Off-peak trains: *2 per hour*

* Plus 3 per hour to London Bridge

Dormansland is slightly smaller than Lingfield, with a population of just under 4,000 if you include **Dormans Park**. It has a post office and one other shop plus a hairdresser, a couple of pubs, a church and a first school. Houses are largely Victorian with a smattering of modern and small council estates. Dormans Park, which is actually closer to the station than Dormansland itself, has a curious history. It grew up when rich Victorians used to come down from London for the weekend to attend Lingfield races. A number of little summer houses were built around the Dormans Hotel (now disappeared), where many of them liked to stay. The summer houses grew grander, and Dormans Park became the sort of place where the playboys of the time liked to entertain their mistresses. Nearly all the houses are large, detached villas in sizeable plots of land surrounded by countryside and they tend to sell for between £300,000 and £400,000. The area is rather secluded, and has no local facilities of its own.

EAST GRINSTEAD

Journey time: *54 min*
Season ticket: *£1672*

Peak trains: *1 per hour**
Off-peak trains: *2 per hour*

* Plus 3 per hour to London Bridge

The town of **East Grinstead** itself retains the characteristics of the market town it once was, though it now has a bypass and other modern appendages. It is in two parts – the old town, which includes much of the high street; and London Road, which contains the new major shops. It is becoming more of an industrial and commercial town, with new offices springing up. East Grinstead draws in people from the surrounding villages for their regular shop, though large or specialist items have to be sought in Croydon or Crawley. The town's old cinema was pulled down, but a new leisure complex is going up on the site which will include not only a new cinema but also a disco and a bowling alley. East Grinstead's theatre has been bought by a security firm, and there is strong local pressure for it to be reopened. One of East Grinstead's attractions to commuters is that its station is at the end of the line, so there's no danger of going to sleep and missing your stop.

There are some pretty old buildings in the centre of the town, including 14 open hall houses in the high street. Particularly handsome is Sackville College, a Sussex sandstone almshouse with high chimneys, a quadrangle and gardens, which is now converted for sheltered housing. Otherwise there is a wide range of housing and quite a number of new estates have sprung up in the last 20 years. Cheap starter homes and flats cost between £55,000 and £80,000. A larger modern mock-Georgian four-bedroom house will cost about £160,000. The best houses are in Imberhorn.

Two manor houses outside the town are put to strangely contrasting uses. Saint Hill Manor, to the south, is the headquarters of the Church of Scientology. Gravetye Manor is one of the best small country house hotels and restaurants in Britain. For fishing, sailing and walking there is Weir Wood Reservoir nearby and to the south is the Ashdown Forest where the countryside becomes very beautiful. Here you come up onto the Weald, where you find some of the last remaining heathland in the south-east, the sort of place where you can walk and see the silver-studded blue butterfly of warm summer evenings.

CHARING CROSS/ CANNON STREET
— TO —
HASTINGS

SEVENOAKS

Journey time: *29 min*	**Peak trains:** *4 per hour**
Season ticket: *£1444*	**Off-peak trains:** *4 per hour*

* Plus 4 per hour to Cannon St

Sevenoaks has been a commuter town ever since the railway first arrived in 1862. Recently it has developed a reputation for wealth, with a survey showing more cars per head of population than any other town in England. The concentration of private schools is another reliable money indicator. There is Sevenoaks School for boys and girls, Solefield for boys, Walthamstow Hall and West Heath for girls, and a clutch of prep schools bringing on the right sort of children. Their fathers are surveyors, accountants, solicitors and other successful professionals. Though the shops are good, and a new Sainsbury is opening nearby, the women of Sevenoaks almost perversely seem to prefer shopping in Bromley or Tunbridge Wells. Other people, however, flock into Sevenoaks for the quaint little shops in Dorset Street, Bank Street and Well Court. Other attractions include the Stag Cinema and Stag Theatre, the swimming and sports centres, two golf courses in town and four more nearby, and The Vine, the ground on which some of the earliest reported cricket matches were played. Sevenoaks Cricket Week happens every July, and if the sound of bat on ball is not music enough to your ears, then there is the Sevenoaks Summer Festival of music, drama and art. Nearby are the wooded walks of the North Downs Way, the lakes and grassland of the Sevenoaks Wildfowl Reserve, and Knole – one of the largest private houses in Britain, set in a vast deer park, where Vita Sackville-West spent her childhood.

Some of the most expensive addresses are on the Wildernesse Estate, where small mansions were developed during the Thirties on huge two-acre plots. Many of these now have smaller modern houses squeezed on to them, often bought by what estate agents refer to as New Money. A five- to eight-bedroom house here will cost upwards of around £400,000. The **Kippington** area is also popular, offering a mix of Victorian, Thirties and post-war housing priced in the £300,000-£400,000 range. Throughout the town you can buy ordinary four-bedroom family houses of varying periods at prices between £170,000 and £225,000. One of the

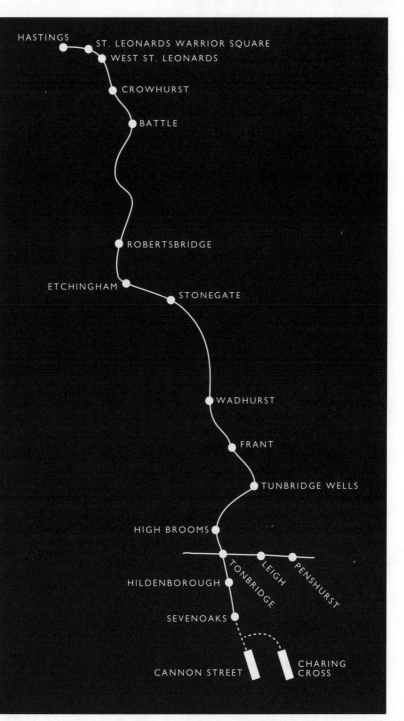

quaintest old streets is Six Bells Lane, where tiny one-bedroom 18th- and 19th-century cottages cost around £55,000. There is a snag here, however. If the cottages score points for charm, they lose them on parking difficulty. The large houses around The Vine cricket ground now tend to be converted into flats, the cheapest of which sell at around £60,000. There are more flats in a purpose-built block also overlooking The Vine, where a spacious apartment with views would cost around £200,000.

HILDENBOROUGH

Journey time: *40 min*

Season ticket: *£1572*

Peak trains: *3 per hour**

Off-peak trains: *1 per hour*

    * Plus 2 per hour to Cannon St

Hildenborough is something of a Cinderella to the wealthy towns around it. It has the occasional shop and garage but no real centre, and the B245 makes it a place to drive through rather than stop in. For affordable housing, however, it's worth a look. A two-bedroom house will cost around £65,000; a three-bedroom one around £80,000.

TONBRIDGE

Journey time: *38 min*

Season ticket: *£1668*

Peak trains: *6 per hour**

Off-peak trains: *4 per hour*

    * Plus 3 per hour to Cannon St

Tonbridge has none of the glamour of Tunbridge Wells, to which it gave its name, though it does have the remains of a motte-and-bailey castle in the town centre. It is a busy one-street town with quite a few businesses and small industries, among which the main local employer is Benn Publications. It also has Tonbridge School, the private school for boys. A studio flat in Tonbridge will cost £28,000; a two-bedroom terrace house £55,000; a three-bedroom detached £70,000.

North Downs Line west to Leigh and Penshurst

No through trains. Trains to Tonbridge: *1 per hour*

Leigh (pronounced *Lie*) is very much a dormitory village. It has a huge green canopied with conker trees, and traditional tile-hung and weatherboarded Kentish houses. There is a general store and post office, supplemented by a mobile butchers and fishmongers. The primary school flourishes, and organised activities range all the way from mothers-and-toddlers to cricket club. Leigh is popular with London solicitors and bankers, which explains why a new development of executive houses is under way. A five-bedroom period property with four reception rooms, granny annexe, tennis court and swimming pool was offered last year at £450,000. **Penshurst** nearby is an attractive, straggly Kentish village with some nice old tile-hung cottages. The heavy influx of commuters here has resulted in a certain them-and-us feeling. Commuters are often referred to as "invisible parishioners", so slight is their involvement in village activities. Support for the village football and cricket teams has dwindled, and the old and new villagers drink in different pubs. Penshurst has its own village school, general store and tourist shop (Penshurst Place and Hever Castle are both very close). Activities include amateur dramatics, bridge, dancing and stoolball (a cross between rounders and cricket, played with a round wooden bat). Property is now so expensive that it is beyond the means of local young people. A two-bedroom cottage might cost around £85,000; a five-bedroom period stone house £348,000; a substantial Queen Anne house may top the £500,000 mark. **Chiddingstone** is also a show-stopping village – the main street, with Chiddingstone Castle at one end, is owned by the National Trust. Prices are similar to those in Penshurst.

HIGH BROOMS

Journey time: *44 min* | Peak trains: *4 per hour**
Season ticket: *£1740* | Off-peak trains: *2 per hour*

* Plus 2 per hour to Cannon St

High Brooms, dominated by the warehouses of Payless and MFI, is the industrial face of Tunbridge Wells – a steep hill lined with streets of Victorian terraces, most of them built in brick from the old Tunbridge Wells brick company. It is within reach of the more elegant part of town, but property prices are significantly lower. A two-bedroom terrace will cost around £50,000; a three-bedroom semi around £80,000. On the eastern side are Sherwood Park and Home Farm, two areas where new housing estates burgeoned during the Eighties. A two-bedroom house here will cost £65,000; a four-bedroom house £100,000.

TUNBRIDGE WELLS

Journey time: *47 min* | Peak trains: *4 per hour**
Season ticket: *£1764* | Off-peak trains: *2 per hour*

* Plus 2 per hour to Cannon St

Royal Tunbridge Wells is to Kent what Bath is to Avon. The gracious crescents and elaborate terraces, designed by Decimus Burton to serve its image as a fashionable 18th-century watering hole, still give it an air of great prosperity. Beau Nash was master of ceremonies at the wells from 1735, and you can still take a foul-tasting sip from the dipper at the Pantiles. For a more complete re-creation of the past there is "A Day At

The Wells", one of those sight, sound and smell museums that aim to leave as little as possible to the imagination. Modern Tunbridge Wells caters for recreational tastes of every kind. There are a couple of art galleries, theatres, a cinema, a lively arts centre and two golf courses, plus a rugby club and Kent county cricket ground. It is a shopper's paradise, with a huge range of specialists including a food hall in the restored Corn Exchange, kitchen shops crammed with cast-iron pots, chocolate shops, tearooms, antique shops, bespoke jewellers and many more.

Undoubtedly the best address in Tunbridge Wells is Nevill Park, where large sumptuous houses, dating from the 1800s to the present day, overlook the town from a ridge. On one side is the green expanse of Tunbridge Wells Common; on the other is Hungershall Park. A grandly proportioned house with five bedrooms, two bathrooms, three reception rooms, large central staircase, high decorated ceilings and perhaps a Victorian conservatory at the back might cost between £350,000 and £500,000. A brand new 5,500sq ft house will be priced at £750,000. Nevill Park is a private road with lodge gates at each end, ten minutes' walk from the station.

Stable block conversion,
near Tunbridge Wells

You would also need a deep pocket if you were to consider one of the exquisitely designed houses by Decimus Burton in Calverly Park. Some of these have been been converted into flats; others sub-divided into two. A four-bedroom half-house might cost around £300,000; double it for a well-maintained whole house. In Calverly Park Crescent, where shops were originally designed into the ground floors beneath heavily gardened balconies, you could find a home for around £240,000.

The imposing private houses built along Mount Ephraim are also sought after, though 70 per cent of them have been turned into flats. A three-bedroom flat with grand reception rooms will cost between £100,000 and £180,000. There are some smaller ones at around £60,000.

Ordinary family houses are to be found in Royal Chase and Culverden Down, behind Mount Ephraim and only a short walk from the station and the shops. Many of them were built during the various building booms of the current century. A four-bedroom, two-bathroom tile-hung house with leaded lights and brick fireplaces, built in 1945 as solid and conservative as Tunbridge Wells knows how, will cost between £200,000 and £300,000. Those of more modest means go east of St John's Sports Centre to the tightly knit area of terraces and semis where a three-bedroom semi with no garage will cost between £85,000 and £135,000.

The reputation of the local schools is another major factor in the town's popularity. They include Skinners, a boys' grammar school; Tunbridge Wells Boys' Grammar; Tunbridge Wells Girls' Grammar; and two comprehensives. All are close to St John's Sports Centre and swimming pool.

Tunbridge Wells is surrounded by rich riding country well provided with bridle-ways and livery stables. The Eridge and South Downs hunt and the pony club are both vigorously attended. **Langton Green**, two and a half miles to the west, is a favourite with local businessmen. It has its own village shops, some old village houses and cottages, plenty of new housing and a popular mixed prep school called Holmwood House. A four-bedroom detached house will cost between £150,000 and £180,000. Two-bedroom cottages cost £60,000. Immediately to the north of Tunbridge Wells is **Pembury**, which has a bypass and offers a large volume of middle-range modern housing. A three-bedroom detached house here would cost around £85,000. See also Penshurst, Leigh and Chiddingstone on the **North Downs Line** (above).

FRANT

Journey time: *56 min* | Peak trains: *2 per hour**
Season ticket: *£1800* | Off-peak trains: *1 per hour*

* Plus 2 per hour to Cannon St

The most striking feature of this hilltop village is its green. Surrounded by superb timber-frame and Georgian houses, it makes a perfect setting for village cricket. The equivalent of the vicarage in **Frant** – a voluminous 10-bedroom house set in two acres – was recently offered at £600,000. A modern four-bedroom house with two bathrooms would fetch around £295,000. The village has its own shops, a restaurant, a bowling green and a well-attended primary school – though many children transfer to private schools when they reach secondary age. The station is actually at Bells Yew Green, and for years the stationmaster ran a wellie-warming service for commuters returning in the evening. Post-journey comfort these days is more likely to be found at the Brecknock Arms, just around the corner.

Lamberhurst is definitely a village worth looking at. Although currently hammered by the A21, there is a bypass on the way and the new air of quiet is likely to push property prices up by 10 per cent. Lamberhurst has some good oak-framed houses, antique shops, a village store, a Range Rover garage and a vineyard. Two-bedroom cottages sell for around £70,000; three-bedrooms for up to £80,000.

WADHURST

Journey time: *55 min*	**Peak trains:** *2 per hour**
Season ticket: *£1856*	**Off-peak trains:** *2 per hour*

* Plus 2 per hour to Cannon St

Wadhurst is a narrow, busy and attractive village, set in an Area of Outstanding Natural Beauty in the High Weald. It is big enough to have around 30 shops including a couple of banks, a good butcher, doctor, dentist, solicitor and so on. Lying on the borders of Sussex and Kent, it offers the choice of two different county education systems. Some people choose Wadhurst's own Uplands Community College, which combines the role of good comprehensive school with adult education and sports centre. Others shuttle their children into Kent to take advantage of the old-fashioned grammar schools in Tunbridge Wells. There are two livery stables, and lots of teenagers ride – the horse population in Wadhurst is between 300 and 400, approximately one for every 10 people.

A two-bedroom village house, old or new, will cost around £60,000 – approximately the same as a one-bedroom flat in one of the small modern developments. Three-bedroom terrace houses built in vernacular style fetch around £140,000; five-bedroom executive houses with 2,400sq ft of space around £245,000. A decent period house with four bedrooms and a garden will be valued at around £200,000; something more lavish with five bedrooms, tennis court and swimming pool will be around £400,000.

STONEGATE

Journey time: *67 min*	**Peak trains:** *2 per hour**
Season ticket: *£1924*	**Off-peak trains:** *1 per hour*

* Plus 2 per hour to Cannon St

Stonegate itself is tiny, with a ribbon of modern estates and council housing. There is a shop and a primary school, but most people would prefer to live in **Ticehurst**. The village is attractively set around a central square in a conservation area. Three horse chestnut trees guard the bus stop which now stands in place of the old village pump. Shops include a village store, baker, butcher, haberdasher, D-I-Y store, dry cleaner and greengrocer. For the last three years a group called Same Sky has visited the village to run art workshops for adults and children in the summer holidays. Ticehurst has its own primary school and a good choice of local societies. Prices are lower than in Wadhurst because it is thought to be more out-of-the-way. A small semi in a cul-de-sac will cost £76,000; a weatherboarded two-bedroom cottage £85,000; a three-bedroom bungalow £155,000. The big house in the village has been split and converted – a four-bedroom slice of it will cost £155,000.

ETCHINGHAM

Journey time: *72 min*
Season ticket: *£1960*

Peak trains: *2 per hour**
Off-peak trains: *1 per hour*

* Plus 2 per hour to Cannon St

Etchingham is popular because it is reasonably good to look at and has the convenience of its own railway station. The village winds up the hill from the railway, offering a sprinkling of traditional weatherboarded properties among the 18th-century houses and a Fifties estate. There is also a modern development opposite the village hall. Etchingham has a general store, post office and a butcher that has been in the same family for generations. There is a much-loved primary school, and the Etchingham Club where people gather for billiards and darts. Haremere Hall, where Shire horses are bred and shown, is a tourist attraction. A small semi in the village might cost between £80,000 and £90,000; a three-bedroom detached house down one of the lanes would be around £100,000 to £150,000.

Burwash is more attractive than Etchingham and is well known for its striking high street of white weatherboarded and tile-hung houses, tearooms, brick footpaths and lime trees. Prices are similar to those in Etchingham – held down by the fact that they are further from the station. On the edge of the village are some five- and six-bedroom modern houses, each one set in half an acre, selling for £245,000. Half a mile away is Bateman's, where Rudyard Kipling lived and wrote *Puck of Pook's Hill*.

To the north-east, back over the border into Kent, is **Hawkhurst**, a village in two halves. Housebuyers would probably avoid the half that contains the junction of two main roads in favour of an area known as The Moor in the neighbouring valley. This has a large village green, playing fields and small shops and cottages. A two-bedroom terrace house will cost around £50,000; a three-bedroom semi £70,000; a four-bedroom detached modern house £120,000; a four-bedroom period house in one of the lanes over £150,000. Both Hawkhurst and its much smaller neighbour, **Sandhurst**, are within the catchment area of Cranbrook

School, one of the most highly respected schools in Kent, run on traditional grammar school lines. Hawkhurst also has a clutch of private schools, including Marlborough House for boys and Bedgebury Lower School for girls.

● ROBERTSBRIDGE

Journey time: *76 min* | **Peak trains:** *2 per hour**
Season ticket: *£2008* | **Off-peak trains:** *1 per hour*

  * Plus 2 per hour to Cannon St

Considering the prettiness of the countryside that surrounds it, **Roberts-bridge** is surprisingly unprosperous. There is no major town or city centre close enough to attract regular commuters, and those who come here tend to want escape. Hastings, it has to be said, does not offer much of a diversion. Robertsbridge's lovely village high street has now been relieved of through traffic by a bypass. It has a sub-post office, butcher, chemist, greengrocer, general store and two hairdressers. The new village hall hosts regular meetings of the archaeological society, playgroups and ballroom dancing classes. There is also football, stoolball for women, and, especially, cricket. The Gray-Nicholls factory makes bats out of locally grown willow (and also the round wooden bats for Sussex stoolball). Property prices in Robertsbridge have been weak for some time. A three-bedroom cottage will cost between £65,000 and £85,000; a three- or four-bedroom modern house between £85,000 and £150,000; and a large country house with extensive grounds between £250,000 and £300,000. Until his death recently, its most famous resident was the journalist and thinker Malcolm Muggeridge. Current residents include the mild-mannered members of a commune who live in the beautifully restored old TB sanatorium. They are very self-contained, make their own clothes and educate their own children. The women distinguish themselves by always wearing a distinctive dark blue spotted headscarf.

● BATTLE

Journey time: *72 min* | **Peak trains:** *2 per hour**
Season ticket: *£2008* | **Off-peak trains:** *2 per hour*

  * Plus 2 per hour to Cannon St

Battle is as self-contained, charming and spirited as any market town in England might have been before the 20th century came along to ruin it. Its most famous asset, of course, is the remains of Battle Abbey, on the site of King Harold's defeat by William the Conqueror in 1066. A spectacular bonfire is lit in the abbey car park on Guy Fawkes Night, big enough to rival the one in Lewes. The town otherwise has a high street full of shops and inns, some of them timber-framed or weatherboarded, and there are some nice old tearooms for connoisseurs of the sticky bun. A first-time buyer could find a one-bedroom period cottage in need of renovation for just under £50,000. Three-bedroom semis come at between £60,000 and £70,000; detached houses at £80,000 to £90,000.

In the lanes around Battle are some rather grand houses in the £200,000 to £500,000 range. For example, a converted oast with 30 acres and a barn for conversion would be likely to fetch in excess of £400,000. Of the neighbouring villages, **Sedlescombe** is particularly pretty with a traditional village green fringed with brick and tile-hung cottages. It has a post office, a grocer, a pub, a hotel, a restaurant, and a good primary school attended by children from surrounding villages. **Catsfield** and **Ninfield** are so popular that most of the house-moves involve people already living there. For utter rural tranquillity there is **Penhurst**, a picturesque hamlet in deep Sussex countryside. Prices in all the villages are roughly similar to those in Battle itself.

CROWHURST

Journey time: *87 min*
Season ticket: *£2116*

Peak trains: *2 per hour**
Off-peak trains: *1 per hour*

* Plus 2 per hour to Cannon St

The station makes **Crowhurst** an extremely sought-after village. The electrification of the line four years ago was followed by an influx of buyers from outside the area (two-thirds of people looking for property at that time were from London). You can now expect to pay £60,000–£70,000 for a small semi; anything from £200,000 to £400,000

Grade II listed
terrace cottage,
east Sussex

for an older detached house. As you come down the hill from Bexhill you see the remains of the old medieval manor house next to the Norman church. There are some lovely tile-hung houses and the oldest yew tree in the county – it may have been here to welcome William the Conqueror. Crowhurst has often been voted best-kept village, though the judges have criticised it for the clods of mud left by the herds of cows that plod through for the morning and evening milkings. The Plough Inn runs an annual pumpkin show, providing plantlets to people on a specific date so that all the competitors start level. The village has a primary school; clubs ranging from Over-60s to Cubs; sports groups from tennis to cricket; a horticultural society which holds three flower shows a year; and a busy drama group. Tesco at Hollington sends a bus to the village each week, and there is a shopping and recreational complex at Glyne Gap, between Bexhill and Hastings.

WEST ST LEONARDS

Journey time: *93 min*
Season ticket: *£2184*
Peak trains: *2 per hour**
Off-peak trains: *1 per hour*

* Plus 2 per hour to Cannon St

ST LEONARDS WARRIOR SQ.

Journey time: *82 min*
Season ticket: *£2184*
Peak trains: *2 per hour**
Off-peak trains: *2 per hour*

Though the stations are only a few minutes apart, many trains do stop at both. The area was created by James Burton and his son Decimus as a bit of early speculative development. **St Leonards** was conceived by them as a dignified residential area, but time has taken its inevitable toll. It now has fish-and-chip shops and restaurants along the sea-front and has been badly hit by the recession. People from South London and Tunbridge Wells tend to move here for the sea air and the comparatively low prices – though the serious retirement area is to the west, at Bexhill-on-Sea. There is an enormous amount of property on the market at the moment, particularly for first-time buyers. Studio flats start at only £12,000, with smarter one-bedroom units at up to £20,000. A sea view can affect prices in boom time, but in a time of glut it tends not to make much difference. Three-bedroom houses of any period tend to cost between £45,000 and £50,000. There are also some very large six-bedroom Victorian houses that sell for £85,000 – very good value when you consider that they were fetching £130,000 during the boom.

HASTINGS

Journey time: *84 min*
Season ticket: *£2184*

* Plus 2 per hour to Cannon St

Peak trains: *2 per hour**
Off-peak trains: *2 per hour*

Hastings has never quite caught the limelight in the way that Brighton has. Much of it has a slightly down-at-heel look, though the population still swells with trippers and holiday-makers during the summer. There are good walks along East Cliff across the gorse-covered valleys to Fairlight. Hastings sea-front is much like any other, with a good pier built in 1872. The castle ruins now tell the 1066 story audio-visual style; the Rock Theatre does a good line in variety shows, concerts and plays, and there is a cinema. The shopping centre has all the major multiples, and draws shoppers in from the neighbouring villages.

Much of the housing is Victorian. Commuters usually prefer to live within walking distance of the station, close enough to the William Parker comprehensive if they have families. A two-bedroom house in this area would cost around £45,000; a four-bedroom house around £65,000. One-bedroom flats in a converted house come at around £20,000. A view, or even a squint of the sea, will add a small premium. A two-bedroom top-floor flat with a sea view would cost around £27,500.

One of the smartest areas is **St Helen's**, close to Alexandra Park, where a three-storey, four-bedroom Victorian house will cost between £60,000 and £70,000; a three-bedroom semi with a 100ft garden between £65,000 and £75,000. For modern properties people look to **Parkstone**. A two-bedroom house here will sell for between £45,000 and £50,000; a four-bedroom detached between £78,000 and £88,000. In other parts of Hastings property prices have fallen steeply. If you don't mind it being in need of repair, you might get a little Victorian house for as little as £30,000. The most expensive area is probably the **Old Town**. Some people find it too claustrophobic, with tourists pressing their noses against the windows in summer, but others find the innate charm of the close ancient streets well worth the extra money. Here you might pay £40,000 for a two-bedroom flat; up to £150,000 for a four-bedroom Edwardian terrace.

CHARING CROSS/ CANNON STREET
— TO —
CANTERBURY

(via Tonbridge and Ashford)

TONBRIDGE

See **Charing Cross/Cannon Street to Hastings** (page 288).

PADDOCK WOOD

Journey time: *52 min*
Season ticket: *£1756*
* Plus 3 per hour to Cannon St

Peak trains: *4 per hour**
Off-peak trains: *2 per hour*

Londoners have always been attracted to **Paddock Wood**. Those with happy memories of hop-picking settled here after the war, and more recently there has been a steady trickle of suburban refugees from Bromley and Orpington. One of the results is that the station car park has a waiting list. Paddock Wood now is a town with little romance, large enough to support a department store and some light industry. Its local comprehensive school has a good reputation and also doubles as an adult education centre. Property prices are lower than in the surrounding area, with three-bedroom semis at between £70,000 and £90,000; four-bedroom detached houses between £90,000 and £110,000; two-bedroom period cottages just under £70,000. It would be misleading to describe all the property here as cheap, however. The convenience of the journey into London means that a large detached house with land could fetch up to £500,000.

Branchline to Maidstone West via Beltring, Yalding, Wateringbury, and East Farleigh

No through trains. Trains to Paddock Wood: *I per hour*
Journey time: *77 min (from East Farleigh)*
Season ticket from East Farleigh: *£1828*
It is also possible to travel to Charing Cross via Strood in the other direction.

Close to **Beltring** station is the Whitbread Hop Farm – it has the largest group of Victorian oast houses in the world, and all the stages

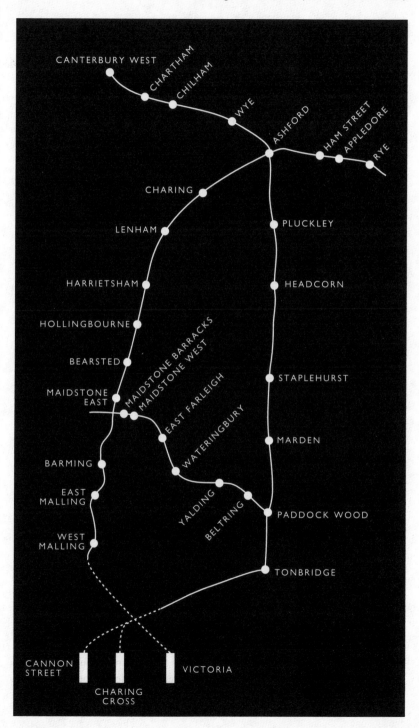

in the production of beer are shown to the public here. Beyond this, Beltring consists of little more than a clump of houses. Nearby **Laddingford** is a true hamlet with a popular Seventies-built development of family houses ranging in price from £100,000 to £120,000.

Yalding is a lovely old village served by winding country lanes, with a few shops, a post office and a Church of England primary school. Two-bedroom period cottages start at around £65,000; a large detached period house with a bit of land would fetch around £300,000; a four-bedroom modern detached house £160,000.

The innate prettiness of **Wateringbury** is marred by the busy A26 Tonbridge to Maidstone road thumping through it. It has some shops, a post office and a Church of England primary school. Its popularity means that even small period cottages can cost as much as £120,000. You would have to pay around £160,000 for a four-bedroom detached house; £200,000 to £220,000 for a larger period detached property. The village contains some fine stone-built Georgian houses but very little modern development.

East Farleigh is much quieter than Wateringbury and just as attractive. It has a few shops, a post office and a county primary school. Again, small cottages are expensive – at least £135,000. A spacious three-bedroom bungalow might cost £235,000; a period detached house with a little land £320,000.

(For **Maidstone**, see page 308.)

MARDEN

Journey time: *58 min*	Peak trains: *2 per hour**
Season ticket: *£1828*	Off-peak trains: *1 per hour*

* Plus 2 per hour to Cannon St

Marden is a pretty village with stone houses, a couple of shops, a post office, library and primary school. Modern three-bedroom semis sell for between £67,000 and £75,000; more mature semis £85,000 to £90,000; new four-bedroom detached houses £100,000 to £120,000. You might find a small three-bedroom period terrace cottage in need of renovation at less than £80,000, but a larger four-bedroom Georgian house will fetch £180,000 at least.

Just over four miles to the south is **Goudhurst**, set on a hilltop surrounded by orchards and cornfields, and with lovely views across the Medway Valley. This is a classic English village with half-timbered cottages and a duckpond at the centre. It is a self-sufficient community (population 2,500) with shops, tearooms for the summer visitors, and its own primary school. Bedgebury, just over two miles to the south, has a private school for girls. Property prices in Marden are similar to those in Cranbrook (see below).

STAPLEHURST

Journey time: *57 min*
Season ticket: *£1856*

Peak trains: *4 per hour**
Off-peak trains: *2 per hour*

* Plus 3 per hour to Cannon St

Staplehurst has a little light industry and a large Mazda warehouse by the station. Sprawling along the A229 south of Maidstone, it is a plain village in comparison with some of the jewels of the Kentish landscape which lie to the south. The busy high street has a pedestrianised section ideal for its population-mix of elderly people and young families. It has its own primary school. On the Sixties estates, three-bedroom semis sell for £85,000 to £95,000; four-bedroom detached houses £140,000 to £150,000. Period properties carry the expected premium, with two- and three-bedroom cottages at £70,000 to £90,000, and larger, more secluded detached houses with pony paddocks around £250,000.

Cranbrook has a special appeal for Londoners worried about schooling. Cranbrook Grammar for boys and girls has a remarkable reputation, sufficient to add a premium to property prices within its five-mile catchment area. Parents living outside it are even prepared to send their children as boarders and pay fees, since it straddles both private and state education systems. Cranbrook is a compact town of weatherboarded houses with a well-preserved black-tarred smock mill at its centre. It used to be cut off in winter because of the deep mud on the roads, and this has given it a lingering feeling of insularity. Small two-bedroom houses, old or new, start at just under £60,000; three-bedroom weatherboarded semis cost £85,000 to £100,000; three-bedroom modern detached houses £100,000; period farmhouses on the outskirts up to £500,000.

A mile up the cramped lanes from Cranbrook is **Sissinghurst** – a pretty one-street village of weatherboarded and half-timbered houses close to Sissinghurst Castle (National Trust), where Vita Sackville-West and her husband Harold Nicolson created their wonderful gardens in the grounds of a ruined castle. **Benenden** is just over seven miles from Staplehurst. This makes it rather far for daily commuters to contemplate, but it deserves mention for its charm. It is a perfect Kentish village set around a green where cricket is played on summer afternoons, beside the William IV and The Bull pubs. There is a handsome range of brick and weatherboarded cottages and old hall houses, clustered in the dominating presence of Benenden, the girls' public school. Prices in both Sissinghurst and Benenden are similar to those in Cranbrook.

HEADCORN

Journey time: *62 min*
Season ticket: *£1880*

Peak trains: *4 per hour**
Off-peak trains: *2 per hour*

* Plus 3 per hour to Cannon St

Headcorn is very popular with commuters, not least for its large station car park. With a population of 3,500 it is big enough to support a busy shopping centre which includes restaurants, though serious shopping means a trip into Maidstone or Ashford. Other assets include a primary school, village green, a vineyard, an aerodrome and the Lashenden Air Warfare Museum. Well-heeled commuters pay over £200,000 for large houses with an acre or two on the outskirts. An old timbered farmhouse with 20 acres and an oast recently went on the market with a guide price of £350,000. Within the village, a period four-bedroom house will fetch around £150,000. There are also some new developments (those built in the Sixties now look rather tatty) where a four-bedroom detached house might be bought for £90,000 to £120,000. A three-bedroom semi right in the centre will cost around £70,000.

Smarden, three miles to the east, is a beautiful, well-kept village with listed cottages grouped around a 14th- to 15th-century church. It is too small to have a shop, but there is a post office, and an annual fair, and the mobile library calls once a week. The village teems with activities based on the primary school and the four churches and chapels. It tends to be a middle-aged village, popular with families. Large, family-sized period houses with big gardens will cost around £200,000. A three-bedroom semi with garage on a modern development might cost just under £80,000; a four-bedroom detached house £150,000.

Biddenden, three miles south of Headcorn, is favoured because of its closeness to Tenterden, a stylish Wealden town that has become something of a local antiques centre. A two-bedroom late 17th-century semi in brick and flint, with leaded windows, might cost £96,000; a converted barn with three bedrooms and four acres would be in the region of £275,000.

PLUCKLEY

Journey time: *73 min* | Peak trains: *2 per hour**
Season ticket: *£1948* | Off-peak trains: *1 per hour*

* Plus 2 per hour to Cannon St

The countryside around **Pluckley** will be familiar to anyone who watched the television serialisation of H.E. Bates's *The Darling Buds Of May*. The influence of the Dering family – previous lords of the manor of Surrenden Dering – is very obvious here. Kentish ragstone was used for many of the older houses, most of which have distinctively arched Dering windows. The village has managed to stay small, with a population of just over 900 served by three shops, a pub, three churches and a Church of England primary school. Leisure opportunities include cricket, tennis, Brownies and Pluckley Pantomime Unlimited. Houses in Pluckley are expensive. The smallest cottage can fetch £100,000; a period manor house on the outskirts up to £500,000. There is also pre-cast concrete council housing which some of the villagers hate.

Bethersden, a couple of miles south of the station, is another pretty conservation village of listed weatherboarded and tile-hung houses. It clusters around two shops, a post office, a church, pub, garage and primary school. Bethersden is cosy and comfortable in character rather than smart like Smarden. A two-bedroom Victorian brick semi will cost just over £70,000; a three-bedroom semi in a quiet lane just under £90,000; a three-bedroom Georgian semi with a half-acre garden £120,000.

ASHFORD

Journey time: *70 min*	Peak trains: *3 per hour**
Season ticket: *£2040*	Off-peak trains: *2 per hour*

* Plus 3 per hour to Cannon St

For **Ashford**, see line via Maidstone (page 312).

Branchline to Rye via Ham Street and Appledore

No through trains. Trains to Ashford: *1 per hour*
Journey time: *100 min (from Rye)*
Season ticket from Rye: *£2308*

Ham Street is something of a main-road village, lacking a real centre even though it has a green and a duckpond by the village hall. It has a primary school, post office/general store, butcher, antique shops and a builder's yard. A two-bedroom Victorian brick house will cost just over £60,000; a modern three-bedroom semi £70,000; a flashy modern four- to five-bedroom house with three reception rooms in a third of an acre £210,000. Just to the north are the Ham Street Woods, a linked series of five woods in a nature reserve.

Appledore is a delightful village, and one of the best places to slip off the main road to enjoy the eery flat landscape of Romney Marsh, which lies just to the east. It has lovely old black-and-white houses and a particularly attractive street, Court Lodge Road, leading to the church and pub. Unfortunately Appledore has lost its primary school – due in part to the incomers' preference for private education. The result is that children are now bussed to Wittersham three miles away. The village has a bric-à-brac shop, a gift shop, a baker and teashop. Hornes Place, the big house on the edge of the village, belongs to the National Trust. The Royal Military Canal – built in the 19th century as a second line of defence inland from the Martello towers – runs along the village margin. Houses sell very quickly here, with buyers always waiting in the wings for an opportunity. A 100-year-old three-bedroom terrace will cost £65,000 to £72,000; a modern four-bedroom detached house £195,000; an old farmhouse with land and stables £280,000. The only things that sell slowly in Appledore are the ex-council houses: you can pick up a three-bedroom semi for £65,000 to £70,000.

Rye is reputedly one of the most picturesque towns on the south coast. Lying two miles into the mouth of the River Rother, it was once a flourishing port huddled behind its protective sea walls. Now its cobbled streets and Tudor, Stuart and Georgian houses attract hordes of summer tourists. It is an intimate place in which to live – most people seem to know what everyone else is doing. There are plenty of shops selling food, antiques and souvenirs, but going to the cinema means a trip into Hastings. Rye has all the usual clubs and societies, including the Rye Players, who perform a Christmas pantomime each year, and a hotel and caterers' association which organises an annual Medieval Week. Well-known local residents include John Ryan, the creator of Captain Pugwash, and Spike Milligan lives nearby in Udimore. Among distinguished past inhabitants of the town are the writers Henry James and E.F.Benson, both of whom, at different times, resided at Lamb House. A two-bedroom Victorian terrace house in Rye will cost £50,000 to £65,000. The picture-postcard street is Mermaid Street, steep and cobbled, where a romantic bow-windowed cottage would cost around £140,000.

Decorative Tudor
cottage, Rye

LINE FROM ASHFORD TO CANTERBURY (see map)

Journey time: *85 min*
Season ticket: *£2088*

Peak trains: *1 per hour**
Off-peak trains: *1 per hour*

* Plus 1 to Victoria and 1 to Cannon St per hour

Wye is possibly the most sought-after village in the Ashford area. Not only does it have the station, but it has a remarkable street called Bridge Street in which many of the medieval houses are reached by steep stone steps. These were designed to raise the buildings above the stream that once ran down the middle. The Great Stour does still run through the village and is overlooked by the Tickled Trout pub. Two-bedroom period cottages here are likely to start at £80,000, with Victorian semis at around £125,000. Larger period houses cost £200,000 or more. There is a small new mews-style development called Taylors Yard, where a three-bedroom house will cost around £95,000.

The village has shops enough for you to buy anything you're likely to need except clothes. There are also two banks, a garage, a primary school and The Wife of Bath restaurant. Wye College, London University's agricultural college, introduces an unusually young, cosmopolitan element. The college has an annual rag week and celebrates Bonfire Night with a torchlight procession to the Crown – a chalk image cut into the Downs. There are good walks along the North Downs Way, which passes through the village, and in the Wye Nature Reserve. The latter contains a deep wooded hollow known as the Devil's Kneading Trough.

CHILHAM

Journey time: *92 min*
Season ticket: *£2116*

Peak trains: *1 per hour**
Off-peak trains: *1 per hour*

* Plus 1 to Victoria and 1 to Cannon St per hour

The central square of 14th- and 15th-century black-and-white houses in **Chilham** is an irresistible draw for tourists, film crews and wealthy househunters. The church is known for its roughly chequered flint tower, and Chilham Castle – a Jacobean mansion with a 12th-century keep – has gardens laid out by the 17th-century botanist John Tradescant. The mulberry trees there are said to be 500 years old. There are falconry displays at the castle in summer. Properties rarely come up for sale in Chilham, but if you were lucky you might snatch a two- or three-bedroom Tudor cottage in the square for £100,000 to £120,000. A Tudor family-sized house will cost at least £200,000. On the outskirts is a small modern development where you might buy a three-bedroom house for £60,000 to £70,000. It is a village with a strong community spirit. There is football, cricket and tennis, and in May the square is closed for a huge fair during which the villagers dress in period costume. Chilham also has the considerable advantage of being only five miles from Canterbury.

Old Wives Lees, a mile to the north, is a cheaper alternative, known to locals as Old Wives Knees. There is plenty of modern development here, with four-bedroom detached houses in the range of £150,000 to £200,000. A converted Methodist chapel with three bedrooms was offered for sale last year at £95,000.

CHARTHAM

Journey time: 95 min	**Peak trains: 1 per hour***
Season ticket: £2116	**Off-peak trains: 1 per hour**

* Plus 1 to Victoria and 1 to Cannon St per hour

The River Stour, which divides before it enters the village, was for centuries the source of power for the local paper mills – one of which is still in production. **Chartham** is not as smart as Chilham. It has a mix of old houses – some of the nicest are by the little green and the 13th-century church – plus Victorian and modern estates built on the sites of old orchards. There is a primary school, and also a mental hospital which is due to close in a couple of years' time. A current planning controversy concerns a proposal for a dry ski slope and golf course on the edge of the village. A three-bedroom terrace house in Chartham would cost between £60,000 and £70,000; a four-bedroom period house £160,000. It is quite a large village with a population of 2,500 served by a handful of small shops.

Petham, three miles to the south-east, also has a mix of old thatched cottages, turn-of-the-century and new houses. It has a pub and a church but no shop. A small period cottage would cost around £70,000; a large barn converted into a family-sized house £220,000.

CANTERBURY WEST

Journey time: 100 min	**Peak trains: 1 per hour***
Season ticket: £2116†	**Off-peak trains: 1 per hour**

* Plus 2 per hour to Cannon St   † Also valid from Canterbury East

For **Canterbury**, see **Charing Cross/Victoria to Canterbury** line (via Rochester) – page 330.

VICTORIA
— TO —
ASHFORD

(via Maidstone)

WEST MALLING

Journey time: *48 min*	**Peak trains:** *3 per hour*
Season ticket: *£1748*	**Off-peak trains:** *2 per hour*

Considering its closeness to London, **West Malling** is surprisingly unspoilt. The old high street, in parts Tudor and Georgian, opens out into what was once the market square. There is a Tesco, a delicatessen, bakers, and a store which sells everything from plimsolls to vests. The village has its own primary school, and a 900-year-old abbey. As always, there are a number of local stalwarts who keep the social wheels turning – organising the beating of the bounds, running the conservation society and fending off new development. The fields that cushion the village from Maidstone are guarded with particular vigilance. The local airfield, an old Second World War fighter station, has been turned into a business park with lavish landscaping. The M20 is close enough to be audible from the nearby woods. A four-bedroom period house in the main street at West Malling is unlikely to cost less than £200,000, though you might pick up a two-bedroom Victorian cottage for as little as £70,000.

EAST MALLING

Journey time: *55 min*	**Peak trains:** *2 per hour*
Season ticket: *£1764*	**Off-peak trains:** *1 per hour*

East Malling is much smaller than West Malling and property prices are about five per cent lower. There are a few timber-framed houses but it's the council properties that tend to dominate. The East Malling Research Station, which develops new fruit varieties, is based in Bradbourne House, a Queen Anne-style mansion.

BARMING

Journey time: *58 min*	**Peak trains:** *2 per hour*
Season ticket: *£1800*	**Off-peak trains:** *1 per hour*

To outsiders, **Barming** may seem like a suburb of Maidstone. To those who live here, however, it is very definitely a village. The old centre has been swallowed up by new development yet it is still extremely popular. A two-bedroom 19th-century cottage will cost just under £70,000; a three-bedroom modern semi around £70,000. A few old houses survive even in the midst of the new estates. A 400-year-old half-timbered cottage with a third of an acre in such a position might cost £175,000.

Detached period house, near Maidstone

MAIDSTONE EAST

Journey time: *55 min*	Peak trains: *3 per hour*
Season ticket: *£1856*	Off-peak trains: *2 per hour**

* Plus I per hour to Charing Cross (j/t: 51 min)

Maidstone looms rather brutishly on the Kentish landscape – particularly if you approach it from the pretty southern villages. Nevertheless, it is a friendly and workmanlike hilly town where people manage to have the time to say Good Morning. Its focus is the River Medway, with the Archbishop's Palace (used as a place of rest on journeys to Canterbury) on the bank. A park-'n'-sail scheme allows boats to be brought upriver from Allington in winter. The remains of some 14th-century collegiate buildings are now occupied by the Kent Music School; the Maidstone Museum and Art Gallery are in Chillington House, a 16th-century manor. The Corn Exchange is a cultural centre too – home of the Hazlitt Theatre and a venue for concerts, dances and conferences.

Maidstone has always had a commercial and agricultural bias. In earlier centuries it supplied hops, linen, paper, ragstone and gin to London. Today it is particularly strong on shopping. The Chequers Centre has a host of major high street names, all gathered together under a single roof; the Royal Star Arcade has more up-market specialist shops, including Hatchards and a delicatessen; Starnes Court is a Victorian-style arcade of designer-shops set around a courtyard. Beside the river on Lockmeadow there are weekly markets for furniture and bric-à-brac, livestock, agricultural produce and secondhand cars. Mote Park, being the former parkland of an old country house, is a popular venue for boating, fishing and football. The new Maidstone Leisure Centre has ice skating and rock climbing as well as leisure pools and health-and-fitness equipment. The town has the benefit of two Kentish grammar schools, one each for boys and girls, plus the Mid-Kent College of Higher and Further Education.

Much of the housing in Maidstone is Victorian. There are terraces of small artisans' cottages where you might pay just over £50,000 for two bedrooms, or just over £55,000 for three. The houses get larger as you move further away from the centre. A four-bedroom terrace house with three reception rooms and a walled garden could cost as little as £90,000.

The huge new Grove Green estate is densely built but popular. You could buy a two-bedroom terrace here for just under £60,000; a three-bedroom semi for around £70,000; a four-bedroom detached house for between £115,000 and £215,000.

To the south-east is **Sutton Valence**, a pretty hilltop village with views over the Weald of Kent. It is marred by the busy A274 running through it but remains popular because of Sutton Valence School, a co-educational private school for older children, and it has a local primary school for younger ones. The village has lost a few of its shops but still has a bakery, village store, newsagent and hardware store. At the centre is an enclave of old houses, black-and-white half-timbered and some weather-boarded, where a four-bedroom Elizabethan house in need of repair might fetch £300,000. On the outskirts are new developments where a three-bedroom semi would cost around £70,000. In the churchyard is a memorial to John Willes, the man who introduced round-arm bowling to the game of cricket.

Due south of Maidstone, and hardly separate from it, is one of those lovely English villages that everyone would dearly love to call home. **Loose** owes its attraction to its position on the steep valley slope of the fast-flowing Loose stream. Old mills litter the wooded streambanks, which are overlooked by the church and pub, and the 15th-century half-timbered Wool House is now administered by the National Trust and open to the public on written application. The village has a primary school but no shops. Half-timbered and weatherboarded cottages rise on terraces over the series of springs which feed the stream. On the outskirts you might find a two-bedroom period cottage for just under £100,000; a fine family-sized Tudor house in the centre would fetch closer to £400,000.

To the north is **Boxley**, a pleasant village close to the M20, with pubs that people from Maidstone drive out to in the summer. Its other benefits include a garden centre and a Tesco superstore. Boxley has a good collection of Thirties houses, some of them in leafy unadopted roads. A classic three-bedroom semi costs around £80,000. Some of the more sought-after properties were built by a firm called Clarke & Epps. These are distinguished by low-pitched tiled roofs, and by very large bay windows with decorative stained-glass lights. A three-bedroom detached Clarke & Epps would cost around £150,000. Alfred, Lord Tennyson, lived at Boxley Place. At the top of Detling Hill a couple of miles away is the Kent County Agricultural Showground.

BEARSTED

Journey time: *61 min*	Peak trains: *3 per hour*
Season ticket: *£1872*	Off-peak trains: *2 per hour*

Bearsted, insulated from Maidstone by a belt of green, is a very popular village, though in recent decades it has become rather bloated with new development. The older part, to the north of the A20, has a core of 17th-century houses around a large green on which is one of the earliest cricket pitches in the county. The poet Edward Thomas lived by the green, close to where the shops now stand – there is a bakery-cum-butcher locally famous for its pies, a hardware shop-cum-post office, a newsagent and a grocer. A small period cottage would cost around £75,000, with a family-sized Tudor house reaching £300,000 or even £400,000.

A disadvantage of Bearsted is that the old and the new sides of the village are rather split, each having its own village hall. But an effort is being made by the old village not to make the new village feel left out. The annual fair, with old-fashioned stalls and silly races, is a great occasion for pulling together. In the new estates to the south, which have their own supermarket and parade of shops, three-bedroom semis sell for an average of just under £80,000.

The first pocket of rural life on Maidstone's eastern flank, but closer to Bearsted, is **Otham**. There is a 900-year-old church, a few ancient half-timbered houses (well over £200,000 to buy), and a tradition of parish life which is maintained in spite of the massing of new houses around the margins. There is a farm shop and a WI hall which also does duty as a village hall and nursery school. There are some pretty walks up the valley around the River Len, where you could keep in training for the egg-and-spoon race at the annual fete. In the Len Valley is **Downswood**, an area of high-density modern housing estates where you might buy a three-bedroom semi for £70,000; a four-bedroom detached for £100,000.

HOLLINGBOURNE

Journey time: **65 min**

Season ticket: **£1900**

Peak trains: **3 per hour**

Off-peak trains: **1 per hour**

Hollingbourne is one of the prettier villages in this part of Kent, breathing more easily now that the threat of the Channel rail-link has been lifted. The high street for practically the whole of its length is lined with half-timbered houses. A small two-bedroom cottage here will cost £75,000; a family-sized house at least £200,000. The upper village clusters around the Elizabethan manor house, with the shops kept in their place at the lower end. There is also a primary school, a football team and an architecturally admired early council housing estate built just after the war. Hollingbourne church contains the 300-year-old embroidered Culpeper cloth. The North Downs Way passes through the village and affords some breathtaking walks.

This is also the station for Leeds Castle. The castle was built in 1192 in the middle of a lake formed by the River Len, and given by Edward I to his wife Eleanor of Castile. It was given to the nation in 1974 and is now a venue for conferences, open-air concerts, balloon events and so on. Prices in **Leeds** are similar to those in Hollingbourne. It merges into the neighbouring village of **Langley**, where there is some council housing and small closes of modern houses. A three-bedroom semi will cost £65,000.

HARRIETSHAM

Journey time: **69 min**

Season ticket: **£1936**

Peak trains: **3 per hour**

Off-peak trains: **1 per hour**

Prices fall again in **Harrietsham**. This is partly because it is split by the A20, and partly because it has been so heavily developed. A three-bedroom semi in a small close will cost around £65,000; a three-bedroom detached just under £100,000. Among the older properties you might stumble across a strange anachronism – a cottage with a flying freehold on a bedroom in the house next door. A two-bedroom cottage with this improbable feature was recently offered for sale at £59,000.

LENHAM

Journey time: **72 min**

Season ticket: **£1960**

Peak trains: **3 per hour**

Off-peak trains: **2 per hour**

Lenham is a large working village with a population of around 3,500. It combines a pretty central market square, surrounded by Wealden hall houses and Georgian-fronted buildings, with a strong industrial base. Marley Tiles established itself here in the 1920s (its three factories are quite well hidden), and in the Seventies the Lenham Storage Company set up Freightflow, one of Britain's first international customs depots. This brings a lot of trans-continental lorries to (but not through) the village. The parish hall is on the square and is heavily used by organised groups ranging all the way from badminton to the British Legion. The village is particularly strong on football – there are several junior teams – and bowls. It has its own primary and secondary schools. Because of the changes in farming methods, ramblers often now find themselves prairie-walking rather than following the ancient footpaths, but the village's saving grace is that it lies just at the foot of the North Downs, which is a designated Area of Outstanding Natural Beauty. Prices don't vary much in the villages between Maidstone and Ashford. Small cottages start at around £75,000, with prices rising to around £400,000 for the larger period properties. For a three-bedroom semi on a modern estate you would have to pay around £70,000.

CHARING

Journey time: *77 min* | Peak trains: *3 per hour*
Season ticket: *£2016* | Off-peak trains: *1 per hour*

At the heart of **Charing** is the old Archbishop's Palace, once used by Archbishops of Canterbury and now a private house. The green – a favourite place to sit in summer – overlooks the market place, where a modern library has replaced the old pig slaughterhouse. The main street with its Elizabethan and Georgian-faced houses is a whole town in miniature. It has two butchers, a baker, two grocers, a watchmaker, an electrician and hardware store, and a doctor's surgery. Charing likes to be thought of not just as a pretty village but as a hard-working one too. A two-bedroom period cottage here would cost £65,000; a large, family-sized period house £300,000; a four-bedroom modern detached house £100,000. There are also some flats in a converted coach house, priced at around £60,000 for two bedrooms. The village has a primary school and a host of clubs and societies which include an angling, gun, and country dancing club. The WI holds a weekly market in part of the Archbishop's Palace.

ASHFORD

Journey time: *85 min* | Peak trains: *3 per hour*
Season ticket: *£2040* | Off-peak trains: *2 per hour*

See **Charing Cross to Canterbury** (page 303), which is the faster route into London.

See **Charing Cross to Canterbury** (page 303)

People are not kind about **Ashford**. If Kent were ever to need an enema, they suggest, then Ashford is where you'd have to insert the tube. In the

Seventies it was designated as a growth area. Thousands of new houses were built, and the population swelled to nearly 100,000. Now British Rail is building its International Passenger Station at Ashford to serve more than a million passengers a year on the Channel Tunnel route. Lydd airport is just a few miles away, and Sainsbury and Tesco are building superstores alongside junctions 9 and 10 of the M20.

Due to the greater distance from London, house prices in Ashford tend to be 10 per cent lower than they are in Maidstone or Tonbridge. A three-bedroom semi with a garage will cost £60,000 to £70,000; a modern four-bedroom detached house between £75,000 and £100,000; a two- to three-bedroom period cottage around the £90,000 mark. Ashford has two good grammar schools, Highworth School for girls and Norton Knatchbull for boys, as well as three mixed high schools. Ashford Girls' School is private and takes both boarders and day-pupils.

To the north, on the slopes of the North Downs, are several tiny hamlets amounting to little more than clusters of houses. **Boughton Aluph** (pronounced Borton Aluf) is rather more substantial. It is centred around a village green on which cricket has been played since 1752. This is flanked on one side by neo-Georgian houses, and on the other by the green-painted, corrugated iron village hall, known as the Iron Room. The village has one or two distinguished Elizabethan houses, but there is no shop and the church (a mile away since the village moved at the time of the Black Death) is used only in summer because it is too expensive to heat in winter. The big house, Eastwell Manor, has become a hotel. A two-bedroom cottage in Boughton Aluph will cost just under £70,000; a family-sized period house over £200,000.

Challock Lees, also in the north, is similarly priced. The Lees which gives the place its name is 19 acres of common land, with a 12th-century church and a primary school but little else – this is another village that moved at the time of the Black Death. Challock proper has a considerable number of new houses squeezed between the old, and there are a couple of modern closes. A large modern detached house will cost around £300,000. Challock is high up on the Downs – 630ft above sea level – and there are some spectacular footpaths and bridle-ways. The price you pay is that it can be very cold, windy and foggy in winter. The village has a post office-general store and a farm shop.

CHARING CROSS/VICTORIA
— TO —
HERNE BAY/CANTERBURY

(via Rochester)

LINE FROM VICTORIA TO MEOPHAM AND SOLE STREET (see map)

MEOPHAM

Journey time: *41 min*	**Peak trains:** *3 per hour*
Season ticket: *£1568*	**Off-peak trains:** *2 per hour*

The cricket green at **Meopham** really grabs all the attention, being overlooked by a marvellous wooden smock mill. The village is long and straggly with a main street that stretches for miles, dotted with 16th- and 17th-century houses mixed with new. You would pay £65,000 for a two-bedroom cottage; £95,000 for a three-bedroom semi built in the Sixties or Seventies.

SOLE STREET

Journey time: *43 min*	**Peak trains:** *3 per hour*
Season ticket: *£1568*	**Off-peak trains:** *2 per hour*

Sole Street is deceptively small and, because it really is very rural, it can be rather expensive. It has a general store, a pub and a little shop that's due to have a post office soon. The Tudor Yeoman's House is owned by the National Trust, though you have to make a written request to see it. Older, two-bedroom Victorian terrace houses sell for around £75,000; four-bedroom modern detached houses for up to £180,000. There are some large individual properties built with large gardens around 1920, for which you would probably have to pay £350,000.

Cobham is a very pretty north Kent village on the crest of a hill in an Area of Outstanding Natural Beauty. The big house, Cobham Hall, is now a girls' boarding school, but the grounds – landscaped by Repton – and deer park are often open to the public in the summer. The Street has a good range of 18th-century houses, some Victorian and some weatherboarded, plus the village hall and the Leather Bottle – a pub which Dickens used as a setting in *Pickwick Papers*. There is also a Victorian flint primary school and a general store that sells meat. It is a very expensive village where a one-bedroom 18th-century cottage will cost £80,000 and one with three bedrooms will cost £140,000 to £150,000. A modern

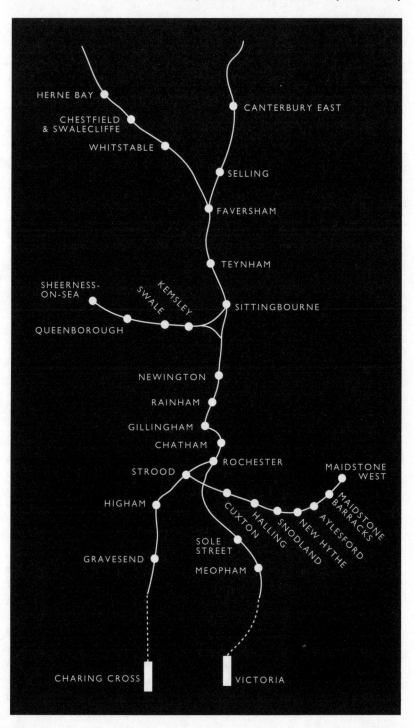

HERNE BAY

CHESTFIELD
& SWALECLIFFE

WHITSTABLE

CANTERBURY EAST

SELLING

FAVERSHAM

TEYNHAM

SHEERNESS-
ON-SEA

KEMSLEY

SWALE

SITTINGBOURNE

QUEENBOROUGH

NEWINGTON

RAINHAM

GILLINGHAM

CHATHAM

ROCHESTER

STROOD

MAIDSTONE
WEST

HIGHAM

MAIDSTONE
BARRACKS

CUXTON

HALLING

SNODLAND

NEW HYTHE

AYLESFORD

SOLE
STREET

GRAVESEND

MEOPHAM

CHARING CROSS

VICTORIA

detached house will be at least £200,000.

MAIN LINE FROM CHARING CROSS TO ROCHESTER
(see map)

GRAVESEND

Journey time: *49 min*	**Peak trains:** *5 per hour*
Season ticket: *£1448*	**Off-peak trains:** *4 per hour*

For centuries the local economy of **Gravesend**, London's trade and defensive gateway, has been bound to the River Thames. Many of the traditional riverside industries have closed down now, but the paper mills and cement works are still going. The riverside part of town is heavily atmospheric, with narrow streets and alleyways peppered with old churches, inns and historic fortifications. The best place to watch river traffic ploughing the Thames is from the Gordon Esplanade gardens, where you can look across the water into Essex.

Efforts to work the London Docklands miracle by replacing old industrial sores with mix-and-match housing somehow haven't quite come off in Gravesend. The district council and Kent County Council together have allocated funds for a town renovation scheme called Impact, but its interest is mainly commercial. There are swathes of Edwardian and Victorian houses, and some handsome Georgian houses (which have been sadly neglected). It is a good hunting ground for first-time buyers. A small two-bedroom Victorian house would cost around £46,000; a slightly larger, typically bay-fronted one, around £55,000 – the same as you would pay for a flat overlooking the river. Almost on the river an old brewery building has been converted into flats selling at around £50,000; and there are some new developments in which two-bedroom flats with river balconies sell for around £75,000. Large Georgian terrace houses with four or five bedrooms can be bought for around £150,000 to £160,000.

Property prices are higher to the south of the town, especially in the Thirties-built roads around the golf course. A large detached house will cost from upwards of £160,000 to around £320,000, for which price you would also get a very large garden. Another more expensive part of Gravesend is the Windmill Hill conservation area, a mile from the town centre, where some of the houses have giddy river views. A two-bedroom Victorian house would cost at least £65,000. Some of the larger houses have been converted into flats. These don't often come on the market, but would command a price of up to £60,000 for a single bedroom. If you were looking for a house on a decent modern estate, the answer could be Riverview Park, built 30 years ago, where a three-bedroom detached house costs £110,000, a three-bedroom semi £80,000, and you might get a good view thrown in.

The village of **Shorne**, two miles east, is pretty and old and therefore extremely sought after since this part of north Kent can sometimes seem rather bleak. It is also close to the A2. Snob value adds to the prices of the 15th- and 16th-century timber-framed cottages; you'd have to pay £80,000 for a single bedroom, £115,000 for a modest three-bedroom in a terrace. There are a few three-bedroom detached Sixties houses, valued at around £150,000.

HIGHAM

Journey time: *57 min* | Peak trains: *4 per hour*
Season ticket: *£1600* | Off-peak trains: *2 per hour*

Higham has one of the best stations for parking, though it is some distance from the rather nondescript village. There are a few older properties, but most of the houses were built in the Sixties and Seventies. A Victorian two-up-two-down will cost around £60,000. A modern three-bedroom semi will cost around £80,000. Gad's Hill Place was Charles Dickens's home from 1856 until the end of his life, and is now an independent girls' school. He left *Edwin Drood* unfinished when he died in 1870.

STROOD

Journey time: *62 min* | Peak trains: *4 per hour*
Season ticket: *£1692* | Off-peak trains: *2 per hour*

In many ways **Strood** is a cut above Rochester, to which it is linked by a bridge over the River Medway. Its bustling high street has a better variety of shops than Rochester's, and the B&Q and Safeway both draw people from over the water. The houses in the centre are flat-fronted, late Victorian terraces which – at between £45,000 and £48,000 for two bedrooms – are attractive to first-time buyers. Close to the station is a surge of Fifties housing, where a three-bedroom home would cost around £72,000. In the more sedate Thirties developments near the fringes of the town a three-bedroom house similarly would cost just over £70,000.

It is a popular area for boating people. Further out along the Medway estuary, the marina at **Upnor** throngs with hundreds of small craft. Developers have begun to cater for the sailors' needs by providing small town houses and semis along the riverbank. Prices are similar to those in Strood. The main street is rather pretty, with old weatherboarded houses. Upnor Castle, now a museum, was built in the mid-16th century to defend Chatham dockyard from across the river. The Isle of Grain, which thrusts out like a hammerhead over the mouth of the estuary, is deeply unattractive, bristling with oil terminals and refineries. North Sea gas is also stored here, and part of it is being developed as a container depot – a venture which may help revive the area's industrial spirits.

Branchline to Maidstone West via Cuxton, Halling, Snodland, New Hythe, Aylesford and Maidstone Barracks

No through trains. Trains to Strood: *3 per hour (peak)/2 per hour (off-peak)*
Journey time: *80 min (from Aylesford)*
Season ticket from Aylesford: *£1780*
You can travel to London via Maidstone East by changing at Maidstone Barracks – a footpath links the two stations

Cuxton is one of the Medway villages that boomed during the 19th century on the back of the cement industry. It has an attractive mock-Tudor station with a hand-operated level crossing and an old-fashioned signal box. Most of the houses are Victorian terraces suitable for first-time buyers, selling for around £50,000 to £55,000 for two bedrooms. There are new developments too, with detached family houses at around £120,000.

Converted oast house

Halling is dominated by the large riverside cement works. There was once a rowing-boat ferry, but it's gone now. This part of north Kent is not very popular, but it does offer the prospect of cheap housing to those who can stand it. **Snodland**, too, has been stigmatised by association with the cement industry, though a bypass now redirects the lorries around the outskirts. It has a plain Victorian centre, where terrace houses sell from just under £50,000 to just over £60,000. On the new developments appearing round the margins you would expect to pay £58,000 for a two-bedroom terrace, £78,000 for a three-bedroom semi.

New Hythe is very close to the old Aylesford paper mills, which have now been converted to light industrial use. Victorian semis and Thirties semis range from £68,000 to £80,000. **Aylesford** is marginally more appealing, and is thought to offer good value for money. It has a 14th-century ragstone bridge and some very old houses overlooking the river. These might sell in the region of £140,000 to £150,000. There are also lots of old terrace properties with two or three bedrooms, selling in the £75,000 to £85,000 range. (For **Maidstone**, see page 308.)

CONTINUATION OF MAIN LINES FROM CHARING CROSS/VICTORIA

ROCHESTER

To Charing Cross	To Victoria
Journey time: *66 min*	Journey time: *54 min*
Season ticket: *£1736*	Season ticket: *£1736*
Peak trains: *4 per hour*	Peak trains: *2 per hour*
Off-peak trains: *2 per hour*	Off-peak trains: *2 per hour*

Most of this apparently seamless string of north Kent towns looks as if it might have detached itself from the north of England and slipped southwards during the night. **Rochester**, however, is something of an exception, having managed to sustain a policy of architectural conservation on the back of the Charles Dickens tourist industry – just as in the past it was able to create fine buildings on the back of its maritime trade. The high street is pedestrianised, and has an intimate villagey atmosphere with tourist shops, gift shops, antique shops and small businesses packing the narrow streets around it. It is pleasant to stroll and enjoy some of the older Elizabethan buildings and excellent Georgian houses. The town is stiff with locations used by Dickens in his novels. The Royal Victoria Hotel is The Bull in *Pickwick Papers*; The Bull is The Blue Boar in *Great Expectations*; Miss Haversham's home was loosely based on Restoration House; *Edwin Drood* was set in Rochester. The Charles Dickens Centre at Eastgate House now has the Swiss Chalet workshop in which he worked while he lived at Gad's Hill. Every year the town dresses itself in 19th-century costume for the Dickens Festival.

One of the most prestigious areas is close to the castle. This was built during the reign of Henry I, and has a well-preserved square keep that overlooks the river. Nearby are the cathedral, largely 12th-century, and

King's School Rochester, the boys' public school. One of the best streets for period properties is St Margaret's Street, where a four-bedroom early Georgian house will sell at around £110,000. In the streets just off it, and lying within the same conservation area, are large, five-bedroom Victorian houses which sell at around £200,000. For less expensive houses you need to travel five or 10 minutes outward from the centre. Here you will find row upon row of Victorian terraces. They front straight on to the pavement and sell at around £45,000 for two bedrooms. New building has been kept at bay, but there are a few small estates where you could buy a four-bedroom, box-shaped detached house for around £100,000. To the south is a large area of Thirties housing, with some bay-fronted terraces and semis, and a few bungalows. The average price for a three-bedroom semi in good condition is £85,000. For a three-bedroom mid-terrace, the price would drop to around £60,000.

You have to suffer a little to commute from Rochester. The one-way system makes driving to the station difficult, and when you get there it is not easy to park the car. For this reason many people prefer to travel from Chatham.

CHATHAM

To Charing Cross	To Victoria
Journey time: *68 min*	Journey time: *43 min*
Season ticket: *£1736*	Season ticket: *£1736*
Peak trains: *4 per hour*	Peak trains: *4 per hour*
Off-peak trains: *2 per hour*	Off-peak trains: *4 per hour*

Little flat-fronted Victorian terraces, ideal for first-time buyers at between £40,000 and £45,000 each, cram the steep hillsides around **Chatham** dockyards, once the industrial heart of the town. Its first ship was launched in 1586, to join the fleet against the Spanish Armada. Four centuries and 400 Royal Navy ships later, the docks were closed in 1984 and handed over to a trust. The 18-acre site, which contains 47 scheduled monuments, is the most complete Georgian and early Victorian dockyard in the world, and there has been much controversy over what should be done with it. Now it is almost as much of an attraction to househunters as it is to tourists. Part of it has been turned into a living museum where you can see rope- and sail-making; other parts have been turned into residential areas with a choice of both restored and new properties. The new developments include one- and two-bedroom flats ranging from £69,000 to £90,000; and town houses modelled on the Georgian officers' terrace, priced at £169,000 to £179,000. There are 12 restored houses in a terrace built on five floors between 1722 and 1732 with relatively plain interiors. The first one on the market had six bedrooms and was confidently expected to fetch £400,000. Old naval stable blocks are being converted into three-bedroom mews houses selling at £120,000. Then there are two tower houses, like small castle keeps, which will have three bedrooms and price tags of £180,000. More period properties are being restored and will be coming on-stream soon. Outside the dockyard you can find ex-naval Georgian town houses selling for around £130,000.

For cheaper modern housing you could look at the Walderslade area, a huge estate with one-bedroom starter homes at £38,000, two-bedroom terrace houses at £47,000, and four-bedroom family houses at £120,000.

GILLINGHAM

To Charing Cross	To Victoria
Journey time: *71 min*	Journey time: *47 min*
Season ticket: *£1764*	Season ticket: *£1764*
Peak trains: *4 per hour*	Peak trains: *4 per hour*
Off-peak trains: *2 per hour*	Off-peak trains: *4 per hour*

Gillingham is the largest of the Medway towns and commercial big brother to Chatham, with which it shares the naval dockyards and depot. The large shopping centre has a pedestrianised high street and contains all the major chain stores. There are very good leisure facilities – an ice rink, leisure centre, leisure pool, indoor bowls and cricket, and Gillingham Football Club, currently playing in the fourth division of the Football League. The dockyard here is ringed by an old Georgian fortification system called the Brompton Lines, one and a half miles of moats and ramparts overlooked by the Napoleonic Fort Amherst.

Many of the tightly packed Victorian streets are still very run down, however, and local comment tends to be disparaging. One of the better areas is Darland, which offers a complete range of properties from small Victorian terraces at £40,000 to four-bedroom detached houses at £200,000.

RAINHAM

To Victoria	
Journey time: *52 min*	Peak trains: *4 per hour**
Season ticket: *£1780*	Off-peak trains: *4 per hour*

* Plus 3 per hour to Cannon St

Rainham is much more suburban in character than either Gillingham or Chatham, with the atmosphere of a dormitory town. It was once popular with hop-pickers coming down from London. The station is large, and the London trains are fast. Housing is a mixed bag, from turn-of-the-century farmworkers' terraces (£40,000 unmodernised) to architect-designed Thirties villas in the Wigmore area. The houses there now sell from around £120,000 upwards. Hempstead is another attractive area with an old villagey heart and a outgrowth of new estates: you can pay from £50,000 for a starter home right up to £250,000 or £300,000 for a large detached house. The Riverside Country Park, which extends along the southern shore of the Medway estuary between Gillingham and Rainham, offers escape from the relentless housing. The park was formed from reclaimed salt marshes and is linked from west to east by the Saxon Shore Way – a coastal footpath which runs 140 miles to link Gravesend with Rye in Sussex.

NEWINGTON

To Victoria
Journey time: *71 min*
Season ticket: *£1828*

Peak trains: *3 per hour*
Off-peak trains: *2 per hour*

The countryside does try to breathe here but it is soon submerged again by Sittingbourne. **Newington** is thought to be more rural, but in fact it's bisected by the busy A2 and is beginning to merge at one end with Sittingbourne and at the other end with Hartlip. You can't call it pretty, but prices are still £5,000 higher than they are in the nearby towns. A two-up-two-down terrace will cost just over £50,000; a modern three-bedroom semi £70,000 to £80,000. Calloways Lane is particularly smart. A large five-bedroom detached house on up to an acre of ground here would sell at around £225,000.

Hartlip, a mile or so to the south-west, is far more sought after since it has more of a villagey feel and is so close to the Medway towns. It is one of the first conveniently placed, nice villages that you reach on your way out of London through this part of Kent. The conservation area in the village centre encompasses a handful of listed buildings, 15th-century thatched cottages and a fine half-timbered pink and white house. The rest is brick and weatherboarding, plus some modern houses built in the Eighties. It is a good address and you pay £300,000 for a four-bedroom period property with an acre of ground, and £200,000 to £250,000 for a modern four-bedroom detached house. There is a primary school with about 85 pupils, a church, a Methodist chapel, village hall and a post office. The village is friendly to newcomers and used to commuters. The main worry is that Gillingham might burst at the seams and engulf it.

SITTINGBOURNE

To Victoria
Journey time: *59 min*
Season ticket: *£1872*

Peak trains: *4 per hour**
Off-peak trains: *4 per hour*

* Plus 3 per hour to Cannon St

Like the Medway Towns, **Sittingbourne** is more affordable for first-time buyers. Much of the town centre looks more like *Coronation Street* than Kent, with terraces fronting straight on to the pavement. A two- or three-bedroom house here could be bought for between £35,000 and £45,000. Yet it is still only 60 minutes by train from London. The favoured side of town is the south, where Thirties detached houses and semis – some of them with good long gardens – sell for between £115,000 and £200,000. There are new estates here too, with three-bedroom semis selling at £65,000 to £75,000, and two- or three-bedroom terraces at just over £50,000.

The high street still betrays something of its history as a market town (there are still Friday and Saturday markets) and coaching stop. The pilgrims used to rest here on their way to Canterbury. The Red Lion, George and Bull inns are still there, and the mile-long high street reveals evidence of Georgian buildings behind the modern facades. Sittingbourne was also once a busy harbour town, and the muddy Milton Creek that runs into town from The Swale is lined with warehouses, factories and reedy inlets. The Dolphin Yard Sailing Barge Museum repairs and restores barges. The town built what wealth it has out of the huge expansion in demand for bricks, paper and cement in the late 19th century. Of these traditional local industries only paper-making now remains: the rest have been replaced by modern light manufacturing. For recreation, there is a huge, multi-million-pound leisure centre called The Swallows.

House prices rise a little as you move out to the villages. To the west is **Stockbury**, where it would be difficult to find a property at less than £100,000 – for which you might be lucky enough to get a two-bedroom bungalow. Most houses will cost around the £200,000 mark, though those closer to the gypsy camp tend to fetch slightly less. Closer to Sittingbourne is **Borden**. It is quite smart, and attracts executives from the Shell research station at Sittingbourne. Some parts of it are very old indeed: a 13th-century church is set in a conservation area which contains some quaint, white-painted weatherboarded cottages. You would pay just under £60,000 for a small period cottage, with four-bedroom detached houses ranging from around £180,000 up to £275,000. Much of the building is in brick, with some timber-frame and some modern infilling. At the heart of the village is the Playstool – an old Kentish name for a playing field on two levels. From the top level you have wonderful views across the countryside. The main street is called The Street and has a pub, post office and general store. The village has a high proportion of elderly people as well as a thriving primary school with about 80 children.

Less than a mile away is **Tunstall**. Prices here are similar to those in Borden, though the village itself is very tiny, with no shops, and has become almost a suburb of Sittingbourne. Due south of here is **Milstead**. Opinions vary about the correct spelling (several maps and guides –

though not the Ordnance Survey – omit the 'a') though there's no doubt about its status as the most sought-after village in the area. It has a truly Kentish feel to it, with leafy lanes on the slopes of the North Downs giving on to a church, a pub, a thatched cricket pavilion, a primary school and old thatched cottages. These sell for around £250,000 and tend to be occupied by well-paid professionals. The village itself is a conservation area and the surrounding countryside is a designated Area of Outstanding Natural Beauty. At the centre is a tiny green with an old cedar tree growing on it, framed by a row of tile-hung cottages, the church and Milsted Manor. It is a busy place. The cricket attracts people from neighbouring villages, and the primary school just outside the village has a swimming pool. It is worried about becoming a dormitory village, though there are truly local families who have lived here for years. A car is essential for all those who don't want to have to use the post bus.

Restored timber-frame house, north Kent

Branchline to Sheerness-on-Sea via Kemsley, Swale and Queenborough

No through trains. Trains to Sittingbourne: *3 per hour (peak)/ I per hour (off-peak)*
Journey time: *80 min (from Sheerness)*
Season ticket from Sheerness: *£1948*

Kemsley was built to house workers from the nearby paper mills and is rather formally laid out with a central square containing a modern social centre built in Queen Anne style. Three-bedroom terrace houses are available in plenty; they cost around £45,000 but they do not sell easily. There is also a large new estate on the outskirts where prices are low: a one-bedroom flat for just over £30,000; a three-bedroom semi for £57,000; a four-bedroom detached house for £75,000.

Swale station is in a bleak and remote spot where the only housing to speak of is the occasional farmhouse on the flattest of horizons. It was named after the channel that separates the Isle of Sheppey from the mainland, now spanned by the Kingsferry Bridge (the central section of which opens up for coasters). The Royal Society for the Protection of Birds' Elmley Marshes nature reserve begins here and stretches across the southern part of the island. At **Queenborough** once again you find the typically north Kentish combination of relentless turn-of-the-century housing in a harbour setting. The high street ends in an esplanade where you can watch the boats coming in and out. It is popular as a safe haven for ships caught in storms but not so much as a place to live. Terrace houses sell for £38,000 to £48,000.

Sheerness-on-Sea, at the north-west tip of the Isle of Sheppey, is protected by a massive sea wall above the shingle beach, from which there are good views over the Thames estuary. The design of the old dockyards was supervised by Samuel Pepys in his capacity as Secretary to the Navy Board in 1665. This is where Nelson's body was brought in HMS *Victory* after the Battle of Trafalgar in 1805. Today Sheerness has a flourishing container port and a car ferry terminal (for the route to Vlissingen in Holland). Most of the town consists of Victorian terrace housing, built for dockyard workers and now selling at around £38,000 for two bedrooms. Ex-council semis sometimes fetch about £10,000 more. **Minster**, two miles to the east, is more popular. Semis and bungalows here tend to sell in the range of £53,000 to £70,000. The place was built up between the wars by speculative developers who sold plots to Londoners in search of seaside homes. Unfortunately some bought them as investments rather than as homes, and Minster still has an unfinished look about it. The coast from Minster to Leysdown on Sea is more or less one continuous run of caravan sites and chalets.

TEYNHAM

To Victoria
Journey time: *82 min*
Season ticket: *£1900*

Peak trains: *3 per hour*
Off-peak trains: *2 per hour*

Teynham is a sprawling village unromantically sandwiched between the A2 and the railway line. It was once 10 hamlets, hence its name. Though only a few trains stop here in peak hours, Teynham is very much a commuter village. Most of the houses were built during the Sixties and Seventies. A three-bedroom semi of that vintage will sell for around

£60,000. There is just one street of older, turn-of-the-century housing where two- or three-bedroom houses sell for around £40,000 to £50,000. Outside the road-rail sandwich lie the hop fields which supply the Faversham breweries.

FAVERSHAM

To Victoria
Journey time: *68 min*
Season ticket: *£1960*

Peak trains: *4 per hour**
Off-peak trains: *4 per hour*

* Plus 3 per hour to Cannon St

Faversham is a hugely popular old market town. The old market place lies within a mainly pedestrianised conservation shopping area, and still has markets on Tuesdays, Fridays and Saturdays. Tudor and Georgian houses exude period charm, and Faversham Creek brings the sights and smells of the river. It was this navigable tidal inlet that earned Faversham its status as one of the Cinque Ports, and the warships built there won it the further title of King's Port. There are still some medieval warehouses left on its banks, though today it is the brewing industry that dominates. Shepherd Neame and Whitbread Fremlins have both settled here in the heart of hop-growing country.

Small plain terrace houses sell for between £40,000 and £50,000. For more expensive property, one of the most sought-after streets is Abbey Street, which contains some of the oldest half-timbered buildings in Kent. They very rarely come on the market, but their current value is probably around the £250,000 mark. People looking for new houses should consider the Preston Park estate in the south-east. This offers a range of housing from two-bedroom terrace houses at around £63,000 to four-bedroom detached at around £155,000.

The villages around Faversham benefit from their proximity to such an attractive and popular town. Stretched along a valley bottom to the south-west is **Newnham**, many of whose 18th- and 19th-century red brick and weatherboarded houses lie within a conservation area. A one-bedroom weatherboarded cottage might fetch £45,000; a two-bedroom period house £65,000; a four-bedroom detached £160,000 to £170,000. Newnham's big house is an interesting Tudor pile with two chalk fireplaces and decorative plasterwork in the form of tumbling leaves.

Eastling, a mile from Newnham, has 14th- and 15th-century timbered hall houses and ancient weatherboarded houses scattered along country lanes. The cheapest two-bedroom weatherboarded house would be likely to cost around £65,000. The village has a pub and a church (with a yew tree reputedly over 900 years old), and a primary school with a toddlers' group, but there are no shops. Though the village barbecue is still a vigorous event, the character of the place has changed over the years as commuters have replaced agricultural workers. Two or three miles away is Belmont House, an 18th-century mansion set in fine parkland which is open to the public.

Boughton Street village, a couple of miles east, has a charming main street lined with period houses, laced with a few shops and a good pub. It has a complete cross-section of people including quite a few commuters. A modern three-bedroom semi with a garage and garden here would sell for just over £60,000, while a larger six-bedroom early Victorian house would be expected to sell for around £160,000.

MAIN LINE FROM FAVERSHAM TO HERNE BAY (see map)

WHITSTABLE

To Victoria
Journey time: *78 min*
Season ticket: *£2056*

Peak trains: *3 per hour**
Off-peak trains: *2 per hour*

* Plus 3 per hour to Cannon St

The sea can be a force to be reckoned with in **Whitstable**, and people have to balance the cachet of sea views against the danger of flood. In the terrible storm of 1953, the waves breached the sea wall and the tide surged miles inland. The oyster-catching industry was severely disrupted too, though this has been built up again to the extent that the harbour area now contains the largest oyster hatchery in Europe. There is an annual oyster festival, and the beginning of the oyster season is marked by the blessing of the sea.

The town centre is full of little Victorian terraces of two-up-two-downs. The shabbier ones sell at £40,000; restored ones at £50,000. There are also some well-established newer developments. Bay View, for example, was built about 20 years ago with some later additions. A neo-Georgian semi here would cost in the region of £60,000 to £70,000. On the sea-front there are some 200-year-old smugglers' and fishermen's cottages with added charm value. Expect to pay £70,000 for a three-bedroom semi. Also overlooking the sea is a small development called Daniel's Court. A one-bedroom flat here costs over £50,000; a larger town house probably over £90,000. As a resort Whitstable is fairly restrained, though there are the usual seaside amusements and it is popular for yachting and watersports. The rows of weatherboarded fishermen's cottages and old boat-sheds along the shingle beach (there is sand to the east and west) are the subject of a Turner sketch.

Tankerton, on the east side of the Whitstable old town, is sedate, slightly more expensive and a popular retirement haven. Houses on the sea-front sell for between £150,000 and £200,000, and overlook the Tankerton Slopes, a wide grassy verge that runs down to the beach.

Extending from the beach is a long shingle spit known as The Street. This is where two tides meet, and at low water you can walk right out along it into the sea. **Seasalter**, to the west, is another retirement area, with its own parade of shops and ration of bungalows. In Joy Lane you will find some of the most expensive houses in the area. This is where Somerset Maugham, whose uncle was the vicar of Whitstable, learned to ride his bicycle. If you fancy one of the large detached houses he must have wobbled past, you'll need to spend anything from £140,000 to well over £200,000.

CHESTFIELD & SWALECLIFFE

To Victoria

Journey time: *83 min*	**Peak trains:** *3 per hour**
Season ticket: *£2068*	**Off-peak trains:** *I per hour*

* Plus 3 per hour to Cannon St

There is a bit of snob value attached to **Chestfield**. It is a cut above the seaside tat, thinks of itself as a village and has a private golf club. It also has some very large period houses that sell for over £500,000. Between these are new developments or individually built modern houses on small plots that sell in the £150,000–£200,000 range. On the Chestfield Park estate, Tudor-style family houses sell from just under £200,000 to £280,000. The village does also have some properties for first-time buyers. Expect to pay around £55,000 for two bedrooms. **Swalecliffe** by comparison is very down-market. It has lots of ex-council houses and some cheaper bungalows in the £50,000–£55,000 range.

HERNE BAY

To Victoria

Journey time: *83 min*	**Peak trains:** *3 per hour**
Season ticket: *£2116*	**Off-peak trains:** *2 per hour*

* Plus 3 per hour to Cannon St

The Victorian seaside resort has spread its tentacles over quite a large area now, and much of **Herne Bay** feels like a retirement town. You could buy a restored, two-bedroom Victorian terrace house for £44,000, or a one-bedroom flat in a larger Edwardian house for £33,000. But if you want a modern home with a sea view you'll need to spend at least £150,000. The compromise solution may be to find a nice house in a road leading down to the sea, for which you may have to pay only £80,000 to £90,000. Herne Bay's long, exposed foreshore can be sealed off when there are severe storms; otherwise it is extremely popular with day trippers, and with sailing and fishing enthusiasts. Sadly the pier, which was the second longest after Southend, was damaged by storms in 1953 and 1978, and demolished in the following year.

One mile inland is the parent village of **Herne**, a collection of pretty white weatherboarded cottages on a hillside with a restored working 18th-century smock mill. A mid-terrace cottage here would cost just over £60,000.

Large seaside family house, Herne Bay

MAIN LINE FROM FAVERSHAM TO CANTERBURY (see map)

SELLING

To Victoria
Journey time: *79 min*
Season ticket: *£2008*

Peak trains: *2 per hour*
Off-peak trains: *2 per hour*

This is a nice position to be in. You are close to the pretty market town of Faversham, near enough to Canterbury for special shopping, and also handy for the sea. The countryside starts to roll south-east of Faversham, and at Perry Wood is a huge area of unspoilt accessible woodland. From the Pulpit, a wooden structure built on a mound at the highest point, you have panoramic views over Kent. There are some very fine half-timbered houses and oasts scattered in the deep lanes round here. A three-bedroom oast conversion might cost £160,000.

CANTERBURY EAST

To Victoria

Journey time: *82 min*	Peak trains: *2 per hour*
Season ticket: *£2116**	Off-peak trains: *2 per hour*

* Also valid for Canterbury West

See also **Charing Cross to Canterbury** (page 306).

Canterbury charmingly combines modernity and tourism with its medieval heritage. The centre was bombed out of it in the Second World War. Beneath the modern shopping precinct that replaced it are Roman mosaics, which are open to the public. Much of the centre is pedestrianised, which makes it a pleasant place to shop, and it is also very beautiful. Much of the old medieval city remains in the narrow streets of timber-framed houses around the cathedral, where Thomas Becket was murdered. The most sought-after area is within the city walls, close to the cathedral and King's public school for boys. This latter occupies many of the buildings that were formerly part of the monastery attached to the cathedral. Grade II listed houses here are snapped up very quickly. Black Prince's Chantry, a three-bedroom house with medieval origins, was put on the market last year with a price tag of £150,000. The price was quite high because it came with a garage. Anything with a garage sells at a premium: parking in Canterbury is a nightmare. At the cheaper end of the market, a tiny turn-of-the-century terrace cottage within the city walls would be likely to fetch between £60,000 and £70,000.

The city margin is ringed with roomy Victorian detached and semi-detached houses. In Ethelbert Road, to the south, the houses have as many as 10 bedrooms and sell for around £400,000. Unsurprisingly, very few of them remain intact as single homes. Many have been converted into flats – priced at around £50,000 for a single bedroom. There are also plenty of modern developments from the Fifties, Sixties and Eighties. A 10-year-old detached house with four bedrooms in the south of the town would cost around £120,000. Within the city walls it would cost £140,000.

The University of Kent, built in the Sixties high on a windy hill just outside the city, attracts a lot of students to the **St Stephen's** area. Many of the bay-windowed Thirties semis here are rented; some are bought by the parents of wealthier students. A three-bedroom house in need of maintenance would cost around £73,000; one in good condition would be nearer £95,000. Students also buy in the area around St Peter's Place, where a flat-fronted turn-of-the-century house may be picked up for £50,000 to £53,000.

North of the city the landscape becomes flat and dull, so people prefer to look to the south. Two and a half miles south-east is the village of **Bridge**, which is extremely pretty and commensurately expensive. It offers a mix of thatched cottages, turn-of-the-century and modern houses, but remains very compact. A small thatched cottage might cost £150,000; a five-bedroom neo-Georgian house on the outskirts £195,000. Further east is **Patrixbourne**, which is very tiny but also very pretty and so sought after that £250,000 half-timbered houses and thatched cottages often sell by word of mouth. The Nail Bourne River runs through it, but it only fills after heavy downpours and for most of the year it is dry.

Looking north-east you find **Wickhambreaux** – a typical Kentish village with a green and an old church on one side, the Little Stour running through it with a watermill now turned into flats, and a manor house. It once formed part of the Kentish estates of Joan Plantagenet, the Fair Maid of Kent, wife of the Black Prince. There are no shops and no bus service, but the village does have a pub and a flourishing Church of England primary school. The annual fete on the green brings the villagers together, and other local entertainments include the WI, Brownie pack and produce association. There has been no new development for 40 years. A large village house with river frontage and a couple of acres would cost £450,000. One way of telling old villagers from new is by the name they give to the main street. Incomers rather grandly call it The Street. To old villagers it is Gutter Street.

At **Stodmarsh**, slightly to the north, the landscape becomes very rural, with good views across the Stour Valley. Stodmarsh itself is a small village with one pub, and very little ever comes on the market. If you were lucky, you might pay £55,000 to £60,000 for a two-up-two-down cottage; £250,000 or more for a converted oast house. The old coal-mining area has been turned into a nature reserve with man-made lakes to attract wildlife.

ROYAL LIFE ESTATE AGENTS

Agent Codes

Allen & Harris	AH	William H Brown	WHB
Barnard Marcus	BM	Roger Platt & Partners	RP
Fox & Sons South	FS	Brown & Merry	BM
Fox & Sons South East	FSE	Brown & Mumford	BMd
Gribble Booth & Taylor	GBT	Shipways	S

AVON

Bath	0225 425111	AH
Bristol	0272 293171	PF
Bristol (Ashton)	0272 662284	AH
Bristol (Apsley Road)	0272 744601	AH
Bristol (Clifton)	0272 731295	AH
Bristol (Down End)	0272 568211	AH
Bristol (Gloucester Road)	0272 232225	AH
Bristol (Hanham)	0272 606118	AH
Bristol (Knowle)	0272 777075	AH
Bristol (Patchway)	0272 697373	AH
Bristol (Stoke Gifford)	0272 798082	AH
Bristol (Queens Square)	0272 227575	AH
Bristol (Westbury-on-Trym)	0272 501555	AH

BEDFORDSHIRE

Bedford	0234 345555	WHB
Biggleswade	0767 600601	WHB
Leighton Buzzard	0525 372021	BM
Luton	0582 400899	WHB

BERKSHIRE

Bracknell	0344 55055	AH
Cookham	06285 24732	RP
Lower Early	0734 876767	AH
Maidenhead	0628 37333/773333	RP
Newbury	0635 521050	AH
Newbury (Kingfisher Court)	0635 521220	AH
Reading	0734 478378	AH
Slough	0753 520304	RP
Thatcham	0635 66111	AH
Twyford	0734 345205	RP
Windsor	0753 851444	RP

Winneresh .... 0734 771111 .... AH
Wokingham .... 0734 794444 .... AH

BUCKINGHAMSHIRE

Amersham .... 0494 725656 .... BM
Aylesbury .... 0296 88111 .... BM
Beaconsfield .... 0494 670770 .... RP
Bletchley .... 0908 371361 .... BM
Bourne End .... 06285 22555 .... RP
Buckingham .... 0280 822711 .... BM
Burnham .... 0628 665252 .... RP
Milton Keynes .... 0908 661601 .... BM
Flackwell Heath .... 06285 30013 .... RP
Gerrards Cross .... 0753 889944 .... RP
High Wycombe .... 0494 464433 .... RP
Marlow .... 06284 75656 .... RP
Newport Pagnell .... 0908 611242 .... BM
Princes Risborough .... 0844 274422 .... BM
Stony Stratford .... 0908 562011 .... BM
Wendover .... 0296 624444 .... BM
Woburn Sands .... 0908 583231 .... BM

CAMBRIDGESHIRE

Cambridge .... 0223 62225 .... WHB
Ely .... 0353 663311 .... WHB
Huntingdon .... 0480 411456 .... WHB
March .... 0354 54545 .... WHB
Market Deeping .... 0778 344441 .... WHB
Peterborough .... 0733 311022 .... WHB
Ramsey .... 0487 815555 .... WHB
St Ives .... 0480 301101 .... WHB
St Neots .... 0480 214115 .... WHB
Wisbech .... 0945 64451 .... WHB
Yaxley .... 0733 244494 .... WHB

ESSEX

Ashingdon .... 0702 549585 .... WHB
Chelmsford .... 0245 262266 .... WHB
Coggeshall .... 0376 561204 .... WHB
Colchester .... 0206 577772 .... WHB
Colchester (St Johns) .... 0206 843464 .... WHB
Epping .... 0378 560464 .... WHB
Great Dunmow .... 0371 876471 .... WHB
Halstead .... 0787 472491 .... WHB

Harwich .... 0255 503125 .... WHB
Ilford .... 081 553 9499 ...... WHB
Leigh on Sea .... 0702 715228 .... WHB
Saffron Walden .... 0799 513516 .... WHB
Shoeburyness .... 0702 298836 .... WHB

GLOUCESTERSHIRE
Cirencester .... 0285 650441 .... AH

HAMPSHIRE
Andover .... 0264 366444 .... AH
Bitterne .... 0703 446724 .... FS
Chandler's Ford .... 0703 252213 .... FS
Eastleigh .... 0703 618522 .... FS
Fareham .... 0329 288425 .... FS
Fordingbridge .... 0425 652121 .... FS
Hedge End .... 0489 785269 .... FS
Lymington .... 0590 675424 .... FS
Portsmouth .... 0705 671110 .... FS
Ringwood .... 0425 472324 .... FS
Romsey .... 0794 513085 .... FS
Southampton (London Road) ... 0703 225155 .... FS
Southampton (Crosshouse) ..... 0703 339466 .... FS
Southampton (The Avenue) ..... 0703 227337 .... PF
Totton .... 0703 862243 .... FS
Waterlooville .... 0705 262447 .... FS
Winchester .... 0962 862121 .... FS

HERTFORDSHIRE
Barnet .... 081 449 4545 ...... WHB
Berkhamsted .... 0442 865421 .... BM
Broxbourne .... 0992 464174 .... WHB
Buntingford .... 0763 71423 .... WHB
Hemel Hempstead .... 0442 213031 .... BM
Hertford .... 0992 586501 .... WHB
Hoddesdon .... 0992 464001 .... WHB
Royston .... 0763 242988 .... WHB
Stevenage .... 0438 351572 .... WHB
Tring .... 044282 4133 .... BM
Ware .... 0920 465411 .... WHB
Welwyn Garden City .... 0707 324361 .... WHB

KENT
Tunbridge Wells .... 0892 25272 .... FSE

LEICESTERSHIRE

Birstall .... 0533 673414 .... WHB
Leicester .... 0533 514131 .... WHB
Melton Mowbray .... 0664 63481 .... WHB
Oadby .... 0533 719671 ...... WHB
Sileby .... 050981 2859 .... WHB

LINCOLNSHIRE

Bourne .... 0778 423316 .... WHB
Grantham .... 0476 66363 .... WHB
Stamford .... 0780 62351 .... WHB

NORFOLK

Diss .... 0379 644719 ...... WHB
Downham Market .... 0366 387638 .... WHB
East Harling *(Norwich)* .... 0953 717681 .... WHB
Kings Lynn .... 0553 771337 .... WHB
Norwich .... 0603 660361 .... WHB

NORTHAMPTONSHIRE

Corby .... 0536 67418 ...... WHB
Kettering .... 0536 518555 .... WHB
Northampton .... 0604 32322 .... WHB
Rothwell .... 0536 710780 .... WHB
Rushden .... 0933 410717 .... WHB

OXFORDSHIRE

Abingdon .... 0235 553777 .... AH
Banbury .... 0295 50390 .... BMd
Didcot .... 0235 812333 .... AH
Faringdon .... 0367 240748 .... AH
Kidlington .... 08675 71616 .... AH
Oxford *(Botley)* .... 0865 790006 .... AH
Oxford *(Bonn Square)* .... 0865 726266 .... AH
Oxford *(Headington)* .... 0865 67414 .... AH
Oxford *(Rose Hill)* .... 0865 711441 .... AH
Oxford *(Summertown)* .... 0865 512582 .... AH
Wallingford .... 0491 35135 .... AH
Wantage .... 0235 771199 .... AH
Witney .... 0993 705915 .... AH

SOMERSET

Castle Cary .... 0963 50116 .... GBT
Frome .... 0373 462999 .... AH

Wincanton .... 0963 32725 .... GBT

SUFFOLK

Aldeburgh .... 0728 452469 .... WHB
Bungay .... 0986 894608/895286 WHB
Bury St Edmunds .... 0284 762131 .... WHB
Framlingham .... 0728 723923 .... WHB
Hadleigh .... 0473 822962 .... WHB
Halesworth .... 0986 872121 .... WHB
Ipswich .... 0473 226101 .... WHB
Leiston .... 0728 832286 .... WHB
Saxmundham .... 0728 603232 .... WHB
Stowmarket .... 0449 613221 .... WHB
Sudbury .... 0787 79372 .... WHB
Woodbridge .... 0394 380280 .... WHB

SUSSEX

Bexhill-on-Sea .... 0424 224243 .... FSE
Bognor Regis .... 0243 864161 .... FSE
Brighton (Ditchling Road) .... 0273 540331 .... FSE
Brighton (Head Office) .... 0273 739201 .... FSE
Brighton (Lewes Road) .... 0273 677544 .... FSE
Burgess Hill .... 0444 232849 .... FSE
Eastbourne .... 0323 410911 .... FSE
Hailsham .... 0323 843554 .... FSE
Hastings .... 0424 722177 .... FSE
Haywards Heath .... 0444 450105 .... FSE
Henfield .... 0273 492505 .... FSE
Hove (Hangleton Road) .... 0273 778455 .... FSE
Hove (Church Road) .... 0273 820280 .... FSE
Kemp Town .... 0273 688148 .... FSE
Lancing .... 0903 766041 .... FSE
Lewes .... 0273 476378 .... FSE
Littlehampton .... 0903 715622 .... FSE
Newhaven .... 0273 513949 .... FSE
Patcham .... 0273 554505 .... FSE
Peacehaven .... 0273 587222 .... FSE
Polegate .... 0323 486561 .... FSE
Portslade .... 0273 423500 .... FSE
Preston Park .... 0273 508761 .... FSE
Rottingdean .... 0273 309968 .... FSE
Rustington .... 0903 783211 .... FSE
Seaford .... 0323 899116 .... FSE

Shoreham-by-Sea .... 0273 461671 .... FSE
St Leonards on Sea .... 0424 722123 .... FSE
Woodingdean .... 0273 604617 .... FSE
West Worthing .... 0903 503906 .... FSE
Worthing .... 0903 209055 .... FSE

WARWICKSHIRE
Leamington Spa .... 0926 883641 .... S
Rugby .... 0788 574641/576778 .... S

WILTSHIRE
Amesbury .... 0980 624155 .... FS
Calne .... 0249 814681 .... AH
Chippenham .... 0242 655255 .... AH
Corsham .... 0249 713877 .... AH
Cricklade .... 0793 750025 .... AH
Devizes .... 0380 729900 .... AH
Downton .... 0725 20449 .... FS
Highworth .... 0793 762407 .... AH
Lyneham .... 0249 891044 .... AH
Pewsey .... 0672 63101 .... AH
Salisbury .... 0722 337691 .... FS
Swindon *(Cheney Manor Road)*   0793 513517 .... AH
Swindon *(Ermin Street)* .... 0793 828900 .... AH
Swindon *(Gorse Hill)* .... 0793 485353 .... AH
Swindon *(Old Town)* .... 0793 643131 .... AH
Swindon *(Stratton Cross)* .... 0793 725523 .... AH
Swindon *(Town Centre)* .... 0793 615105 .... AH
Swindon *(Wroughton)* .... 0793 814702 .... AH
Trowbridge .... 0225 764161 .... AH
Warminster .... 0985 213121 .... AH
Westbury .... 0373 822457 .... AH
Wootton Bassett .... 0793 853333 .... AH

INDEX OF STATIONS, TOWNS AND VILLAGES

British Rail stations are in capital letters

E

F

M

Stoke Lyne 139
STOKE MANDEVILLE 131
Stoke Poges 157
Stoke-by-Nayland 24
STONEGATE 292
Stoneygate 106
Stony Stratford 120
Storrington 253
Stotfold 78
Stow-on-the-Wold 152
STOWMARKET 30
Stratton Audley 139
Streatley 144
Stretham 61
STROOD 317
Stutton 28
SUDBURY 22
SUNNINGDALE 183
Sunninghill 183
SUNNYMEADS 178
Sutton, Cambs 61
Sutton, W Sussex...................... 253
Sutton Green 228
Sutton Valence........................ 309
Swaffham Bulbeck 59
Swaffham Prior 59
Swainswick 173
SWALE 324
Swalecliffe 328
SWAYTHLING 222
SWINDON 165
    Broome Manor 165
    Old Town 165
    The Lawns 165

TACKLEY 147
Tandridge 278
Tankerton 327
TAPLOW 158
Tempsford 80
Tewin 68
TEYNHAM 325
Thame 138
THATCHAM.............................. 194
Thaxted 54

The Lee.................................. 130
THEALE 192
Therfield.................................. 75
Thornborough 115
Thornbury 177
Thorney 85
Thorpe 182
THORPE BAY 42
Thorpe Langton........................ 105
THORPE-LE-SOKEN 24
Thorpeness.............................. 29
THREE BRIDGES 249
THURSTON 30
Ticehurst................................ 292
Tilbury 44
TILBURY RIVERSIDE 44
TILBURY TOWN 44
TILEHURST 144
Tillingham 37
Tingrith 98
Toddington 98
Tollesbury 20
TONBRIDGE 288
TOTTON.................................. 226
Towcester 123
TRING 111
Tring Station 112
TROWBRIDGE 170
TUNBRIDGE WELLS 289
Tunstall 323
Tur Langton 105
TWYFORD.............................. 162

UCKFIELD 283
Uffington................................ 165
Ufford, Cambs 86
Ufford, Sflk 29
Ugley.................................... 54
Upnor 317
Upper Heyford 148
Upper Lambourne...................... 195
Upper Slaughter 151
Upper Weald 121
Upper Woodford 217
Upper Wraxhall 174

Y